SMALL ENGINES

SMALL ENGINES

L.J. Reid

McGraw-Hill Ryerson Limited

Toronto

Montreal   New York   London   Sydney

Johannesburg   Mexico   Panama   Düsseldorf

Singapore   Rio de Janeiro   Kuala Lumpur   New Delhi

SMALL ENGINES

ISBN   0-07-092535-6

2 3 4 5 6 7 8 9 10   MP72   10 9 8 7 6 5 4

Printed and bound in Canada

CONTENTS

This text has been compiled for the beginning student. It presents information with respect to the principal instructions and mechanical operation of the modern air-cooled engine and the water-cooled outboard engine. The review questions after each chapter are intended as home work assignments.

Small motors may be brought in to the class to be used in practical assignments given by the teacher. At crucial points in assignments, instructors should inspect the work. The equipment and tools used should be basic and available in any junior automotive mechanics' shop. One other thing that is very important to these small engine mechanics is the adaptation and use of the special tools that are used in the small engine trade.

LOUIS J. REID

PART 1
AIR-COOLED ENGINES

CHAPTER 1
THEORY OF GASOLINE ENGINE OPERATION

The remarkable progress made in travel on land, air, and water has been made possible almost entirely by the development of the gasoline engine. These compact, powerful engines have found a multitude of uses in transport of all kinds — trucks, motor boats, airplanes, racing cars. They provide the power for machinery for an endless range of other uses — lawnmowers, chainsaws, water pumps, concrete mixers, generators, and excavators. Small engines — particularly two-stroke cycle engines — are ideal motors. They are small; their uses are limitless; they can generate any amount of power needed.

The process that produces mechanical motion or power in a gas engine is based on a fundamental law of physics which states that gas will expand when heated. If the gas is confined or compressed without an outlet for expansion as it is heated, the pressure of the gas will be increased.

The term "gas-engine" means an internal combustion engine using natural gas or the vapour of gasoline as fuel. It is distinguished from an oil engine such as the diesel which uses kerosene or heavy, low-grade oils as fuel. The gas engine is one of two forms of "heat-engines," since it operates by means of the expansion of a gas which has been subjected to the action of heat.

These two types of heat-engines are:

> *External Combustion* engines like the steam engine, which operate from the expansion of vapour outside the engine;
> *Internal combustion* engines, which get their power from the expansion of gases inside the engine cylinder.

There are two ways in which gasoline burns:

> *Combustion* is a constant action that occurs when a mixture of fuel and air is ignited. A good example of natural, or free, combustion is the common bonfire. Even here, there must be a proper mixture of air and fuel. A pile of magazines will not burn satisfactorily unless the pages are separated to permit air circulation. In a sense, this separation of the pages is a form of controlled combustion. Combustion is the first action to take place in the cylinder chamber of the gas engine.
> *Detonation* is an almost instantaneous action that causes a very sudden rise in temperature and pressure. In gas engines, this occurs after combustion has spread partially across the cylinder chamber.

The easiest way to understand the operation of a gasoline engine is to see what happens when combustion occurs within a confined area.

One or two drops of gasoline are placed in an empty metal or unbreakable container. A cork is fitted with a pair of wires whose inner ends are spaced about the thickness of a dime apart. The container is then sealed with the cork and shaken to create a gasoline vapour. When these wires are charged with electricity, a spark occurs at their ends inside the container. The result is commonly called an explosion. It actually is sudden combustion producing a high degree of heat inside the container and resulting, in this case, in the cork being forcefully ejected from the mouth of the container. Because the fuel is burned right inside the container, this process is referred to as "internal combustion."

The mixture of air and fuel which is introduced into the container is called the "charge." In actual engine operation, the mixing of air and fuel in proper amounts to create the charge is done outside the engine. This charge is then introduced at a predetermined interval. The act of igniting the charge is referred to as "ignition" or "spark," since it is caused by an arc of electric current from a "spark plug" that has been energized by the ignition system. This spark also occurs at a predetermined interval.

THEORY OF THE FOUR STROKE CYCLE

A metal container with a movable bottom, like the one in Figure 1-1, can be used to illustrate the movement of a piston in a gas engine. This illustration shows the container itself; A, a spark plug; B, an opening through which a charge of gasoline air-fuel mixture may be admitted and then sealed; and C, a bottom which can be moved up or down in the container.

In this device, combustion occurring within the container would force the bottom away from the top. Since the mechanical, downward motion derived from the combustion is needed to create a circular motion on a shaft, a simple arrangement of a connecting rod and crankshaft is used, as shown in Figure 1-2. A flywheel mounted on the crankshaft develops momentum as the shaft revolves. This momentum should be sufficient to keep the shaft turning, thus returning the base to its former position at the top of the container. Therefore, if the pressure from combustion is sufficient, the movable part of this engine will be driven down, then up, cranking the shaft 360 degrees.

Figure 1-3 shows the names of the engine parts. These will be used from this point.

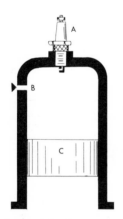

Figure 1.1 Parts of the Combustion Chamber

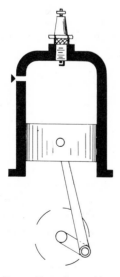

Figure 1.2 Power Transfer to Keep Momentum

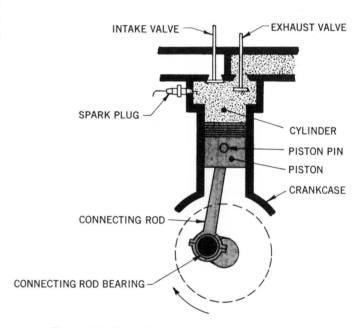

Figure 1.3 Parts of a 4-stroke-cycle engine cutaway

The action of the piston, moving away from the top of the cylinder, is a *stroke*. The number of strokes that a piston makes in order to complete a series of events is called a *cycle*. The events which complete the cycle for a gasoline engine are:

1. *Intake stroke.* The fuel-air charge is admitted to the cylinder.
2. *Compression stroke.* The charge is compressed between the head of the cylinder and the top of the piston.
3. *Power stroke.* The air-fuel mixture ignites and explodes.
4. *Exhaust stroke.* Burned gases are expelled from the cylinder.

In order to see the operational sequence for a complete cycle of events similar to those in an engine, refer to

Figure 1-4 where the events are demonstrated by the loading and firing of an antique cannon. Here we have:

1. The *charge* being injected;
2. *Compression* being administered by tamping the charge;
3. *Ignition* of the charge with consequent power driving the ball from the muzzle;
4. *Exhaust* of burned powder and gases.

All internal combustion engines are separated into one of two groups: two-cycle and four-cycle engines. Both groups operate on the theory that heated gas expands and have common, but not identical, features. Engines are grouped by the number of strokes required by their pistons to complete one cycle. A two-stroke cycle engine requires two strokes of the piston in order to complete one full cycle, whereas the four-stroke cycle engine completes the cycle in four strokes of the piston. The names for these engines have been shortened to four-cycle and two-cycle engines in common usage.

Operating Principles
The Four-Cycle Engine

Four-cycle engines require fuel intake and burned-gas exhaust valves. In the following illustrations of a single cylinder, four-cycle engine, the intake and exhaust valves are located on opposite sides of the cylinder — intake valve on the left and exhaust on the right. These valves are operated by lifting devices which are operated by a gear arrangement driven by the crankshaft. They are timed to the piston so that they remain shut most of the time and open only to perform certain actions during the cycle.

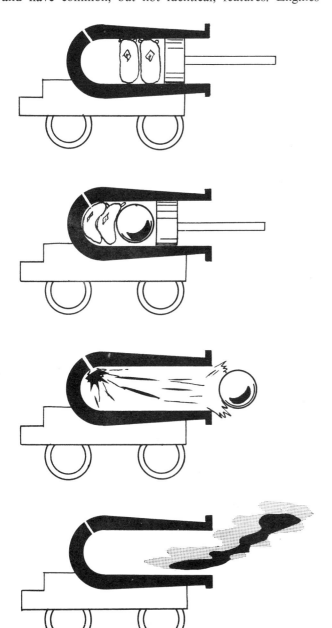

Figure 1.4   Operation Order for a Cycle

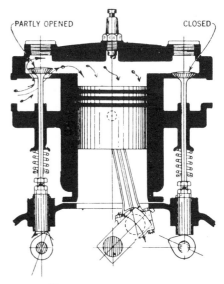

Figure 1.5   Intake Stroke

The initial starting action for any engine must be acquired from an outside source — by a hand crank, a manually operated pull cord, or by an electric starting motor. For this instruction, assume that the engine is being hand cranked.

The cranking motion on the crankshaft in these figures is clockwise, pulling the piston down on the intake stroke and pushing the intake valve up. The exhaust valve is closed. As the piston gains speed on its downward stroke in the cylinder, a rapid enlarging of the cylinder space sucks in the charge; that is, a free flow of the fuel-air mixture is drawn into the combustion chamber through the intake valve.

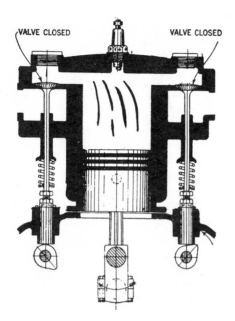

Figure 1.6   Piston at BDC

on the compression stroke. Remember — compressed fuels develop a greater pressure when ignited. Both valves are closed to prevent the charge from escaping, and confine it to a space about 1/6 to 1/10 of the original displacement volume.

The piston has now reached the lowest point that it may travel in the cylinder (BDC—bottom dead centre) and must make a full stop before coming up the cylinder. The intake valve and the exhaust valve are closed, trapping the charge in the combustion chamber. In actual fact, the intake valve does not close entirely until the piston is well beyond the bottom dead centre point, pulling in a maximum charge. This is made possible by the speed of the charge coming through the intake valve into the chamber as the piston is dropped.

Figure 1-7 shows the piston travelling up the cylinder

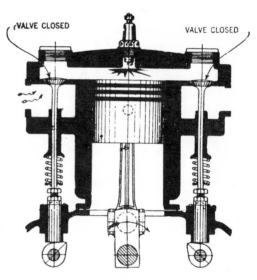

Figure 1.8   Ignition

In Figure 1-8, the engine is still being manually cranked. The piston has reached its highest point in travel up the cylinder (TDC — top dead centre). The spark occurs with the resulting combustion of the charge. In normal operation, the spark usually occurs when the piston is on top dead centre while it is being hand cranked. As speed increases and the engine becomes self-operating, the spark usually occurs slightly before the piston reaches the point of top dead centre. This

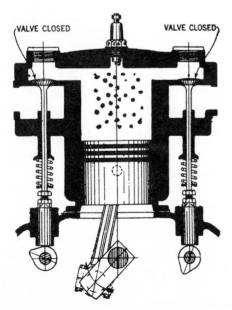

Figure 1.7   Compression Stroke

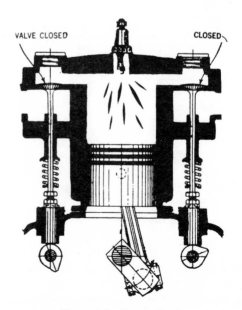

Figure 1.9   Power Stroke

gives the charge a slight interval to ignite and develop pressure by the time the piston has reached top dead centre or slightly past it. The full impact of the pressure will, therefore, be delivered to the piston just as it begins its downward stroke.

In Figure 1-9, the piston is now subject to pressures from the expanding gases. Both valves are still closed. The piston is travelling down on its power stroke, being pushed by the force of the combustion expansion, developing whatever mechanical energy is available. Not all of the heat is used, simply because the perfect machine has not yet been created. Much of the heat is absorbed by the metal of the engine and carried off to the atmosphere by cooling water or air. More heat is lost during the next stage in the cycle.

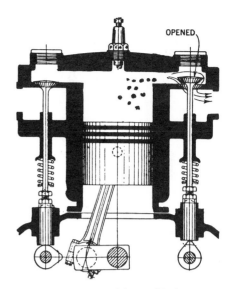

Figure 1.11   Exhaust Stroke

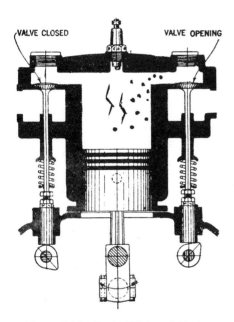

Figure 1.10   Start of Exhaust Stroke

The intake valve is closed as Figure 1-10 shows. The piston has reached bottom dead centre. The exhaust valve started to open slightly before this time, and is fully open when the piston is at bottom dead centre. Since some of the pressure remains in the cylinder chamber, burned gases start to escape. Exhaust, at this point under some pressure, tends to carry off much of the carbon residue.

Figure 1-11 shows the piston on its upward stroke as it forcefully exhausts all remaining gases. The intake valve is still closed and the exhaust valve is fully open. The escaping heat subjects the exhaust valve to a greater temperature than the intake valve. Therefore, the exhaust valve must have a larger clearance adjustment than the intake valve.

When the piston reaches top dead centre, the exhaust valve is almost closed and the intake valve starts to open. The engine is ready to begin another cycle. By now, the crankshaft has made two complete revolutions — 720 degrees. The four-cycle engine always, therefore, follows this sequence to complete one full cycle:

DOWN - Intake stroke
UP - Compression stroke
DOWN - Power stroke
UP - Exhaust stroke

Sufficient momentum has been provided from the power stroke of the first cycle to carry the piston down on the intake stroke of the next cycle. Therefore, if combustion occurs during the first cycle, the next and subsequent strokes will be under their own power as long as the engine continues to receive a supply of fuel.

Lubrication

Since tremendous heat is developed inside the cylinder chamber, the piston must be kept lubricated; otherwise, it will expand and seize against the sides of the cylinder. In the four-cycle engine lubricating oil is stored in the crankcase. The crankshaft stirs the oil continually, and spreads it upward to cool the piston at the bottom of each stroke.

THEORY OF THE TWO-STROKE CYCLE

Although the two-stroke gasoline engine gets its mechanical motion from the same heat expansion that drives the four-cycle engine, it differs in many mechanical features from its usually larger counterpart. Compare the two engines illustrated in Figure 1-12. The two-cycle engine does not have as many moving parts, such as camshafts, timing gears, push rods, valves and springs, and gear trains for the operation of its camshafts. All of

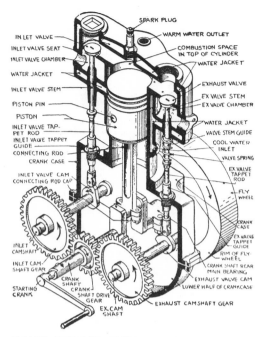

FOUR-STROKE-CYCLE ENGINE

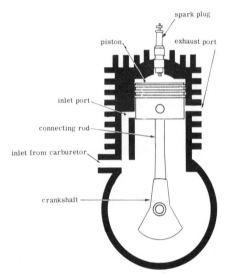

TWO-STROKE-CYCLE ENGINE

Figure 1.12 Comparison of 2-stroke and 4-stroke-cycle Engines

these parts are necessary in any four-cycle engine, whether of the older design which used two separate camshafts, one each for the intake valve and the exhaust valve, or of the more modern design which operates both valves from one camshaft with two separate cams.

The simplicity of design gives the two-cycle engine a greater versatility in such smaller, portable machines as chainsaws, power mowers, and outboard motors. Although gas engines themselves are not interchangeable (that is, a lawn-mower engine could not be used in an outboard motor), a majority of their components are

sufficiently similar that they may be interchanged if they are the same size.

Operating Principles The Two-cycle Engine

The two-cycle gasoline engine accomplishes in two piston strokes the work done by four strokes in the four-cycle engine. A study of the following illustrations describes how this is accomplished. Once again, it may be assumed that the engine receives its initial motion when the crankshaft is turned manually.

Figure 1-13 shows the cycle of events that begins with the piston in bottom dead centre position. Note that a charge of fuel is in the *crankcase* and is moving into the combustion chamber on the right side of the cylinder. When the piston starts on its *upward* or *compression* stroke, most of this charge has been displaced from the crankcase to the combustion chamber.

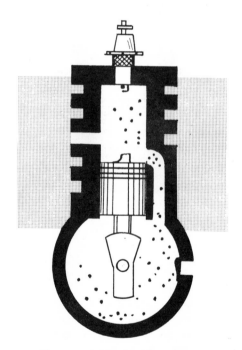

Figure 1.13 Intake to Cylinder

In Figure 1-14, the piston is at the point of top dead centre with all ports into the cylinder closed by the piston itself. The charge is compressed. An intake valve into the crankcase is opened, admitting a fresh fuel charge there.

Ignition with the resulting combustion occurs, driving the piston *down* on the *power* stroke. As well as developing mechanical motion on the crankshaft, the downward motion of the piston is compressing the fuel trapped in the crankcase. Before reaching bottom dead centre, the piston passes and opens an exhaust port on the left side

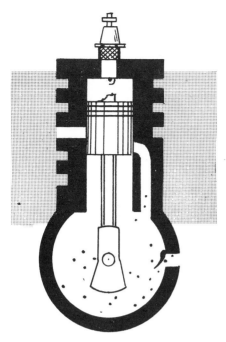

Figure 1.14   Intake to Crankcase—Compression in Cylinder

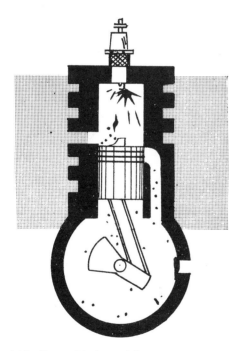

Figure 1.15   Power Stroke and Compression in Crankcase

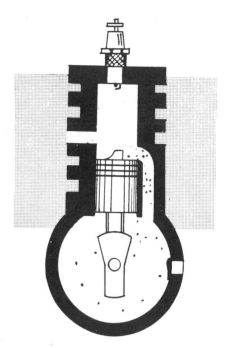

Figure 1.16   Both Ports Open—Piston at BDC

of the cylinder. Since some pressure from combustion still remains, the burned gas and carbon dust escape through this port.

In Figure 1-16, the piston has reached bottom dead centre. Both exhaust and intake ports are opened. The piston head is made in such a way that burned gases are directed toward the exhaust port and the fresh charge, under pressure from the descending piston, is deflected upward into the combustion chamber. The pressure from the fresh charge also drives out remaining burned gases.

At this stage, the piston has made two complete strokes, turning the crankshaft 360 degrees. The two-cycle engine always, therefore, follows this sequence to complete one full cycle:

UP - intake and compression.
DOWN - power and exhaust.

Lubrication

The piston in a two-cycle engine is lubricated and cooled by oil mixed with the gasoline in the storage tank and introduced to the piston from the carburetor. Oil grades and types, and mixture ratios are very important. This subject will be discussed in another chapter.

Types of Two Cycle Engines

There are two basic types of two-cycle engines: the two-port engine and the three-port engine. The two-port type is easier to start because the charge reaches the combustion chamber faster.

Figure 1-17 offers a comparison of the two types. Note that the major difference is in the method of fuel admission to the crankcase.

The two-cycle engine delivers a power stroke for every 360 degrees of the crankshaft travel, whereas the four-cycle engine has one power stroke for every 720 degrees. Theoretically, then, the two-cycle engine would have twice the power output as a four-cycle engine of the

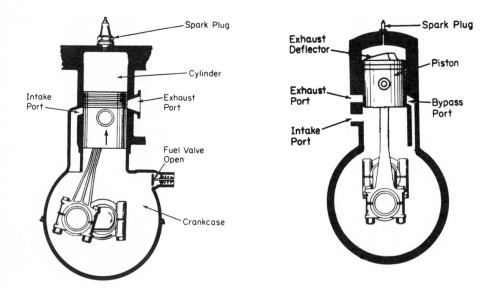

Figure 1.17 Comparison of Two- and Three-port Two-cycle Engines

same size operating within a certain period of time. This is not so. Fuel and power are wasted in the two-cycle engine when some of its incoming fuel combines with the exhaust and escapes. This reduces its efficiency considerably.

The stroke-cycle relationship applies to any cylinder in an engine. In other words, regardless of the number of cylinders in an engine, each one delivers a complete cycle of intake, compression, power, and exhaust.

The number of cylinders in an engine has no relationship to the stroke-cycle designation of that engine. It is possible, therefore, to encounter two-, four-, or six-cylinder engines in either a two- or four-cycle variety. The advantages of a multi-cylinder engine are restricted to power output and smoothness of operation.

REVIEW QUESTIONS

1. Explain in your own words the meaning of internal and external combustion engines.
2. How many degrees of revolution does a crankshaft turn for every power stroke in a four-cycle engine?
3. Define the following terms:
   i) TDC   v) Cycle
   ii) BDC   vi) Cylinder
   iii) Compression   vii) Piston
   iv) Stroke
4. In point form, list the four strokes of the four-cycle engine and list the action that is taking place.

5. Describe the basic difference in operation of a two-cycle and four-cycle engine.
6. What is the name given to the volume above the piston in a cylinder?
7. What are the principal moving parts of a two-cycle engine?
8. Explain what we mean by the "charge" in a cylinder.
9. What event is taking place in a four-cycle engine when both exhaust and intake valves are closed and the piston is travelling up the cylinder?
10. What is the purpose of the cams on a camshaft in a four-cycle engine?
11. When the engine is operating under its own power does the spark occur immediately before or after TDC?
12. Explain how an engine receives a maximum charge in the intake cycle.
13. How large is the area in the combustion chamber at TDC compared to the area at BDC?
14. What actually forces the piston down the cylinder?
15. Why does the exhaust valve need a larger clearance than the intake valve?
16. What is the purpose of the flywheel on a gasoline engine?
17. How does the gasoline engine, both two- and four-cycle, manage to keep its pistons from seizing as a result of the tremendous heat accumulated?
18. Make a diagram of a two-cycle piston head and explain its operation.

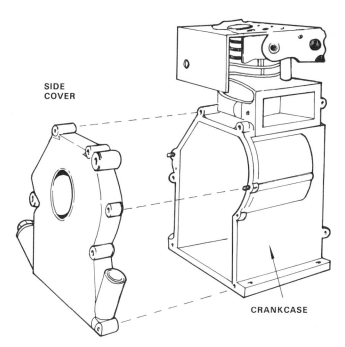

Figure 2.2   Crankcase and Side Plate

CHAPTER 2
PARTS OF THE SMALL AIR-COOLED ENGINE

The cylinder block is the main body of the engine. All other parts are fastened to it or are moulded on at the same time. The cylinder block is molded into its complicated shape in either aluminum or cast iron; the lower horsepower engines are usually molded from aluminum or other lightweight metals. The cylinder block serves as an enclosure for cylinders and the crankcase. It also contains valves, pistons, valve springs and seats.

The cylinder is the portion in which the piston travels up and down. Its diameter is called the *bore.*

The crankcase is the lower part of the cylinder block. It houses the crankshaft, camshaft, and valve lifters, and acts as an oil sump in the four-cycle engine, while in a two-cycle engine, it acts as a primary compression chamber for the fuel mixture entering the combustion cham-

ber. Sometimes, the crankcase is bolted to the cylinder block; in most cases, it is molded to the cylinder block as a unit. The crankcase is composed of two parts in vertical shaft engines: the lower part of the crankcase is called the *sump;* the upper part is called the *cylinder, or block, assembly.* In horizontal shaft engines, one part is called the *block assembly* and the other part is called the *side-plate assembly.*

The cylinder head serves several purposes. It acts as a cover for the cylinder, provides a threaded hole for the spark plug, and is hollowed underneath to provide the combustion chamber over the piston.

Cooling fins are attached to air-cooled cylinder heads so that air passing over the fins will keep the cylinder head cool. Water-cooled cylinders have passages, called water-jackets, cast in the head to provide a path for water to pass through to cool the engine.

Cylinder heads are cast from the same materials as the crankcase and cylinder block. They are usually bolted to the cylinder block, with an asbestos gasket between them, although they may be cast as a single unit with the cylinder.

The piston moves up an down in the cylinder. It is the first moving part to receive the push of the burning and expanding gases in the cylinder.

Some pistons are cast from iron but these are too heavy for high-speed engines. The majority of small engine manufacturers employ a lightweight aluminum alloy instead. Light pistons can be moved up and down in the cylinder faster and less wastefully.

Pistons come in a wide variety of sizes and have dif-

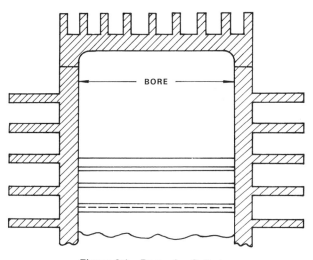

Figure 2.1   Bore of a Cylinder

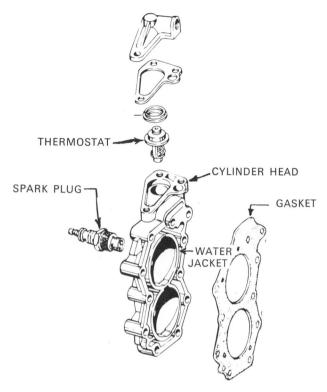

THERMOSTAT

SPARK PLUG

CYLINDER HEAD

GASKET

WATER JACKET

Outboard Marine Co. Ltd.

Figure 2.3　Water-cooled Cylinder Head

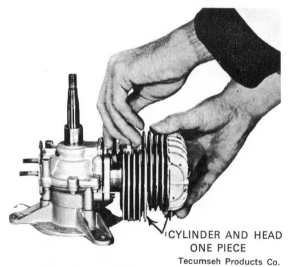

CYLINDER AND HEAD ONE PIECE

Tecumseh Products Co.

Figure 2.4　One Piece Cylinder and Head

ferent shaped heads. The top of the piston is called the *piston head* and the lower part is called the *skirt. Grooves* are cut around the head of the piston and *rings* are fitted into these grooves to provide a seal between the piston and cylinder wall. A hole on either side of the piston is heavily reinforced to support the piston pin and lock rings. These holes are called *piston-pin bosses.*

The piston rings are very important to the operation of the engine. They are usually made of steel and are some-

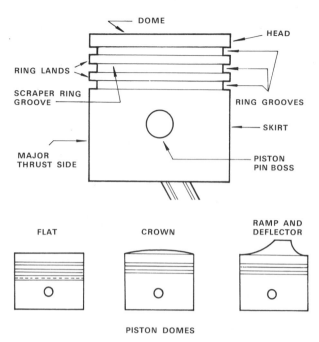

DOME

HEAD

RING LANDS

SCRAPER RING GROOVE

RING GROOVES

SKIRT

MAJOR THRUST SIDE

PISTON PIN BOSS

FLAT　　CROWN　　RAMP AND DEFLECTOR

PISTON DOMES

Figure 2.5　Parts of a Piston

times coated with chrome to increase their life. They provide three services for the engine. They seal the space between the piston and cylinder wall in order to keep the gases from escaping from the combustion chamber; they control the flow of oil over the cylinder walls. A further study will be made in detail in a later chapter.

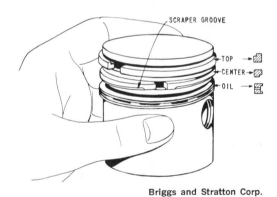

SCRAPER GROOVE

TOP

CENTER

OIL

Briggs and Stratton Corp.

Figure 2.6　Piston Rings and Assembly on Piston

The connecting rod, sometimes referred to as the "con-rod," is joined to the piston by the piston pin that is fitted through the pin bosses of the piston and the top of the connecting rod. The rod joins the piston to the crankcase. It has a removable cap at the lower end so that the rod can be bolted to the crankshaft. The ends of the connecting rod are usually machine drilled to act as a bearing, although in some cases needle type bearings are used.

The crankshaft is located in the crankcase directly below the cylinder. Each end of the crankshaft is supported

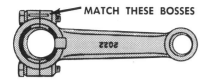

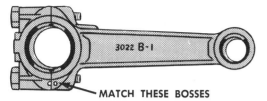
MATCH THESE BOSSES

MATCH THESE BOSSES

Clinton Engine Co.
Figure 2.7 Connecting Rods

Tecumseh Products Co.
Figure 2.8 Connecting Rods with Cap Removed

by a bearing, plain or ball, called the *main journal*. The part of the crankshaft where the connecting rod is fastened is known as the *rod journal* (a crankshaft may have one or several rod journals). The purpose of the crankshaft is to change the up and down movement of the piston and connecting rod to a rotating movement. A person riding a bicycle accomplishes the same thing. The up and down motion of the rider's legs changes to the circular motion of the drive sprocket. The crankshaft is usually made of forged steel — steel that has been heated until red-hot and then hammered or pressed into the proper shape.

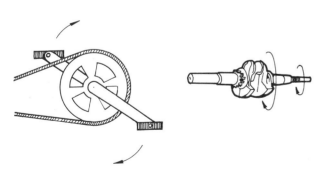

Figure 2.9 Up and Down Movement Changed to Rotating Movement

The camshaft is located in the crankcase to one side of the crankshaft. It has two off-centre *lobes* for each cylinder of the engine. These lobes push the valve lifters at a predetermined time, to allow intake or exhaust valves to open. The camshaft can be driven by two methods: by a gear arrangement and by sprockets and a timing chain. Sprockets are built on both the camshaft and crankshaft, and are connected by a drive chain that

Briggs and Stratton Corp.
Figure 2.10 Camshaft

works like a bicycle's chain and sprockets. In the gear arrangement, one gear, the *driving gear,* is mounted on the crankshaft; the other, the *driven gear,* is on the camshaft. The *bearing journals* of the camshaft are similar to the crankshaft bearings.

The timing gears will be mentioned briefly in this section but will be covered more thoroughly in another chapter. There are two gears, the *camshaft gear* and *crankshaft gear*. The gear on the camshaft has twice as many teeth as the gear on the crankshaft. The camshaft, therefore, turns at half the speed of the crankshaft.

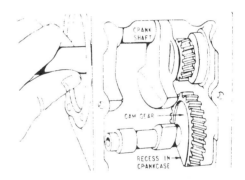

Figure 2.11 Timing Gears

The valves and lifters are located in the crankcase directly above the camshaft with their lower ends resting on the cam lobes of the camshaft. The valve lifters slide up and down in *lifter guides,* which are cylindrical holes in the cylinder block above the camshaft. In some engines the guides are removable. The action between the cam and the lifter is a rolling motion. The bottom of the lifter, therefore, has to be hard enough to withstand wear.

Figure 2.12 Valve Lifter

The valves. The valves are mushroom-shaped pieces of steel used to open or close a port or hole. The engine valves are located in the exhaust and intake ports and extend, by means of a stem, down to the valve lifters.

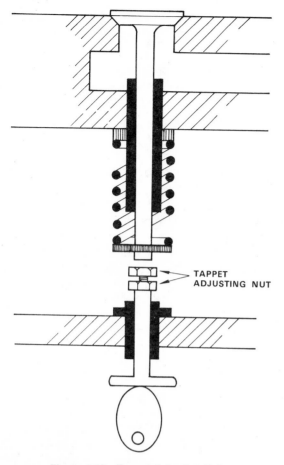

Figure 2.13   Tappet Adjusting Nut

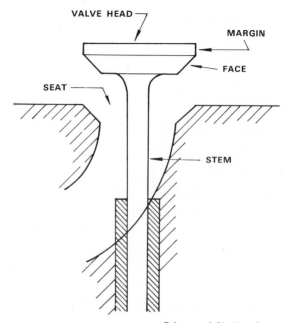

Briggs and Stratton Corp.

Figure 2.14   Parts of a Valve

In the smaller of the air-cooled engines, the valves are not adjustable for clearance distance between lifter end and valve stem end; in larger horsepower engines, the tappet adjustment nut provides adjustment.

The valves are very important in the operation of an engine; they must, therefore, be made of special metal. The *exhaust valves* must be able to withstand the tremendous heat of the exhaust gases, and so they are made of special heat-resisting alloy of nickel, tungsten, and silicon-chrome steel. Some exhaust valves are hollowed out and filled with sodium to help to disperse excess heat. The *intake valves* are made of chrome-nickel steel. The chrome gives hardness and wear-resisting qualities to the steel, and the nickel increases the strength.

The valve is composed of several parts. The wide part of the valve is the *valve head* and below it is the *valve stem*. The tapered part of the valve head is called the *valve face*, and the tapered part of the port where the valve fits is called the *valve seat*. The valve face and seat are usually tapered 30 or 45 degrees. The portion of the valve head, or edge, that is left is known as the *valve margin*.

The valve springs. The valve springs are located on

the valve stem and are fastened at the end by a pin, a split collar, or a slotted collar. The purpose of the springs is to keep the valves tightly closed when they are not being opened by the action of the camshaft and lifters. The exhaust valve springs are made of hardened spring steel. The exhaust spring is slightly larger and stiffer than the intake spring because it must withstand a greater amount of heat.

The carburetor. The carburetor is the device used to mix gasoline and air in the proper portions to operate the engine. Gasoline is in a liquid form in the storage tank, but when it enters the throat of the carburetor it is broken into tiny particles or vaporized. When it has been vaporized, it is mixed with the proportion of air that is required to operate in the cylinder for combustion. These proportions vary slightly for different makes of

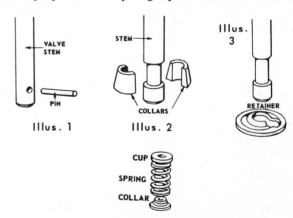

Briggs and Stratton Corp.

Figure 2.15   Valve Spring Retainer Locks

engines, but the average volume would be 10,000 gallons of air to each gallon of gasoline.

The carburetor consists of three basic parts: first, the tube, called an *air horn,* through which the air is drawn in; second, a *throttle valve* that can be adjusted to regulate air passage through the air horn, and a nozzle through which gasoline is fed into the air horn; third, a narrowed portion in the air horn called the *venturi.* The carburetor will be studied in detail in Chapter 5.

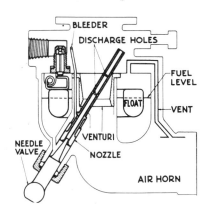

Briggs and Stratton Corp.

Figure 2.16   Part of a Carburetor

The spark plugs have a steel shell case that is threaded on one end so that it may be screwed into the threaded hole of the cylinder head. A porcelain *insulator* is placed inside the steel shell, then sealed. The lower portion, or *electrode,* is welded to the steel shell and is called the ground electrode. The centre electrode passes through the centre of the porcelain to the *high-tension lead.* A round nut is sometimes screwed on the outside end.

The magneto is the heart of the small engine. It is made up of a few component parts that will be examined more closely in a later chapter. The magneto, along with many other parts which operate in the same system, supplies a spark between the electrodes of the spark plug. This spark must occur at the proper time in the combustion chamber to ignite the fuel vapours.

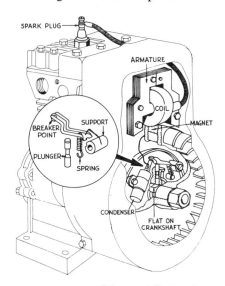

Briggs and Stratton Corp.

Figure 2.18   Magneto of an Engine

The air shroud is another important part of the small engine. It serves several important duties: it keeps foreign objects from catching or coming in contact with the flywheel; it directs the air currents from the flywheel fins over and around the cylinder fins to cool the engine in operation. An air-cooled engine, for safety's sake, should never be operated without the shroud securely fastened in place.

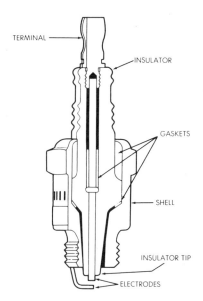

Figure 2.17   Spark Plug—Sectional View

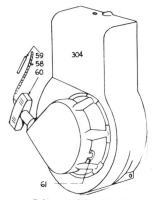

Briggs and Stratton Corp.

Figure 2.19   Air Shroud with Recoil Starter

REVIEW QUESTIONS

1. Name the two metals that are used to mold engine blocks.
2. What is the bore of an engine?

3. What purpose does the crankcase serve in the four-cycle engine?
4. What purpose does the crankcase serve in the two-cycle engine?
5. List the three uses of a cylinder head.
6. Name one reason that cast iron pistons are not used in small air-cooled engines.
7. Draw the three piston heads and name them.
8. What are the piston bosses and where are they located?
9. Name three functions of the piston rings.
10. Give another name for the "connecting rod."
11. How does the crankshaft change the motion of the piston?
12. What is forged steel?
13. What is the purpose of the camshaft of the small engine?
14. List two ways of driving camshafts.
15. What is the ratio of camshaft speed to the speed of the crankshaft?
16. Where are the valve lifters located in the small engine?
17. Describe in your own words the shape of an engine valve.
18. List three ways of locking a valve spring in place.
19. Which of the two valves of a single cylinder engine is subjected to the most heat?
20. List the three basic parts of the carburetor and state the purpose of each.
21. Where is the venturi located?
22. Describe the spark plug and its parts.
23. What is the purpose of the magneto?
24. How are foreign objects kept out of the flywheel?
25. What is used on a small engine to direct air currents over the cylinder fins?
26. What is the safety precaution concerning the air shroud?

CHAPTER 3
HAND TOOLS
AND FASTENERS

This chapter gives a full description of the hand tools, fastenings, bearings, gaskets, and general safety practices that are used in service and repair procedures. A thorough knowledge of this information is necessary in repairs and service of small engines.

HAND TOOLS

The small engine mechanic must have a sound knowl-

edge of the use of hand tools. He must learn to care for the tools and use them in the correct manner. A good mechanic chooses the correct size and kind of tool for the job it was designed to do. There are two excellent rules to remember: choose the proper tool for the job and do not abuse these tools at any time.

An efficient mechanic owns a large variety of tools. His tool kit consists of various types and sizes of wrenches, pliers, punches, chisels, files, screw drivers, feeler gauges, and hammers.

Wrenches

Wrenches come in a great variety of sizes and types, each one designed for a special operation. The proper wrench size must be picked to match the nut or capscrew, or a personal injury may occur.

The manufacturers always observe a simple rule when designing a wrench: wrench handle leverage is usually 12 inches for every one inch of socket size.

The student must learn to apply the proper amount of pressure on the wrench handle to avoid breaking either the wrench or the nut he is tightening.

The *socket wrench* is the best type to use because it is both efficient and safe.

The socket is round outside and has either six or twelve sides inside for easier positioning. Sockets are manufactured in a standard length or a deep length, and have a square opening at one end to adapt to various number of styles of handles. The socket fits closely around the nut or bolt head to help to prevent slipping.

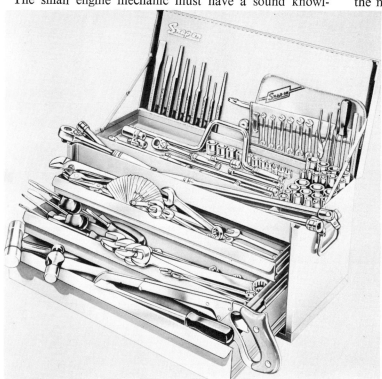

Snap-on

Figure 3.1   Mechanics Tools

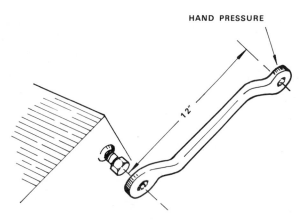

HAND PRESSURE

12"

Figure 3.2   Leverage of a Wrench

Socket drive handles are designed for many different purposes. The handles are designed to do a specific operation and are easily changed. A *speed handle* is shaped like a carpenter's brace. It is used only on smaller nuts and bolts because it does not supply enough leverage for larger ones. It is called a speed handle because it does the job more quickly than other types.

The *nut spinner handle* is recommended for use on sockets of 5/8 inch and over because greater leverage can be applied.

A *ratchet handle* resembles the nut spinner handle except for its ratcheting device which allows the handle to turn in one direction and to return without the socket. It is more efficient than the spinner handle and allows the mechanic to work in a confined area.

The *torque wrench* resembles the rachet handle and the nut spinner handle. It is designed to measure the amount of pressure applied to a nut or bolt. The torque or twist, is measured in either inch-pounds or foot-pounds. An inch-pound equals one pound of pressure applied one inch from the socket.

The *open-end wrench* is designed with a U-shaped opening at either end of its body. The openings are set at an angle to allow use of the handle in a small area. It is used when a socket cannot be placed over the nut

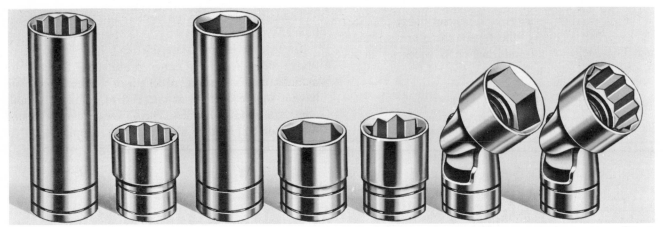

Snap-on

Figure 3.3   Types of Sockets

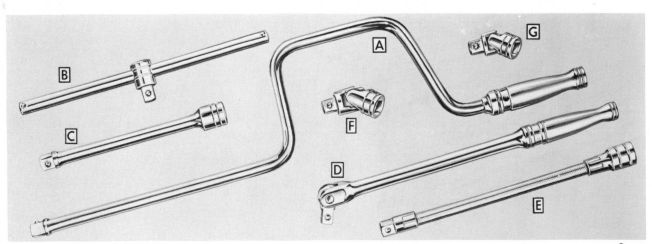

Snap-on

Figure 3.4   Speed Handles

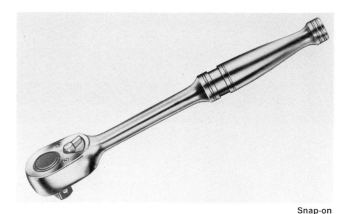

Figure 3.5   Ratchet Handle

Figure 3.6   Torque Handle

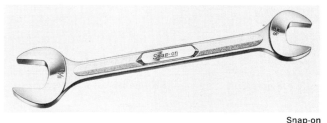

Figure 3.7   Open-end Wrench

or bolt. Open-end wrenches are machined so that they will fit one size of nut or bolt precisely. The proper size must be used to avoid spreading the wrench jaws or damaging the bolt or nut.

A *tappet wrench* is almost the same as the open-end wrench except that it is thinner and longer. It is normally used for adjusting valve tappets, but could be used on small engines in very narrow openings where a thin long wrench could be used with little pressure.

The *box-socket wrench* is commonly called the box-end wrench. This wrench has a socket-type opening on either end of the wrench body. It is used in preference to the open-end wrench in places where the socket wrench does not fit.

The *combination wrench* received this name because it is a combination of two wrenches in one: a box socket at one end and an open-end at the other. The two openings are generally the same size but there are several manufacturers who make these wrenches with one end one size smaller than the other.

The *adjustable wrench* is made with one movable smooth jaw. It does not fit snugly on a nut or bolt and, therefore, it should not be used unless no other wrench will fit.

Pliers and Their Uses

There are four types of pliers commonly used in the small engine trade.

Sidecutting or diagonal pliers are used for cutting electrical wire or pulling cotter pins.

Combination slip-joint pliers are used to grip only round stock that is unfinished. The teeth on the jaws will spoil a polished surface.

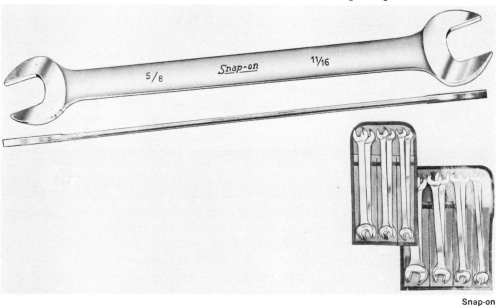

Figure 3.8   Tappet Wrenches

Snap-on

Figure 3.9   Needle Nose Pliers

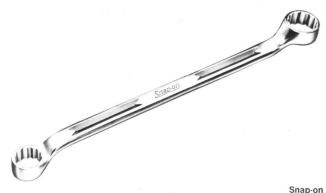

Snap-on

Figure 3.10   Sidecutting or Diagonal Pliers

Snap-on

Figure 3.11   Box Sockets

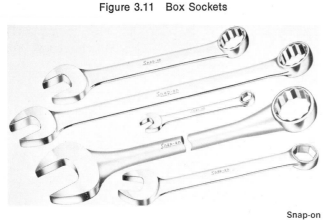

Snap-on

Figure 3.12   Combination Wrenches

Vise-grip pliers are used in place of a clamp or a pipe wrench, but they never should be used in place of a wrench.

Needle-nose pliers are used for fine instrument or electrical work inside the magneto system.

Pliers are never used on nut or bolt heads as they will damage the hexagonal sides of the nuts or bolts.

Snap-on

Figure 3.13   Adjustable Wrench

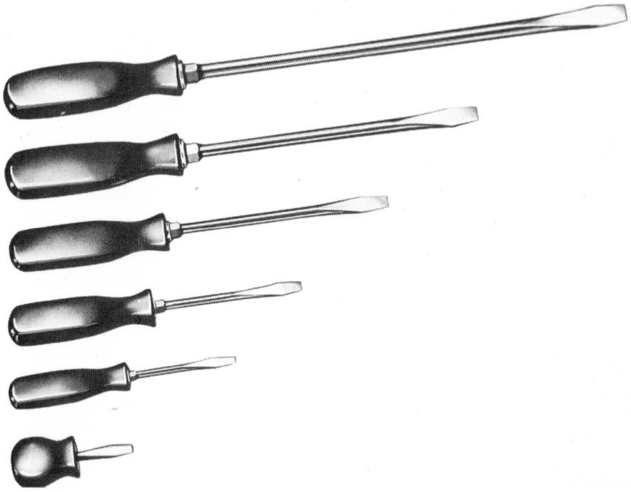

Snap-on

Figure 3.14   Standard Flat-bladed Screwdrivers

Screwdrivers

Screwdrivers must not be used for prying or chiseling, as the shank may bend or the blade may be twisted. The screwdriver must be used only to turn screws.

The end of the screwdriver is ground flat and square to fit the slot of the screw without slipping. The mechanic should be careful to choose the proper size of screwdriver for the screw slot to avoid damaging both the tip of the screwdriver and the screw slot.

The most common type of screw in general use is the straight slot, but in small engine work most of the mechanical parts are fastened to the engine block by a Phillips screw or a capscrew.

Hammers

The *lead or plastic-tipped hammer* is used specifically on surfaces that must not be damaged.

The *steel ball-peen hammer* is used to drive or strike a punch or chisel with great force.

The *rubber-tipped hammer* is used for removing or replacing seals to avoid damage to the area surrounding the seal.

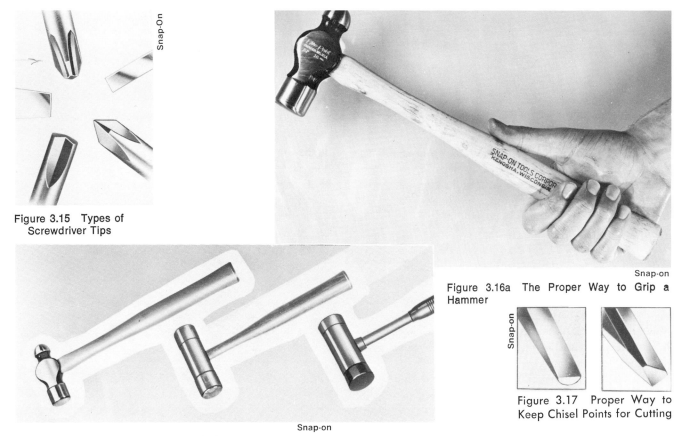

Figure 3.15 Types of
Screwdriver Tips

Figure 3.16a The Proper Way to Grip a
Hammer

Figure 3.17 Proper Way to
Keep Chisel Points for Cutting

Figure 3.16b Types of Hammers

To use any hammer properly, you should hold it near the end of the handle.

Punches

A *centre punch* is used for marking steel or making an indentation to centre a drill bit.

A *pin punch* is used to drive out a shaft or locating pin: for example, a tapered camshaft that has to be driven out of the engine block. Pin punches are available in ¼-, 5/16-, and ⅜-inch sizes.

A *starter punch* is used to free or "start" a shaft or locating pin. It is heavier than a pin punch and can therefore stand heavier blows of the hammer.

Chisels

The cold chisel is used to cut bolts or pieces of metal. It never should be used in place of a punch. Care must be taken when using it on the small engine, as the metal of the engine is soft and easily damaged. The chisel, like the screwdriver, must be properly ground and kept sharp. The mushroom heads of the chisel and punches should be removed by grinding; otherwise, a piece could break off and cause an injury.

Files

Manufacturers have designed files to perform different operations. A coarse file is preferred for removing large

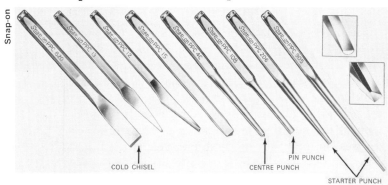

Figure 3.18 Punches

COLD CHISEL CENTRE PUNCH PIN PUNCH STARTER PUNCH

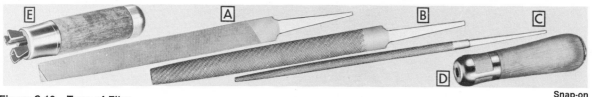

Figure 3.19   Type of Files

amounts of metal, whereas the fine file is used to produce a smoother finish. Files are manufactured in various shapes, each designed to do a specific operation: flat, round, half-round, three-cornered, and square. Their sizes are determined by the lengths of their blades.

Selecting the proper file for the job is very important. The first consideration is the amount of metal that must be removed. The single-cut file, which has teeth cut diagonally in one direction, is used for filing on a lathe or drawfiling where only small amounts of metal are removed. A double-cut file has teeth crossing one another. It is used where large amounts of metal must be removed because it has twice the cutting action. However, it leaves a rougher surface finish.

The second problem is the surface finish that is required. File teeth are cut in varying degrees of coarseness, from heavy, to medium, to the smooth cut for fine work.

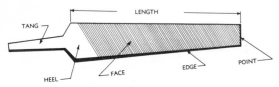

Figure 3.20   Parts of a File

Allen Wrenches

Mechanics seldom use this type of wrench except in the small engine, where it is used extensively.

Hacksaw

The hacksaw is an important tool to the mechanic. He most often uses it to cut off a bolt or for cutting a piece of metal to make a part fit.

The hacksaw is made up of the following parts: the frame, which is adjustable in length; the handle, which can be either pistol grip or straight grip; the blade, which has the teeth facing forward; and the thumbscrew for tightening the blade.

The blade breaks easily if care is not taken in the operation of the saw. The major causes of blade breakage are twisting the blade, excessive pressure on the blade, tilting the blade, and using a coarse blade on thin work.

The hacksaw blade should have fairly rigid tension.

Slight pressure should be applied to the forward stroke only and relaxed on the back stroke. The stroke should be long, passing almost the entire length of the blade over the work with a slow, steady movement.

The blade is usually 8, 10, or 12 inches long. There are blades with 14, 18, 24, and 32 teeth per inch but 18 and 32 teeth per inch blades are commonly used in the small-engine trade.

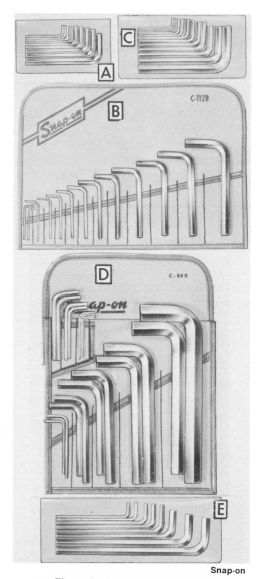

Figure 3.21   Allen Wrenches

Figure 3.22 Pistol Grip Hacksaw

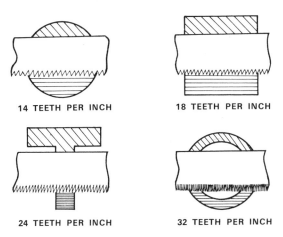

14 TEETH PER INCH   18 TEETH PER INCH

24 TEETH PER INCH   32 TEETH PER INCH

Figure 3.23 Number of Teeth per Inch

SPECIAL TOOLS AND POWER EQUIPMENT

The mechanic has a very large variety of tools, but he cannot afford to own all the tools of the trade. The shop owner usually supplies the special tools and power equipment needed to repair the units that are sold by his shop.

These special tools, sold by small engine manufacturers, include valve-spring compressors, special pliers, flywheel holders, and flywheel wrenches. Other special tools required by the service shops are dial indicators, micrometers, taps, and dies.

The special tools mentioned above are both expensive and delicate. A student must learn to use these tools with great care and store them carefully afterwards to prevent damage.

Valve-spring Compressor

The intake and exhaust valve are held in place by a stiff spring, retainer, and lock. The valve-spring compressor squeezes the spring to allow the easy removal of the spring retainer and lock.

Figure 3.25 Valve Spring Compressor

Feeler Gauge

Feeler gauges are needed to measure accurately the distance between two surfaces. They are manufactured in several ways. They may be a long flat strip, or a round hardened wire in the shape of an "L". Both types are set up in sets or books and vary in thickness from .001 inch to .050 inch.

There is another type of feeler gauge manufactured called a "GO" and "NO GO" gauge. This type of gauge is used in ignition service or for measuring air-gap on magneto systems. The blade is flat and thinner at one end than at the other.

Figure 3.24 Feeler Gauges

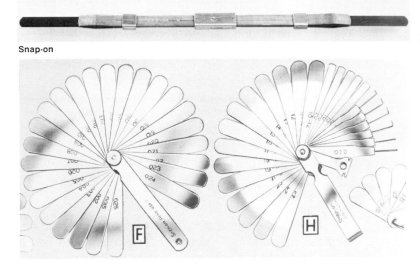

Piston-ring Compressor

The piston-ring compressor is a band-like device made of spring steel. The piston is placed inside the compressor; then the compressor is tightened by an Allen wrench. As the compressor is tightened, it pushes the piston rings into their grooves. The piston and rod assembly are placed in the cylinder. A light tap with the wooden handle of a hammer will slide the piston into the cylinder.

Figure 3.26   Piston Spring Compressor

Dial Indicators

The dial indicator is a very delicate tool and requires special care in handling and storing. This tool is important for measuring the trueness of a shaft, the wobble of a pulley or gear, and the amount of backlash of a gear. It shows these to thousandths of an inch.

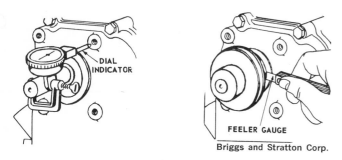

Briggs and Stratton Corp.

Figure 3.27   Dial Indicators

Micrometer

The micrometer is a delicate precision tool. It also requires special care in handling and storing to avoid damage to the adjustments.

The micrometer measures in thousandths of an inch.

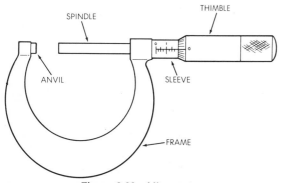

Figure 3.28   Micrometer

It is used for measuring machined parts or comparing part size to manufacturers' specifications.

Power Tools

Power tools required for small engine repair include valve seat and valve grinders, electric drill (hand and stand), and electric bench grinder. All these tools are expensive and easily damaged.

Pullers

The puller is used in many repair operations in the small engine trade. Each operation requires a different puller; the mechanic, therefore, must always refer to the master manual for the specific puller to use.

FASTENERS

The most common fastening device is the nut and bolt. It is used to hold one or more parts together so that these parts may be removed for repair or replacement.

The nut and bolt threads are described below.

The National Fine Thread has many threads per inch. It is therefore more resistant to vibration.

The National Coarse Thread has a greater thread depth, therefore it is used where greater holding power is required.

The capscrew is a finished machine screw generally used without a nut. It is manufactured in both coarse and fine threads. The coarse thread is used mainly for cylinder heads; the fine thread for other parts. Today, the capscrew is often used in place of the stud.

Studs are made of steel with a coarse thread on one end and a fine thread on the other. It is threaded into a cylinder block; the cylinder head is placed over the studs and tightened down with nuts.

Hexagonal nuts are the most popular type of nut in the small engine trade.

Other types of nuts that are manufactured are plain (square), castellated, self-locking, and slotted. Slotted and castle nuts are used to lock a rotary mower blade on a shaft. A cotter pin is placed through the slots that line up with a hole in the threads.

The self-locking nut comes in different types; they cannot be used a second time:
1. Upper threads are slightly deformed to create a friction or binding between the threads to hold the nut in place.
2. Fibre or plastic is placed near the top to create a friction when the nut is tightened on the bolt.
3. Slots are cut in the top part of the nut. Thus the upper part of the nut is smaller in diameter than the bolt, causing the slotted part to press tightly against the bolts.

Bolt and capscrews are sized according to the measurements indicated in Figure 3-35. The thread on a bolt is die cut to size to fit the inside tapered thread on a nut.

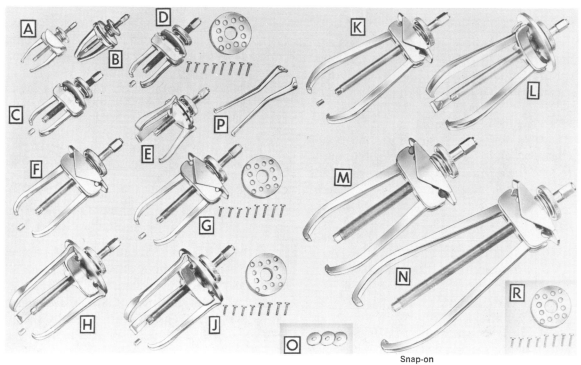

Figure 3.29 Types of Pullers

J. C. Adams Company Limited

Figure 3.30 Fine Thread

J. C. Adams Company Limited

Figure 3.31 Coarse Thread

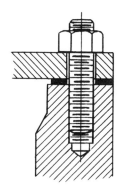

Figure 3.32 Stud

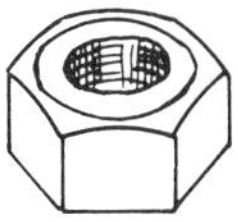

Figure 3.33 Hexagonal Nut

SQUARE

CASTLE
(CASTELLATED)

SLOTTED HEX

SELF-LOCKING

Figure 3.34 Types of Nuts

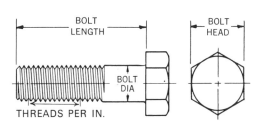

BOLT
LENGTH

BOLT
HEAD

BOLT
DIA

THREADS PER IN.

Figure 3.35 Bolt Measurement

Select the Proper Wrench

When the mechanic has memorized the standard nut and bolt sizes, he will then be able to select the proper size of wrench by sight. For bolts 1/4 to 7/16 inch, the stem diameter is 3/16 inch smaller than the head diameter; for bolts 1/2 to 3/4 inch, the stem diameter is 1/4 inch smaller than the head diameter.

The table of sizes below should be memorized to speed up the selection of wrenches for the bolt or nut:

Bolt and Nut Size	Wrench Size
1/4 inch	7/16 inch
5/16 inch	1/2 inch
3/8 inch	9/16 inch
7/16 inch	5/8 inch
1/2 inch	3/4 inch
9/16 inch	13/16 inch
3/4 inch	1 inch

Screws

A great variety of screws are used in the small engine trade, including the machine screw, self-tapping screw, and metal screw. The location and strength of the fastener will decide the type of head, the type of thread and the size of the screw.

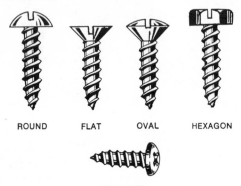

ROUND   FLAT   OVAL   HEXAGON

PHILLIPS
Spae-Naur Products Limited
Figure 3.36   Types of Screws

Locking Device

Locking devices are important to small engines because of the vibration set up in a single cylinder engine. The locking device helps to keep nuts and bolts tightly in place.

The cotter pin is a round metal split pin with an eye head. When the pin is placed through a slotted nut and a hole in the bolt, the ends are spread apart, preventing the nut from coming loose.

Figure 3.37   COTTER PIN

Lockwashers are made of spring steel and are severed so that the ends spring up in opposite directions. A great pressure is then formed under the nut when it is tightened to keep it from coming loose. A flat washer is the most common type of washer and is used to protect the metal surface from damage by the turning of the bolt head or nut.

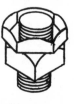

Figure 3.38   Washers: left, Flat Washer; right, Lock Washer

Locknuts and palnuts are used when vibration is extreme. A locknut is simply one plain nut tightened against another to prevent loosening. The palnut is almost identical except that it is a very thin, one thread, steel nut that is tightened against the first nut. It cannot be reused.

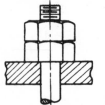

Figure 3.39   Left, Lock Nut; right, Pawl Nut

Tongued washers are simply flat washers with a square projection on the inner edge. The *"D" Washer* is another type of tongued washer, having a flat side on the inner edge. The tongue is formed to fit a special groove or the flat side of a bolt or shaft to prevent a nut from turning. The rotary action of a mower blade fastened to the threaded crankshaft may have both a "D" washer and a self-locking nut. *A wire locking device* is used to lock a series of bolt heads together to keep them from turning. A hole is drilled in the bolt head and a wire is placed through the holes and twisted together. Sometimes a seal is placed over the twisted end of wire.

Figure 3.40   Tongue Washer

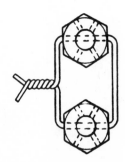

Figure 3.41   Wire Locks

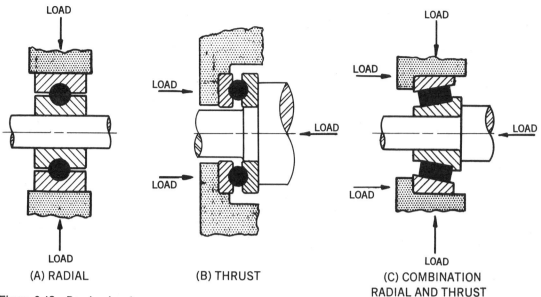

Figure 3.42   Bearing Loads

(A) RADIAL   (B) THRUST   (C) COMBINATION
                                            RADIAL AND THRUST

Bearings

Almost every metal part that moves or rotates against another is designed to use some type of bearing. This bearing surface, if lubricated sufficiently, will help to reduce wear and friction. Bearings have to support three types of loads:

Radial loads are loads at right angles to the shaft.
Thrust loads are loads parallel to the shaft.
Combination loads are both radial and thrust loads.

There are three general types of bearings used in the small engine industry to carry the radial, thrust, and combination loads.

Plain bearings. They are sometimes called friction-type bearings and may be made or faced with a large number of different types of alloys or materials ranging from copper to nylon, or they may even be a plain, polished drilled hole in the housing. They need plenty of lubrication and are capable of carrying a fairly heavy load. The design of the bearing governs whether it will carry a radial, thrust, or combination of both loads. In the larger engines, this bearing is one commonly used for connect-

Figure 3.43   Plain Bearing

ing rods and main bearings. The plain bearing may be split as it is for connecting rods and main bearings, or it may be in the form of a bushing or a solid bearing.

Ball bearings. Ball bearings are classed as anti-friction bearings because the point of contact between the two surfaces is a rolling ball. They are classified in three groups:

(a) Annular ball bearings are used mainly when radial loads are encountered. The bearing may consist of more than one row of balls; in that case, it is often called a double-row ball bearing.

(b) Cup and cone ball bearings can be adjusted to some degree because of their angular construction. They take light thrust loads as well as carrying their regular radial load.

(c) Thrust ball bearings support a load parallel to the shaft and therefore carry no weight at right angles.

ANNULAR
BALLBEARING

CUP-AND-CONE
BALLBEARING

THRUST

Canadian SKF Company Limited

Figure 3.44   Anti-friction Bearings

Roller bearings. Roller bearings employ a steel roller rather than a ball as the point of contact between two surfaces. This bearing usually has the rollers enclosed in a race or a cage. In some cases, when the rollers are very small, the bearing is known as a needle bearing. There is no race or cage in some of these needle bearings. The rollers may be straight to carry a radial load or they may be tapered to carry a combination load. These bearings can carry a heavier load than the ball bearing as they have line contact.

Figure 3.45   Roller Bearing

Canadian SKF Company Limited

General Bearing Information

Since all bearings are precision-made, dirt is one of their worst enemies. It is very important that absolute cleanliness be maintained wherever bearings are handled.

Some bearings are prelubricated. This means that they are packed with a lubricant when they are assembled at the factory and then sealed. This type of bearing should never be submerged or cleaned in a solvent since such treatment will ruin the lubricant and, eventually, the ball bearing. It is necessary that all bearings be properly lubricated; the manufacturer's specifications give correct directions.

Another main reason for ball bearing failure results from incorrect installation and adjustment. As mentioned above, manufacturer's directions are most important.

Gaskets

A gasket provides a seal between two pieces of metal. The cost of machining the metal surfaces to prevent oil or air leaks is so great that a thin, pliable material is used to complete the seal instead. There are many types and styles of gaskets. One type is neoprene rubber O-rings. They are set in a groove to prevent leakage.

Gaskets can be made from a special gasket paper—the manufacturer stamps out the shapes and sizes that are required. Gaskets can also be stamped out of sheets of cork, copper, asbestos (especially for cylinder heads), and card paper. Card paper gaskets are treated with oil to make them soft and flexible.

Always check with engine specifications for the thickness of gaskets required for shimming. Shimming gaskets vary in thickness from .003 inches to .015 inches.

Tubing, Connector and Fitting Accessories

Tubing is necessary in a small engine to provide a path for fuel from the tank to the carburetor, or to permit oil to move under pressure to a remote part of an engine to provide lubrication. The tubing can be made from preformed steel, copper, or neoprene flexible hose depending on the job it is to perform.

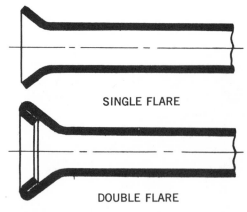

Figure 3.46   Single Flare and Double Flare Tubings

The steel tubing is shaped to the manufacturers specifications and cannot be reshaped.

Copper tubing is the most common type of metal tubing used by small engine manufacturers as it provides a certain amount of flexibility. The ends may be cut and flared with a simple flaring tool. Flexible neoprene tubing is used when a fuel tank is set some distance from the engine. The hose has little or no pressure; therefore, no clamps are required. Some engine manufacturers use a spring clip or clamp to be sure the hose does not leak because of vibration wear.

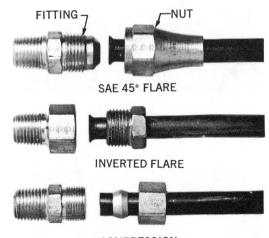

COMPRESSION
The Weatherhead Company of Canada Ltd.
Figure 3.47   Styles of Fittings

Tube Sizes and Flaring

Sizes are indicated by the outside diameter of the tube. Different thicknesses of tube walls are used for different pressures required. The tubes are connected by special connectors using a flare on the tube and compression nut tightened on a fitting.

Two types of flares are used: the single flare on copper tubing and double flare on steel tubing. The double is the stronger of the two flares.

Connectors and Fittings

Many types of connectors and fittings are available to connect the metal lines to the units. The manufacturer may use 45-degree flared, inverted flare, compression, double compression, or the regular pipe fitting. Other shapes are straight, 45-degree, and 90-degree elbow and T shape. Each fitting mentioned will have a male fitting, a seal, and a female nut. The male fitting usually has a pipe thread on one end and a special thread on the opposite end. It is impossible to mismate the connectors because each fitting has its own thread.

CARE OF TOOLS AND EQUIPMENT

Hand Tools

Hand tools are expensive to replace. An efficient mechanic always takes care of his tools. The tools should be cleaned before storage in his tool box. All worn and loose ratchets should be repaired or replaced. Drills should be properly ground and kept sharp to prevent drill bits from overheating. Hammers should have good tight handles, free from cracks and splinters.

The Successful Mechanic

The successful mechanic respects his employer's tools and equipment as well as his own. The steps to follow are
1. Keep work area clean and neat.
2. Clean and return special tools to storage area immediately after use.
3. Report any faulty equipment.
4. Try to be cheerful and respectful to both fellow workers and customers.
5. Do not take chances; follow safety precautions at all times.

SAFETY IN THE SHOP

Safe working habits are one of the most important assets to any working man.

If the mechanic applies himself to the rules listed below, he will be following safe working habits. Not every shop has the same working conditions, so this list can be expanded.
1. Fire is the greatest hazard to business. If gasoline is used, it should be stored with special care. If any fuel is spilled, it is important to wipe it up immediately, and place the rags in a metal container outside the shop. Oily wipers and damp clothes must be kept in covered metal receptacles. The fire department will be glad to explain and demonstrate the use and placement of fire extinguishers.
2. Carbon monoxide, the creeping killer, is a product of exhaust fumes. The operation of engines in a shop

without proper ventilation is playing with death. If an exhaust system is not provided in the shop, windows and doors should be kept open during the engine operation and for at least ten minutes after the engine has stopped.
3. If it is necessary to operate a lawnmower, rotary, or reel in a shop to test its operation, a 2- by 6-inch hardwood frame should be placed around the mower base. If the blade should come off for any reason, it will strike the hardwood frame and stop without injury to the operator or damage to the immediate shop area.
4. It is wise to wear safety glasses at all times in any shop. Safety goggles or shields should be at all machines, especially grinders.
5. Before any engine is started all the component parts should be in proper operating condition. There should be no tools lying near or under the machine. Oil levels, belts, and other moving parts should be checked. The manual will explain the proper operation of an unfamiliar make of engine.
6. An important rule to follow is—Don't push it, pull it. If you push a wrench instead of pulling it, your hand might slip, and your fingers may go into the machine.
7. If the engine is to be placed on a bench as a complete unit, be sure the spark plug wire is disconnected before lifting it. Otherwise the engine might start accidentally.
8. Do not lift anything that is too heavy—ask for help.

REVIEW QUESTIONS

1. List at least ten different tools an efficient mechanic has in his tool kit.
2. Describe in your own words what a speed handle looks like, and explain where it is used.
3. Describe the method for finishing a piece of metal by filing.
4. How should the cutting edge of a chisel be ground?
5. When should a box-end wrench be used?
6. What is the purpose of the torque wrench?
7. When should pliers not be used?
8. Name four types of pliers.
9. Name two common screwdrivers.
10. Explain, in your own words, why it is important to study the use of the hand tools.
11. Where do you use the micrometer and dial indicator?
12. Name three types of hammer, and tell where each is used.
13. List the parts of a hacksaw.
14. Name three causes of blade breakage in hacksaws.
15. What hacksaw blades are most common in the small engine field?
16. List some special tools required by the shop.

17. What is the purpose of the following tools?
    (a) Piston-Ring Compressor
    (b) Valve-Spring Compressor
    (c) Socket Wrench
18. What are the two types of threads used on nuts and bolts?
19. What are five steps to being a successful mechanic?
20. What is a capscrew and where is it used?
21. Draw at least three locking devices.
22. Can locknuts be used again?
23. State, in your own words, the difference between a plain bearing and a roller bearing.
24. Which of the bearings in question 23 will carry a greater load?
25. Draw the following bearing loads: (a) radial, (b) thrust, (c) combination.
26. What is a prelubricated bearing?
27. Describe the two-tongued washers and tell where they are used.
28. What variation in thickness will the shimming gasket give?
29. What is the purpose of tubing?
30. List some ways to prevent fire in a shop, besides the ones already mentioned.
31. What is another name for carbon monoxide?
32. How can carbon monoxide poisoning be prevented?
33. What safety precaution should be followed before lifting a small engine unit to a bench?
34. Add at least two new safety precautions to the list in the text book.
35. How do you select a wrench for a bolt head or nut?

CHAPTER 4
PISTONS, RINGS, AND VALVES

Before studying the piston, its problems, and its purpose, we must understand its basic parts and its function.

The piston is a cylindrical, hollow aluminum or iron part, closed on the top and open at the bottom, fitting closely within the engine cylinder or sleeve and capable of being driven alternately up and down in the cylinder. The piston transmits the force of expanding combustion gases through the piston pin to the connecting rod and crankshaft throws. Piston rings are fastened around the piston.

PISTON TERMS AND COMPONENTS

The *lands* are the parts of the piston above the top ring or between ring grooves. The lands confine and support the piston rings in their grooves.

The *heat dam* is a narrow groove cut in the top land of some pistons to reduce heat flow to the top ring groove. This groove fills with carbon during the engine operation and reduces the heat flow to the top ring.

The *compression distance* or *height* is the distance from the centre of the pin hole to the top of the piston.

The *ring belt* is the area between the top of the piston and the pin hole where grooves are machined for the installation of piston rings.

The *piston head* is the top piston surface against which the combustion gases exert pressure. The piston head may be flat, concave, convex, or irregularly shaped.

The *piston pins* (wrist pins or gudgeon pins) join the upper end of the connecting rod and the piston. Pins may be held in one of three ways:

1. Anchored in position; the bushing in the upper end of the connecting rod oscillates on the pin.
2. Clamped in the rod; the pin oscillates in the piston.
3. Full floating in both connecting rod and piston; lock rings or other devices prevent the pin from contacting the cylinder wall. This full floating type is most commonly used in small gasoline engines.

The *skirt* of the piston is located between the bottom ring groove and the open end of the piston. The skirt forms a bearing area in contact with the cylinder wall.

The *pin hole* is the opening through the piston skirt that carries the piston pin.

The *major thrust face* is that portion of the piston skirt which carries the greatest thrust load. This is on the right-hand side when viewing the engine from the flywheel with the crankshaft rotating counterclockwise.

The *minor thrust face* is the portion of the piston opposite to the major thrust face.

The *piston pin bushing* is the bushing that is fitted between the piston pin and the piston pin hole to provide a better bearing material. This is used particularly with iron pistons.

The *oil ring groove* is cut into the piston around its circumference, at the bottom of the ring belt or at the lower end of the piston skirt. Oil ring grooves are usually wider than compression ring grooves and generally have holes or slots through the bottom of the screw for oil drainage to the interior of the piston.

The *compression ring groove* is cut in the piston

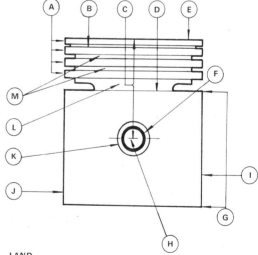

A. LAND
B. HEAT DAM
C. COMPRESSION DISTANCE
D. RING BELT
E. PISTON HEAD
F. PISTON PINS
G. SKIRT
H. PIN HOLE
I. MAJOR THRUST FACE
J. MINOR THRUST FACE
K. PISTON PIN BUSHING
L. OIL RING GROOVE
M. COMPRESSION RING GROOVE
Perfect Circle Piston Rings

Figure 4.1 Parts of the Piston

around its circumference, in the upper part of the ring belt. The depth of the groove varies depending on the piston size and types of rings used. The groove depth is the distance from the cylinder wall to the bottom of the ring groove with the piston centred in the cylinder.

The *land diameter* is the diameter of the land being measured. In some piston designs, all lands are equal in diameter and in others they may increase from top to bottom.

The *land clearance* is the difference between the diameter of the land and the cylinder diameter.

The *skirt clearance* is the difference between the piston skirt diameter and the cylinder diameter.

Th *offset pin hole* on some pistons is set to one side of the piston centre line.

Top groove spacers are steel spacers installed above the ring in a reconditioned groove to reduce the side clearance to the recommended dimension. When badly worn, top ring grooves must be machined before installing a new ring.

The *piston skirt taper* is the difference between the diameter of the piston at the top of the skirt and at the bottom of the skirt, that diameter being measured in the thrust direction.

The *piston skirt* is manufactured in a cam shape to provide proper cylinder contact and running clearance under all normal conditions of temperature and load.

PISTON CONSTRUCTION
Materials

A piston may be constructed of cast iron, semi-steel, or aluminum. The piston must be strong enough to stand up against the stresses which may be imposed and it must have a melting point above the cylinder operating temperature. It must expand at the same rate as the cylinder and, when properly lubricated, will not generate excessive friction. Cast-iron and semi-steel pistons work well, but they are quite heavy. Therefore, most modern pistons are made of aluminum because it is lighter than cast iron, is easily cast and machined, and does not generate excessive friction in the cylinder. However, aluminum pistons expand much more rapidly than cast iron when subjected to the heat of operation. They also have a much lower melting point.

When aluminum pistons were first used, they were noisy because they had to be fitted in the cylinder with considerably more clearance than the cast-iron pistons. This caused a piston slap and rattle in a cold engine until the piston could expand to fit the cylinder. This difficulty was finally overcome by making the piston skirt from a flexible aluminum alloy.

The aluminum piston has now been developed to a point where its advantages outweigh its disadvantages;

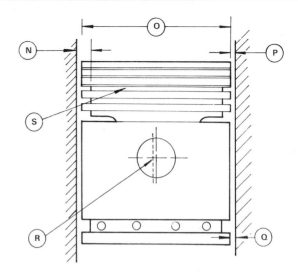

N. GROOVE DEPTH	Q. SKIRT CLEARANCE
O. LAND DIAMETER	R. OFFSET PIN HOLE
P. LAND CLEARANCE	S. TOP GROOVE SPACER

Perfect Circle Piston Rings

Figure 4.2 Piston Measurements

they are almost universally used in small engine construction.

A lighter piston involves less force or less work for the reciprocating parts and, therefore, gives a higher speed for the engine along with better acceleration. This lessened work load also decreases bearing loads at high speeds and reduces the side thrust on the cylinder walls. Because of the greater heat conductivity of aluminum, the piston head runs cooler and often allows the use of higher compression ratios.

Aluminum pistons also have the desirable characteristic of conducting the heat away from the combustion chamber far more rapidly than the cast iron ones, but they also melt at a much lower temperature. Pistons of aluminum alloys seldom melt entirely, but their strength lessens very rapidly as the temperature increases. In some cases of stuck or broken rings, the top edge of the piston or the aluminum lands between the rings may soften and be blown away by the hot gases in the combustion chamber.

Severe and continued detonation is also responsible for broken pistons and wedged rings. When overheated, the aluminum become soft and plastic enough to allow the ring grooves to deform. The strength of the aluminum pistons may be increased by alloying aluminum with other metals and through heat treatment processes. Some of the materials added to aluminum are copper, nickel, silicon, and magnesium.

Design

It was mentioned before that the piston head comes in many different designs. The piston head or dome is the surface against which the force of the expanding gases is exerted. The piston dome may be flat, concave, convex, or irregular. A great variety of shapes are needed, especially in two-cycle engines, to promote or direct turbulence and to control combustion. A groove is sometimes cut into the piston to serve as the heat dam to reduce the amount of heat reaching the top piston ring.

The piston ring grooves are usually located above the piston pin but, sometimes, there is another groove below the piston pin. The piston rings are carried in these grooves. There are two types: compression rings and oil rings. The upper ring or rings prevent compression leakage while the lower ring or rings control oil leakage to the combustion chamber. The lower ring grooves usually have holes drilled at the back of them to permit oil drainage from behind the ring.

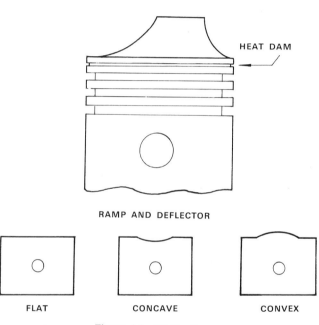

RAMP AND DEFLECTOR

FLAT   CONCAVE   CONVEX

Figure 4.3   Piston Domes

The main section of the piston which we have described as the skirt forms a bearing area with the cylinder wall and takes the thrust of the crank shaft. Pistons are internally braced to make them as strong as possible to withstand the tremendous pressure exerted on the top of the piston.

In some cases, the piston skirt is extended downward on the thrust sides to form a *slipper piston*. This design increases the area of piston contact with the cylinder wall on the thrust faces.

Some pistons are also cut away or partially cut away around the piston pin holes. This is known as a relief. It is intended to provide additional clearance to avoid the danger of seizing if the piston become over-heated and expands excessively.

Pistons are designed in many different ways. Some have a *T-slot split skirt;* some have the *U-slot split skirt.* These slots are placed on the minor thrust side of the piston to provide flexibility in the piston skirt. By this means the piston can be fitted more closely when cold and can expand when hot without damaging the piston or the cylinder.

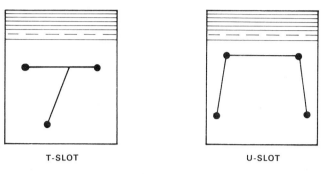

T-SLOT   U-SLOT

Figure 4.4   Styles of Pistons

Another type of piston design is the *strut type.* This piston has a steel alloy insert cast into the aluminum piston to control the expansion of the aluminum and to maintain a constant clearance. Such pistons are skeleton-like and do not contact the cylinder walls around the piston pin holes.

Another design is known as the *steel belted type.* In these pistons, a steel ring is cast into the aluminum piston above the piston pin hole to help control expansion.

Many aluminum pistons are cam-ground, or oval shaped. The skirts will be out of round when the piston is cold. The thrust faces, therefore, will have the greater diameter. The skirt will become more nearly round when the piston expands at operating temperatures.

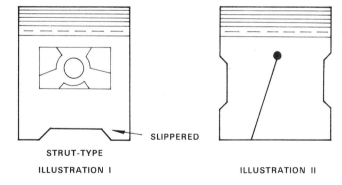

SLIPPERED

STRUT-TYPE
ILLUSTRATION I   ILLUSTRATION II

Figure 4.5   Styles of Pistons

Tolerances

Pistons are also slightly tapered in most cases. The dome becomes much hotter than the skirt and, therefore, is tapered to a smaller diameter. The piston is always smaller above the top ring. If the entire piston is not tapered, the top lands are, at least, smaller in diameter than the skirt because the skirt needs less clearance.

There is no set rule on the amount of clearance to be provided between the piston and the cylinder. It depends on the design of the cooling system, the piston design, the material and to a certain extent, the service conditions under which the engine is to operate. It is customary to fit solid-skirt, cast-iron pistons to about .00075 to .001 per inch of diameter of piston. A four-inch piston would therefore be .003 to .004 inches smaller than the cylinder. Aluminum pistons can be fitted much more closely. The fit, however, depends largely on the design of the piston and on the instructions of the manufacturer's specifications.

The clearance between the cylinder and piston can be measured in different ways. First of all, a feeler gauge can be inserted between the piston and the cylinder wall. The strip or feeler gauge should be about a half inch wide and long enough to extend the full length of the cylinder. The measurement with the feeler gauge should be taken on the thrust side of the skirt.

The piston clearance can also be measured by subtracting the maximum diameter of the piston from the minimum diameter of the cylinder as measured by inside and outside micrometers. Measurement must be made at several points in the cylinder and on the piston. All piston clearance recommendations are made for use when the temperature is approximately 70 degrees Fahrenheit.

Resizing Pistons

As a piston wears and becomes overheated, it is likely to become smaller in diameter. When this happens, the piston will slap in the cylinder and will allow oil to by-pass the rings. This will place an undue load on the oil control rings. As a result, oil may be pulled out of the crankcase and burned; this is called oil pumping.

There are several ways to resize a piston. One method consists of heating the piston and expanding it. However, as this method requires specialized equipment, it is not often used. A more popular method *knurls* the outside of the piston with a variety of equipment and tools.

Knurling raises the metal in ridges or cross patterns along the piston and thereby increases the piston diameter. In addition, this method creates pockets on the piston surface which gather and retain a film of oil to assist in lubricating and sealing.

When pistons are inspected for wear after the engine has been disassembled the cylinder should always be checked. A visual inspection will show if there are any cracks, stripped bolt holes, broken pins, or scores. An inside micrometer, or a telescoping gauge and micrometer, will determine the size of the cylinder bore. The manufacturer of the engine usually supplies tables or

Perfect Circle Piston Rings

Figure 4.6   Knurled Piston

specifications with lists for standard cylinder sizes. The measuring faces of the instrument must be placed so that a line between them forms a right angle with the walls of the cylinder.

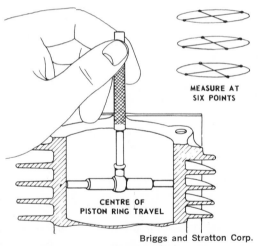

MEASURE AT SIX POINTS

CENTRE OF PISTON RING TRAVEL

Briggs and Stratton Corp.

Figure 4.7   Measuring Cylinder Bore

Resizing Cylinder Bores

Some small engine companies state that a cylinder must be resized if the bore is more than .003 inches over size, or if .0015 inches out of ground on cast iron cylinders, or .0025 inches out of ground on the aluminum light-weight cylinders.

Resizing a cylinder bore to the next over-size is a comparatively easy operation. It is always resized to exactly .010 inches, or .020 inches, or .030 inches over-standard-size as shown by the manufacturer's specifications. If this is done accurately, the stock size over-sized piston and rings will fit perfectly and proper clearances will be maintained.

The cylinder, either cast iron or light-weight, may be quickly resized with a good hone as recommended by the manufacturer for the various engine models to produce the correct cylinder wall finish.

If a boring bar is used, a hone should be used after the boring operation to produce the proper cylinder wall finish.

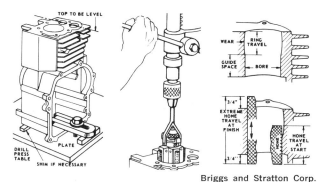
Figure 4.8   Honing a Cylinder

Honing can be done with a portable electric drill, but it is usually easier to use a drill press. If equipment is not available, it may be done by an outside machine shop. The sequence for honing a cylinder is outlined below. The cylinder is cleaned of all burrs and bits of gasket, and then fastened to a heavy iron plate. Shims may be necessary.

The drill press spindle is aligned to the bore by using a level.

The drill press table must be well oiled. The cylinder and plate are set, but not fastened, on the table and the hone drive shaft is put into the drill chuck. If a portable drill is used, the cylinder and plate are placed on the floor.

The hone is put into the cylinder, connected to the drive shaft on the drill, and set so that it can extend only one inch from the top and bottom of the cylinder. On a portable drill, a wooden block can be used as a stop for the hone. In the cylinder, the hone should fit in the middle and be adjusted until it is snug with the cylinder wall. The hone must now be on centre and aligned with the drive shaft and spindle.

When the drill is started, the hone must not be forced. It should move at 300 to 700 rpm's. The first operation should be at the bottom of the cylinder. The wear is minimal there, but the cylinder is round and will guide the hone to a straight bore. Gradually, the strokes are lengthened until the hone is moving the whole length of the cylinder; it must not, however, extend more than one inch beyond the end of the cylinder.

Whenever the cutting tension drops, the hone is tightened. The bore is constantly checked with a micrometer. The final cut should be .0005 inches larger to allow for shrinkage when the cylinder cools. A finishing stone is used when the cut is within .0015 inches of the final bore. Always bore .010 or .020 or to the exact over-size dimensions above the manufacturer's specifications. The cylinder, when finished, should have a cross-hatched appearance that will allow proper lubrication and ring break-in. This can be produced by the use of the proper stones, the proper lubrication, and the proper spindle speed within the cylinder during the last few strokes.

After the honing, the cylinder must be washed in a solvent such as kerosene to rid it of the shavings. The bore should also be washed with a brush, and soap and water.

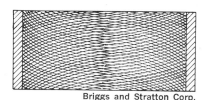
Briggs and Stratton Corp.
Figure 4.9   Bore Cross Hatching

REMOVING THE PISTON AND CONNECTING ROD

First of all, the connecting rod locks are bent down; then the connecting rod cap and any carbon or ridge around the top of the cylinder bore are removed. This will keep the rings from breaking. The piston and rod are pushed out through the top of the cylinder.

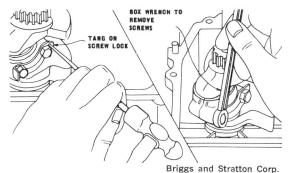
Briggs and Stratton Corp.
Figure 4.10   Removing Capscrews from Rod Cap

Figure 4-11 shows the type of wear that may have taken place on the piston.

To Remove Connecting Rod

The piston pin locks are removed with needle-nose pliers. One end of the piston pin is usually drilled to help with the removal of this lock.

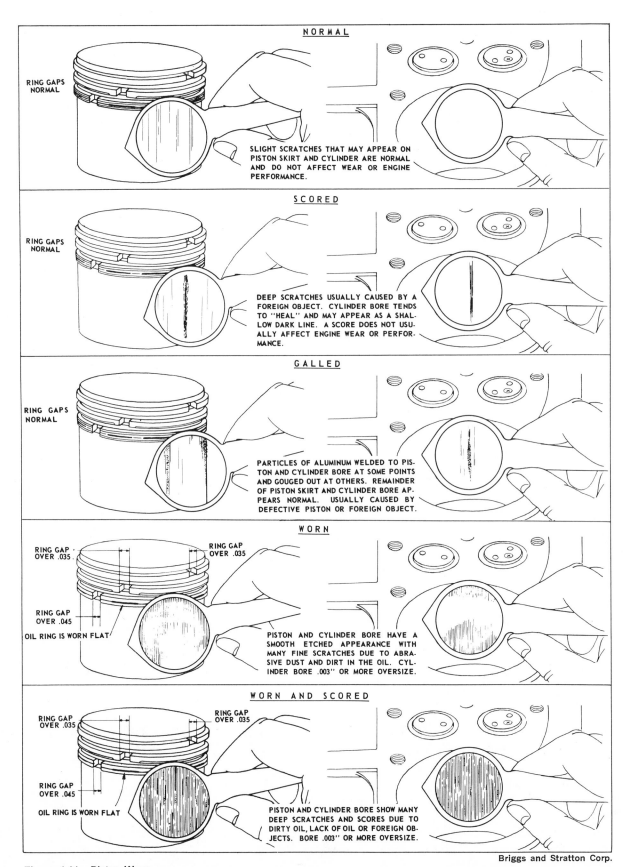

NORMAL

RING GAPS NORMAL

SLIGHT SCRATCHES THAT MAY APPEAR ON PISTON SKIRT AND CYLINDER ARE NORMAL AND DO NOT AFFECT WEAR OR ENGINE PERFORMANCE.

SCORED

RING GAPS NORMAL

DEEP SCRATCHES USUALLY CAUSED BY A FOREIGN OBJECT. CYLINDER BORE TENDS TO "HEAL" AND MAY APPEAR AS A SHALLOW DARK LINE. A SCORE DOES NOT USUALLY AFFECT ENGINE WEAR OR PERFORMANCE.

GALLED

RING GAPS NORMAL

PARTICLES OF ALUMINUM WELDED TO PISTON AND CYLINDER BORE AT SOME POINTS AND GOUGED OUT AT OTHERS. REMAINDER OF PISTON SKIRT AND CYLINDER BORE APPEARS NORMAL. USUALLY CAUSED BY DEFECTIVE PISTON OR FOREIGN OBJECT.

WORN

RING GAP OVER .035 RING GAP OVER .035

RING GAP OVER .045

OIL RING IS WORN FLAT

PISTON AND CYLINDER BORE HAVE A SMOOTH ETCHED APPEARANCE WITH MANY FINE SCRATCHES DUE TO ABRASIVE DUST AND DIRT IN THE OIL. CYLINDER BORE .003" OR MORE OVERSIZE.

WORN AND SCORED

RING GAP OVER .035 RING GAP OVER .035

RING GAP OVER .045

OIL RING IS WORN FLAT

PISTON AND CYLINDER BORE SHOW MANY DEEP SCRATCHES AND SCORES DUE TO DIRTY OIL, LACK OF OIL OR FOREIGN OBJECTS. BORE .003" OR MORE OVERSIZE.

Briggs and Stratton Corp.

Figure 4.11   Piston Wear

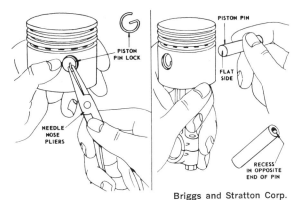

Briggs and Stratton Corp.

Figure 4.12   Removing Piston Pin

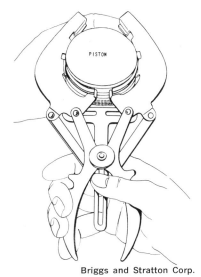

Briggs and Stratton Corp.

Figure 4.13   Removing Rings

The rings are taken off one at a time, and slipped over the ring lands. A ring expander prevents damage to the ring and piston.

If the bore is to be resized, there is no reason to check the piston, since a new over-sized piston assembly will be used.

If, however, the cylinder is not to be resized and the piston shows no signs of wear or scoring, the piston should be checked.

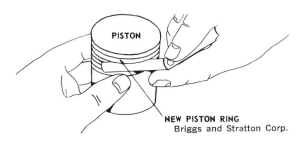

NEW PISTON RING
Briggs and Stratton Corp.

Figure 4.14   Checking Ring Land Clearance

To check the piston the carbon should be cleaned from the top ring groove. A new ring is inserted in the groove, and the remaining space in the groove checked with a feeler gauge. If a .005 inch feeler gauge can be inserted on all models, the piston is worn and should be replaced.

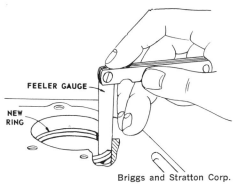

FEELER GAUGE

NEW RING

Briggs and Stratton Corp.

Figure 4.15   Checking Ring End Gap

To check the rings, all the carbon should be cleaned from the ends of the rings and from the cylinder bore. The old rings are placed, one at a time, one inch down into the cylinder and the gap measured with a feeler gauge. If ring gap is greater than shown in the table of manufacturer's specifications, the rings should be rejected.

Checking the Connecting Rod

If the crank pin bearing in the rod is scored, the rod must be replaced. The rejection sizes of crank pin bearing hole and piston pin bearing holes are shown on the tables in the engine manual. Oversize piston pins are available in case the connecting rod and piston are worn in the piston pin bearing. If, however, the crank pin bearing in the connecting rod is worn, the rod should be replaced. The rod should never be filed or fitted.

Reassembling the Piston and Connecting Rod

The piston pin is a push-fit in both the piston and connecting rods on some models of engines. On models using a solid piston pin, one end is flat and the other is recessed. Some engines use a hollow pin. A pin lock is put in one of the pin hole grooves, and the piston pin inserted through the pin hole in the opposite side of the piston until it stops against the pin lock. If a solid pin is used, the flat end is inserted first. Either end of a hollow pin may be inserted first. Needle-nose pliers are used to assemble a pin lock in the remaining end (recessed, if a solid pin is used) of the piston pin. The lock must be firmly set in the pin hole groove.

Assembling Piston Rings

The engine specifications should be checked for the various rings and for the proper positioning of each. Take

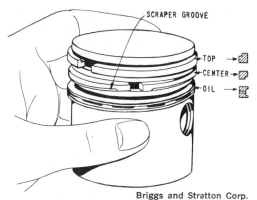

Briggs and Stratton Corp.

Figure 4.16   Proper Ring Installation

note especially of the centre compression ring. The scraper groove should always be down toward the piston skirt. The oil return holes must be clean and carbon removed from all grooves. In aluminum alloy engines, the expander ring must be installed under the oil ring in the sleeve.

The rings and piston skirt must be oiled and the rings compressed with a ring compressor.

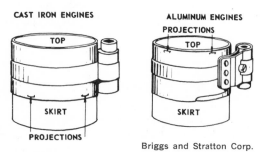

Briggs and Stratton Corp.

Figure 4.17   Using Ring Compressor

The piston and compressor are turned upside down on the bench and pushed downward, so the piston head and edge of the compressor band are even when tightening the compressor. The compressor is tightened fully to compress the rings; then the compressor is loosened very slightly. No attempt should ever be made to install a piston and ring assembly without the ring compressor.

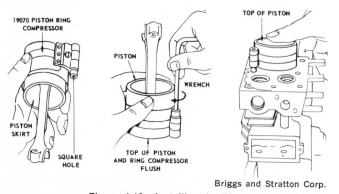

Briggs and Stratton Corp.

Figure 4.18   Installing the Piston

Installing Piston and Rod Assembly

The connecting rod and piston assembly with its rings compressed are put into the cylinder bore. The piston and rod are pushed into the cylinder. The crankshaft is oiled. The connecting rod is pulled against the crankshaft and then the rod cap is assembled so that the assembly marks are aligned. Some rods do not have assembly marks and the rod and cap will fit only in one position.

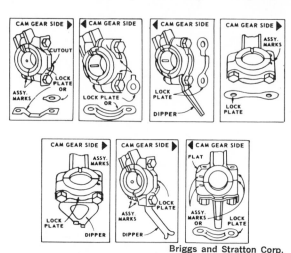

Briggs and Stratton Corp.

Figure 4.19   Match Marks

The capscrews and screw locks are assembled with the oil dipper, if one is used. The capscrews are tightened to the torque required by the engine manufacturer. The crank shaft is rotated two revolutions to guarantee that the rod is correctly installed. If the rod strikes, the connecting rod has been installed incorrectly or the cam-gear is out of time. When the crankshaft operates freely, the screw locks should be bent against the screw heads.

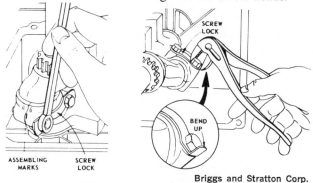

Briggs and Stratton Corp.

Figure 4.20   Securing Rod Gap

The rod screws should be tightened securely. After the rod screws are tightened, the rod should be able to move sideways on the crank pin of shaft. If not, the rod screws should be adjusted. A torque wrench should be used to prevent loose or over-tight cap screws which result in breakage and scoring.

PISTON RINGS

Piston rings are cut from a soft circular piece of metal, under spring tension. They are installed in the piston grooves to provide a movable seal between the combustion chamber and the crankcase.

Piston rings prevent the escape of the gases that have been expanded by the heat of combustion in the cylinder. Because these seals keep the expanded gases from escaping, pressure builds up in the cylinder, and (when translated through the piston and rod assemblies, this pressure rotates the crankshaft. At the same time, piston rings prevent excess oil loss into the combustion chamber and they maintain a thin film of oil in the cylinder walls to lubricate them.

Piston rings provide this movable seal while operating under widely variable conditions of speed and acceleration. They are exposed alternately to a partial vacuum and then to pressures as high as 800 pounds per square inch from the hot corrosive gases which may approach 4,000 degrees Fahrenheit. They must change diameter rapidly in order to conform to the variations in the cylinder wall.

The metal used for piston rings must meet a number of requirements. It must be a good bearing material and it must have a low rate of wear. All wear faces must be coated with such material. The metal must be suitably hard and strong, yet readily machinable. It must be good spring material and resistent to fatigue. These ring materials must be able to carry high loads and able to operate under *boundary location conditions,* conditions of backward and forward motion. The metal must retain its mechanical strength while working at the high temperature and pressure in the engine; it must tolerate hot corrosive products of combustion without wearing excessively.

To satisfy all these requirements, the rings are made from nearly 15 different types of cast iron and steel. Piston rings are an outstanding example of a high-precision product manufactured at a moderate cost.

Ring sides must be smooth and must fit flat against the piston ring grooves around the entire circumference. When rings are confined inside the cylinder diameter, the ring faces must conform to this cylinder wall. The ring tension must be accurately controlled during design and and manufactured to ensure proper unit pressure against the cylinder wall. Too much pressure will cause rapid wear and perhaps scuffing or scoring. Too little tension will result in a loss of oil and blow-by control. Blow-by is a slight leakage of burned gases through the ring end clearance. The ring manufacturer must pay constant attention to the surface finishes, the tolerances and the metallurgic qualities of the ring material in order to ob-

tain all these desired characteristics. For example, the tolerance on ring width on production runs is held to one half to one thousandth of an inch. Strict quality control and a full visual inspection of the finished product ensure that only rings of proper quality are packaged and shipped.

History of the Piston Ring

Until as late as 1920, most engines used only plain compression rings. There were no specialized oil rings. Since driving or operating speeds were low, compression rings satisfactorily controlled the small amount of oil splashed on the cylinder walls by connecting rods. As operating speeds and engine revolutions increased, and as pressure-fed lubrication systems were introduced, a problem arose. Connecting rod bearings, even when new and operating with minimum clearance, threw more oil onto the cylinder walls than the simple compression rings could control. Small engine operators naturally complained of the constant oil consumption and added expense. At the same time, they wanted still higher top speeds which further increased such oil consumption. Finally, the problem of excessive engine oil consumption became so general that a solution had to be found.

The slotted oil ring was introduced in 1921. This ring was made with a continuous channel around its face. Slots were milled through this channel. Small holes were drilled to the bottom of the grooves to permit the oil which collected in the channel to drain back to the crankcase.

This early oil ring development introduced two important principles of oil control still valid today.

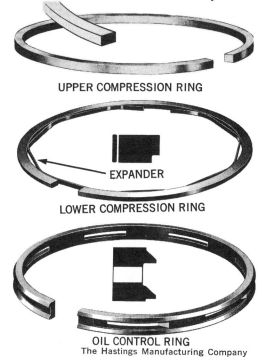

UPPER COMPRESSION RING

EXPANDER

LOWER COMPRESSION RING

OIL CONTROL RING
The Hastings Manufacturing Company
Figure 4.21 Piston Rings

1. Narrow ring faces provide hard unit wall pressure to restrict the passage of oil past the rings.
2. Openings to the oil rings and piston grooves provide for oil collection and drainage.

Following the introduction of the first slotted oil ring, there was a gradual evolution of ring materials and machining processes, but no major design improvements until another type of oil ring was introduced in 1931.

This slotted oil ring had a much narrower face than the earlier model and provided almost twice the unit wall pressure to cope with the ever-increasing engine speeds, horsepower, and compression ratios.

Improved oil rings were very helpful in controlling blow-by and excessive oil consumption, but a need arose for improved compression rings as well.

In solving one problem, another arose. Insufficient oil in the compression ring area caused excessive blow-by and rapid wear, while too much oil caused excessive oil consumption when plain compression rings were used. The solution seems simple with the benefit of hindsight. Oil rings must meter sufficient oil past themselves for compression ring lubrication and sealing. Compression rings must provide not only a combustion gas field but also an effective final oil control.

Research was directed at the stroke-by-stroke investigation of piston ring action in the engine cycle. Let us review their findings.

Cylinder walls are lubricated on upward compression and exhaust strokes of the piston by oil thrown off by the connecting rod bearings. Much more oil is usually thrown onto the cylinder walls than is required for lubrication. Most of it must be wiped away by the rings and

returned to the crankcase. The excess oil wiped from the cylinder walls helps to keep the walls, pistons, and rings clean by trapping and carrying away any particles of carbon, dirt, and engine wear debris.

The rings below the top ring wipe most of the oil from the cylinder wall as the piston starts down. Each successive ring cuts the oil film on the cylinder wall a little thinner. The oil rings remove most of it, however. The difference in pressure between the partial vacuum in the combustion chamber and the atmospheric pressure in the crankcase tends to force oil upward past the rings. As the piston continues downward, the top compression ring rests against the upper surface of the ring groove. The lower outer edge of the ring wipes oil from the cylinder wall. This oil is forced or wedged into spaces below and behind the ring in the piston groove. In spite of the wiping action of all the rings, an oil film is left on the entire cylinder wall area through which the rings have travelled.

In the compression stroke, the compression pressure at the beginning of the stroke forces the top ring downward to form a seal between the lower side of the ring and the groove.

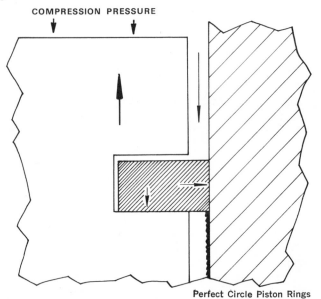

COMPRESSION PRESSURE

Perfect Circle Piston Rings

Figure 4.23 Seal Is Formed Between Side of Ring and Side of Groove

Compression pressure acting on the top of the ring is added to ring tension to force the ring outward; this forms a better seal between the cylinder wall and the ring face. Near the upper end of the compression stroke, ignition occurs and in a few thousandths of a second, the temperature reaches a peak of approximately 4,000 degrees Fahrenheit.

On the power stroke, the piston commences its downward movement; the combustion chamber pressure rapidly increases to 800 pounds per square inch or more.

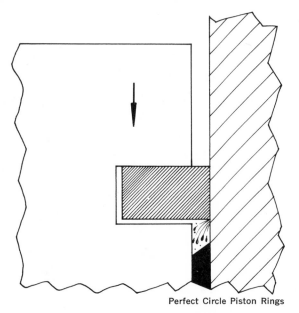

Perfect Circle Piston Rings

Figure 4.22 Lower Outer Corner of Ring Wipes Oil from Cylinder Wall

This pressure acts on the back of the ring to force it out toward the cylinder wall with the full force of the combustion pressure. Both the ring tension and combustion pressure, therefore, work together to seal combustion gases above the piston.

A small amount of blow-by is normal. It occurs during the momentary lag before a complete side seal is obtained. Expansion of the combustion gas forces the piston ring quickly downward in the cylinder. The wiping action of all the piston rings is controlled so that a thin film of oil is left on the cylinder wall over the entire area included in the ring travel to lubricate the rings and the cylinder wall.

The intake air-fuel mixture contains a small percentage of extremely fine, gritty dust, some of which passes through the air cleaner. Part of this gritty dust sticks to the oil film on the cylinder wall.

Some of these abrasives adhering to the oil on the cylinder wall. In addition, hot combustion gases partially burn and carbonize the oil film left on the cylinder wall. The piston starts upward on the exhaust stroke, the ring wipes part of the carbonized surface from the oil film on the cylinder wall including any gritty dust. The balance of this mixture is left on the cylinder wall and is passed over by the ring as it moves upward. This mixture of partially burned and carbonized oil and gritty dust acts as a cutting compound and is responsible for increasing the rate of wear of both the cylinder wall and the face of the ring. Early tests proved conclusively that, on the one hand, an extremely thin film of oil left on the cylinder wall would definitely slow down this rate of wear on the cylinders, rings, and pistons. On the other hand, thicker films tend to trap more abrasives and to carbonize excessively on the cylinder wall.

Investigations to determine the oil film thickness necessary to meet the requirements of both oil economy and lubrication have shown that when a film of oil one-tenth of a millionth of an inch thick is lost from the cylinder wall during each firing stroke, the result is a consumption rate of 2,500 to 3,750 hours per gallon — excellent oil economy. On the other hand, if the oil film that is lost is one-millionth of an inch thick, oil consmption amounts to 250 to 375 hours per gallon — very poor economy. The option, therefore, must be an oil film thickness on the cylinder wall less than one-millionth of an inch, in order to satisfy the requirements of adequate lubrication and satisfactory oil economy.

Since the top ring is exposed to the highest temperature and pressure, sufficient oil must be permitted to pass upward and provide an oil film between the top ring and the cylinder wall, even at the top of the ring travel. Otherwise, the cylinder will wear at an excessive rate in this area and scuffing or scoring may occur. The top must also act as a final oil control ring and wipe back the oil not required for lubrication to prevent it from being burned and lost. The downward wiping ability of the ring depends upon its maintaining a positive contact between the ring face and the cylinder wall.

Ring Terms

Ring width is the distance from top to bottom of the ring as measured in fractions of an inch.

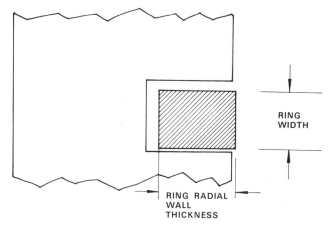

Figure 4.24   Ring Clearances

Radial Wall Thickness is the distance, in thousandths of an inch, from the face to the back side of the ring. There are four classifications of radial wall thickness:

1. *Thick wall rings* have a radial thickness equal to the cylinder diameter divided by twenty.
2. *"D" wall rings* have a radial thickness equal to the cylinder diameter divided by 22.
3. *SAE wall rings* have a radial thickness in accordance with SAE published recommendations. Ring size determines wall thickness and there is no constant ratio of wall thickness to diameter.
4. *Shallow wall rings* have special radial walls which are less than SAE specifications. These must be used with some type of expander ring or in shallow groove. There

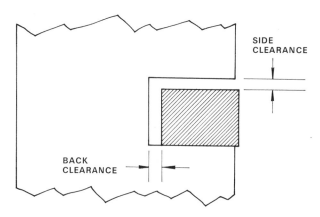

Figure 4.25   Ring Clearance

are no industry standards for shallow wall rings, since each manufacturer has its own specifications.

Side clearance is the axle, or up and down, clearance between the side of the ring and the ring groove.

Back clearance is the clearance between the back of the ring and the bottom of the ring groove when both piston and ring are centred in the cylinder.

End clearance is the distance between the ring ends when the rings are confined in a cylinder of diameter specified for the ring being measured. End clearance is often called "ring gap." Manufacturer's tables specify proper end clearance. It varies with ring size and type of application.

Use of Piston Rings

The number of rings installed on a piston may vary with different manufacturers. Some use two compression rings and one oil control ring and others use two of each.

Compression rings, located in the top grooves of the piston, actually have a double purpose. The first is to prevent the escape of engine compression down past the piston and the second is to prevent the passage of heat along the side of the piston. If the compression rings are to do a good job, engine oil must be used to help seal the expanding gases above the piston. It is important that the amount of oil getting to the compression rings be controlled, as mentioned before.

The lower grooves in the piston which accommodate oil control rings are drilled so that the oil can go through the slots in the ring and then through the drillholes, and down into the oil pan. The size of the drill holes in the piston, along with the size of the slots in the oil ring, regulates the amount of oil returned to the pan. These openings also fix the amount of oil allowed to reach the compression rings; the oil then helps the rings to make their seal.

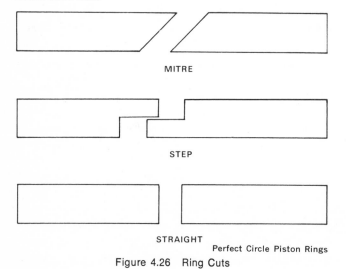

MITRE

STEP

STRAIGHT

Perfect Circle Piston Rings

Figure 4.26 Ring Cuts

The sealing effect of the piston ring is accomplished by placing a slight strain on the original casting. After the rings have been machined to the correct dimensions and then severed, the ends of the ring will "spring apart." This space created by the ends of the rings springing apart is called "ring-gap" or "end-gap." There are several methods of severing the rings: mitre, step, and straight.

CLEANING THE PISTON

The piston should be cleaned and examined for scuffing and scoring, cracks on the head or skirt, and bent or broken lands. A damaged piston must be discarded.

If carbon is allowed to remain on the sides of the piston grooves, side clearance will be reduced and ring sticking will be aggravated. Excessive carbon in the bottom of the groove will make a ring protrude from the ring land far enough to make installation a problem and to cause scoring when the engine is started.

The end of a broken ring filed to a sharp edge makes an excellent tool for cleaning ring grooves. It is used to remove as much carbon as possible from the grooves, and then the piston is soaked in a good liquid cleaning solution. After the remaining carbon has been softened in the cleaning tank, the groove is cleaned again; care must be taken not to scratch the sides of the grooves. A wire brush might score the ring-to-groove seal with scratches and should not be used. The bristles will also round the outside corner of piston lands and result in less support for the rings and decreased efficiency of the piston and ring combination.

TOP GROOVE WEAR

After it has been cleaned, the top groove of a used piston should always be checked for wear. Since it is exposed to the highest temperature and pressure in the cylinder, as well as to all airborne abrasives that enter the engine, the top groove area is subject to the most wear.

New compression rings should never be installed in grooves worn beyond allowable limits. New rings simply cannot form a seal against excessively worn and uneven piston groove sides.

A new ring in a worn groove will sag, causing the upper corner of the ring face to contact the cylinder wall. Then, on four-cycle engines, the ring will whip oil up into the combustion chamber instead of down into the crankcase. In addition, constant deflection of a new ring in a worn groove will eventually result in ring fatigue and breakage.

Checking Ring Grooves For Wear

A fast and accurate check to determine when ring grooves are worn beyond allowable limits can be done with a wear gauge. Designed as go, and no-go gauges, the flanges are .006 inches greater than standard ring widths. If the appropriate flange will enter the groove at any point, the piston must be replaced or the groove reconditioned. Several points around the circumference of the groove should be checked because grooves wear unevenly.

If a wear gauge is not available, groove wear can be checked by installing a new ring in the groove. If a .006-inch feeler gauge can be inserted between the upper surface of the ring and the land, 1/16 inch in from the face of the land, the groove is worn too much.

Briggs and Stratton Corp.
Figure 4.27   Checking Ring Groove Clearances

Correcting Top Groove Wear

The Perfect Circle Manulathe can be used to regroove pistons that are 2-1/16 inches in diameter or larger (except those designed for pinned rings) so they will accept a new standard width ring and a .024 inch steel top groove spacer. Top groove spacers, installed above new top rings, actually reduce groove and top ring side wear.

Correcting Piston Skirt Wear

Most pistons that have been in service for any length of time have excessive clearance because of cylinder wall wear and piston skirt wear or collapse. This condition allows pistons to rock in the cylinder, causing piston noise and incorrect ring face to cylinder wall contact. When a piston is to be reused, piston skirts should be resized by knurling to maintain the proper clearance between the piston and cylinder wall.

This process increases the piston diameter by displacing metal on the two thrust faces of the piston skirt. Besides increasing the piston skirt diameter, knurling produces an interrupted surface that provides greater resistance to scoring and raises the load-carrying capacity under boundary lubricating conditions.

Correcting Connecting Rod Alignment

Piston pin fit and connecting rod alignment should always be checked and corrected if necessary. Wear at the bottom of the piston skirt, on one pin side and at the top land on the opposite pin side are signs that the rod is bent. When a connecting rod is bent or twisted, rings do not make proper face contact with the cylinder wall, pistons wear rapidly and unevenly, oil consumption is increased in four-cycle engines, and scuffing and scoring are likely to occur.

Perfect Circle Piston Rings
Figure 4.28   Aligning Rod

It is also important to check all bearing surfaces for burning or scoring and to correct bearing clearances. All specifications for tolerances should be rigidly followed.

VALVES: FOUR-STROKE-CYCLE ENGINE

The valve is one of the most important units used to maintain good compression in the four-stroke engine. Valves operate under more severe conditions than any other engine part. This is particularly true of the exhaust valve.

Briggs and Stratton Corp.
Figure 4.29   Timing of Valves

The valves open and close in little less than one revolution of the crankshaft. When the engine is operating at 3,000 revolutions per minute, each valve opens and closes in about 1/50 of a second.

Valves have to seal well enough to withstand pressures up to and beyond 500 pounds per square inch. Under full load, the exhaust valve is exposed to temperatures high enough to cause it to operate at a red heat. The temperature of the valve under these conditions may be 1,200 degrees Fahrenheit or more. The intake valve is cooled by the incoming fuel mixture, but the exhaust valve is subjected to high temperatures by exhaust gases passing over it on their way out of the cylinder. It is, therefore, very

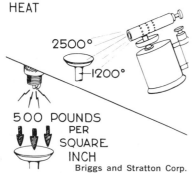

Figure 4.30   Heat and Pressure on Valves

difficult to cool the head of the exhaust valve. The cylinder head, the cylinder, and the top of the piston are exposed to this same heat, but these parts are cooled by air from the flywheel fan and the oil from the crank case. Very special steel is required in the exhaust valve to help it to withstand the corrosive action of the high temperature of the exhaust gases.

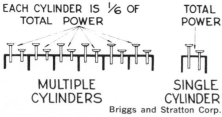

Figure 4.31   Relative Importance of Valves

The most popular small engine has a single cylinder and two valves. There are often twelve or sixteen valves in an automotive engine. The fewer the valves, the more important they become.

In a one cylinder engine, one bad valve can cause a considerable drop in horsepower or even cause the engine to stop entirely. In a multi-cylinder engine, one valve may fail and only one-sixth or one-eighth of the power is affected; the bad cylinder may even be forced to operate by the other good cylinders.

Valve Maintenance

The first requirement is good equipment. A valve refacer and a valve seat grinder are necessary if a good precision job is to be obtained. If the shop does not have them, arrangements can be made, instead, with a machine shop to do this work.

After the valves are removed, they should be thoroughly cleaned on a wire brush wheel to remove all carbon deposits. All carbon should be removed from the valve guides as well. When the valves are cleaned, they should be visually inspected. Valves usually fail because they are burned, dished, or necked.

As mentioned before, when a valve becomes defective

Figure 4.32   Valve Failures

in a multi-cylinder engine, the bad cylinder is motorized by the other cylinders. This may cause serious damage to the valve and seat. The small engine valves, however, are seldom subjected to such extremes of abuse. While the valves may burn to some extent, valve seats and faces are seldom severely burned, and dished or necked valves are almost never found.

Causes of Valve Failure

A *burned valve seat* is usually caused by an accumulation of carbon or fuel lead either on the valve stem or on the valve face, or from insufficient tappet clearance. These deposits on the valve stem or on the face will hold the valve open, allowing the hot flames of the burning fuel to eat away at the valve face and seat.

A *dished valve* is one that has a sunken head. This is caused by operating at too hot a temperature or by too strong a spring, or the head may be eroded away by highly leaded fuels.

A *necked valve* is one that has the stem directly beneath the head eaten away badly by heat; at times, the stem has been stretched.

Valve sticking is caused by fuel lead, gum, or varnish forming on the valve stem and in the valve guide. Since the amount of lead in different fuels varies, the rate of deposit accumulation naturally will vary also. When excess deposits prevent proper closure of exhaust valves, the hot gases that escape from the combustion chamber heat up the valve stem and valve guide excessively. This causes the oil on the valve stem to oxidize into a thick varnish which holds the valve partially open and causes burning on the stem. Intake valves sticking may be caused by the use of fuels having a high gum content. Fuels that are stored for too long may contain high amounts of gum. It is very important that fuels not be stored more than thirty days.

If burning occurs in rather a limited area on the valve face, it indicates that something may have caused the valve to tip, because of a bent valve stem or a deposit on one side of the valve seat or stem.

If such a condition left an opening for the passage of hot gases, the valve could be burned so badly that it could not be refaced. If this type of failure occurs, the valve must be discarded.

General Repair Procedures

The important parts of the valve are the head, the mar-

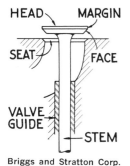

HEAD MARGIN
SEAT FACE
VALVE GUIDE
STEM

Figure 4.33 Valve Part Names

Briggs and Stratton Corp.

gin, the face, and the stem. They make contact with the seat and the valve guide in the cylinder. The margin is the edge of the valve head. As a general rule, the valve should be discarded when the margin becomes less than one half of the original thickness.

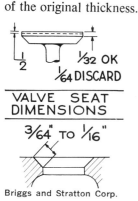

Figure 4.34 Margin Dimensions

$\frac{1}{2}$ $\frac{1}{32}$ OK $\frac{1}{64}$ DISCARD

VALVE SEAT DIMENSIONS
$\frac{3}{64}''$ TO $\frac{1}{16}''$

Briggs and Stratton Corp.

If the valve is bent, the face will be ground unevenly. If the valve margin becomes too thin on one side, again the valve should be discarded. A valve with a thin margin will not be able to withstand the heat and will quickly crack and burn. After facing the valves and the valve seats to a 45-degree angle, a little fine grinding compound is placed on the valve face, and the valve tapped very lightly to the seat. A fine grinding compound will remove any grinding marks, but on completion, it must be removed from the seat and valve.

The valve seat width is usable up to 5/64 inch, but a new seat should measure between 3/64 inch and 1/16 inch, and it should be in the centre of the valve face. (Check engine manufacturer's specifications for this measurement.) After the valve seat and faces are ground, the valve should be installed in the guide, the cam-gear turned to the proper position, and the tappet clearance checked. (Check engine specifications for tappet clearance.) Usually, the clearance is too small, and the end of the valve stem on some small engines has to be ground off to obtain the proper clearance. Some engines have tappet adjustments which are made with small nuts and adjusted to proper clearance. Care should be taken to avoid overheating the end of the valve stem while grinding is taking place and to be sure that the end is square with the stem.

It is recommended that valve springs and spring retainers be assembled immediately after setting the tappet clearance to keep dirt from getting under the valve seat.

VALVE REPAIR SEQUENCE
To Remove Valves

The accompanying figure shows three methods used to hold the valve spring retainers. A compressor is used to remove types shown in the illustration, adjusting the jaws until they touch the top and bottom of the valve chamber. This will keep the upper jaw from slipping down into the coils of the spring. The compressor is pushed in until the upper jaw slips over the upper end of the spring. The jaws are tightened to compress the spring. The collars to

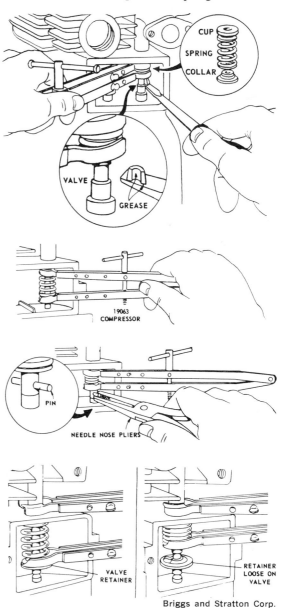

Briggs and Stratton Corp.

Figure 4.35 Removing Valve Spring Retainer Locks

the pin are then removed and the valve is lifted out. Compressor and spring can then be pulled out.

A retainer is used to remove valves. The upper jaw of the compressor is slipped over the top of the valve chamber, and the lower jaw between the spring and retainer. The spring is compressed and the retainer removed. The valve is pulled out and the compressor and spring removed.

To Check and Adjust Tappet Clearance

The valves are inserted in their respective positions in the cylinder and the crankshaft is turned until one of the valves is at its highest position. Then the crankshaft is turned one revolution, and the clearance checked with a feeler gauge. Manufacturer's tables provide the proper clearance specifications. This procedure is repeated for the other valve. The end of the valve stem can be ground to obtain proper clearance if no other means of adjustment is available. Clearances when valves are cold must also be checked.

To Install Valves

Some engines use the same spring for intake and exhaust valves, while others use a heavier spring on the exhaust side. Springs should be compared before installation.

If retainers are held in by a pin or a collar, the valve spring and retainer are placed into the valve spring compressor, and then the spring is compressed until it is solid. The compressed spring and retainer (and cup, when used) are put in the valve chamber. Then, the valve is dropped into place, with the stem pushed through the retainer. The spring is held in the chamber and the valve is balanced, and the retainer pin inserted with needle-nose pliers; otherwise, the collars are put in the groove on the valve stem by using grease. The spring is lowered until the retainer fits around the pin or collar, then the spring compressor is pulled out. Pin or collars must be in place.

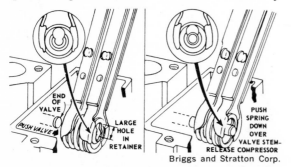

Figure 4.36   Removing Slotted Valve Spring Retainer

If a self-lock retainer is used, the retainer and spring are squeezed with a compressor. The large diameter of the retainer should be toward the front of the valve chamber, and the compressed spring and retainer placed in the

valve chamber. The valve stem is dropped to the larger area of the retainer slot and the compressor moved so that the small area of the valve retainer slot is centred onto the valve stem shoulder. The spring tension is released and the compressor removed.

To Repair Valve Guides

If the flat end of a valve guide plug gauge can be inserted in the valve guide for a distance exceeding the manufacturer's specifications, the valve guide is worn and should be rebushed. The reamer set out by the engine manufacturer reams the worn guide, and should go only 1/16 inch through the valve guide bushing. Do not ream all the way through the guide.

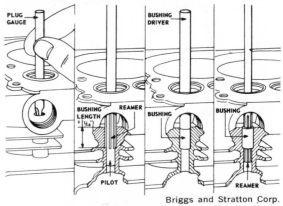

Briggs and Stratton Corp.
Figure 4.37   Rebushing Valve Guides

The valve guide bushing is driven until the top end of the bushing is flush with the top end of the valve guide, with a soft, brass or copper driver supplied by the engine manufacturer so that the top end of the bushing is not peened over. The bushing is finished with the finish reamer provided in the tool kit. The guide is now rebushed and a standard valve can be used. In some engines, the valve guide is removable; therefore, by pressing out the old valve guide, a new valve guide can be installed.

Valve Seat Inserts

Cast iron cylinder engines are equipped with an exhaust valve insert, which can be removed to install a new insert. The intake side must be counterbored to allow installation of an intake valve seat insert. Aluminum alloy cylinder models are equipped with inserts on both exhaust and intake sides.

To Remove A Valve Seat Insert

A valve seat puller and the proper puller nut are chosen according to the engine's specifications. The puller body must not rest on the valve seat insert. The bolt is turned with a wrench until the insert can be pulled out of the

Briggs and Stratton Corp.

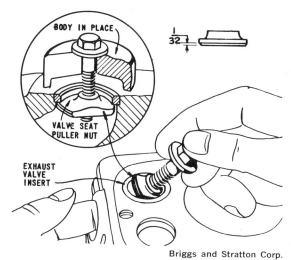

Figure 4.38 Valve Seat Puller

cylinder. On aluminum alloy cylinder models, it may be necessary to grind the edges of the puller nut to a suitable thickness to allow it to slip under the valve insert.

To Install A New Valve Seat Insert

The proper valve seat insert and the correct pilot and driver are selected according to engine specifications. One side of the seat insert is chamfered at the outer edge. This side should be placed down in the cylinder.

Briggs and Stratton Corp.

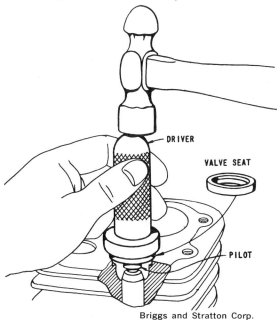

Figure 4.39 Installing Valve Seat

The pilot is inserted into the valve guide, and the valve insert driven into place with the driver. The seat should be ground lightly, the valve and seat lapped lightly with a grinding compound, and then cleaned thoroughly. When inserts are installed on aluminum alloy engines, the old insert is used as a spacer between the driver and the new insert. The new insert is driven until it bottoms. The top of the insert will be slightly below the cylinder head gasket surface.

Briggs and Stratton Corp.

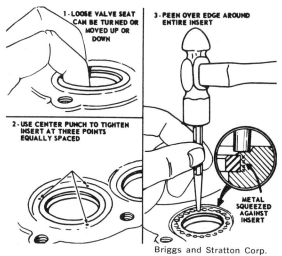

Figure 4.40 Peening Around Valve Seat

The Valve and Valve Operating Mechanism

Valves are very important for the proper functioning of an engine. They are opened by the camshaft, which travels at one-half the speed of the crankshaft, and has one cam for each valve to be operated. The shape of this cam governs the speed at which the valve opens, the time it remains open, and the length of time it takes to close. The camshaft may be driven by the crankshaft, by a chain drive, or by gear-to-gear contact.

Figure 4.41 Timing Gears

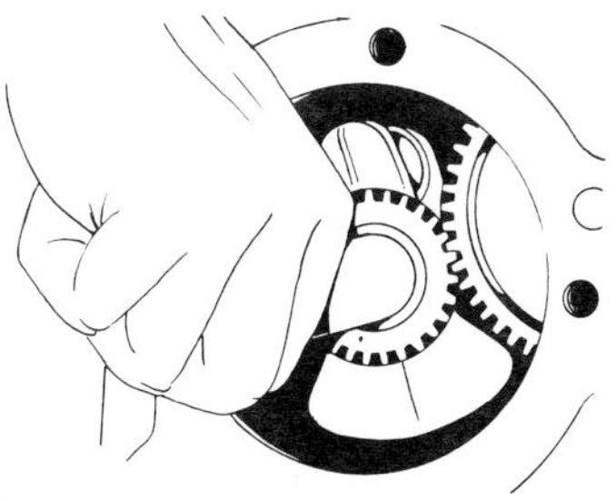

Briggs and Stratton Corp.

The gears and sprockets are fastened to the shaft in many ways and maintain a definite time relationship between the camshaft and the crankshaft to ensure that the valves open exactly at the right time in relation to the piston position. When installing timing gears it is necessary to line up the timing marks on the gears. Where timing chains are used, the marks on the sprockets are lined up with each other and with the centre of the shafts.

On removal of a cam-gear, the gear teeth are inspected for wear and nicks. The camshaft and cam-gear journals and lobe rejection sizes will be shown by engine manu-

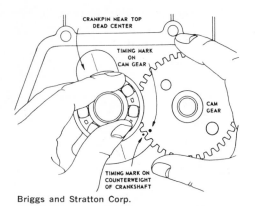

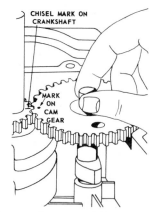

CRANKPIN NEAR TOP
DEAD CENTER

TIMING MARK
ON
CAM GEAR

CAM
GEAR

TIMING MARK ON
COUNTERWEIGHT
OF CRANKSHAFT

Briggs and Stratton Corp.

CHISEL MARK ON
CRANKSHAFT

MARK
ON
CAM
GEAR

Figure 4.42   Timing Marks

facturers. The small engine camshaft and gear may be seated on either a bushing bearing or a drilled hole in the crankcase body.

When the cam gear is reinstalled to mesh with the crankshaft gear, care must be taken to line up the matching timing marks. One tooth is punch marked and this must match between the two punch marks on the accompanying teeth.

As discussed before, the cam raises the tappet in the insert, which in turn raises the valve in its seat. The engine manufacturer furnishes the exact valve tappet clearance specifications in all cases, and they should be followed explicitly. If the specified clearance is not followed, the efforts of the design engineer who built efficiency into the engine are wasted. These specifications are so precise that they state whether the engine should be cold or at operating temperature when the adjustment is made.

In the two-cycle engine, the piston acts as the valve. On its upward movement, the piston compresses fuel in the cylinder chamber. On its downward movement, first the exhaust port is uncovered and then gradually the intake port is uncovered allowing fuel to come into the combustion chamber. As the fuel enters, it drives out the remaining exhaust gases.

REVIEW QUESTIONS 1

1. In your own words describe the piston and the cylinder and construction. Be sure to show all major parts of the piston and cylinder.
2. Draw the piston and name all parts: show lands, heat dams, compression distance or height, ring belt and other major parts.
3. List three ways that piston pins might connect the rod to the piston.
4. How would you determine which side of the piston skirt has the major thrust force?
5. What is a piston pin bushing and when is it used?
6. Describe in your own words the oil ring and where it is located.

7. How is the depth of the compression ring groove measured?
8. Are all piston lands equal in diameter and, if not, how may they differ?
9. Draw a picture or diagram of the piston skirt showing the taper and the difference of the taper.
10. In a short paragraph describe the principles of piston construction.
11. What are the advantages of the aluminum piston and a cast iron piston?
12. What problems did the early aluminum piston manufacturer have in small engines?
13. How did the engineers overcome the piston problem?
14. Name some of the materials added to aluminum to make aluminum alloys.
15. Describe in your own words piston head design and explain the reason behind some of these designs.
16. Give a reason for holes drilled at the back of the lower ring groove.
17. What is a slipper piston and what is its purpose?
18. Some pistons have the relief cut in the side of the skirt to keep the piston from seizing if it becomes overheated. What do we call these pistons?
19. What is a cam-ground piston?
20. If a four-inch piston is .003 to .004 inches smaller than the cylinder, how much smaller would a three-and-a-half inch piston be?
21. List two ways in which a clearance between cylinder and piston may be measured.
22. When a piston begins to slap in the cylinder, what problem might arise in the engine?
23. Name the two methods of resizing pistons to overcome a piston slap.
24. Describe in point form a method of resizing pistons by honing.
25. What is "knurling"?
26. What tool is used to measure the inside of the cylinder wall and at what position should measurements be taken?

27. At what speed should the drill operate for honing a cylinder wall?
28. Why is cross-hatching important in the cylinder wall?

REVIEW QUESTIONS 2

1. Give a definition of piston rings.
2. In a short paragraph explain the purpose of the piston rings and why they are so important to any engine.
3. At what temperature are the hot corrosive gases in the combustion chamber?
4. List the requirements that a metal must meet in order to be used for piston rings.
5. Why is it important to have the proper ring tension?
6. What clearance on a ring width is required in manufacture?
7. What problems arose after 1920 with the compression rings on engines, and how did the ring manufacturers overcome this problem?
8. Explain the following terms: (a) compression rings; (b) oil consumption; (c) oil ring grooves, ring face; (d) tension; (e) corrosive; (f) circumference; (g) cylinder diameter; (h) blow-by; (i) metallurgy.
9. Explain how cylinder walls are lubricated by the piston.
10. What effect has the burned and carbonized oil on the cylinder wall and face of the ring?
11. Is a thin film of oil more advantageous than a thick film of oil on the cylinder wall?
12. What is a poor oil consumption according to ring manufacturers.
13. Explain the following ring terms: (a) ring width; (b) radial wall thickness; (c) side clearance; (d) back clearance; (e) end clearance. What does the term SAE mean?
14. In your own words, explain the purpose of the compression rings and the lower control rings.
15. How do piston manufacturers put the slight spring in the ring?
16. What are the methods of severing the rings?
17. Draw the three methods of severing the rings.

REVIEW QUESTIONS 3

1. What is the purpose of the piston in the cylinder?
2. List the parts of the piston, draw a diagram, and name the parts on the diagram.
3. Give two other names for piston pins and list the three ways the piston pins may be held.
4. What is meant by an offset pin hole on some pistons?
5. Why must the piston have a melting point at the cylinder operating temperature?
6. What is the purpose of using aluminum for pistons?

7. List two names for pistons whose skirts are slotted and tell where the slots are on the piston, and what their purpose is.
8. What is a strut type piston?
9. Name the two ways in which the clearance between the cylinder and piston can be measured.
10. What are the two ways to resize a piston?
11. In your own words list the steps in honing a cylinder wall.
12. List the steps to remove a piston and connecting rod.
13. What do we watch for in checking a connecting rod that has been removed from an engine?
14. In point form, explain the assembly of rings to a piston.
15. What is a cam-ground piston?
16. How does the ring manufacturer accomplish what we call ring tension?
17. Where are the following rings on the piston: (a) compression ring, (b) oil ring? Why are they located there?
18. Why should a connecting rod be checked on disassembly of an engine?
19. Draw the three methods that the ring manufacturers use for cutting the ring to produce the "ring gap."

REVIEW QUESTIONS 4

1. Why is the valve so important to a single cylinder small engine?
2. Name the three common valve failures that an engine may have.
3. Valve seat burning is caused in several ways. List some precautions that may be taken to overcome this valve seat burning.
4. What happens when a valve margin becomes too thin? What is the rejection size?
5. In point form, describe the repair procedure for removal and repair of the valves.
6. How do we check and adjust tappet clearance.
7. Are all engines equipped with the same valve spring on intake and exhaust?
8. List three methods in which valve springs and retainers are held in place.
9. What procedure should be taken if a new valve seat has to be istalled?
10. Explain how the valve is operated in the small engine.
11. How are the timing gears lined up for proper valve openings and closings?
12. In your own words, explain what takes the place of the engine valves in a two-cycle engine. Draw a diagram to support your theory on this question.

CHAPTER 5
CARBURETION

An engine will not operate unless a combustible fuel charge is applied to the engine cylinders at the proper time. In a carburetor-type engine this fuel charge is formed by a mixture of air and vapour resulting from the vaporization of a volatile liquid fuel — usually gasoline. The process of vaporizing or atomizing the liquid fuel and mixing it with the proper amount of air is called carburetion and the device for doing this is called a carburetor.

In this chapter, carburetors from three manufacturers will be studied. Their theory and operation seem somewhat similar but the student will see the difference as he studies each carburetor. Although all carburetors use the same physical laws to accomplish the same result, the methods used to achieve this result differ from manufacturer to manufacturer.

PURPOSE OF THE CARBURETOR

The basic purpose of a carburetor is to produce a mixture of fuel and air on which an engine will operate, and to do so is relatively easy. However, maintaining economical fuel consumption and smooth engine operation over a wide range of speeds creates the need for a mechanism more complicated than a mere mixing valve. There is an additional problem—cost—for the price of a carburetor must be held in proportion to the price of the engine. The price of most small engines is not much greater than the price of a carburetor on an automobile.

Atmospheric Pressure

The force of atmospheric pressure and the principals of the venturi and the air foil can be used to obtain functional and inexpensive carburetion.

Atmospheric pressure, while it may vary slightly because of altitude or temperature, is a constant, potent force which tends to equalize itself in any given area. The weight of the air that pushes down and out in all directions exerts a force between thirteen and fifteen pounds per square inch. In addition, air moves from a high-pressure area to a low-pressure area.

To use this force of atmospheric pressure in a carburetor, a low-pressure area is artifically created to move either the air or the fuel.

The greater the difference in pressure between the two areas, the greater is the velocity of the fuel-air mixture. The increase in pressure increases the distance the fuel can be raised.

The terms "vacuum" or "suction" are often used when a difference in air pressure is being described.

Venturi

What is a venturi? Notice how a wind, blowing through a narrow space between two buildings, always seems to be much stronger there than out in the open. In other words, the velocity is greater. The same thing can be seen in a river. The current is always faster in narrow, shallow places than in deep, wide pools.

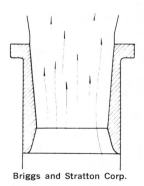

Figure 5.1   Venturi

Briggs and Stratton Corp.

In a way, these narrow places are like a venturi. The great bulk of air or water suddenly pours through a constricted space and has to accelerate in order to maintain the volume of flow. That is the way a venturi acts in a carburetor. The shape is carefully designed to produce certain air-flow patterns.

Air Foil

What is an air foil? Figure 5-2 shows a tube in an air stream. When there is no air movement, the pressure is equal on all sides. When the air moves, an air pattern is formed, as seen in Figure 5-2, creating both a high-pressure area and a very low-pressure area.

These principles of the venturi and the air foil and the theory of atmospheric pressure can be used to explain the functions of the three common types of carburetors:

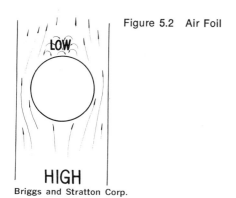

Figure 5.2 Air Foil

Briggs and Stratton Corp.

the gravity-feed float type, the suction feed type, and the newer fuel pump type.

BRIGGS AND STRATTON GRAVITY/FEED CARBURETORS

The first type of carburetor that should be studied is the gravity-feed float type. It is one of the simplest types of carburetors on the market today. The tank is located above the carburetor and gravity causes the fuel to flow into the carburetor. There is an air-vent hole in the tank cap that allows air to flow into the tank as the fuel flows out. There is also a vent hole in the carburetor bowl that allows air to flow out as the fuel flows in. If one or both of these holes were plugged, the flow of fuel would cease and the engine would stop.

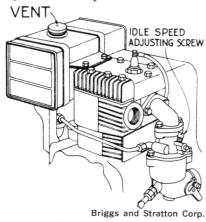

Briggs and Stratton Corp.
Figure 5.3 Vent Holes

As the fuel enters the carburetor bowl, it raises the float. The float, in turn, raises the needle in the float valve. When the needle touches the seat, it shuts off the fuel flow, and the position of the float at this time is called the float level.

Float Level

In general, the float level should be high enough to allow an ample supply of fuel at full throttle and yet low enough to prevent flooding or leaking.

The level in the carburetor is set by inverting the upper body so that the float and the body are parallel. If they are not, the tang on the float should be bent until the float is parallel to the body. The actual difference between the float and the gasket on small carburetors is 5/16 of an inch. On large models it is 3/16 of an inch. It is seldom necessary to measure this distance. The float level here is not as critical as on some carburetors. There should be only one gasket between the float valve seat and the carburetor.

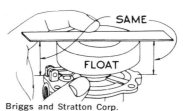

Figure 5.4a Float Setting

Briggs and Stratton Corp.

Fuel Nozzles

By now, the fuel is in the bowl of the carburetor. Figure 5-4b shows the position of the nozzle and the fuel level. The fuel in the bowl seeks its own level, which is well below the discharge holes in the venturi, the place of the greatest air velocity. As the piston in the cylinder moves down, with the intake valve open, it creates a low pressure area that extends down into the carburetor throat and venturi. Two things start to happen.

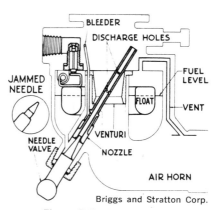

Briggs and Stratton Corp.
Figure 5.4b Needle Valve

The air pressure above the fuel in the bowl pushes the fuel down in the bowl and up in the nozzle to the discharge hole. At the same time, the air rushes into the carburetor air horn and through the venturi where the velocity is greatly increased.

The nozzle extending through this air stream acts as an air foil, creating a still lower pressure area on the upper side. This allows the fuel to stream out of the nozzle through the discharge holes in the venturi where it mixes with the air and becomes a combustible mixture ready for firing in the cylinder.

A small amount of air is allowed to enter the nozzle through the bleeder. This air compensates for the difference in engine speed and prevents too rich a mixture at high speed.

The story of carburetion would end here if the engine were to run at only one speed and under ideal conditions. However, since smooth and economical operation is desired at varying speeds, some additions must be made to the carburetor.

The ideal combustion mixture, by weight, is about fourteen or fifteen pounds of air to one pound of gasoline. An engine operating under a heavy load requires a richer fuel mixture than it does under a light load. In order to regulate the mixture, a threaded needle valve with a tapered point which projects into the end of the nozzle is placed in the carburetor.

Needle Valve

To adjust the carburetor for maximum power, the engine should, first of all, be run at the desired operating speed; then the needle valve is turned in until the engine slows, indicating a lean mixture. The position of the needle valve is noted. Then the needle valve is turned out until the engine speeds up and then begins to slow down, indicating a rich mixture. The position of the needle valve is again noted and the needle valve then turned to midway between these lean and rich positions. The mixture should be adjusted for each engine. Too lean a mixture is not economical. It causes overheating, deterioration, and short valve life. Since there is no accelerator pump, the mixture must be rich enough so that the engine will not stop when the throttle is suddenly opened. Engines which run at constant speeds can use slightly leaner mixtures than those engines that change speed.

When the needle valve is turned in too far, a square shoulder is produced on the taper. Such a jammed needle is shown in Figure 5-4b. It is possible, of course, to adjust the carburetor with the needle valve in this condition, but it is quite difficult because a small movement of the needle makes a big difference in the amount of fuel that can enter a nozzle. If it is eventually adjusted, the vibration of the engine will soon put the adjustment out.

Throttle

To allow for different speeds, a flat disc, called a butterfly, is mounted on a shaft and placed in the carburetor throat above the venturi. This is called the throttle valve.

The throttle in a wide open position does not affect the air flow to any extent. However, as the throttle starts to close, it restricts the flow of air to the cylinder and this decreases the power and the speed of the engine. At the

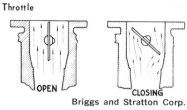
Briggs and Stratton Corp.
Figure 5.5   Throttle Valve

same time, it allows pressure in the area below the butterfly to increase. This means that the difference between the air pressure in the carburetor bowl and the air pressure in the venturi is decreased and the movement of the fuel through the nozzle is slowed down. The proportion of the fuel and air remain approximately the same. As the engine speed slows down to idle, this situation changes.

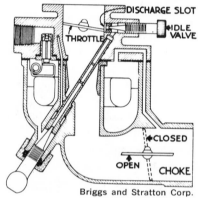
Briggs and Stratton Corp.
Figure 5.6   Idle Valve and Throttle Position

At idle speed, the throttle is practically closed, very little air is passing through the venturi, and the pressure in the venturi and the float bowl is about the same. The fuel is not forced through the discharge holes, and the mixture tends to become too lean.

Idle Valves

To supply fuel for the idle, the nozzle is extended up into the idle valve chamber. It fits snugly into the upper body to prevent leaks. Because of this tight fit, the nozzle must be removed before the upper and lower bodies are separated, or the nozzle will be bent. This is not true in all carburetors, but it is true with the Briggs and Stratton float-type carburetor.

The idle valve chamber leads into the carburetor throat above the throttle. Here the pressure is low, and the fuel rises in the nozzle past the idle valve and into the carburetor throat through a discharge slot. The fuel flow quantity is adjusted by turning the idle valve in or out until the proper mixture is obtained. If the needle is screwed in too far, a damaged idle needle will result.

The adjustment of the idle valve is similar to that of the

needle valve, but it should be made after the needle valve has been adjusted. The idle speed is not the slowest possible running speed of the engine. On some small engines, the recommended idle speed is around 1,750 rpm, while on some larger engines, the idle speed may be as low as 1,200 rpm. A tachometer is used to set the speed and check the recommended idle revolutions per minute with the engine manufacturer's specifications.

The idle speed adjusting screw on the throttle shaft is turned until the desired idle speed is obtained. The throttle is held closed. The idle valve is turned in until the speed decreases, then out again until the speed increases and again decreases. Then the idle valve is turned to a point midway between these two settings. Usually the idle speed adjusting screw will have to be reset to the desired idle speed.

Choke

The next problem in carburetion is starting the engine in different temperatures and with different fuels. A butterfly, mounted on a shaft, is placed in the air horn. With this choke the air horn can be closed, or almost closed, and a low pressure area produced in the venturi and float chamber.

A rush of fuel flows into the nozzle together with a relatively small amount of air. Even with low vaporization, this rich mixture enables the engine to start easily. Only a portion of the fuel will be consumed while choking, and a large portion will remain in the cylinder. This raw gas dilutes the crankcase oil and may even cause scuffing by washing away the oil film from between the piston rings and the cylinder wall. For this reason, prolonged choking should be avoided at all times.

BRIGGS AND STRATTON SUCTION FEED CARBURETOR

The fuel tank may be located below the carburetor, and obviously the fuel will not flow by means of gravity; therefore, the force of atmospheric pressure has to be

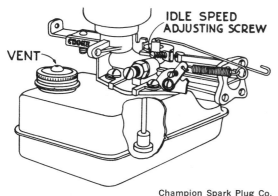

Champion Spark Plug Co.
Figure 5.7 Suction Feed Carburetor

used. The fuel is drawn directly from the gas tank to the needle valve. Therefore, there is no float bowl, floats, or fuel chamber.

Again, there is a vent hole in the fuel tank cap to allow the pressure in the tank to remain constant. Before a carburetor is adjusted, the tank should be half full. The distance that the fuel has to be lifted will affect the adjustment of most small engines. A half-full tank represents an average operating condition, and the adjustment will be satisfactory if the engine is run with the tank either full or nearly empty.

As the piston goes down in the cylinder with both the intake valve and throttle valve open, a low pressure area is created in the carburetor throat. A slight restriction is placed between the air horn and the carburetor throat at the choke. This helps to maintain the low pressure.

The difference in pressure between the fuel tank and the carburetor throat forces the fuel up the fuel pipe, past the needle valve and through the two discharge holes. The throttle is placed in such a way that a venturi effect is created at this point, aiding vaporization. A spiral is placed in the throat to help acceleration and to keep the engine from dying when the throttle is opened suddenly.

The amount of fuel at operating speed is metered by the needle valve and seat. Turning the needle valve in or out changes the setting until the proper mixture is obtained. The adjustment must be done while the engine is running at operating speed, not at idle speed. While the needle

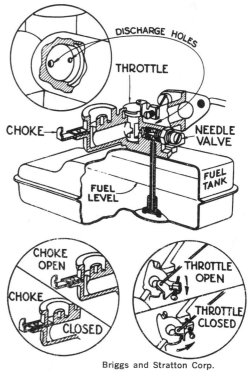

Briggs and Stratton Corp.
Figure 5.8 Throttle Valve

valve may look like an idle valve because of its position, it is a true high-speed mixture adjusting valve.

Since no accelerator pump is used on the suction-feed carburetor, and since many of these engines are used on lawn mowers where rapid acceleration is needed, the mixture should be rich. The needle valve is turned in until the engine begins to loose speed, indicating a lean mixture. Then the needle valve is opened past the point of smooth operation until the engine just begins to run unevenly. Since this setting is made without load, the mixture should operate the engine satisfactorily under load.

Suction-feed carburetors do not have an idle valve; the mixture at idle speed is controlled in a different way. As the throttle closes to an idle, the leading edge takes a position between the two discharge holes. The larger of the discharge holes is now in the high-pressure area and the flow of fuel to it will cease. The small hole will continue to discharge fuel, but the amount will be in the proper proportion to the reduced air flow. For this reason it is important that the small discharge hole be the correct size. The needle valve will allow much more fuel to pass than should go through the small discharge hole. A number 68 drill can be used as a plug gauge to check the small hole diameter. A number 56 drill can be used to check the larger hole. This can de done with the needle valve and seat removed.

A small section is milled out of the throttle where it meets the discharge hole. This concentrates the flow of air past the hole and assures good vaporization.

The idle speed adjusting screw should be set to obtain an idle speed of 1,750 rpm. This may seem fast in comparison with automobile engines, but it is necessary in order to have fast acceleration. It also aids engine cooling and lubrication. A slight unevenness may be noticed at idle speed, but this is normal, and no readjustments of the needle valve should be made.

The choke is the slider plate mounted at the outer end of the carburetor. The choke is pushed in to close the air intake for starting but should be pulled out as soon as the engine starts. The use of this choke should be understood clearly. Many complaints of engine trouble, upon investigation, proved to be nothing more than failure to use the choke properly, especially where the choke is operated by a remote control linkage. The choke must close fully.

The latest engines with the suction feed carburetor incorporate a ball check in the fuel pipe which ensures a steady flow of fuel to the needle valve and discharge holes.

BRIGGS AND STRATTON FUEL PUMP TYPE CARBURETOR

The fuel pump type carburetor is a full carburetor incorporating a diaphragm-type fuel pump and a constant-level fuel chamber.

The fuel tank, the fuel pump, and the constant level fuel chamber serve the same functions as the gravity feed tank, the float, and the float chamber of conventional "float type" carburetors.

Figure 5.10   Fuel Below Venturi

Briggs and Stratton Corp.

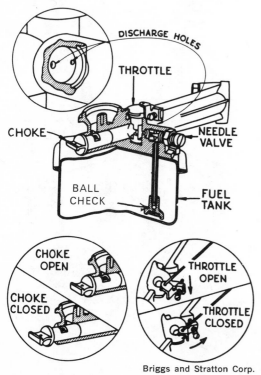

Briggs and Stratton Corp.

Figure 5.9   Choke Slider Plates

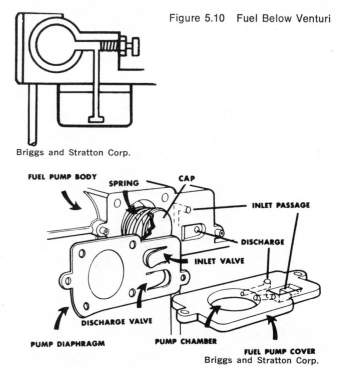

Briggs and Stratton Corp.

Figure 5.11   Part of Fuel Pump Carburetor

This design makes it possible to obtain just as much horsepower from the fuel pump carburetor as is obtained from a more complex "float type" carburetor. This is due to the fact that the fuel pump provides a constant fuel level in the fuel chamber situated directly below the venturi. With this design, very little fuel "lift" is required to draw gasoline into the venturi. The venturi can be made larger, permitting a greater volume of fuel air mixture to flow into the engine with a consequent increase in horsepower.

A low-pressure area created in the carburetor elbow by the intake stroke of the piston pulls cap "A" and pump diaphragm "B" inward and compresses spring "C." The vacuum thus created on the "cover" side of the diaphragm holds gasoline in the suction pipe "S" and under intake valve "D" into the pocket created by the diaphragm moving inward.

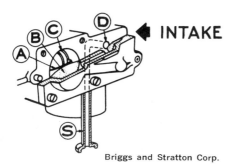

Briggs and Stratton Corp.

Figure 5.12   Operation of Fuel Pump Carburetor

When the engine's intake stroke is completed, spring "C" pushes plunger "A" outward. This causes gasoline in the pocket above the diaphragm to close inlet "D" and open discharge valve "E." The fuel is then pumped into fuel cup "F."

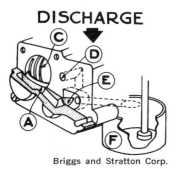

Briggs and Stratton Corp.

Figure 5.13   Fuel Pump Carburetor Showing Fuel Cup

On the next intake stroke, the cycle is repeated and this pulsation of the diaphragm keeps the fuel cup full. Excess fuel flows back into the tank.

The venturi of the carburetor is connected to the intake pipe "I" which draws gasoline from the fuel cup "F."

Since a constant level is maintained in the fuel cup, the

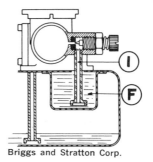

Figure 5.14   Fuel Cup

Briggs and Stratton Corp.

engine gets a constant air-fuel ratio no matter what the fuel level is in the main tank.

From this point on, the carburetor operates and is adjusted in the same manner as the suction feed carburetor, except that the fuel tank does not have to be half full when adjustments are made. It can be full or almost empty and adjustment will be the same, since the fuel level in the small cup is always the same. There are no valve checks in the fuel pipes. Flaps on the diaphragm serve as ballchecks.

Fuel Recommendations

The use of fresh, clean "regular" gasoline is recommended. Store gas, naptha or other such low-test fuels that have a rating below 80 octane should not be used. Nor is it necessary to use highly leaded premium fuels.

It is also recommended that fuel be purchased in amounts that will be used up within a short time. Stale gasoline can produce gum or varnish in the fuel tank, carburetor, and combustion chamber. It will also cause valve sticking and other serious problems. If the engine is not used for a period of thirty days or more, the fuel tank and carburetor should be drained to avoid these gum deposits.

The air entering the engine through the carburetor is important to engine performance and engine life. Power will decrease three and a half percent per thousand feet above sea level.

Power will also decrease one percent for every ten degrees Fahrenheit above the standard temperature of sixty degrees Fahrenheit. In addition, ambient temperature is important in the cooling of the engine. (Ambient temperature is the temperature of the air immediately surrounding the engine.) If the ambient temperature is too high, the engine will seize.

Air Cleaners

One of the causes of engine wear is dirt that gets into the engine. A small three-horsepower engine operating at 3,600 rpm uses about 390 cubic feet of air an hour; this air enters at the rate of about 24 miles an hour. Many such engines operate in very dusty conditions. A large amount of dust and dirt can enter an engine if it does not have an air cleaner or if the air cleaner is not functioning properly. If dirt gets past the air cleaner, it enters the combustion chamber. Although some may be blown through the muffler, some may adhere to the cylinder, where it will create ring wear. It may also work down the cylinder walls into the crankcase, where it will cause wear on all moving parts.

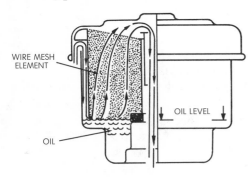

Figure 5.15   Oil Bath Cleaner

Regular and proper maintenance must be conducted on this important device. Occasionally, operators add oil to the exact centre of the air cleaner body. Of course, this fills the air cleaner elbow and the carburetor with oil, causing starting trouble and excess smoking. The operator should add oil to the air cleaner body only and he should not fill above the oil level mark.

It is also very important to see that the breather is vented on all engines used in dusty surroundings.

Oil Foam No-Spill Air Cleaners

For many years, the oil bath cleaner, illustrated in Figure 5-15, was considered the best type of cleaner; recently, small engine manufacturers have developed the oil foam no-spill air cleaner. This cleaner employs a polyurethane element. The important patent feature is that it is sealed. Some cleaners are made with a simple polyurethane element, but they are merely blocks of material with no seals of any kind, and sometimes allow air and dirt to by-pass the element. The Briggs and Stratton Corporation have developed a cleaner which uses the edges of the

element as a gasket so that the air must pass through the element itself.

There are two other important features of the no-spill cleaner. Oil will not spill if the engine is tilted. If the element becomes loaded with dirt, the air supply will be shut off so the engine will lose power or stop entirely. Then the element can be cleaned, re-oiled and reinstalled. The element must be re-oiled after cleaning.

Air Cleaner Servicing

A properly serviced air cleaner protects the internal parts of the engine from dust particles in the air. It is very important that this problem of the small engine be stressed repeatedly. If the air cleaner instructions are not carefully followed, the dirt and dust which should be collected in the cleaner will either be blown into the engine and become part of the oil film, or will choke the engine, causing an excessively rich fuel mixture.

Either condition is very detrimental to engine life; dirt in the oil forms an abrasive mixture which wears the moving parts instead of protecting them. No engine can stand up under the grinding action which takes place when this occurs. A choked-off air cleaner can cause raw gasoline to wash oil off the cylinder walls, thereby causing poor lubrication. The air cleaner on every engine brought in for a check-up or repair should be examined and serviced. If the cleaner shows signs of neglect, it should be shown to the customer before cleaning and he should be instructed on the proper care to ensure long engine life.

Air cleaner gaskets and mounting gaskets that are worn or damaged should be replaced to prevent dirt and dust from entering the engine because of improper sealing. Bent mounting studs should be replaced or straightened.

Servicing Oil Bath Air Cleaner

The old oil is poured from the bowl, and the element thoroughly washed in solvent and drained dry. The bowl is cleaned and refilled with the same type of oil used in the crankcase.

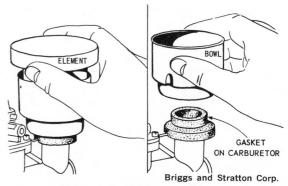

Briggs and Stratton Corp.

Figure 5.17   Oil Bath Air Cleaner

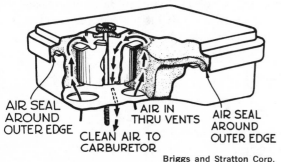

Briggs and Stratton Corp.

Figure 5.16   Oil Bath No-spill Air Cleaner

Servicing Air Foam Air Cleaner

The element is washed in a solvent such as kerosene or a detergent and squeezed dry and re-oiled liberally with engine oil. It is squeezed again to spread the oil throughout the element. It is reassembled, and the screen, if used, is placed with the edge up. The element should not be washed in carburetor cleaner.

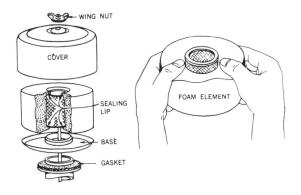

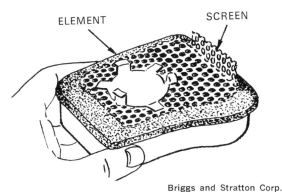

Briggs and Stratton Corp.
Figure 5.18 Air Foam Air Cleaner

Servicing Dry Type Air Cleaner

The cleaner element can be cleaned by tapping on a surface as illustrated. This should be done after twenty-five hours of operation. It should not be tapped hard enough to deform the element, immersed in a cleaning solvent or blown out with compressed air. It should be replaced when damaged or excessively dirty.

The dry type air cleaner must not be oiled.

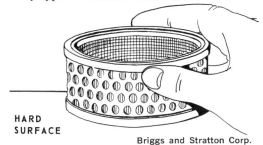

Briggs and Stratton Corp.
Figure 5.19 Dry Type Air Cleaner

Cleaning the Fuel System

Gummy or dirty fuel tanks, lines and carburetors should be cleaned in a carburetor cleaner. Acetone should not be used. The parts should not be soaked for extended periods. Diaphragms or plastic parts should not be soaked in the cleaner. Before any carburetor is removed for repair, signs of air leakage from mounting gaskets that are loose, have deteriorated, or are otherwise damaged should be noted.

Note the position of governor springs, governor length, remote control, or other attachments to facilitate reassembly. The links should not be bent or the springs stretched.

FUEL SYSTEMS
Kerosene Operated Engine Carburetors

In some areas, small engines are operated with kerosene for economy. Engines operated on kerosene use two head gaskets to lower the compression ratio.

Model series 23-A and 23-C on Briggs and Stratton use three cylinder gaskets. The power will be approximately 15 to 20 percent less than when operated on gasoline. Fuel consumption will be approximately the same.

Because of the low volatility of kerosene, those engines operating on kerosene-gasoline fuel systems can be started on kerosene only when the engine is at its operating temperature. Cold engines must be started on gasoline and

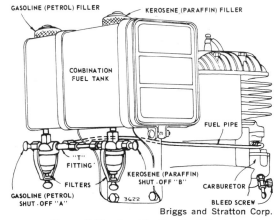

Briggs and Stratton Corp.
Figure 5.20 Combination Fuel Tank

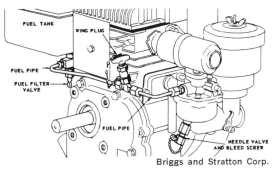

Briggs and Stratton Corp.
Figure 5.21 Kerosene Fuel System

then switched over to kerosene operation only after the engine is warmed up. After the warm-up and during the kerosene operation, the carburetor needle valve is adjusted to a point where the engine runs smoothest and accelerates without hesitation when the throttle is quickly opened. When the engine is shut down, the carburetor must be emptied of kerosene so that the engine may be started on gasoline.

On these units, the filter valve is closed and the bleed screw in the needle valve is opened to drain the carburetor. The bleed screw is then closed and the wing plug removed to fill the fuel line and carburetor with gasoline. As shown in Figure 5-22 the gasoline shutoff valve "A" is opened and the kerosene shutoff valve "B" closed two or three minutes before shutting off the engine. This will stop the flow of kerosene to the carburetor and will admit gasoline to the carburetor.

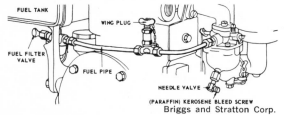

Figure 5.22   Kerosene Fuel System

Liquid Propane Gas Fuel System

A cylinder of liquid propane gas should be available so that an engine may be run and adjusted after repairs. Adjustment should be made in a well ventilated area away from any flame or fire.

Checking the Fuel System

The fuel line is loosened at the primary regulator, and the valve on cylinder opened for an instant to ensure that there is pressure in the fuel cylinder. Escaping gas can be heard.

The fuel line is removed between the primary and secondary regulator (the fuel controller). A pressure gauge is attached to the outlet primary regulator, while leaving the gauge connection loose enough to permit a slight leakage of gas. (This will permit an adjustment of the regulator under conditions of actual gas flow). The top or cap of the primary regulator is taken off.

The fuel cylinder valve is opened and the pressure regulator screw turned in the primary regulator, until a pressure of one and a half pounds is obtained at the pressure gauge. The fuel cylinder valve is turned off, and the cap reassembled. The pressure gauge is removed. The secondary regulator bracket is taken off the carburetor, and the secondary regulator pulled away from the carburetor so that the short rubber fuel line is disconnected. The fuel line between the primary and secondary regula-

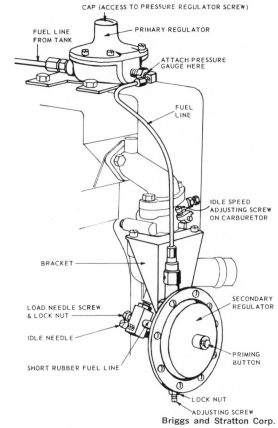

Figure 5.23   L. P. Fuel System

tors is assembled. The secondary regulator must remain mounted so that the diaphragm is in a vertical plane.

The fuel cylinder valve is opened. Soap suds are put on the barbed outlet at the centre of the secondary regulator to which the rubber fuel line has been attached. If a bubble forms, it indicates that the valve is leaking or is not locking on. If no bubble appears, the primer button can be pressed. A bubble should appear, indicating that the fuel is flowing into the regulator. The soap suds should be applied to the barbed outlet again, and the adjusting screw at the bottom of the secondary regulator turned counter-clockwise until a bubble forms at the barbed outlet. Then the adjustment screw is turned in (clockwise) slowly until the soap bubbles no longer form on the outlet. The adjusting screw is held at this point and the locknut tightened. The primer button is pushed to start the fuel flow, released and soap suds again put on the outlet to ensure that the fuel flow shuts off. This is repeated several times. If a bubble should form when the primer button is pushed, the adjusting screw should be turned in until the fuel flow stops and the soap bubble does not break or enlarge. The fuel line between the regulators is loosened and the secondary regulator reassembled onto the carburetor with the short rubber fuel line in place. The fuel line is tightened.

Adjusting the Carburetor in a Liquid Propane Fuel System

The locknut on the load needle screw is loosened and the needle screw turned in until it seats. It must not be forced. The needle valve is then opened two and a half turns. The idle is turned in until it seats, and then opened one turn. If the engine will not be required to idle, the idle needle can be closed. The primer button is momentarily depressed, the engine started, and allowed to warm up before the final adjustment. With the engine running at normal operating speed, the load needle screw is turned in (clockwise) until the engine starts to miss, indicating a lean mixture. Then the load screw is turned out past the point of best operation until the engine begins to run unevenly on a rich mixture. Then the load screw is set so that the engine will run smoothly. The load screw is held while the locknut is tightened. The throttle is kept at an idle position, and the locknut tightened. The engine should accelerate quickly and smoothly when the throttle is held at idle and then released.

If the engine will be required to run at idle, the idle speed adjusting screw on throttle is adjusted until the engine runs at the proper idle speed for the engine model. The throttle is held at this point and the idle turned slowly in or out until the engine runs at maximum idle speed. Then the idle speed adjusting screw is readjusted until proper idle speed is obtained. The engine should accelerate quickly and smoothly when the throttle is opened. If not, the load screw is adjusted, usually to a richer mixture. To stop the engine, the fuel supply valve at fuel cylinder is turned off.

Starting the Engine

To start the engine the prime button is momentarily depressed, and the engine immediately started. In cold weather, it may be necessary to partially close the choke valve to permit the engine to run smoothly until the engine warms up. Otherwise, the choke is not used.

Cleaning the Liquid Propane Gas Filter

The filter head is unscrewed from the filter body, and the element assembly removed from the head. The element is washed in a commercial solvent cleaner or gasoline. If the accumulated dirt is gummy, a short soaking period in a solvent cleaner is recommended. The element should then be rinsed in a clean gasoline and blown out with compressed air.

Always use reverse flow from the inside out. Never use compressed air on the outside surface of the element. Never dip the element in an acid solution.

To assemble the filter, the element is inserted into the filter head with the round washer entering first. The

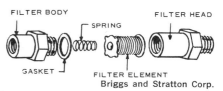

Figure 5.24 L. P. Fuel System

gasket is put on the filter body. The spring is located in the filter body so that when the filter body and head are put together, the spring will hold the element against the head. The body and head are tightened with 75 foot-pounds of torque. After the filter has been reassembled to the engine the area at the gasket and the other line connections should again be checked with soap suds, with the fuel turned on, to ensure that there are no leaks.

Automatic Choke Adjustment

The choke shaft is held so that the thermostat lever is free. At room temperature, the screw in the thermostat collar should be in the centre of the stops. If not, the stop screw should be loosened and readjusted.

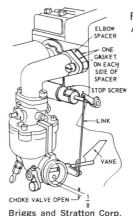

Figure 5.25 Automatic Choke Adjustment

The set screw on the lever of the thermostat assembly is loosened and the lever pushed to right or left on shaft to ensure free movement of the choke link in any position. The thermostat shaft is rotated clockwise until the

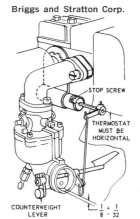

Figure 5.26 Automatic Choke Adjustment

stop tube strikes the tube, and held in position, and the lever on the thermostat shaft set so that the choke valve will open about 1/8 inch from its closed position. Then the set screw in the lever is tightened.

The thermostat shaft is rotated counter-clockwise until the stop screw strikes the opposite side of the tube. The choke valve is opened manually until it stops against the top of the choke link opening. The choke valve should now be open approximately 1/16 inch from its closed position.

The position of the counterweight lever is checked. With the choke valve in wide open position (horizontal), the counterweight lever should always be in a horizontal position with the free end toward the right.

The choke should be manually operated to guarantee that all parts are free to move without binding or rubbing

THE CLINTON ENGINE CARBURETOR THEORY

Earlier in this chapter, we have studied one type of theory —the Briggs and Stratton Carburetion Theory using a venturi, a combustible mixture, a float type carburetor, a fuel pump type carburetor, and a suction feed carburetor. Now we will discuss the theory based on the Clinton float type carburetor. This theory applies generally to most small air cooled engines using gasoline. Although all carburetors operate in a similar manner, each manufacturer varies the mechanical structure somewhat in order to suit the design characteristics of his engine.

Atmospheric Pressure

To understand why air moves from one area into another we have to know something about pressure and pressure differential. The atmospheric pressure at all areas around and in a cylindrical piece of mailing tube is equal, so we have no air movement. If a solid cylinder is placed inside the mailing tube, and then pulled from the mailing tube, there is an air movement into the open end of the mailing tube as the solid cylinder moves. The air flow is caused by the low atmospheric pressure behind the solid cylinder,

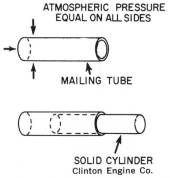

ATMOSPHERIC PRESSURE
EQUAL ON ALL SIDES

MAILING TUBE

SOLID CYLINDER
Clinton Engine Co.

Figure 5.27   Equal Atmospheric Pressure

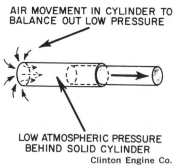

AIR MOVEMENT IN CYLINDER TO
BALANCE OUT LOW PRESSURE

LOW ATMOSPHERIC PRESSURE
BEHIND SOLID CYLINDER
Clinton Engine Co.

Figure 5.28   Balance of Air Pressure

thus causing the outside atmospheric pressure to rush in the tube to balance the low pressure.

If a piece of light paper is put over the end of the mailing tube and the solid cylinder removed again, the outside atmospheric pressure will force the paper inside the tube.

In carburetion, the artificially created low atmospheric pressure caused by the piston's downward travel in the cylinder of an engine is used in the movement of air and fuel into the combustion chamber.

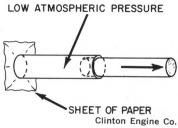

LOW ATMOSPHERIC PRESSURE

SHEET OF PAPER
Clinton Engine Co.

Figure 5.29   Demonstration to Show Low Pressure

The High-Speed Circuit

The high-speed circuit in a carburetor is used when the engine is operated at working speeds. The high-speed circuit is an important part of the carburetor, in that it has to supply a combustible mixture to the engine under full, partial or no load conditions and at various engine speeds. The high-speed circuit consists of a metering jet, high-speed adjustment screw, main nozzle and air jet. To explain the high-speed circuit, we can start with the low atmospheric pressure in the throat of the carburetor created by the downward travel of the piston in the cylinder when the throttle butterfly is wide open, or almost wide open. With the low atmospheric pressure now concentrated behind the venturi, fuel is being forced through the metering jet, around the high-speed adjusting screw and into the main nozzle where air from the air jet blends with the fuel. From the nozzle, the fuel-air mixture moves up into the throat of the carburetor where additional air, coming in from the front of the carburetor, helps to move the fuel-air mixture into the combustion

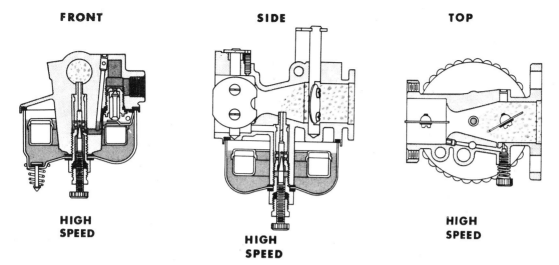

FRONT   SIDE   TOP

HIGH
SPEED

HIGH
SPEED

HIGH
SPEED

Figure 5.30   High Speed Circuit

chamber. The amount of fuel being supplied by the main nozzle is controlled by the high-speed adjustment screw, located below the main nozzle. The carburetor throttle assembly controls the engine speed by changing the fuel pressure in the main nozzle area. When the fuel pressure is reduced in the main nozzle area, the engine will slow down and the movement of the fuel-air mixture will slow down in the high-speed circuit.

The Low-Speed Circuit

The low-speed circuit is used when the engine is being operated at a slow rpm (normally below 2,900 rpm, no load). The idle circuit is so calibrated that the proper mixture of air and fuel is supplied at speeds ranging from 1,400 rpm through 2,900 rpm. The idle-speed circuit consists of a fuel metering jet, air jet, primary idle port, in-

termediate idle port, and adjustment screw. The low-speed circuit starts to function when the throttle butterfly is closing or almost closing the throat of the carburetor. At this time, the low atmospheric pressure is now concentrated behind the throttle butterfly, causing fuel to move through the fuel metering jet into the idle passage where air is mixed with the fuel. At this point, the fuel-air mixture is ready to be moved into the primary or intermediate port area of the carburetor. The amount of fuel-air mixture to be supplied to the carburetor throat is controlled by the idle adjustment screw located in the primary port area. The primary idle port operates independently from the intermediate port up to approximately 2,200 rpm, no load. Beyond that, the intermediate port starts to supply fuel mixture to the idle circuit. If the intermediate idle port were not functioning, there would be a

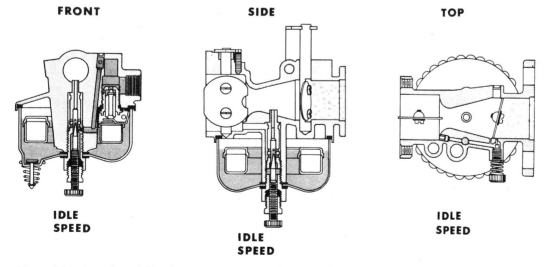

FRONT   SIDE   TOP

IDLE
SPEED

IDLE
SPEED

IDLE
SPEED

Figure 5.31   Low Speed Circuit

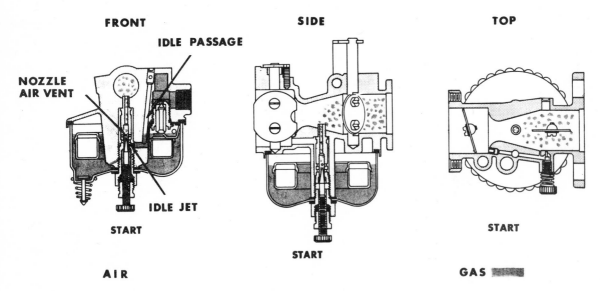

FRONT   SIDE   TOP

NOZZLE AIR VENT — IDLE PASSAGE — IDLE JET

START   START   START

AIR   GAS

Figure 5.32 Choke Circuit

hesitation, or a flat spot, in the operation of the engine from 2,200 rpm to 2,900 rpm where the high-speed circuit blends in.

The float-circuit controls the level of fuel in the carburetor bowl, so that a sufficient amount of fuel is available at all times for both idle and high-speed operation. The float circuit consists of a metal float, inlet needle, and seat. The float inlet needle and seat assembly are calibrated to control the level and amount of fuel supplied to the carburetor bowl, with either a pump or a gravity feed fuel supply. The float level is very critical—the setting must be correct. If the proper float level is not maintained the whole carburetor system will be out of balance. The engine will start hard, idle badly, surge on the governor, and fail to develop maximum horsepower.

The Choke Circuit

The choke circuit is used in starting the engine in different temperatures and with different fuels. The device for choking the engine is located in the air intake side of the carburetor and consists of a shaft and butterfly. With this choke we can close, or almost close, the throat of the carburetor and produce a low-pressure area in the venturi area of the carburetor. When this is done, a reduced amount of air is supplied along with an increased amount of fuel, all of which is moved into the venturi area of the carburetor. Even with a low vaporization, this rich mixture will let the engine start easily. Prolonged choking is not recommended as the rich mixture will have a tendency to wash the oil film from the cylinder walls, to cause scoring or scuffing of the piston, and to dilute the crankcase oil.

Since the piston, on its downward travel in the cylinder, creates a low atmospheric pressure, the preceding circuits

of a carburetor are used to supply the fuel-air mixture necessary to supply a combustible mixture to the engine.

Fuel Systems

There are two types of fuel used in Clinton engines: LPG and natural gas.

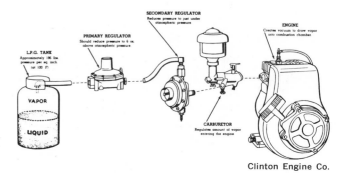

Figure 5.33 L. P. Gas System

LPG or Liquefied Petroleum Gas is butane, or propane, or any mixture of the two. In the operation of a small gasoline engine, the operating characteristics are the same. Figure 5-91 shows a typical hook-ups for LPG on a

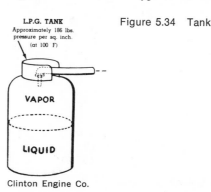

Figure 5.34 Tank

Clinton engine. These hook-ups are either factory installed or available in kit form for adaptation by service accounts.

There are two types of LPG hook-ups used on small engines:

1. liquid operating, and 2. vapour operating.

Clinton engines use the vapour operating.

Natural gas operation is basically the same as LPG except that the primary regulator is not required. Natural gas flows through the meter and is released from the meter at 6 ounces pressure. The secondary regulator, carburetor, and engine are the same and adjustments should be made in the same way as on LPG engines.

There are five components of the Clinton LP Gas fuel system:

1. The tank
2. The primary regulator
3. The secondary regulator
4. The carburetor
5. The engine

The LPG vapour flows from the tank under high pressure to the primary regulator, where this pressure is reduced from approximately 186 pounds per square inch to 6 ounces above atmospheric pressure. The vapour then flows to the secondary regulator where this pressure is reduced to just less than atmospheric pressure; now no vapour will be released unless there is a vacuum which attracts the vapour through the carburetor and into the combustion chamber of the engine.

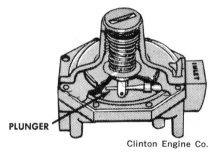

PLUNGER

Clinton Engine Co.

Figure 5.35   Primary Regulator

The Tank

Only a vapour withdrawal tank should be used. Care should be used that the connection for removal is at the top so that only vapour is withdrawn and not liquid. When the tank valve is opened, it should be opened slowly. If opened too quickly, the safety valve inside the tank may close and not allow the vapour to be released from the tank. If this happens, the valve should be closed and then opened slowly. The line from the tank to the primary regulator should be at least 1/4 inch in diameter and 250 pound test. If the line is too small, it may refrigerate and restrict the flow of vapour.

Some equipment manufacturers place a safety shut-off

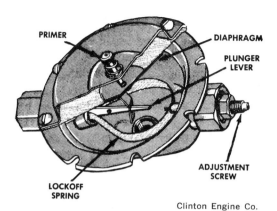

PRIMER   DIAPHRAGM

PLUNGER LEVER

ADJUSTMENT SCREW

LOCKOFF SPRING

Clinton Engine Co.

Figure 5.36   Secondary Regulator

in the line between the tank and the primary regulator that is operated either by crankcase pressure or by an electrical device.

The Primary Regulator

The purpose of the primary regulator is to reduce the pressure of the gas to six ounces above atmospheric pressure. Care should be taken that the air vent on the side of the regulator be kept open and not plugged with dirt. Leaks may be detected, caused by a punctured diaphragm or by dirt under the plunger.

Some units use a special primary regulator set to 5 pounds pressure instead of 6 ounces. The same secondary is used but it requires a different setting.

The Secondary Regulator

The secondary regulator reduces the pressure (6 ounces) to just below atmospheric pressure. The adjustment screw requires one full turn to shut off the flow of the fuel. The regulator should be disassembled and checked. The air around the engine then must be kept clean and the dia-

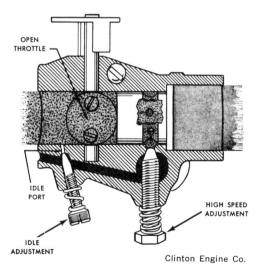

OPEN THROTTLE

IDLE PORT

IDLE ADJUSTMENT

HIGH SPEED ADJUSTMENT

Clinton Engine Co.

Figure 5.37   Carburetor

phragm free of holes. Dirt can get under the plunger lever causing a fuel leak. The fuel should be shut off and the adjustment screw turned one-eighth to one-quarter turn more. Use soap bubbles on the outlet to check shut-off.

The Carburetor

The carburetor should be opened one turn on the high speed and one-quarter to three-eighths of a turn on the idle screw. After the engine is started and warmed up, the carburetor should be adjusted in the same way as any other carburetor.

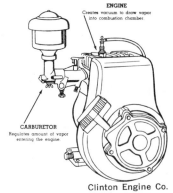

Figure 5.38 Closed Breather System

The Engine

An engine equipped for LPG should have a stellite (specially cooled steel) valve and seat in the exhaust and a standard exhaust valve in the intake. The shorting clip should also be removed since an LPG unit should be shut off only at the tank. The spark plug gap should be set at .018 for better starting. The engine should be equipped with the new style breather assembly in the valve chamber cover. It is also recommended that a closed breather system be used.

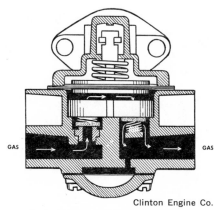

Figure 5.39 Fuel Pump

Starting Procedure For LPG Equipped Engines

All regulators are preset on engines built at the factory.
1. Turn on the valve at the fuel tank slowly.
2. Completely depress the primer on the secondary regulator and bleed the line until gas is smelled at the air cleaner (15 to 20 seconds).
3. Start the engine in the normal manner. If the unit does not start on the first pull, depress the plunger for three or four seconds on every other attempt to prevent flooding.
4. After the engine has started, allow it to warm up and then adjust the carburetor in the normal manner.

Clinton Fuel Pumps

Fuel pumps are used on engines that use a remote fuel tank or have a tank mounted to the engine in such a way that a gravity fuel system will not work. Clinton uses two types of fuel pumps, the mechanical and diaphragm types.

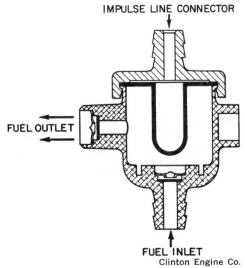

Figure 5.40 Clinton Old Style Fuel Pump

Mechanical fuel pumps are activated by an eccentric cam on the engine crankshaft. This type of fuel pump will lift fuel approximately 48 inches. Mechanical fuel pumps are used on the 700, 900, 1200, 494, 498, 1600, 1800, 2500, 2790, 414, 418, 420, and 422 series Clinton engines.

Diaphragm fuel pumps. Part number 403777 fuel pump was first used on the E-65 go-cart engines with float carburetors. The fuel pump screwed into the inlet side of the carburetor and was activated by use of an impulse tube connected to the crankcase. This fuel pump is designed to lift fuel six inches.

Part Number 220-145-5 fuel pump, a newer type fuel pump, is used on 900, 412, and 413 series engines. This pump also screws into the inlet side of the carburetor, but

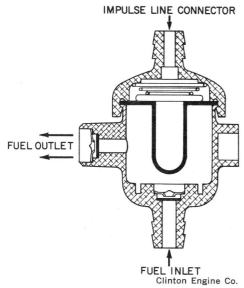

IMPULSE LINE CONNECTOR

FUEL OUTLET

FUEL INLET
Clinton Engine Co.
Figure 5.41 Clinton New Style Fuel Pump

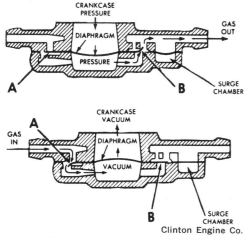

CRANKCASE
PRESSURE

DIAPHRAGM

GAS
OUT

PRESSURE

A

B

SURGE
CHAMBER

CRANKCASE
VACUUM

GAS
IN

A

DIAPHRAGM

VACUUM

B

SURGE
CHAMBER
Clinton Engine Co.
Figure 5.42 Clinton Fuel Pump

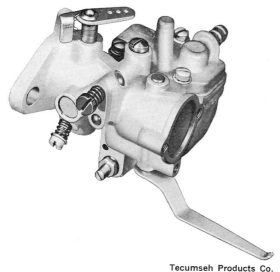

Tecumseh Products Co.
Figure 5.43 Typical Float Feed Type Carburetor

it is activated by an impulse tube connected to the intake manifold. This pump is designed to lift fuel six inches.

The 403777 and 220-145-5 fuel pumps cannot be repaired; if defective they require complete replacement.

The diaphragm fuel pump used on VS-1200, V-1200, and 299 series engines is not supplied as a complete assembly; the individual parts have to be acquired. This fuel pump is attached to the engine crankcase and cover and is activated by the crankcase vacuum and pressure. This pump is designed to lift fuel 12 inches.

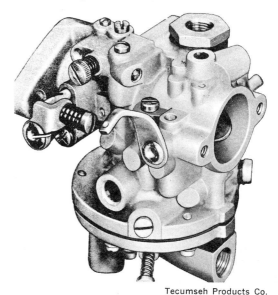

Tecumseh Products Co.
Figure 5.44 Typical Diaphragm System Carburetor

TECUMSEH PRODUCTS COMPANY

General Information: Fuel System Service

The fuel system of Lauson and Power Products engines consists of a carburetor, air cleaner, fuel tank, and fuel lines.

Though a number of different models of carburetors are used on Lauson and Power Products engines, basically they operate in one of two ways. The one type uses a float feed system, while the other uses a pressure differential system. All models of the float feed system operate in the same general manner and all models of the pressure differential system operate in the same general manner.

Float Feed Carburetors

Float feed carburetors use a hollow metal float to maintain the operating level of fuel in the carburetor. As the fuel is used, the fuel level in the carburetor bowl drops and the float moves downward. This activates the inlet needle valve to allow fuel to flow by gravity into the fuel bowl. As the fuel level in the bowl again rises, it raises

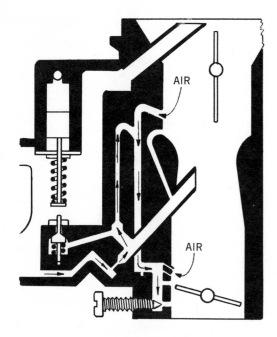

(A) THE IDLE SYSTEM

(B) THE LOW SPEED SYSTEM

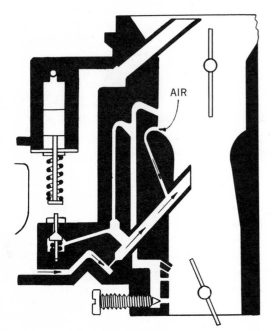

(C) THE HIGH SPEED SYSTEM

(D) THE POWER SYSTEM

Figure 5.45 Typical Carburetor Operation

Atlas Supply Company of Canada

the float. This float motion closes the needle valve to stop the fuel flow at the proper level.

Two main types of float feed carburetors are used. One type uses a cylindrical float while the other uses a ring-shaped circular float. The cylindrical type float will operate within a tilt range of 35 degrees without disturbing fuel feed. The circular float will allow the engine to be tilted as much as 45 degrees during operation.

Pressure Differential or Diaphragm System Carburetors

Pressure differential or diaphragm type carburetors have a rubberized nylon diaphragm that is exposed to crankcase pressure on one side and to atmospheric pressure on the other. As the crankcase pressure decreases during the compression portion of the engine cycle, the diaphragm moves against the diaphragm lever. The lever pivots around the pivot point; the end of the lever moves away from the inlet needle, allowing the inlet needle to move from its seat. This permits the fuel to flow through the inlet valve to maintain the correct fuel level in the fuel chamber.

Some models also have a fuel pump diaphragm. This diaphragm is exposed to crankcase pressure on one side, causing the diaphragm to pulsate in conjunction with pressure changes in the crankcase. The chamber on the opposite side of the diaphragm has an inlet to the fuel tank and an outlet to the carburetor fuel intake. These openings are fitted with check valves to permit fuel to flow only in the inlet-to-outlet direction. When the diaphragm moves upward, the inlet check ball moves from its seat and permits fuel to flow into the chamber. When the diaphragm moves downward, the inlet check valve closes and fuel is forced from the chamber through the outlet check valve and into the carburetor fuel inlet. The advantage of the diaphragm system carburetor over the float feed system is that the diaphragm system will operate over a much wider tilt range.

Carburetor Operation

The carburetor is designed to provide the correct fuel mixture to the engine at any operating speed. During idling a relatively small amount of fuel is required to operate the engine. At idle, the throttle is almost closed, shutting off the fuel supply from all except the one idle fuel discharge hole, so that the suction created by the engine draws fuel only from that opening.

During intermediate operation a second opening is uncovered as the throttle shutter opens and more fuel is allowed to mix with the air flowing into the engine.

During high-speed operation, the throttle shutter is fully opened. Air flows through the carburetor at high speed. The venturi, which decreases the size of the air passage through the carburetor, further accelerates the air flow. This high speed movement of the air decreases the air pressure, and fuel is drawn into the air stream through the main nozzle that opens into the venturi, mixing the air in the air passage. As the engine load increases, air is automatically bled into the main nozzle through the air bleed tube located in the air horn. This allows liquid fuel to be metered freely from the main nozzle.

In the choked condition, the choke shutter is closed, and the only air entering the engine enters through the hole drilled in the shutter. As the starting device is operated to start the engine, the air pressure in the carburetor is reduced as air is drawn into the engine. Since the air passage is blocked by the choke shutter, fuel is drawn from the main nozzle and from both idle fuel discharge ports and mixes with the air that passes through the small hole in the throttle shutter. This makes a very rich mixture which is needed to start a cold engine.

REVIEW QUESTIONS

1. What is the basic purpose of the carburetor for the small engine?
2. Why is a simple mixing valve not enough for the small engine, and what additional problem has the small engine manufacturer with the carburetor?
3. What is atmospheric pressure?
4. Explain the following terms: (a) venturi, (b) air foil, (c) low-pressure area, (d) velocity, (e) vacuum.
5. Name the three types of carburetors that small engine manufacturers use on their motors.
6. Describe a gravity feed carburetor and explain how it operates.
7. What is the measurement between the float and the body when they are parallel?
8. Why is it seldom necessary to measure the distance between the float and the body?
9. When the fuel is down in the bowl of the carburetor, how does it get into the cylinder of the motor?
10. What is an ideal combustion mixture for a small engine?
11. Explain how you adjust the carburetor for maximum power at the desired operating speed.
12. What happens when the needle valve is turned in too far?
13. What is the purpose of the throttle valve? Describe how it operates in the carburetor.
14. Describe in your own words how the carburetor operates at idle speed.
15. Explain the procedure used to start a small engine in cold weather. What might happen if the engine is choked excessively?
16. Why must the suction feed carburetor have a half-full tank of gas?
17. Explain the operation of the fuel pump carburetor on the small engine.
18. What advantage has the fuel pump carburetor over the suction feed carburetor or the gravity feed carburetor?
19. Why is it recommended to use fresh, clean regular gasoline?
20. What would the horsepower loss be on a small engine at 6000 ft. above sea level at 80 degrees Fahrenheit?
21. Name the three types of air cleaners used on Briggs and Stratton engines and name the one which is the most efficient in your estimation.
22. What is the basic difference between the suction feed carburetor and the gravity feed carburetor?
23. Why must we have a vent hole in the fuel tank cap and in the carburetor bowl?

24. Explain in your own words how the fuel pump carburetor operates.

25. What advantage has the fuel pump carburetor over the gravity feed carburetor and the suction feed carburetor?

26. Why is it not recommended that fuel be kept for any length of time?

27. What will happen to the cylinder walls if the air cleaner becomes dirty and chokes the engine excessively or causes a rich mixture?

28. What precautions should be taken when cleaning fuel tanks and carburetors?

29. If the small engine operates on kerosene, will there be any power loss and what will the fuel consumption be?

30. Explain the operation procedure for starting a kerosene engine.

31. Why is it necessary to check all line connections on an LP gas fuel system?

32. Why is soap applied to the connections rather than clean water?

33. Are the needle valve adjustments the same on an LP gas fuel system as they are on a standard gasoline fuel system and if not, what is the setting for the idle valve and the load needle screws?

34. What precaution should be taken when removing a Pulsa-Jet carburetor from the engine?

35. What is the proper procedure for checking the operation of a choke-a-matic linkage?

36. When starting a Pulsa-Jet engine for the first time, why is it necessary to prime the engine?

37. In point form, list the procedure for replacing a fuel pump diaphragm.

CHAPTER 6
ELECTRICAL AND IGNITION SYSTEM

MAGNETISM

For an understanding of the operation of an electrical or ignition system on a small engine, magnetism must be studied.

Magnetism is the name given to a force of attraction that was first observed in connection with certain iron ores. Although its exact nature is almost unknown, the rules that govern its behaviour are very well established and it has been turned into a very useful working force.

Natural Magnets

The people of the ancient world discovered that certain bits of stone had a property of attracting small bits of iron. A very large number of these stones were found near a city called Magnesia, in Asia Minor, and thus the name "magnet" was attached to them. The people of China are given credit for being the first to suspend these stones so that they would swing, making them a useful guide for their ships at sea. The ability of these stones to guide the ships in a direct path led to the name "leading stones," or lodestones. They were the forerunners of our magnetic compasses. Natural magnets were seen to have the ability to attract ferrous metals at the ends and these ends are called poles. One end is called the north-seeking pole because it continually turns to the north, and the opposite end, of course, is the south-seeking pole because it turns south.

Permanent Magnet

Permanent magnets may be purchased in any shape or size. They are made of hardened steel, and they retain magnetism indefinitely. These magnets are used to assist us today in many ways; they are used in electrical instruments, magnetos, and compasses.

ELECTROMAGNETISM

The concept of electromagnetism may be explained in the following manner. Whenever a current of electricity is flowing in a conductor, a magnetic field is set up about the conductor (the wire). Every wire containing a current possesses this magnetic field. This may be seen in several ways. If a compass needle is held near the wire, the needle will point to the wire. If a wire, through which the current is flowing, is placed through a piece of paper and sprinkled with iron filings, the filings will arrange themselves in concentric circles with the wire at the centre. In other words, there are magnetic lines of force around the wire. The cylindrical whirl of metal filings shows how the strength of the magnetic lines of force decreases as the distance from the wire increases.

By coiling the wire, however, a much stronger magnetic force is obtained through the centre of the coil. The magnetic field of each and every loop of wire no longer acts as an individual force, but joins the rest to produce one large field of greater magnetic force.

A still stronger magnet may be produced by placing a piece of iron in the centre of the coil of wire. This creates an *electromagnet*. The strength of this electromagnet will be governed by the amount of current flowing in the wire and the number of turns of wire in the coil itself.

The polarity of the electromagnet will be governed by the direction of the current flow and by the winding of the coil — either right or left. A decision as to which polarity is used is left to the designer of the engine. Manufacturer's specifications should always be followed when replacing any electrical (magnetic) unit in the circuit.

The law of magnetic attraction and repulsion states that like magnetic poles repel each other and unlike poles attract.

THE FORMS AND KINDS OF ELECTRICITY

The first type of electricity that should be studied is static electricity. It is the form of electricity that is commonly felt or noticed. This is produced by friction and remains normally at rest until allowed to escape to some other body or to the ground. Most people are familiar with the charge developed from walking over a rug or drawing a hard rubber comb through dry hair, or the electric discharge of lightning during a thunder storm.

Current electricity is electricity in motion, developed by a mechanical generator or chemical cells. It must have a complete path if the current is to do its work.

The movement of electricity may be explained by the

electron theory, which states that the flow is from negative (—) to positive (+); or it may be explained by the conventional current theory in which the current is considered to flow from positive to negative.

To aid in understanding the laws governing electrical circuits, the flow of electricity in a conductor is often compared to the flow of water in a pipe. It is important to remember, however, that electricity is not a liquid; by comparing it to water, the characteristics of the electric flow are described more clearly.

It is always important to remember that in an electric circuit, a source is needed. In a small engine, there are two sources: the battery and the magneto unit. These sources develop a pressure which causes a flow of current when the circuit is complete.

SMALL ENGINE ELECTRICAL TERMS

A *conductor* is usually a path in which electrical current will travel. The size of the conducting material will vary depending on the cost, on the amount of current to be carried and on the distance which the current has to travel. Some small engine conductors include copper, aluminum, steel, iron, and tungsten. One of the best conductors is silver, although the high cost of this material makes the use of copper and other materials more common.

An *insulator* is a material that will resist the flow of an electric current. The type of material used as insulators in small engines will be governed by the strength of the electrical pressure in the circuit. Some of these insulators are rubber, nylon and rubber, cotton, fiberglass, bakelite, and porcelain.

A *volt* is the unit by which electric pressure can be measured. The more volts that are acting in a circuit, the greater the pressure of the electricity. This *voltage* is measured by an instrument called a voltmeter.

An *ampere* is the unit by which electric current can be measured. It is usually a rate of flow and consists of a stated number of electrons passing a given point in the conductor at a given time. This *amperage* is measured by an instrument called an *ammeter*.

In all electric circuits there is a tendency to resist the flow of the current. The unit of measure for this *resistance* is called an *ohm*.

An *alternating current* (A.C.) flows in one direction through the engine circuit and then it is reversed and flows in the opposite direction through the circuit. It does this many times in a second, and the number of times it changes per second is called the *frequency*.

A *direct current* (D.C.) flows in one direction only.

The *ground* is the common base for the electric circuit. In the small engines this common base or earth ground

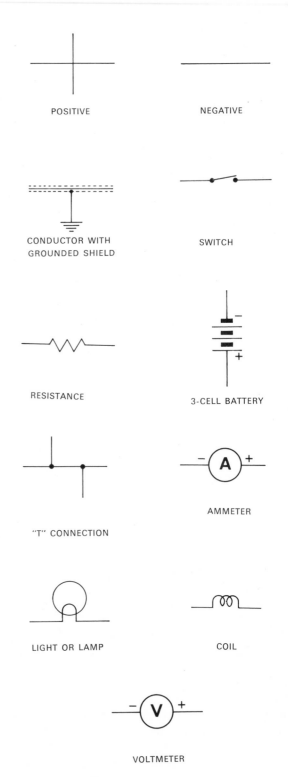

Figure 6.1 Electrical Symbols

is the block or the frame on which the engine is mounted. The ground returns current to the source.

An *electric circuit* is the path followed by an electric current from its source through its conductors to a load, or use, then back to its source. The circuit should have a control. It must be complete since the current will flow only through a complete circuit. There are two types of circuits.

A *series circuit* is set up when two or more electric units are connected so that the same current will flow though all of them at the same time without an alternate path. These types of units are said to be connected in series.

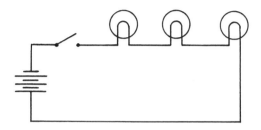

Figure 6.2a   A Series Circuit

A *parallel circuit* is set up so that two or more electric units are connected to the same source of current supply in such a way that they will provide more than one path for the flow of current. The units in this circuit are said to be connected in parallel.

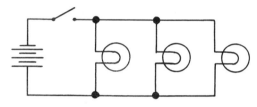

Figure 6.2b   A Parallel Circuit

An *open circuit* is a circuit which is broken so that the flow of current is interrupted. This open circuit might be a switch or a break in the wire.

A *closed circuit* is a circuit which is complete and so allows the current to flow in an uninterrupted course.

A *short circuit* is caused when two or more loops of wire in a coil touch each other, allowing the current to take a shorter path back to the source. It may also occur

when a fault in the insulation or a crack in the conductor allow the bare wire to touch the ground or base.

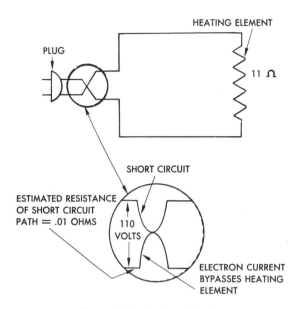

Figure 6.2d   A Short Circuit

SMALL ENGINE MAGNETO IGNITION

A magneto in a sense consists of two simple circuits: one called a primary circuit and the other a secondary circuit. Both circuits have windings which surround the same iron core and the magnets in the flywheel or rotor act through both circuits. Currents can be induced in each by changing the magnets in or around the coils of the circuit.

The primary circuit has relatively few turns of heavy wire. The circuit includes a set of breaker points and a condenser.

The secondary circuit has a coil with many turns of lighter wire which are wound around the outside of the primary winding, and include the spark plug. There are approximately 60 turns in the secondary circuit to each turn in the primary.

A permanent magnet is mounted on the flywheel or the

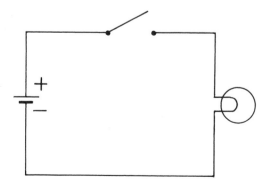
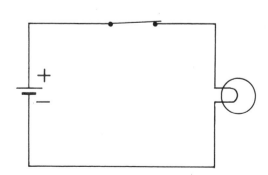

Figure 6.2c   An Open Circuit and A Closed Circuit

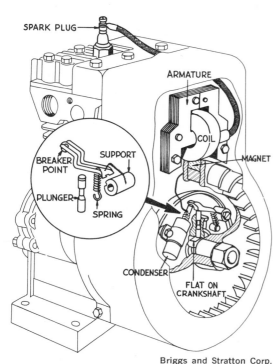

Briggs and Stratton Corp.

Figure 6.3   Magneto System

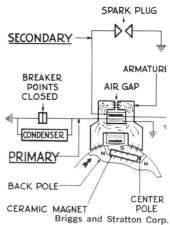

Briggs and Stratton Corp.

Figure 6.5   Step 2. Operation of the Magneto System

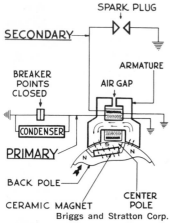

Briggs and Stratton Corp.

Figure 6.4   Step. 1. Operation of the Magneto System

rotor. As the flywheel rotates, the magnet is brought into proximity with the coil and the core.

The Briggs and Stratton new ignition magneto system differs from the ordinary magnetos in that the voltage produced is tailored to the needs of the engine.

Ceramic magnetos which develop a very high magnetic strength in a very short distance are used in this system. The length of this magnet is three-eighths of an inch as compared with Alnico magnet length of seven-eighths of an inch.

Figure 6-5 shows the flow of magnetism through the iron core of the coil as the magnet in the flywheel approaches the armature. The arrows indicate the direction

in which the lines of magnetic force act. It will be noticed that there is very little magnetism acting through the upper part of the core. This is because the air gap at the top of the coil lamination causes a resistance. In this position, the breaker points close.

The flywheel continues to rotate. The magnetism continues to act in the same direction and magnitude through the centre of the core because of the primary circuit. However, the magnetism acts in an opposite direction through the outer portion of the core and through the top air gap because of the change in the flywheel position. Since the shunt air gap provides a path for the flux from the armature legs and the core, the required current flow through the primary circuit is low, assuring, therefore, a long breaker point life.

At this position, the breaker points open, the current stops flowing in the primary circuit, and the electromagnetic effect ceases. The magnetism instantaneously changes from the action shown in Figure 6-6 to that shown in Figure 6-4. Note the opposite direction of the arrows indicating a complete reversal of magnetism,

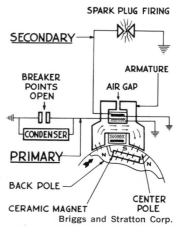

Briggs and Stratton Corp.

Figure 6.6   Step 3. Operation of the Magneto System

which has happened so fast that the flywheel magnet has not had a chance to move to any noticeable degree.

The rapid change in magnetism produces approximately 170 volts in the primary winding. A voltage is also induced in the secondary but in proportion to the turns ratio—for example, 60:1 or approximately 10,000 volts. This voltage is more than ample to fire across the spark plug electrodes. This rapid magnetism change is very short. The flow of current, therefore, across the spark-plug gap is both as long as necessary, and short enough to afford long electrode life. The engineers have achieved the aims of full power plus long life and dependability.

THE CONDENSER

The condenser is a safety valve in the primary circuit. It is connected across the breaker points to prevent the current from jumping the breaker point gap, or arcing, as it is called.

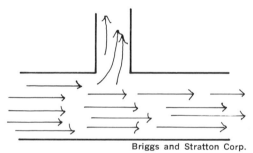

Briggs and Stratton Corp.

Figure 6.7   Water Under Pressure in Pipe

Suppose that there is a large pipe through which water is forced at a high rate of speed. (This corresponds to the primary circuit.) A much smaller pipe branches out from this pipe. (This is the secondary circuit.) As long as the large pipe is unobstructed, the water is free to flow and only some of it flows out the smaller pipes.

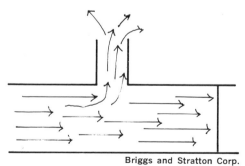

Briggs and Stratton Corp.

Figure 6.8   Obstruction in Water Pipe

Now, suppose that the large pipe is suddenly shut off by a valve. The water will stop flowing through the large pipe but the inertia of the water back in the large pipe will force the water out through the small pipe at a tre-

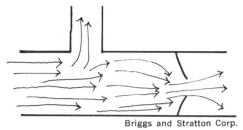

Briggs and Stratton Corp.

Figure 6.9   Obstruction or Valve Breaking

mendous velocity until the pressure is dispersed. This corresponds to the high voltage in the secondary circuit.

Suppose, however, that the valve could not stand the pressure and should break. This would correspond to arcing across the breaker points. The flow would continue through the large pipe, and very little would flow through the small pipe.

If another small pipe were put near the valve, and a strong rubber bag were placed over its end, an equivalent to the condenser would be constructed. When the valve is closed, the pressure on the valve would be partially absorbed by the rubber bag. The valve would not break and water would stream out the small pipe as intended.

The rubber bag must be the proper size and strength. If it is too small, it will not absorb enough of the pressure and the valve will break. If it is too large, it will hold too much water and there will not be enough pressure to force the water out through the small pipe.

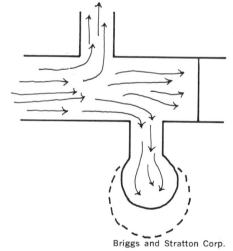

Briggs and Stratton Corp.

Figure 6.10   Small Pipe with Rubber Bag Attached

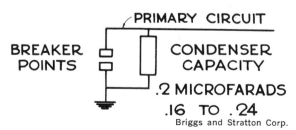

Briggs and Stratton Corp.

Figure 6.11   Condenser in Circuit

This also applies to the condenser. The proper capacity should be about .2 microfarads or .16 to .24. This is just the right size to prevent arcing at the points and still stop the flow in the primary current.

SPARK-PLUG CABLES

The spark-plug cables (or high tension leads) are molded into the coil so that moisture cannot shut out the spark. This has happened on some of the older coils that have such an open connection between the coil and the spark-plug cable.

At one time, some mechanics tried to judge the condition of the magneto system by the brightness and the noise or "snap" of the spark. This is not a good method as can quickly be demonstrated by using a resistor-type spark plug and a regular-type spark plug. If they are laid on top of the cylinder head of the engine and the spark-plug cable connected to first one and then the other and the flywheel spun, the spark across the electrodes of the resistor plug will be much thinner and will make less noise. Yet these engines run very well on this type of plug.

The magneto can be tested by placing the spark-plug tester between the ignition cable and the spark plug. If the flywheel is spun vigorously, the spark should jump the .166 inch gap.

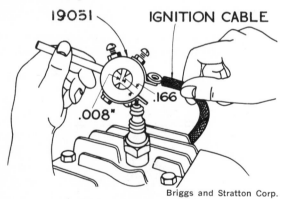

Briggs and Stratton Corp.

Figure 6.12   Testing Spark Strength

This test can also be performed with the engine running but the cable should be shifted quickly from the spark plug to the tester or from the tester to the spark plug. Damage to the coil can result if the engine spins more than just a few revolutions with the cable disconnected. This running test should not be performed on the Briggs and Stratton engine models 9, 14, 19 & 23 with the magnematic engine system.

On small engines, the flywheel key must not be partially sheared since this can put the timing off enough to cause difficult starting, or a failure to start at all. However, a steel key must not be used. A soft metal key is used so

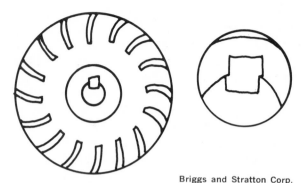

Briggs and Stratton Corp.

Figure 6.13   Flywheel Key Partially Sheared

that if the flywheel should become loose, the key will be sheared, allowing the flywheel to shift and stop the engine before any further damage occurs. The flywheel key is a locater and not a driver.

THE SPARK PLUG

The spark plug serves only one function: namely, to introduce the spark into the combustion chamber for the ignition of the fuel mixture. The spark plug does not ignite; it only supplies the gap for the current to jump. Since the insulator of the spark plug is delicate, care should be taken to avoid damaging it while handling the plug.

Spark plugs come in various sizes according to the diameter of their thread, the length of the thread and the type of seat.

The lower part of the thread should not extend down into the combustion chamber or it will cause a hot spot. Spark plugs also come in different heat ranges so that a suitable type may be chosen for different types of engine operations. Manufacturer's specifications should be followed in the choice of the plug.

The arrows in Figure 6-14 show that heat takes longer to travel from the tip of the centre electrode to the cooling zone on a hot plug than on a cold one. In other words, the hotter the plug, the longer the nose on the insulator. Should the spark plugs have to be serviced, they should be

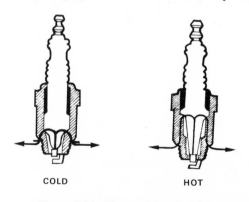

Figure 6.14   Types of Spark Plugs

serviced by trained men; their correct function is important if good engine performance is to be expected. Plugs should be removed regularly, checked and adjusted, and replaced according to the manufacturer's specifications.

The ease of engine starts, the smoothness of its operation, its acceleration and its fuel consumption, all of these depend to a great extent on the condition of the spark plug. All spark plugs decrease in efficiency as they are used. Constant exposure to burning fuel and high temperatures, and the accumulation of combustion deposits eventually cause misfiring, poor engine performance, and high gas consumption. More often than not, this gradual decrease in efficiency is not noticed by the operator.

Why Spark Plugs Should be Replaced

All spark plugs waste gas, cause hard starting, loss of power and acceleration when they misfire. There are many reasons why spark plugs misfire, especially after long hours of service.

Worn, eroded electrodes result when corrosive gases, formed by combustion of the fuel, attack the electrodes in the intense engine heat. The high voltage spark itself tends to blast the electrodes like continuous bolts of lightning. Both of these forces tend to wear away the electrodes and increase the distance that the spark must jump.

Champion Spark Plug Co.
Figure 6.15 Worn Eroded Electrodes

Spark plugs in this condition require more voltage to fire, often more voltage than the ignition system can produce. Cleaning and re-gapping the electrodes will help, but if they are badly worn, they cannot be filed or re-gapped to new plug sharpness, and should be replaced.

A spark plug with a *fouled or blistered insulator tip*

Champion Spark Plug Co.
Figure 6.16 Fouled Blistered Insulator Tip

can cause misfiring because the deposit tends to short the spark-plug gap. These deposits sometimes provide a path for the electricity to ground itself to the steel shell of the plug and it fails to fire.

Cleaning can sometimes remove these deposits if they are not too heavy. But if the deposits are heavy or burned into the insulator nose, it is virtually impossible to remove them completely. The plug should be replaced.

A spark plug with a *cracked or broken insulator* will misfire, particularly on new acceleration or at high speed. Such insulator breakage may be hidden inside the steel shell; the crack may be difficult to see. Careful visual examination or bench testing will reveal this damage. The plug must be replaced for satisfactory engine performance.

Champion Spark Plug Co.
Figure 6.17 Cracked or Broken Insulator

Only the best quality spark plugs, kept in good operating condition by cleaning and re-gapping after the specified hours of service, can provide the "spark" of a good engine performance. But when the spark plugs are worn out or damaged, they should be replaced; usually new plugs are needed after every 50 hours of operation on small engines.

Spark-Plug Heat Range

Spark-plug heat range is the primary factor governing spark-plug performance under various service conditions. The term "heat range" simply refers to the classification of spark plugs according to their ability to transfer heat from the firing end of the plug to the cooling system of the engine.

The rate of transfer, or heat range, is controlled by the distance between the inside gasket seat and the insulator tip.

A *cold* type plug has a relatively short insulator nose and transfers heat very rapidly into the engine's cooling system. Such a plug is used in heavy duty or continuous high-speed operation to avoid overheating.

The *hot* type plug has a much longer insulator nose and transfers heat more slowly away from its firing end. It runs at higher temperature and burns off combustion; deposits which may tend to foul the plug during prolonged idling or low speed operation.

New design factors which affect the efficient heat range of spark plugs include high thermal conductivity of the insulator, improved thermal conductivity of the electrode, uniform heat transfer between the electrode and the insulator, a scientifically designed insulator tip, and larger clearance volume between the insulator tip and the shell.

Spark plugs, both regular and projected core-nose types, are made in several heat ranges (*hot and cold plugs*) to suit requirements of individual engines in operating conditions.

Spark-Plug Numbering System

Spark plugs are designed in several thread sizes and *reaches* of which 14MN and 18MN thread sizes are the most popular. Thread reach is the distance between the gasket seat and the end of the shell. The thread size is the diameter of the threads.

Manufacturer's manuals indicate the meaning of their size codes.

Checking Spark Plugs Visually

A survey shows that at least half the units in service need new spark plugs at the present time. Within any 12-month period, all units need new spark plugs.

The spark-plug chart shows up the two most common causes of misfire: deposits of oil or carbon on insulator tips, and electrode gaps that are too wide.

It does not take long to remove one plug, usually less than 60 seconds in any small engine. Even in the toughest motor it might take less than three minutes if the proper wrench and socket are used.

One plug almost always indicates the general condition of the plugs in the engine. Exceptions to the rule are no problem. If the plug that has been removed appears to be in good condition and the engine performance is satisfactory, the plug is probably all right. If the plug looks worn, it should be checked for service or replacement.

When a chart is used, the mechanic has a standard for himself and the operator to use in judging the necessity for new plugs. If the old plug is held next to the matching chart, it will probably match one of the illustrations.

Procedure for Removing, Regapping and Installing Plugs

The spark plug is loosened several turns after the ignition cable is disconnected. A proper wrench and socket must be used.

The dirt around the spark plugs should be air blasted away to prevent it from entering the cylinder head thread when the plugs are removed.

The spark plug is removed and checked as it is removed. The cylinder number is marked on the rack so that service conditions may be analyzed if the engine has more than one cylinder.

If cleaning is required, an abrasive blast in the cleaner is used for three to six seconds and the plug is wobbled. Then it is air blasted. Plugs with cracked insulators should be discarded.

The electrode sparking areas are filed vigorously to bright, flat parallel surfaces. Plugs with badly worn electrodes should be discarded.

The gap is reset to the required spacing by bending only the side electrode with a bending fixture provided by the spark-plug company.

Each gasket seat in the cylinder head should be wiped with a clean dry cloth. The spark plugs are screwed in finger tight and then tightened as shown in the table below:

Plug Thread Size	No. of Turns
10 mm.	3/4 to 1
14 mm.	1/2
18 mm.	1/2 to 3/4
7/8" - 18 mm.	1/2 to 3/4

Analyzing Spark-Plug Conditions

Quick diagnoses of many engine troubles are possible by removing and examining new spark plugs. There is a spark plug in the heat range that is right for any engine, in any kind of operation.

Normal plugs have brown to greyish deposits and slight electrode wear indicating correct spark-plug heat range and mixed periods of high and low operations. Spark plugs having this appearance may be cleaned, re-gapped and re-installed.

Worn-out, eroded electrodes and pitted insulators are indications of many hours of operation. Spark plugs

Champion Spark Plug Co.
Figure 6.18   Normal

Champion Spark Plug Co.
Figure 6.19   Worn Out

should be replaced when these conditions are observed for better gas consumption, quicker starting and smoother engine performance.

Carbon fouled plugs show dry fluffy black deposits which may result from over-rich carburetion, overchoking, a sticking manifold valve or a clogged air cleaner. Faulty breaker points, weak coil or condenser, and worn ignition cables can reduce voltage and cause misfiring. Excessive idling, slow operation speeds under light load can also keep plug temperatures so low that normal combustion deposits are not burned off. In such a case a hotter spark plug will better resist carbon deposits.

Champion Spark Plug Co.
Figure 6.20   Carbon Fouled

Wet oily deposits on *oil-fouled* plugs may be caused by oil leaking past worn piston rings. The break-in of a new or overhauled engine before the rings are fully seated may also produce this condition. A porous fuel pump diaphragm or excessive valve stem clearance can also cause oil fouling. Usually these plugs can be degreased, cleaned and re-installed. While hotter spark plugs will reduce oil fouling, an engine overhaul may be necessary to correct this condition properly.

Champion Spark Plug Co.
Figure 6.21   Oil Fouled

High-speed glazing may cause misfiring. The shiny deposit is usually yellow or tan in colour. It suggests that temperatures may have suddenly risen during a hard acceleration. As a result, normal deposits do not get a chance to fluff off the plug; instead, they melt and form a conductive coating. If this continues to recur, a colder heat range should be used, along with regular spark-plug cleaning.

Burned or blistered insulator nose and badly eroded

Champion Spark Plug Co.
Figure 6.22   High Speed Glazing

Champion Spark Plug Co.
Figure 6.23   Burned Electrodes

electrodes are indications of spark-plug overheating. Improper spark timing or low octane fuel can cause detonation and overheating. Lean air fuel mixtures, cooling system stoppages or sticking valves may also result in this condition. Sustained high speed, heavy load service can produce high temperatures which require use of a colder spark plug.

Fuel scavenger deposits may be white or yellow in colour. They may appear to be bad, but this is the normal appearance with certain brands of fuel. Such materials are designed to change the chemical nature of deposits to lessen misfire tendencies. The accumulation on the ground electrode and shell areas may be unusually heavy, but the material is easily flaked off. Such plugs can be considered normal and may be cleaned by standard procedures.

Champion Spark Plug Co.
Figure 6.24   Scavenger Deposits

Initial pre-ignition damage is caused by excessive temperatures. This produces a melting of the centre electrode and, somewhat later, the ground electrode. Insulators will appear relatively clean of deposits. The spark plug is like an electric fuse; when it melts, it is a warning of other trouble. A check for the correct plug heat range, for over-advanced ignition timing and for similar reasons for overheating should be conducted.

Champion Spark Plug Co.
Figure 6.25   Pre-ignition

Sustained pre-ignition damage usually involves melting of the ceramic firing tip. Since this requires temperatures above 1,700 Fahrenheit, it is probable that other components of the engine have also been damaged by pre-ignition. This is another sure sign that careful inspection of the engine and its adjustments is required.

Champion Spark Plug Co.
Figure 6.26   Sustained Pre-ignition Damage

Splashed fouling may sometimes occur after a long-delayed tune up. Deposits that have accumulated after a long period of misfiring may suddenly loosen when normal combustion temperatures are restored upon installation of new plugs. During a high-speed run, these materials that are shedding off the piston are thrown against the hot insulator surface. They may be removed with a

Champion Spark Plug Co.
Figure 6.27   Splash Fouling

good regular cleaning and the plugs reinstalled with good results as the engine has scavenged itself.

Chipped insulators usually result from bending the center electrode during the re-gapping of the plug. Under certain conditions, severe detonation can also split an insulator firing end. In a four-cycle engine, a piece of ceramic like this is easily blown out through the exhaust. Obviously, the plug must be replaced.

Champion Spark Plug Co.
Figure 6.28   Chipped Insulator

Mechanical damage to the firing-end is caused by a foreign object in the combustion chamber. Since small objects can travel through the cylinder, the engine performance should always be checked to prevent recurrence of this damage. Whenever work is being done on an engine, the carburetor throat and the spark-plug hole must be well covered.

Champion Spark Plug Co.
Figure 6.29   Mechanical Damage

Pressure type gap tools, if improperly used, impose a tremendously high unit pressure on the centre electrode.

Champion Spark Plug Co.
Figure 6.30   Pressure Gap Tool Damage

Champion Spark Plug Co.
Figure 6.31   Reversed Coil Polarity

This is caused by the compression being exerted between the end of the centre electrode and the top of the shell. If too much force is applied through leverage multiplication, the centre electrode seal on any type or brand of spark plug is liable to be damaged. There are several of these pliers on the market.

Reversed coil polarity can often be detected by "dishing" of the ground electrode. The centre electrode is not worn badly. This source of misfiring and rough idle can be corrected by reversing the primary coil leads.

MAGNETO THEORY

Out of all that is not known about electricity and magnetism, one thing at least is sure. They have a close relationship with each other. Every time an electric current flows, it sets up a magnetic field. Every time a magnetic field is increased, decreased, or changed in direction, an electric voltage is set up in any nearby conductor. If electricity flows through a coil around an iron core, it will make an electromagnet out of the iron core. If the direction of magnetism passing through an iron core is reversed, a voltage will be generated in the windings of a coil of wire around this core.

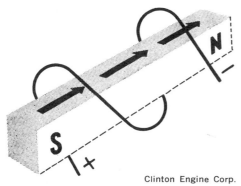

Clinton Engine Corp.

Figure 6.32   Coil of Wire on Iron Core

A magneto is simply a specialized form of an electric generator which uses this principle in order to generate electricity. Permanent magnets are used to produce the magnetic field. The magnets do not have to give up any magnetism in order to produce the electricity. They simply produce a magnetic field in one direction through the iron core of a coil and then reverse this direction.

What is a Magnet?

As explained in the last paragraph, any time a current passes through a coil of wire around a piece of iron, it turns the iron into an electromagnet. If it is a piece of soft iron, the magnetism will be lost as soon as the current stops flowing. If the direction of the current is reversed, the direction of the magnetic field in the iron will be reversed.

If, however, the piece of iron is hardened, it will retain a certain amount of magnetism after the current is shut off. In fact, the new Alnico alloys retain a very large

portion of the amount of magnetism that they had when the current was flowing in the coil; therefore, they are nearly as strong as permanent magnets or electromagnets.

A number of different metals can be magnetized to a certain extent, but by far the most common one, and the one which is most easily magnetized, is iron in one of its forms or alloys. This is explained by some scientists by the fact that the iron atom has spinning electrons which act like a tiny magnet. The axes on which these electrons rotate in an ordinary piece of iron are pointed in all directions, so that the magnetic effect of each of them neutralizes the others. However, if a magnetic field is applied (for example, by a coil with current flowing through it) most of the elementary magnets have their axes lined up in the same direction, and they add their magnetic forces together to turn the iron into a magnet. In a soft piece of iron, these electrons return to their miscellaneous arrangement as soon as the outside magnetic action stops. In a hardened piece or in a special alloy, they remain in line for a longer period of time, depending on the characteristics of the alloy. The iron becomes a more permanent magnet with established north and south poles.

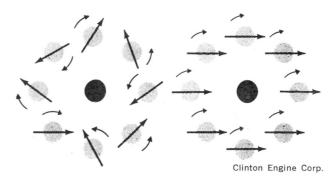

Clinton Engine Corp.

Figure 6.33   Electrons in a Magnet

The field of a magnet is indicated by arrows pointing from the north end through the outside path to the south end. The field will concentrate itself as much as possible in the shortest possible distance between the two poles, but particularly it will concentrate itself within the iron.

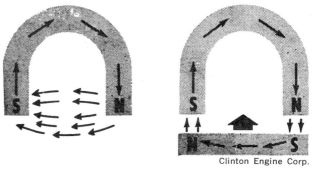

Clinton Engine Corp.

Figure 6.34   Magnetic Fields

It will pull a piece of iron into place to reduce the length of the path through the air. In fact, it is this preference of the magnetic field for iron that the coil core employs. The core leads the magnetic design and concentrates it inside the coil.

What is a Magneto Coil?

About 175 turns of heavy wire form the primary coil. One end of the primary is connected to the frame of the magneto as a ground, and the other end is connected to the live insulated breaker point. The secondary coil usually has about 10,000 turns of very fine wire wound outside of the primary. The inside of the secondary coil is grounded with the primary ground. The outside is connected to the spark plug wire.

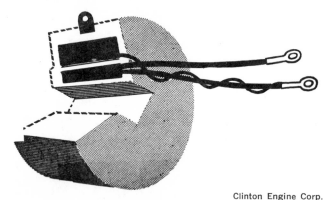

Clinton Engine Corp.

Figure 6.35   Magneto Coil

What is a Condenser?

A condenser is a storage reservoir for electricity. It consists of two strips of foil with paper insulation between them. They are wound together so that one of the strips of foil can be grounded and the other connected to the live breaker point. At the instant of breaker point opening, the insulating paper between the two strips of foil acts as a storage reservoir for electricity during an extremely small fraction of a second before the arc across the breaker points is extinguished.

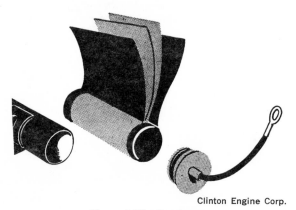

Clinton Engine Corp.

Figure 6.36   Condenser

Why is the Core Laminated?

The core has magnetism concentrated in its first in one direction and then, rapidly reversed, in the other. Because iron itself is an electrical conductor, large eddy currents would in themselves act as electromagnets and oppose the change of direction of the magnetic field in the iron, thus slowing it down. By splitting the iron core into a series of thin laminations, the build-up of any one large electrical path for an eddy current is prevented. The slight amount of oxide between each lamination acts as sufficient insulation to prevent the eddy currents from travelling across between one lamination and the next.

The Magnetic Current

In the magneto design, the Alnico magnets are charged in a radial direction and the iron flywheel rim forms a part of the magnetic circuit that connects magnetically the two magnets. The right-hand pole can be considered as north. The left-hand pole can be considered as south. The magnetism acts in a direction from the left-hand magnet pole, along the iron flywheel rim connecting the two magnets and then downward inwardly to the right-hand north pole. The poles are of soft, cold-rolled steel, and they allow the transfer of the magnetic field from end to end, as needed, to match the coil core.

If an ordinary generating coil is put on the coil core in place of the ignition coil and the flywheel rotated, the magneto acts as a generator. The north pole is over the centre leg of the core and the direction of magnetism acts from the north pole down through the centre leg to the left-hand leg of the core and to the south pole magnet— completing its circuit through the flywheel. A few degrees of revolution later, the north pole is over the right-hand leg of the coil core and the direction of magnetism is from the north pole through the right-hand end of the core and up through the centre leg to the south left-hand magnet

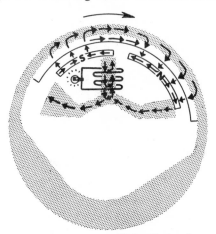

Clinton Engine Corp.

Figure 6.37   Magnetism in a Coil

pole. The reversal of the magnetism generates electricity in the generator winding and operates a light as indicated. The intensity of the voltage generated in each turn of the coil depends on the force of the magnetism and the speed with which it is reversed in direction.

In a Magneto

When the magneto with the ignition coil condenser and points are in operation, the magnetism (as in the case of the generator,) first establishes itself from the north right-hand pole downward through the centre leg to the left-hand south pole.

Clinton Engine Corp.

Figure 6.38 Direction of Magnetism Flow

The Primary Coil Resists a Change of Direction

As the flywheel rotates and the north pole passes the centre leg and the south pole, in turn, approaches it, there is an attempt on the part of the magnetic circuit to reduce and reverse the direction of the magnetism in the centre leg. However, as soon as there is even a slight reduction in the amount of magnetism in the centre leg, a current passes through the primary coil. This current

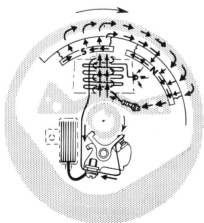

Clinton Engine Corp.

Figure 6.39 Magnetism in Suspension

makes the primary coil an electromagnet and its magnetism acts in opposition to a change in the direction of the magnetism through the core. There is, therefore, a condition wherein the primary of the coil (with the breaker points closed) is acting like a choke, throttling the efforts of the permanent magnets to reverse the friction of the magnetism through the centre leg of the coil, and virtually holding the magnetism through the centre leg in a state of momentary suspension.

When the Points Open, the Reversing of the Magnetic Field Creates a Large Voltage In the Secondary Coil

A primary coil is only called upon to hold this choking effect for a very brief fraction of a second. Just as soon as the south magnetic pole has sufficient coverage over the end of the centre leg, the breaker points are opened by the cam. The opening of the points instantly stops the flow of the current in the primary circuit, releasing its choking effect. The built-up magnetic forces, therefore, surge through the centre leg, instantly reversing the direction of the magnetic field from its former direction, top to bottom, to a direction from bottom to top. This sudden surge of magnetism through the centre leg establishes an enormous voltage in the secondary coil, allowing it to break down the air resistance of the spark plug and to pass a spark across the spark plug gap.

The Moment that the Points Open

At the same instant that the breaker points open, the condenser comes into play. It acts as a momentary reservoir for the surge of current in the primary which, if it had nowhere to go, would continue to arc across the breaker points. With the condenser available, the current surges into this reservoir momentarily, and then surges out again, further contributing to the change of the magnetic field in the coil core and thus to the voltage of the secondary output.

Magneto Edge-Distance

Normally, this distance need not be checked as it is preset and will not give problems unless there is a worn or damaged part in the magneto assembly. Of course, the magneto edge-distance is affected by point setting, and if the points are set too wide, the edge-gap becomes much less than it should be for the magneto to provide sufficient output to fire under compression. As points become too close and edge-gap becomes wider, the distance becomes too wide for the magneto to spark.

Quite often, the reason that an engine will start after the points are reset is that the edge-distance is re-established because of a proper point setting.

Many things can ruin the proper edge-distance setting: a worn breaker cam, a breaker cam with a worn key, a breaker cam installed upside down, a split breaker cam, a worn flywheel or a crankshaft keyway, a crankshaft twisted from the impact that affects or causes the flywheel to twist the crankshaft on the magneto side, wide crankshaft keyways, wide flywheel keyways, a partially sheared key, a lack of torque on the flywheel, wide point settings, wrong points, wrong breaker cam, improperly positioned points.

When a magneto has been carefully checked as to coil, condenser, points, point setting and cleanliness, and flywheel magnet, and when a problem still occurs in the engine, the edge-distance can be checked readily. In the case of a *no fire* or a weak fire, when it is questionable that the realtionship between the flywheel magnets and the lamination is correct, the relationship can be checked by marking the position of the lamination on the bearing plate or block.

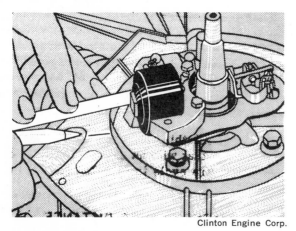

Figure 6.40   Marking Position of Lamination Plate

CAUTION: The direction of rotation of the flywheel should be marked with a small arrow since, when the flywheel is turned over to mark out the trailing edge of the lamination, it will appear correct but will be backwards and possibly be marked wrong.

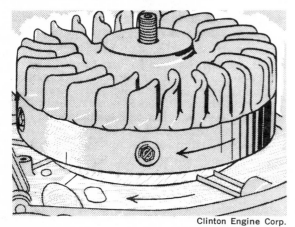

Figure 6.41   Direction of Flywheel Rotation

After the relationship has been marked between the core through the coil and the pole laminations to the flywheel magnet, tthe points should be set according to the service clearance. Then the crankshaft should be rotated in the direction of normal engine operation until the points just break or are open .001 of an inch with the original .020 point setting. The time at which the points break is when edge-distance is measured, and this can be accomplished by using a magneto tester (which will indicate when the points first open) or by using something that is .001 of an inch thick between the points.

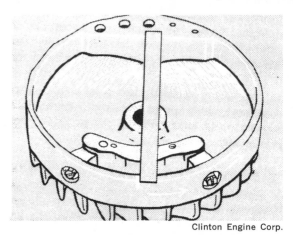

Figure 6.42   Measuring Distance Between Lines

After the crankshaft has been rotated so the points (that are pre-set at the proper setting, for example .020) open .001, the flywheel key should be put into the crankshaft keyway and the flywheel carefully set down on the crankshaft taper and tapped lightly into place. Caution should be taken not to move the crankshaft. By measuring the distance between the two lines, the edge-distance of the magneto can be determined.

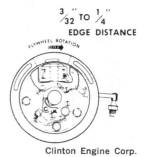

Figure 6.43   Measuring Edge Distance

The edge-distance on an engine can also be checked by measuring the fire at .020 (if that is the recommended point setting). The point setting is moved to .014 and the fire checked again, and then to .026. In this way, it can be determined at which point setting the best magneto output is secured. It is recommended (when edge-distance is a problem) that it be marked out carefully and the defective, worn, or wrong part be replaced.

In the event that the engine has suffered from an impact, trouble may start in the crankshaft. When engines run with loose flywheels, it may be caused by the flywheel, flywheel key, and possibly the crankshaft. The first thing to check on an engine with the edge-distance disturbed would be the breaker cam. Replace it if necessary.

Air Gap

Another thing that may affect the magneto's operation is an improper air-gap. This is the distance between the stationary lamination and the rotating flywheel magnets. The proper clearance is .007 to .017 on engines under five horsepower, and .012 to .020 on engines over five horsepower.

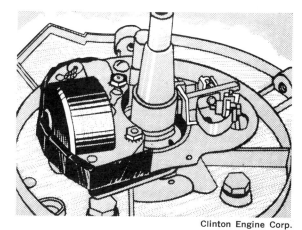

Clinton Engine Corp.

Figure 6.44 Taping Laminations for Air Gap

The air-gap can be checked by using plastic tape over the laminations. In other words, one layer of plastic tape, after its thickness is measured, is applied to the laminations carefully, then the flywheel is replaced on the crankshaft (using care to have the relation of flywheel magnets to the stationary lamination separated by 1/2 turn), and the flywheel is tightened with the flywheel nut. Then the flywheel is rotated twice and returned to its original position.

If the flywheel magnets have cut through the tape, the air-gap is too small and the high spots on the stationary laminations can be dressed down with a file. If this is done, care should be taken because each of the three legs of the lamination must be equidistant from the rotating flywheel magnets.

If the magneto is not operating properly and one strip of tape does not touch the flywheel, another strip can be applied. It should contact or show contact from rubbing on the two thicknesses of tape since the tape is usually .008 to .009 or larger per layer.

If there is too much air-gap, either the flywheel or lamination assembly should be replaced.

The flywheel magnets should be as close as possible to the stationary laminations. They must not, however, rub together.

Timing

From time to time, it may seem necessary to check the magneto timing to the piston. This can be done accurately if the top dead centre of the piston travel is located. It is not easy to find exact top dead centre. If a dial indicator is available, note that as the piston goes over top dead centre there is a definite spot where the piston seems stationary even though the flywheel moves. Top dead centre can be found quite accurately by moving the flywheel back and forth—thus moving the piston over top dead centre. With the dial indicator, it will show at which points the piston apparently stops. A reference mark is put on the bearing plate or block in line with a mark on the flywheel. The piston starts to move again when the flywheel is turned counter-clockwise. The bearing plate and block are marked a second time as the piston starts to move when the flywheel is turned clockwise. Half the difference between the two marks would be an exact top dead centre of the crankshaft.

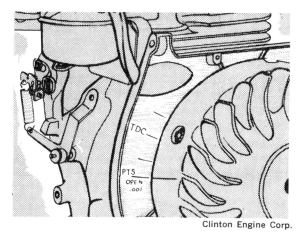

Clinton Engine Corp.

Figure 6.45 Timing an Engine

When exact top dead centre is found, the flywheel should be removed. The points should then be set to the recommended service clearance. The crankshaft should then be rotated in the direction of engine rotation until the points break at .001 of an inch (which can be checked by the same method as edge distance is checked). The flywheel key and flywheel then should be carefully replaced. The difference between the reference mark on the flywheel and the centre mark on the bearing plate or block is the magneto timing position.

The number of degrees before top dead centre can be figured by counting the number of flywheel fins and dividing them into 360 degrees. For example, if there are 20 flywheel fins, 20 is divided into 360 degrees, and the distance between each fin will be 18 degrees. And if the mark on the bearing plate or clock is approximately one flywheel fin from the mark on the flywheel, the magneto timing to piston will then be approximately 18 degrees.

If it is more or less than this, the distance between two fins can be marked out into three degrees, six degrees, or whatever is desired by measuring the distance and dividing the distance into three parts which would give six degrees, six parts which would give three degrees, and so on. With a different flywheel having a different number of fins, the original division of the total 360 degrees will vary. This procedure is a method of checking magneto timing accurately as to piston travel.

REVIEW QUESTIONS

1. What do we mean by a magnetic field?
2. What is another name for a magneto?
3. What is a magneto coil?
4. Approximately how many volts are produced by a magneto coil?
5. Why is the core of the magneto coil laminated?
6. Explain in your own words how a magneto circuit operates.
7. What happens in the magneto and the secondary windings when the points open?
8. What do we mean by the term "magneto edge distance?"
9. List at least eight things which may cause the edge distance of a flywheel to be off.
10. Draw a diagram showing the direction of rotation of a flywheel. With small arrows, join the flow or current through the flywheel magnets on to the coil and condenser into the secondary circuit with the spark plug.
11. What is the proper clearance between the laminations of the coil and flywheel magnets?
12. Make a list in step form showing how the magneto timing is checked to the piston.
13. At how many degrees before top dead centre should the flywheel fin be set before the nut is tightened?
14. List two ways of checking compression in small engines.
15. If a plug is oil-fouled, what two causes may produce this fouling and what can we do to overcome this problem?
16. If a small motor has burned electrodes in the spark plug, explain what problem has arisen or could arise because of this malfunction.
17. In the small engine magneto system, what part is sometimes called the reservoir or storage compartment of the ignition?
18. What difference has been made in the construction in new models of secondary high-tension leads to coils from the older models?
19. Where were magnets supposedly discovered?
20. Who were the first people to put the magnet to work?
21. Explain, in your own words, the following terms: a) open circuit; b) closed circuit; c) short circuit; and d) parallel circuit.
22. Describe the difference, by using a diagram, between a hot plug and a cold plug.

CHAPTER 7
TROUBLESHOOTING

THE FOUR STEP PROCEDURE

The following steps should be taken when troubleshooting to try and localize trouble in the electrical system.

(A) The magneto output is checked with a wide gap spark plug.

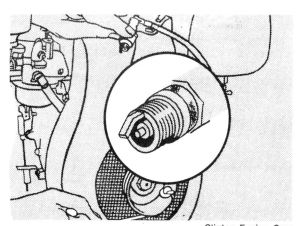

Clinton Engine Corp.
Figure 7.1   Check Magneto Output

One of the first checks that should be made on a small gasoline engine is the magneto output. The check we recommend on the magneto output is done with an 18 MM spark plug with the gap set between the centre electrode and ground electrode at (.156) 5/32 to (.187) 3/16. The high-tension lead should be fastened to the spark plug, the plug grounded to the engine, and the engine cranked over.

The use of the wide gap plug is recommended for several reasons. The amount of magneto output that is required to fire a .028 gapped plug under compression is 7 kilo-volts. The 18 MM spark plug, gapped at (.156) 5/32 to (.187) 3/16, requires approximately 10 kilo-volts of electricity to jump the gap, more than enough to fire the .028 gapped plug in the engine under compression. The magneto assembly on some engines is capable of putting out approximately 15 kilo-volts, providing the assembly is in good condition. In the event the magneto output is not adequate to jump the wide gap plug, the componet parts that made up the magneto should be checked, and replaced as required.

(B) The compression is measured with compression gauge.

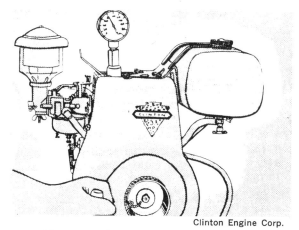

Clinton Engine Corp.
Figure 7.2   Checking Engine Compression

The compression on a one-cylinder engine is very important. Without the required amount, the engine would be hard starting and would not develop maximum horsepower.

The recommended way to check the compression is to remove the spark plug from the cylinder head. The gauge is held or screwed (depending on what type of gauge is used) into the spark plug hole. The engine is cranked over at normal cranking speed. The gauge reading should be above (60 P.S.I. 2-cycle) (65 to 70 P.S.I. 4-cycle above 4-1/2 H.P.). In the event that the compression reading is below what is required, the valves, seats, cylinder, piston, or gaskets should be reworked or replaced as required.

(C) The supply of fuel to carburetor should be checked.
If the carburetor is equipped with a bowl drain, this valve can be pressed to let a small amount of fuel leak out on to the deck or into a flat container. If it does not leak out of the carburetor bowl, it is likely that there is an obstruction in the fuel supply tank or line. When fuel leaks out of the bowl drain, it should be checked for puddles of water or other foreign elements; if any are present, consideration should be given to servicing the carburetor, fuel tank, and line.

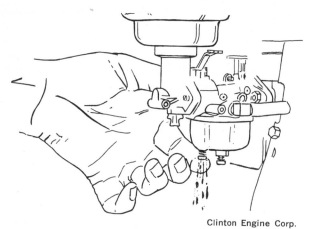

Clinton Engine Corp.

Figure 7.3   Checking Fuel in Carburetor

(D)   *The spark plug conditions should be checked.*
During any inspection of the engine, the spark plug should not be overlooked since it can cause an engine to fail to start or the misfire when it is running. This can be a visual inspection in which a check should be made for carbon buildup, burned electrodes, an improper gap between electrodes, (which should be (.028) to (.033) 2-cycle (.025) to (.028) 4-cycle engines), cracked insulation, and carbon between electrodes. If a spark plug has heavy carbon deposits, burned electrodes, or cracked insulation, it should be replaced with a new one.

By making the four checks, it can be determined what part of the engine needs repair or adjusting. Item (A) would indicate if the magneto is functioning. Item (B) would indicate if the valves and head gaskets are in order. Item (C) would indicate if the fuel is being supplied to the carburetor. Item (D) would indicate if the carburetor is supplying fuel to the combustion chamber or if the plug is functioning properly.

If the steps outlined are followed, a lot of time can be saved by working only on the part of the engine that needs repair.

In addition to the four-step procedure outlined, there are checklists that can be used to diagnose the cause of malfunction or failure, and corrective steps to take. One such list is given below.

ENGINE FAILS TO START OR STARTS HARD

CAUSE	*CORRECTION*
1. No fuel in tank.	Fill tank with clean, fresh fuel.
2. Fuel shut off valve not open.	Open fuel shut-off valve.
3. Fuel line to carburetor blocked.	Clean fuel line or remove and replace with a new one.
4. Water or foreign liquid in tank.	Drain tank. Clean carburetor and fuel lines. Dry spark plug points. Fill tank with clean, fresh fuel.
5. Stale fuel in tank.	Drain tank. Clean carburetors and fuel lines. Dry spark plug points. Fill tank with clean, fresh fuel.
6. No fire or insufficient fire to spark plug.	Check points, condenser, coil, high-tension lead, and flywheel keyway and magneto charge. Rework or replace as necessary.
7. Spark plug fouled or defective.	Replace spark plug with new.
8. Stop device in the off position.	Move stop device to ON position.
9. Engine flooded.	Open choke. Remove air cleaner, clean and service.
10. Choke valve not completely closing in carburetor.	Adjust control cable travel, and/or speed control lever.
11. Carburetor idle needle or power needle not properly adjusted.	Reset idle and power needles to the recommended preliminary settings.
12. Carburetor throttle lever not open far enough.	Move speed control lever to fast or run position; check for binding linkage or unhooked governor spring.
13. Low or no compression.	Check for a blown head gasket, damaged or worn cylinder, and valves that are stuck open, burned, not properly adjusted, or badly seated. Rework, or replace as necessary.
14. The engine fails to crank over quickly enough.	Inspect for a broken or weak impulse starter spring, or for excessive drag on the driven equipment. Replace broken or weak spring, and remove belts, chains, or release clutch.

15. Carbon blocking exhaust ports (in a 2-cycle engine). Remove muffler and clean carbon from ports.
16. Reed broken off (in a 2-cycle engine). Replace reed or reed assembly.
17. Oil seals leaking (in a 2-cycle engine). Replace oil seals with new.
18. Carburetor dirty. Remove and clean carburetor in a recommended cleaning solvent.
19. Loose blade (in a vertical shaft engine). Tighten blade.

ENGINE MISSING UNDER LOAD OR LACK OF POWER

CAUSE

CORRECTION

1. Weak or irregular fire to spark plug. Check points, condenser, coil, high-tension lead wire, flywheel, keyways, and flywheel charge.
2. Defective spark plug. Remove and replace with new.
3. Choke not completely open. Open lever to full choke position.
4. Carburetor idle or power needle not properly adjusted. Reset idle and power needles to the recommended preliminary settings.
5. Restricted fuel supply to carburetor. Clean tank, open gas tank cap vent, or clean or replace fuel lines.
6. Valves not functioning properly. Reset or reface valves, clean guides and stems of valves, and reset valves to tappet clearance.
7. Stop device not in the positive ON position. Move stop device to the ON position or adjust.
8. High-tension lead wire loose or not connected to spark plug. Adjust high-tension lead wire terminal, or connect to spark plug.
9. Air cleaner dirty or plugged. Clean or replace air cleaner element.
10. Not enough oil in crankcase (in a 4-cycle engine). Drain and refill with the proper type and quantity.
11. Improper fuel oil mix (in a 2-cycle engine). Drain tank and carburetor, and refill with the correct clean, fresh fuel mix.
12. Engine needs major overhaul. Overhaul engine.
13. Too much drag on driven equipment. Adjust clutches, pulleys or sprockets on driven equipment.
14. Obstructed exhaust system or use of a muffler not designed for the engine. Remove obstruction or replace muffler with the correct one.
15. Weak valve springs (in a 4-cycle engine). Replace weak valve springs with new.
16. Reed valve assembly not functioning properly (in a 2-cycle engine). Replace or adjust reed assembly.
17. Crankcase gaskets or seals leaking (in a 2-cycle engine). Replace gaskets or seals in question.

ENGINE NOISY OR KNOCKS

CAUSE

CORRECTION

1. Piston hitting carbon in combustion chamber. Remove head and clean carbon from head and top of cylinder.
2. Loose flywheel Torque flywheel nut to recommended torque.
3. Loose or worn connecting rod. Replace rod or crankshaft if tightening the rod bolt does not correct the condition.
4. Loose drive pulley blade, or clutch on power take-off end of crankshaft. Replace, tighten, or rework as necessary.
5. Rod lock or rod bolt hitting cam gear or block. Crimp rod lock or tighten rod bolt.
6. Main bearings worn. Replace worn bearings or crankshaft if necessary.
7. Rivet that holds oil distributor to cam gear hitting counterweight of crankshaft. Replace cam gear or grind head of rivet off.
8. Rotating screen hitting housing flywheel. Centre screen on flywheel.

ENGINE SURGES OR RUNS UNEVENLY

CAUSE

1. Fuel tank cap vent hole-obstructed.
2. Carburetor float level set too low.
3. Restricted fuel supply to carburetor.

4. Carburetor power and idle needles not properly adjusted.
5. Governor parts sticking or binding.
6. Engine vibrates excessively.

7. Carburetor throttle linkage, throttle shaft or, butterfly binding or stitching.

CORRECTION

Remove obstruction or replace with new cap.
Reset float level.
Clean tank, fuel lines, inlet needle, and seat of carburetor.
Readjust carburetor power, and idle needles.

Clean, and if necessary, repair or replace governor parts.
Check for bent crankshaft or poorly balanced condition on blades, adaptors, pulleys, sprockets, and clutches. Replace or rework as necessary.
Clean, lubricate or adjust linkage and de-burr throttle shaft or butterfly.

OVERHEATING

CAUSE

1. Carburetor settings too lean.
2. Improper fuel.
3. Over-speeding or running too slowly.
4. Overloading engine.

5. Not enough oil in crankcase (in a 4-cycle engine).
6. Air flow to cooling fins and head and block obstructed.
7. Engine dirty.

8. Too much carbon in combustion chamber.

9. Obstructed exhaust system or the use of a muffler not designed for engine.
10. Engine out of time (in a 4-cycle engine).

CORRECTION

Reset carburetor to proper setting.
Drain tank and refill with correct clean, fresh fuel.
Reset speed control or adjust governor to correct speed.
Review the possibility of using a larger horsepower engine.
Drain and refill with the proper type and quantity.
Clean debris from rotating screen, head, or cylinder cooling fins.
Clean grease and dirt from cylinder block and head exterior.
Remove head and clean carbon deposits from combustion chamber.
Remove obstruction or replace muffler with correct type.

Time the engine.

ENGINE VIBRATES EXCESSIVELY

CAUSE

1. Engine not mounted securely.
2. Bent crankshaft.
3. Blades, adaptors, pulleys, and sprockets out of balance.

CORRECTION

Tighten mounting bolts.
Replace crankshaft with new.
Rework or replace parts involved.

ENGINE FAILURE

CAUSES

1. Broken or damaged connecting rods, and scored pistons.

CORRECTION

Engine has run low on oil (in a 4-cycle engine).
Rod bolt locks not crimped securely.
Engine operated at speeds above the recommended RPM.
Oil pump, line and passage obstructed with debris (in a 4-cycle horizontal engine).
Not enough oil in fuel mix (in a 2-cycle engine).
Oil in crankcase not changed regularly (in a 4-cycle engine).

2. Excessive wear on parts. This includes valves, valve guides, cylinders, pistons, rings, rods, crankshafts, and main bearings.

3. Main bearing failure.

Air cleaner not serviced regularly.
Oil not changed often enough in crankcase.
Air cleaner element improperly installed in air cleaner body, or element needs replacing.
Air cleaner body not making good seal to carburetor.
Engine has run low on oil.
Excessive side loading of crankshaft.
Oil in crankcase not changed often enough (in a 4-cycle engine).
Blades, adaptors, pulleys, and sprockets out of balance.

CHAPTER 8
GOVERNORS

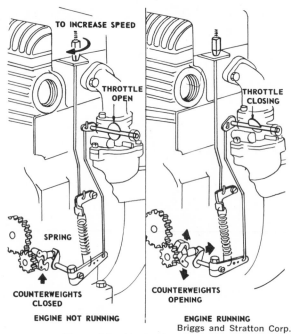

Figure 8.2   Mechanical Governor

While some people think that a governor on an engine is used to prevent overspeeding, its real purpose is to maintain a desired speed regardless of load. With a fixed throttle position, the engine speeds up if the load is lightened; if the load is increased, the engine slows down or even stops. A governor closes the throttle if the load is lightened or opens the throttle to obtain more power if the load is increased.

Basically, governors consist of two types—the pneumatic or air-vane type and the mechanical or flyball weight type.

The pneumatic governor is operated by the force of the air from the flywheel fins. When the engine is running, the air from the fins pushes against the air vane. The air vane is connected to the carburetor throttle by a link. The force and movement of these parts tend to close the carburetor and to slow the engine speed.

Opposed to this force and movement is the governor

spring which tends to pull the opposite way, opening the throttle. This spring is usually connected to an adjustable control of some kind so that the tension on the spring can be changed by the operator. Increasing the tension of the spring will increase the engine speed. Decreasing the tension will lower the engine speed. The point at which the pull of the spring equals the force of the air vane is called the *governed speed*.

The mechanical governor works in a similar manner except that, instead of using the force of the air that blows against the vane, it employs the centrifugal force of flyball weights opposing the governor spring.

The operation is the same. As the load on the engine increases, the engine starts to slow down. As soon as this happens, the centrifugal force of the flyball weights lessens. This allows the governor spring to pull the throttle open wider, increasing the horsepower to compensate

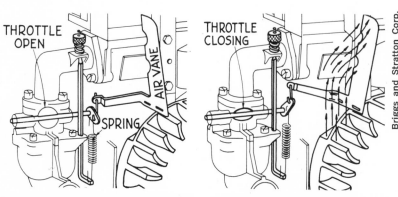

Figure 8.1   Air Vane Governor

for the increased load and thus maintaining the desired governed speed.

If the load on the engine lessens, the engine starts to speed up. This increases the pressure of the centrifugal force. The spring is stretched a little farther, closing the throttle and reducing the engine power. A properly functioning governor maintains this desired governed speed within fairly close limits.

MECHANICAL GOVERNORS

The governor spring tends to pull the throttle open. The force of the counterweights, which are operated by centrifugal force, tends to close the throttle. These two forces balance each other at the governed speed. The governed speed can be changed by changing governor spring tension.

Disassembly. The two mounting screws are loosened to remove the governor housing. The cup can be pulled off the governor gear and the gear will slide off the shaft. The roll pin is driven out at the end of the governor lever; the governor crank bushing is removed. Then the governor crank may be pulled out of the housing.

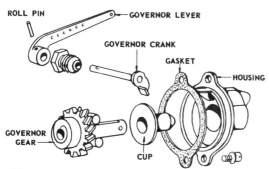

Figure 8.3 Governor Housing and Gear Assembly

Re-assembly. The governor crank is pushed with lever end forward into the housing. The bushing is slipped on to the shaft and threaded into the housing and tightened securely. The lever is placed on the shaft, and the governor gear on the shaft in the cylinder. A gasket is put on the governor housing. Then the governor housing is assembled on to the cylinder and tightened in place with two mounting screws.

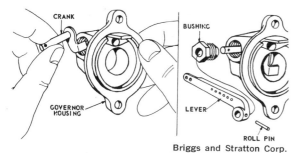

Briggs and Stratton Corp.

Figure 8.4 Install Crank and Lever

Adjustment. There is no adjustment between governor lever and governor crank on most of these engines. However, governor action is changed by inserting the governor link or the spring in different holes in the governor and throttle levers; in general, the closer to the pivot end of the lever, the smaller the difference between load and no load engine speed. The engine will begin to "hunt" if the spring is brought too close to the pivot point. The further from the pivot end, the tendency to "hunt" is lessened but the speed drops faster under an increasing load. If the governor speed is lowered, the spring can usually be moved closer to the pivot.

Manufacturers' manuals should be checked for detailed instructions on specific models.

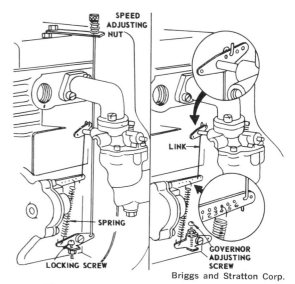

Briggs and Stratton Corp.

Figure 8.5 Mechanical Governor Linkage

AIR VANE GOVERNOR

The governor spring tends to open the throttle. Air pressure against the air vane tends to close the throttle. The engine speed at which these two forces balance is called the governed speed.

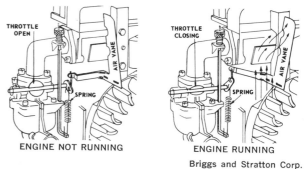

Briggs and Stratton Corp.

Figure 8.6 Air Vane Governor

Check and Adjust Pneumatic Governor. The governor shaft bearings must be in alignment and free on the shaft.

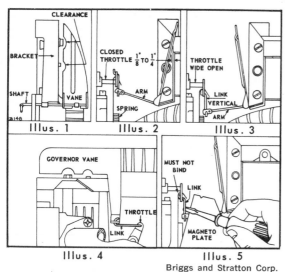

Illus. 1   Illus. 2   Illus. 3

Illus. 4   Illus. 5

Briggs and Stratton Corp.

Figure 8.7   Adjust Governor

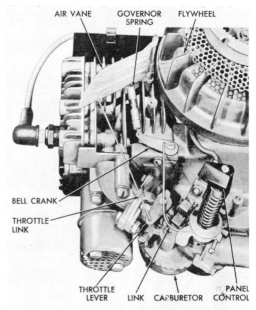

Tecumseh Products Co.

Figure 8.8   Air Vane Governor Assembly

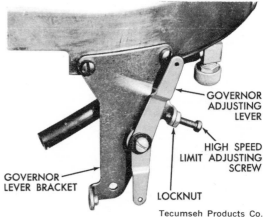

Tecumseh Products Co.

Figure 8.9   Governor Adjusting Lever

If they have been forced out of line, the bracket must be straightened and the bearing enlarged to restore free movement. The governor vane should be checked for the clearance of both edges so that it does not reach either the bracket, the blower housing, or the flywheel. To restore clearance throughout the vane travel, it may be necessary to straighten the bracket and shaft. The vane should stop at approximately 1/8 inch to 1/4 inch from the magneto coil when assembled and linked to the throttle shaft. This clearance may be adjusted if the vane is sprung carefully while the shaft is held. If the soldered joints have broken loose, they may be resoldered.

With the throttle wide open, the link connecting governor blade arm to the throttle lever should be in a vertical position on horizontal crankshaft engines and in a horizontal position on vertical crankshaft engines. If the above adjustments have been made and the end of the link binds to the throttle lever, it may be relieved by bending the governor end of the link until the link bends slightly and any binding is eliminated.

On models equipped with a nylon governor blade, no adjustment is necessary.

Air Vane Governor Operation
General Repair Procedure

The air vane governor controls the engine speed by controlling the setting of the carburetor throttle. It acts in conjunction with either a governor adjusting lever or a panel control to operate the engine at the required speed, regardless of load conditions.

The air vane is mounted on the cylinder block near the flywheel. It is operated by the air movement from the fins on the flywheel which tend to pivot the air vane away from the carburetor. The governor adjusting lever exerts a force against the air vane directly through the governor spring, tending to keep the air vane pivoted toward the carburetor. When a panel control is used, this force is exerted through the link, bell crank, and governor spring.

The air vane is connected to the carburetor throttle lever by the throttle link. When the air vane is pivoted toward the carburetor, the throttle is in the wide-open position. When the air vane is pivoted away from the carburetor, the throttle is closed. The greater the tension applied by the governor adjusting lever or the panel control through the governor spring, the greater the speed of the engine.

As the engine speed increases, the amount of air that is directed against the air vane by the fins on the flywheel increases, tending to pivot the air vane away from the carburetor against the tension of the governor spring. This movement is transferred to the throttle lever through the throttle link, which rotates the throttle shaft to partially close the throttle. As the throttle closes, the fuel flow to the engine is decreased, and the engine speed immediately decreases. As the engine speed decreases, the amount of air that is directed against the air vane decreases, and the throttle spring becomes tighter and pivots the air vane toward the carburetor. This movement is transferred to the throttle lever of the carburetor to open the throttle, increasing the fuel flow to the engine. As fuel flow increases, engine speed increases. In this manner, engine speed is stabilized and the engine maintains a constant speed regardless of engine load.

Adjusting Governors on Four-Cycle Engines

Air Vane Governors

The engine is operated with the governor adjusting lever or panel control set to the highest speed position and the engine speed measured with a tachometer. If the top engine speed is not within the limits recommended for application, the governed speed should be adjusted.

To adjust the top engine speed on models that use a governor adjusting lever, the locknut on the high speed limit adjusting screw is loosened and the adjusting screw turned out to increase the top engine speed. The adjusting screw is turned in to decrease top engine speed. The locknut is tightened to secure adjustment.

Early engines were manufactured with a governor blade pivot shaft that was screwed into a tapped hole in the cylinder block. In later production, the position of the governor blade pivot shaft was changed and mounted to the cylinder by a press fit. Until recently, the tapped hole for governor blade pivot shaft has been provided in all replacement cylinders. This is discontinued.

If the engine uses a governor blade pivot shaft, the service procedures that are followed are listed below:
a) Centre punch boss provided on cylinder.
b) Drill 3/4" deep with No. 29 drill.
c) Tap out drilled hole with 8-32 tap.
d) Screw in governor blade pivot shaft.
Caution: Use drill press to assure proper alignment of pivot shaft to cylinder boss.

Mechanical Governors

The adjustment procedure is listed below for vertical crankshaft engines.
a) The governor shaft is twisted to the left (counterclockwise) until tight.
b) The governor lever is attached to the linkage from the carburetor throttle.
c) The linkage is pulled, closing the throttle lever. The governor lever is slipped on the governor shaft. The throttle is held closed.
d) The governor shaft is twisted left (counterclockwise) with pliers until tight. It must not be forced.

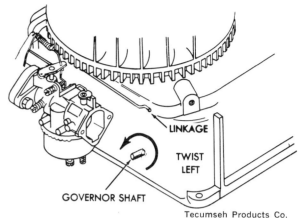

Figure 8.10   Mechanical Governor Vertical Crankshaft Engine

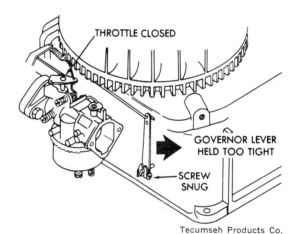

Figure 8.11   Adjusting Governor Lever on Rod

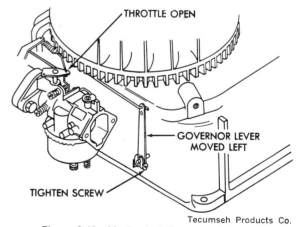

Figure 8.12   Mechanical Governor Adjustor

e) The screw in the governor lever is turned until the lever is snug on the governor shaft.
f) The governor lever is moved to left (counterclockwise) with the fingers until carburetor throttle lever is in the wide open position. The screw in the governor lever is then tightened.

On horizontal crankshaft engines, the adjusting procedure is as follows.

a) The governor shaft is twisted to the right (clockwise) until tight.

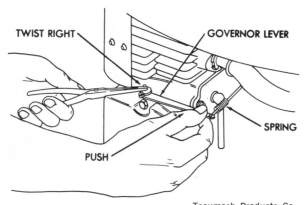

Figure 8.13   Adjusting Mechanical Governor

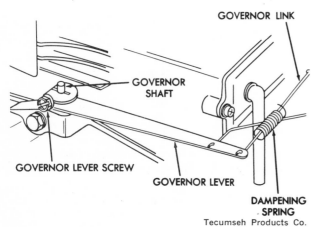

Figure 8.14   Mechanical Governor on Horizontal Crankshaft Engines

b) The governor lever is attached to the linkage from the carburetor throttle.

c) The linkage is pulled, closing the throttle lever, and the governor lever slipped along the governor shaft. The throttle is held shut.

d) The governor shaft is twisted right (clockwise) with pliers until tight. It must not be forced.

e) The screw in the governor lever is turned until the lever is snug on the governor shaft.

f) The governor lever is moved with the fingers to the left (counterclockwise) until the carburetor throttle lever is in a wide-open position. The screw in the governor lever is then tightened.

Caution: The governor spring, the links from the throttle or the governor lever should never be removed without a marking on the proper hole. Failure to replace the spring or link properly can cause serious damage.

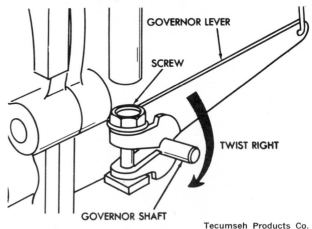

Figure 8.15   Governor Throttle Adjustment

MECHANICAL FLYBALL GOVERNORS

A practical example is necessary to illustrate the operation of the flyball governor. This checklist provides one.

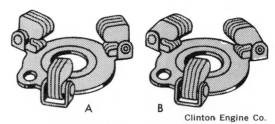

Figure 8.16   Counterweights

1. Start the engine and set the speed adjusting lever (or remote control throttle) to a point where the engine is operating at approximately 3,600 rpm.

2. Place a load on the power take-off shaft of the engine. The engine will appear to slow down momentarily, but will quickly regain its former speed because of the governor action.

3. As the engine begins to slow down, the sets of centrifugal governor weights which are mounted on pivot pins on the side of the camshaft or governor gear will allow the governor yoke to move toward the cam or governor gear.

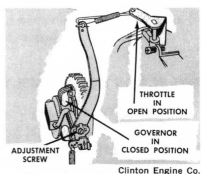

Figure 8.17   Closed Governor

4. This lateral movement of the yoke activates the governor shaft assembly which transmits the action through the connecting linkage to open the throttle. Movement of the governor shaft and the amount that the throttle is opened will be proportionate to the loss of engine speed. The throttle will open just enough to restore lost speed.

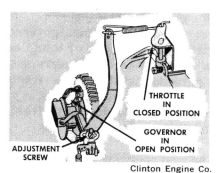

Figure 8.18   Open Governor

5. When the load is removed from the engine drive shaft, the governor will reverse the operation to prevent racing in the engine.

6. When the engine is stopped, the governor weights fall toward the centre of the camshaft or governor gear, allowing the governor yoke to move against the cam or governor gear. (This causes the movement of the governor spring and connecting linkage to open the throttle position.)

7. The governor throttle spring is the control or balance acting against the centrifugal force produced by the governor weights. The speed of the engine depends upon the initial tension applied to this spring, either by the speed adjusting lever or by the remote control throttle lever. The spring has been carefully selected and is calibrated to permit only permissable engine speeds.

Inspection and Assembly

It is best, when reassembling an engine equipped with the centrifugal weight governor, to inspect both the governor shaft bearing in the block and the governor arm assembly that goes through the bearing, for wear. If necessary, they should be replaced. After inspection, the arm is inserted through the bearing and the arm and weight assembly fastened into the bearing.

Care should be taken on installation of this arm and weight assembly since they may be locked to the outside linkage at 180 degrees from the correct position. This would tear out the centrifugal weights and damage the arm and weight assembly upon operation of the engine. The weight and arm or yoke should be as close to the cam axle or governor gear as possible for proper installation. In this position, it will operate against the governor collar or thimble assembly and will move in conjunc-

tion with the governor spring tension and the centrifugal force of the weights which are attached to the camshaft or governor gear.

The collar and the weight assembly should be inspected for wear and possible damage or for bending in the weights or the weight supports.

When a centrifugal governor is serviced, it should be checked to ensure that the collar or thimble operates freely on the camshaft or governor gear and that the governor shaft moves freely in the bushing. When the governor rod bushing in the block is replaced, the freedom of shaft must be inspected since the bushing may become distorted in installation. The governor shaft can also be bent easily on disassembly, reassembly, or in usage. The range of movement of the collar or the thimble must be checked after assembly of the camshaft or the governor gear to determine that these parts do not lock against the block.

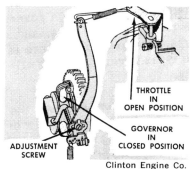

Figure 8.19   Closed Governor with Open Throttle

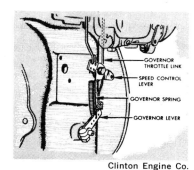

Figure 8.20   Governor and Throttle Linkage

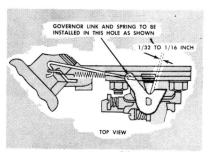

Figure 8.21   Governor Link and Spring

The adjustment screw is an important part of the governor. By loosening this screw, the governor weight's travel can be set to the throttle travel. Figure 8-21 illustrates the position of the throttle and the governor arm, with the engine in a stopped position and with tension on the governor spring. The throttle lever should be locked together in this position.

Older engines do not have this screw for balancing the throttle valve to the governor travel. On these, therefore, the loop in the governor link should be opened or closed to produce the same results.

The 1/32 to 1/16 inch distance between the throttle plate and the carburetor casting is critical. If this adjustment is ignored, it is possible to tear out the governor weights or to damage them.

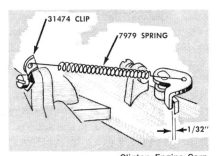

Figure 8.22   Throttle Back Lash Spring

On most of the horizontal cast-iron engines, a governor backlash spring is used in conjunction with the governor link between the throttle and the governor arm. The hookup of this spring is very important. Its function is to move the throttle open as the engine speed drops. The link is used to close the throttle as the engine goes overspeed. If the spring is hooked over the link in any way, it will give a "sloppy" linkage in the governor arm or throttle plate which will bring a surge into the engine operation from the extra travel of the governor arm prior to any response from the throttle.

AIR VANE GOVERNOR

The air blast created by the finned flywheel operates the air vane governor. The air vane is located inside the blower housing and linked directly to the throttle lever. The air vane governor is positioned to the air blast by a light coil spring attached to the throttle lever or, in some instances, to the governor link. When a load is applied to an engine drive shaft, the flywheel begins to slow down, causing a reduced air blast. The governor spring will move the linkage (and the air vane) in proportion to the engine speed reduction. The air vane, in turn, opens the throttle enough to restore the lost engine speed.

When the load is removed, this action is reversed and

Figure 8.23   Air Vane Governor

the governor operates to prevent the engine from running away.

The governor spring is the balancing force of the governor. The engine can be set to run at any desired speed within the operating range by adjusting the initial tension of the governor spring.

A heavier or lighter spring must not be used. This would seriously affect governor action. Maximum engine speed should not be above 3,600 rpm.

Inspection and Assembly

After the bearing plate and the flywheel plus magneto parts have been reassembled, and prior to replacement of the blower housing, the carburetor (or manifold with carburetor attached) should be replaced, hooking the linkage between the carburetor and air vane. Thus the linkage can be reassembled without bending. If a governor link is bent, it should be replaced with a new link.

The air vane should be inspected visually when reassembling and replaced if bent or damaged. The linkage should be replaced if it has been bent or if it is distorted, and care should be used in the hook-up of the air vane link and the throttle plate so that they move freely and do not drag at the connection or on the bearing plate or blower housing. Many of the air vane governors have a spring inside the vane at the pivot. The spring gives a dampening affect on the vane movement. This spring can be replaced if the engine has been out for a period of time. If it is not replaced, it can be stretched slightly so that it retains the pressure on the bushing or vane.

When servicing an air vane governor, the condition of the blower housing is important. Dents and bends should be removed from it so that the air stream moves as it should to the air vane. The air vane must be in the same condition as when new and replaced if bent because the governor spring tension and the vane are balanced. If the vane does not position itself properly in the air blast, the spring is too strong to be stretched by the air vane.

As the engine is reassembled, tension should be applied to the governor spring and the throttle closed manually. The throttle must move open freely, and not bind at the governor linkage, air vane, pivot post, bushings, bearing plate, or blower housing. It should move freely from closed to open position by governor spring tension.

It is always important to caution the customer to keep the air intake open and not to allow grass, weeds, or other debris to pile up on the intake. If the air is blocked from going into the flywheel through the opening in the blower housing of recoil starter, there is less available air and the air stream from the flywheel is reduced. As the air blast from the flywheel is reduced, the engine will increase and cause damage to the engine from excessive rpm. Obviously, any reduction of the air intake would affect the cooling as well, but the engine speed is also very important

A wide variation in speed (surge) can be caused by improper carburetor adjustment as well as from binding linkage, or from improperly installed linkage or governor spring.

A slight opening of the idle adjustment needle can often minimize surge. Governor surge after an engine is repainted can be caused by paint on the links. It is recommended that a new engine or rebuilt engine be operated for a period of time at "no load" to wear off any paint on the governor mechanism, as well as to seat the rings for better compression.

REVIEW QUESTIONS

1. What is the real purpose of a small engine governor?
2. List the two types of governors in a small engine and describe in your own words how they operate.
3. Define the word "governed speed".
4. What is wrong with an engine that surges or hunts, and what would be the procedure to overcome this problem?
5. When reassembling the small engine governor lever to the lever shaft, what is the degree or angle of degree required?
6. Give the step form for adjusting the governor lever to the governor crank.
7. Define the following words:
   a) pneumatic governor
   b) air vane governor
   c) governor lever
   d) tension
   e) centrifugal
   f) flyball weights
8. Explain in your words how to adjust an air-vane governor for operation.
9. Where is the air vane governor mounted on the small engine?

10. Where is the mechanical governor usually installed on a small engine? List the parts required in the mechanical type governor.
11. Where is the governor spring tension fastened?
12. What is the proper rpm setting on a small engine with no load?
13. What precaution should be taken when removing the governor spring or link from the throttle or governor lever? What might happen if you fail to take this precaution?
14. On inspection and before reassembling an engine equipped with a centrifugal weight governor, what parts should be inspected for wear?
15. On a horizontal cast iron engine, what type of spring is used in conjunction with the governor link between the throttle and the governor arm?
16. In studying the governor operation for air vane governors, of what importance is the blower housing to the operation of a small engine?
17. What would happen to a small engine if a heavy spring were substituted in the governor?
18. What would happen to the small engine if a lighter spring were substituted in the governor system?
19. If a governor link has been bent, is it advisable just to straighten it and reassemble it to the system?
20. On removal of the blower housing or shroud, what visual inspection can be made on the small air vane type governors?
21. In reassembly of the air vane type governor, what unit should be inspected for operation at the same time?
22. If you were operating a small engine shop, what advice could you give to the customer about the operation of his lawnmower to care for the blower housing?
23. What section of the Service Manual should be consulted when adjusting or repairing or even replacing parts of the governor system?
24. What section of the Service Manual should be consulted when settings for the governors are required?
25. What is a fixed throttle position on a small engine?
26. What effect will poor compression have on governor operation?
27. On a lawnmower, what precautions must be taken to insure correct engine speed is made?
28. List the advantages of a mechanical governor over the air vane governor.
29. In your estimation, which would be the better governor for the average small engine operator?
30. If the flywheel pin becomes clogged with dirt or foreign matter, what effect would this have on the air vane type governor?
31. If the flywheel becomes clogged with foreign matter,

what effect would this have on the mechanical type governor?

32. What units do we use for checking engine speed at different throttle openings?

33. What adjustments can be made to the air vane governor blade?

34. Does the nylon type governor blade require adjustment?

CHAPTER 9
LUBRICATION

The importance of lubrication in small engines is an aspect of their operation that must be seriously studied. Any study of lubrication must start with an examination of *friction*. Friction is resistance to motion caused by the contact of surfaces; it exists in varying degrees between all moving bodies and masses. Friction exists whenever two masses or bodies have movement relative to each other, as for example when a piece of metal is dragged along another piece of metal. This friction prevails in so many places throughout the small engine that examples are too numerous to mention. The purpose of lubrication in a small engine is to reduce this drag, and to keep the resulting friction heat to a minimum.

If friction could be entirely overcome we would have *perpetual* motion. It is impossible, however, to machine metal surfaces to such a smooth finish that a great number of projections and uneven spots will not show up under strong magnification. When two pieces of metal slide against one another, therefore, the high spots of one piece bump into the high spots of the other, setting up a resistance force which is converted to heat as this movement is increased.

The amount of friction between two objects depends

on many factors, such as the load or weight of the objects, the material of which the objects are made, and the degree of smoothness of the objects. Friction will also be affected by the temperature, the amount of clearance, and such additions as water, gasoline, oil, or dirt.

Lubrication in the small engine aims at reducing the direct contact between metal surfaces that would otherwise rub together and, therefore, at minimizing friction and wear. Other objectives include the dispersal of excess heat, the sealing of certain areas, and the cushioning and cleaning of the parts being lubricated.

A good lubricant must have adhesive and cohesive qualities. *Adhesion* is the oil's attraction or ability to stay on surfaces. A good lubricant will stick to the surfaces which it separates. *Cohesion* differs from adhesion; it refers to the force of attraction between the particles of the lubricant. It is often described as the *viscosity,* or body, of the oil. This viscosity is a very important factor of all lubricating oils.

It is necessary that lubricants have some fluidity. This means that they must be able to flow freely through all oil lines and to spread effectively over all bearing surfaces. This fluidity has to be controlled since the lubricant would damage some areas if it touched them.

A lubricant has to be engineered for a specific job, taking into consideration such facts as heat, speed, the weight of the bodies which are to be supported, and the kind of metals involved. Lubricants must be resistant to carbon formation, foaming oxidation, and water.

ENGINE LUBRICATION

Lubricating oil is distributed to the moving parts of an engine in various ways. It may be mixed with a fuel, splashed on to the parts, or forced to the parts; it may even form an oil fog or drip on to the surfaces needing lubrication. Most modern four-stroke-cycle engines are lubricated by pressure, and all two-stroke-cycle engines are lubricated by adding the oil to the fuel in various amounts.

Pressure System

There is a wide range of pressure systems, each one dependent on the number of parts which are to be fully lubricated. The older engines combine a pump and splash system. This old system used dippers on the end of the connecting rod which splashed oil to certain parts of the engine which could not be fed by the pressure pump. Even in the modern pressure system, a number of parts are lubricated by splash gravity and oil fog systems.

A pressure system consists of a pump which is usually driven by a gear on the crankshaft or the cam shaft. The pump draws oil from the top of the oil pan or sump, then through a floating oil strainer and forces it through drilled

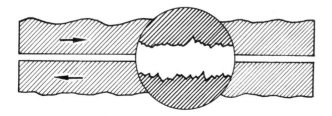

Figure 9.1   Moving Pieces of Metal Magnified

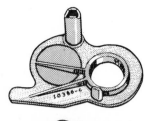

Figure 9.2   Oil Pump

Clinton Engine Corp.

passages to the place to be lubricated. These main lubrication areas are the connecting rod bearings, the cam shaft bearings, the connecting rod journals and the crankshaft bearings. The oil fog lubricates the valve guides, cam lobes, and timing gears.

Oil pressure is maintained by a special relief valve which is usually located in the main line or part of the pump.

The older intake was a floating unit. The floating intake took clean oil from the top of the oil sump and allowed all the sediment to remain in the bottom. This was a decided improvement over the previous pump which took oil from a fixed position in the bottom of the pan or sump.

Some of the older engines used just a straight splash system. This was a dipper fastened to the bottom of the connecting rod; the engine revolutions literally splashed the oil over the various parts that needed it.

ENGINE OILS AND LUBRICANTS

Engine oil for small engines is rated on a scale similar to that of automobile oils: MS, ML, MM, DG, and DM. These ratings come in different grades of 10, 20, 30 and 40.

Clinton Engine Corp.

Figure 9.3   Oil Types

MS Oil

This oil is useful in gasoline engines used under unfavourable or severe types of operating conditions. It is used under those conditions where an engine needs special lubrication to control bearing corrosion and engine deposits. Some of these operating conditions include frequent stopping and starting, high speed operation of an engine (as on a lawnmower) during summer when the engine will become very hot, and very heavy load operation as on a small tractor or a pump.

MM Oil

This oil is used for medium service such as high speed operations for short periods of time, long operations at average speed, and cold temperature operation where the unit is used for long or short periods. The service rating is for moderate to severe conditions, but does not include extensive operation under such severe types of low engine temperature service as prolonged idling and frequent starting and stopping of the engine.

ML Oil

ML service is the type needed by gasoline engines used under light and favourable operating conditions. These include moderate speed or moderate load operation most of the time, with no severe high or low engine temperature variation. Most operating periods are longer than 20 minutes.

DG Oil

DG and DM rated oils are high detergent lubricants. DG oil is used in diesel engines that operate where there are no severe requirements. This oil is also commonly used in automobiles and especially those with hydraulic valve lifters.

DM Oil

This oil is also used in diesel engines and in automobiles using hydraulic valve lifters. Unlike DG oil, this rating is suitable for engine operation under severe conditions.

Viscosity

The viscosity of the oil as specified by the manufacturer is stated as S.A.E. 20, S.A.E. 30, and so on. In the higher number categories the viscosity, or rate of flow, is heavier and slower. S.A.E. viscosity numbers specify viscosity only, and should not be confused with the type of oil. Most small engines need a grade 30 oil in the summer and a grade 10 oil in the winter.

Oil Change

The period of time between oil changes depends on the operating conditions of the engine; the speed, the atmospheric condition including the amount of dust in the air, and the mechanical condition of the engine. Under perfect operating conditions, the oil may be used for many hours of operation while under very poor conditions it should be changed very frequently.

Gear Lubricants

The lubrication used for gears on small engines must be

heavy enough to withstand extreme pressures without separating and must flow at low temperatures so it will not channel and allow gears to make metal-to-metal contact. In some units, such as gear differentials in small tractors, riding lawnmowers, pumps, and generating plants, it is necessary for the lubricant to withstand extreme pressures. It also has to overcome a sliding action or the transmission gears will come in contact. It must resist being pushed off the gears in high speed operation. A lubricant which will withstand these extreme pressures has certain added chemicals and is called an extreme pressure or E.P. lubricant.

Grease

It is necessary to lubricate some engine parts with a heavy grease. Grease is actually oil to which thickening agent has been added. The oil lubricates and the thickening agent simply holds the oil in place.

The material used for a thickening agent is sometimes called soap. It may be one of several metallic compounds, depending on the job the grease is expected to do.

Some grease is called fibre grease; it clings tightly to rotating parts such as external gears on a small engine; this is also called a soda grease.

Calcium grease is thickened with a calcium compound. This lubricant is called a cup grease; it has a tendency to separate into a liquid oil and a solid soap at high temperature. For this reason, it is not often used in small engines.

Aluminum grease is generally used for lubrication on the parts of the engine that may be exposed to moisture.

A grease may be a blend or mixture of any two of these greases. Each grease has a certain characteristic and blending it with others helps to obtain a grease which will perform almost any particular job.

The manufacturer's lubrication specifications must be followed if satisfactory results are to be obtained from an engine.

LUBRICATION FOR BRIGGS AND STRATTON ENGINES

Oil has four purposes. It cools, cleans, seals, and lubricates. Briggs and Stratton engines are lubricated with a gear-driven splash oil slinger, a connecting rod dipper, or a gear-driven open spade pump.

A high quality detergent oil with the American Petroleum Institute (API) classification for MS service should be used. Detergent oils keep the engine clean and retard the formation of gum and varnish deposits.

For operating temperatures above 40°F., an S.A.E. 30 or an S.A.E. 10 W-30 should be used. For operating temperatures below 40° F., S.A.E. 5W-20 is needed. Nothing should be added to the recommended oils.

Oil Slinger - Aluminum Alloy Engines

The oil slinger is driven by the cam gear.

Older slingers used a diecast bracket assembly with a steel bushing between the slinger and the bracket. A replacement bracket on which the oil slinger rides with a diameter of .490 inch or less should be used. The steel bushing must be replaced if worn.

The new style oil slingers have a stamp steel bracket. The unit is made from one assembly. The gear teeth in both the old and new style should be inspected. The gear must be replaced if they are worn.

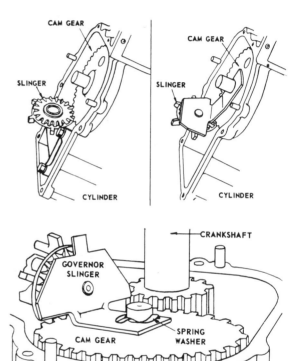

Briggs and Stratton Corp.

Figure 9.4   Oil Slinger and Bracket—Vertical Crankshaft Engines

Oil Dipper - Aluminum Alloy and Cast Iron Engines

In this splash system, the dipper goes into the oil reservoir in the base of the engine. It has no pump or moving parts. The connecting rod in the dipper for this engine model is shown in Figure 9-5.

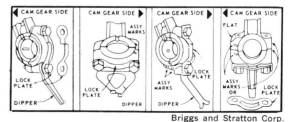

Briggs and Stratton Corp.

Figure 9.5   Connecting Rod Installations—Horizontal Crankshaft Engines

Oil Slinger Cast Iron Engines

The oil slinger is mounted in the oil sump on a screw, lock washer, washer, and bushing. The slinger should have .010″ end play on the bushing when cold. If there is less than .010″ end play, a small end of the slinger gear hub may be ground on a piece of emery cloth laid on a flat surface.

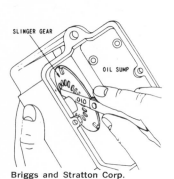

Figure 9.6 Checking Slinger Gear End Play

Briggs and Stratton Corp.

Figure 9.7 Grinding Off Slinger Gear Hub

Briggs and Stratton Corp.

Idler Gear

The idler gear is held in place in the cylinder by a shoulder screw and is driven by the crankshaft gear. The head of the shoulder screw should be against the idler gear. The screw should be tight. The idler gear should have .010″ end play on the shoulder when cold. If the clearance is less than .010″, a small end of the gear hub may be ground on a piece of emery cloth laid on a flat surface. This will prevent the gear from locking when the engine warms up.

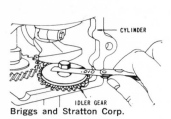

Figure 9.8 Checking Gear End Play

Briggs and Stratton Corp.

Figure 9.9 Grinding Off Gear Hub

Briggs and Stratton Corp.

Oil Pump

If the oil pump has been flushed out, it should be primed by squirting oil into the inlet opening. The oil pipe is assembled to the pump with the compression nut left loose. The oil pump is inserted into the sump.

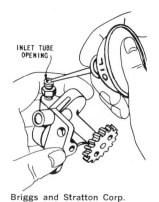

Figure 9.10 Priming Oil Pump

Briggs and Stratton Corp.

The pump is tightened in place with two mounting screws, and centred in the opening in the sump. Then the compression nut is tightened. The pump can be checked by placing oil in the sump up to the level of the screen at the end of the oil pipe, and then spinning as shown in Figure 9-12.

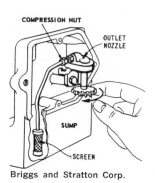

Figure 9.11 Installing Oil Pump

Briggs and Stratton Corp.

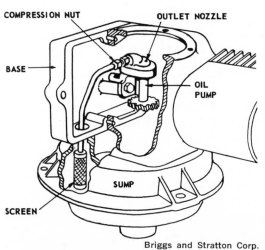

Briggs and Stratton Corp.

Figure 9.12 Installing Oil Pump

Individual Oil Levels

The amount of oil in the crankcase should be checked. On some of the vertical shaft engines used in tillers, the rear wheels may have to be set on blocks to obtain a level in the engine oil. Some of the models require 1 pint of oil to fill the crankcase properly. Many models require $1\frac{1}{4}$ pints. The manufacturers' specifications give exact information. On vertical shaft engines, when engine is on perfect level, the crankcase is filled until the oil in the filler hole is level at the top. That is sufficient in many engines. The oil level is often correct when the oil is even with the top of the filler plug.

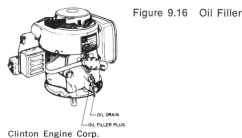

Figure 9.16   Oil Filler

Clinton Engine Corp.

Figure 9.13   Oil Filler

Clinton Engine Corp.

Some engines require 2 pints to fill the crankcase. These have a dip stick on the bottom of the filler plug; when checking the oil level, the plug should not be screwed into the threads but placed on top of the casting while the level is being measured.

The No. 412 Clinton, requires $2\frac{1}{2}$ pints of oil to fill the crankcase properly. There is a dip stick on the bottom of the filler plug. The same procedure is used when a reading is taken with the dip stick.

Figure 9.14   Oil Filler

Clinton Engine Corp.

Figure 9.15   Dip Stick

Clinton Engine Corp.

Some models have a combination filler plug-dip stick, and these models require 3 pints of oil. In checking the oil level, the dip stick must not be screwed in the threads but just placed over the filler plug hole, then removed and the indicated level read.

The largest of the Clinton engines require $4\frac{1}{2}$ pints.

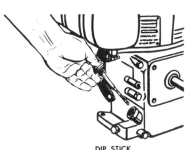

Figure 9.17   Dip Stick

Clinton Engine Corp.

Clinton Oil Pumps

On present production vertical Long Life engines, a replaceable sleeve bearing is used. The lubrication to the bearing plate is the same. Prior to removal of the cam shaft in the vertical shaft Long Life engines, the oil line is moved toward the magneto side and the pump swung from under the line. To reassemble, the cam shaft is re-

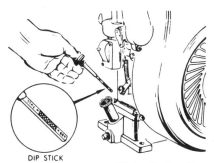

Clinton Engine Corp.

Figure 9.18   Dip Stick

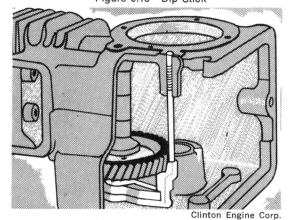

Clinton Engine Corp.

Figure 9.19   Oil Feed

Clinton Engine Corp.
Figure 9.20   Oil Channels

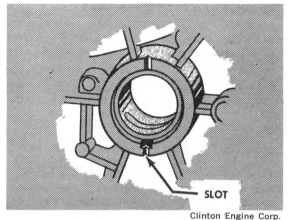
SLOT
Clinton Engine Corp.
Figure 9.22   Oil Slot in Main Bearing

placed and the assembly pumped. Then the spring and line are replaced.

The line must be down in the adapter or the oil flow to the bearing plate will be reduced or stopped.

A variation of this lubrication is illustrated later in this section. Figure 9-21 illustrates lubrication of the vertical shaft Gem to the centre of the block bearing. The hole in the bearing must line up with this lubrication passage if this bearing is to be lubricated.

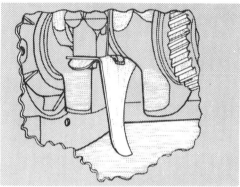
Clinton Engine Corp.
Figure 9.23   Oil Dipper

The lubrication on the VS-300 will be shown later in this section where variations on this engine have been illustrated. The VS-700, VS-750, and VS-800 use a slinger on the cam shaft to move oil throughout the engine. This slinger should be inspected, and if bent or damaged, replaced. It can be removed, if damaged, by removing the pin and replacing with a new slinger.

Clinton Splash Oil System

The horizontal 300 series engines use a splash system, but the vertical shaft series use an oil impeller. Prior to removal of the crankshaft on the vertical shaft 300 series engines, the lower PTO housing should be removed. This will expose the oil impeller. The impeller should be removed next and will expose the pin that fits into the crankshaft and drives the impeller. The pin is then taken out, and the crankshaft removed. For reassembly, the pin must be replaced, the impeller placed over the pin, and the lower housing replaced. When installing the lower housing, the oil return from the crankcase to the impeller must be lined up with the oil return hole in the PTO housing.

The previous parts must be removed on this assembly,

Clinton Engine Corp.
Figure 9.21   Oil Channels

The horizontal Gem feeds in a similar way, but the oil is moved to the bearing by a splash system. In servicing horizontal diecast (Gem series) engines, slotting the block, with care taken not to burr the bearing, may aid in minimizing seal problems that occur due to steady thrust toward the magneto side.

The vertical shaft Clintalloy has the same lubrication system as illustrated in Figure 9-20. The horizontal Long Bearings should be placed so that the oil can move through the channels for lubrication or a bearing will fail due to lack of lubrication.

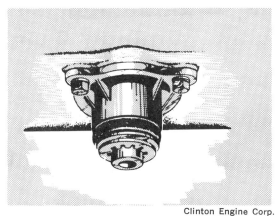

Figure 9.24 PTO Housing

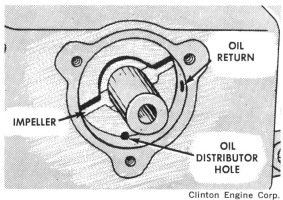

Figure 9.25 Oil Channels

as driving the pin through the bearing will damage the bearing and may damage the crankshaft as well.

The oil is moved by the impeller through a brass nozzle into the crankshaft and rod travel for lubrication of the VS-300 series engine. This nozzle must always be installed in the block, and it should not be drilled out or removed. If the nozzle is in questionable condition, it can be removed and replaced. It is listed in the parts breakdown for the vertical shaft 300 series engines.

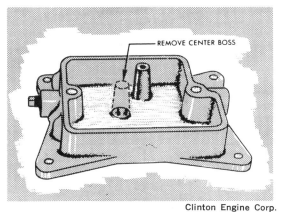

Figure 9.26 Restyled Engine Sump

The first production of the 700-A series engines had a plunger type oil pump. It is recommended that, when these engines are serviced, this engine be converted to a splash system.

The oil pump and the centre boss are removed. There must be at least 1/8 inch between the oil distributor and the boss. Prior to reassembly, it will be necessary to install a new baffle plate No. 3559 and hold it in place with a rivet No. 3569. The rivet hole will have to be cleaned out with a .140 drill prior to installing baffle. Use No. 4007 oil distributor as well. Figure 9-27 illustrates the position of the oil distributor to the rod cap on the horizontal cast iron engines.

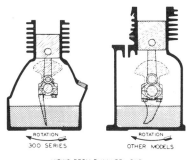

Figure 9.27 Oil Dipper Lubrication

A 3/16 inch vent hole was used between the crankcase and the valve chamber on some of the early engines. When these engines are serviced the 3/16 inch hole can be opened to 3/8 inch. The breather assembly can then be installed.

LUBRICATION IN TECUMSEH ENGINES
Tecumseh Barrel-type Lubrication Pump System

The barrel-type lubrication pump is driven by an eccentric cam on the cam shaft. Lubricating oil is drawn by the pump through the hollow camshaft that extends into the oil sump in the engine base. This occurs when the pump is making its intake stroke. During this time, the passage through the cam shaft to the sump is aligned with the pump opening.

As the cam shaft continues to rotate, the eccentric cam causes the pump to start its pressure stroke, during which time the plunger is driven down into the pump body, forcing out the oil. At this time, the other port in the cam shaft is aligned with the pump and the oil is directed through the drilled cam shaft passage to the other end of the cam shaft.

At the end of the cam shaft opposite the pump, the oil is forced through a crankcase passage to the top main bearing oil groove. The drilled crankshaft passage is aligned with the top main bearing oil groove, and oil is

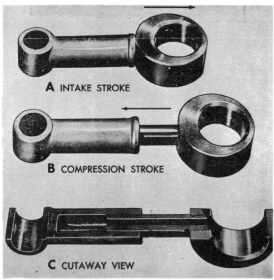

Figure 9.28   Barrel Type Lubrication

Briggs and Stratton Corp.

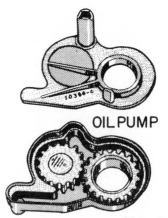

OIL PUMP

Clinton Engine Corp.

Figure 9.29   Oil Pump

directed through this passage to the crankshaft connecting rod journal. Spillage from the connecting rod lubricates the cylinder walls, and normal splash lubricates the other internal parts of the engine.

A pressure relief valve is installed in the crankcase to relieve any excessive pressures that might build up in the lubrication system. This valve opens at 28 psi, and is not likely to operate unless oil viscosity is extremely heavy due to cold temperatures, or unless the system becomes plugged or damaged. The normal pressure created by the lubrication system is 7 psi.

The bottom bearing receives its lubrication through a long and deep oil groove in the bearing. This constant lubrication of the working parts of the engines ensures that the engine will be able to handle heavy loads for extended periods of time without danger of bearing damage.

Tecumseh Gear-type Lubrication Pump System

The gear-type lubrication pump is a positive displacement pump driven by the crankshaft gear. It pumps oil from the oil sump in the engine base to the cam shaft, through the drilled cam shaft passage to the top cam shaft bearing, through a passage to the top main bearing, and then through the drilled crankshaft to the connecting rod journal on the crankshaft.

Spillage from the connecting rod lubricates the cylinder walls, and normal splash lubricates the other internal working parts. There is a pressure relief valve identical to the one described in the barrel type lubrication system.

General Repairs Checklist

REMOVAL OF TECUMSEH BARREL TYPE OIL PUMP AND REASSEMBLY

A.   Remove the barrel-type oil pump as follows:
1. Remove the mounting flange or the cylinder cover.
2. Slide barrel type oil pump from cam shaft and from stationary pin on cylinder.
3. Remove pump plunger from pump barrel.
B.   Clean and inspect pump parts as follows:
1. Wash pump parts with solvent.
2. Inspect pump plunger for rough spots or wear. If pump plunger is scored or worn, replace entire pump.
3. Inspect pump barrel for scoring or wear of inner barrel or bearing surfaces; replace entire pump if scored or worn.
C.   Reassemble oil pump as follows:
1. Liberally lubricate working parts of pump with engine oil. Manually operate pump to make sure plunger slides freely in barrel.
2. Lubricate stationary pin and eccentric on cam shaft. Position bearing end of barrel on stationary pin and position bearing end of plunger on eccentric on cam shaft. If the oil pump has a chamfer only on one side, that side must be placed toward the cam shaft gear.
3. Install mounting flange or cylinder cover.

GEAR TYPE OIL PUMP REMOVAL AND REASSEMBLY

A.   Remove gear type oil pump as follows:
1. Remove the mounting flange or cylinder cover.
2. Remove the three screws and lockwashers that hold the oil pump cover, oil pump gear, and displacement member.
B.   Clean and inspect the oil pump parts as follows:
1. Wash all parts in solvent.
2. Inspect the oil pump drive gear and displacement member for worn or broken teeth, scoring, or other

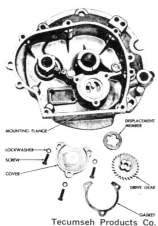

Tecumseh Products Co.
Figure 9.30   Parts of an Oil Pump

damage. Inspect shaft hole in drive gear for wear.

3. Inspect the pump cover for cracks, wear, or scoring.

4. If any of the parts are worn, replace the entire pump as an assembly.

C. Reassemble gear type oil pump as follows:

1. Position the oil pump displacement member and oil pump gear on shaft.

2. Flood the pump parts with engine oil to insure proper priming during the initial starting of the engine.

3. The gasket between the cover of the oil pump and body provides clearance for the drive gear. With a feeler gauge, determine clearance between cover and oil pump gear. The clearance desired is .006″ to .007″.

4. If it is necessary to obtain the proper clearance use either a shim or a gasket No. 28803 (.010″ thick), or a combination of the two.

5. Position the oil pump cover on the mounting flange; secure it with three screws and lock washers.

6. Install the mounting flange on the cylinder assembly.

REVIEW QUESTIONS

1. Explain how engine oil removes heat from the engine.

2. How does engine oil reduce friction in the small engine?

3. What does cohesion in lubricants mean?

4. What is another term for cohesion?

5. What is lubricant adhesion?

6. List the various ways in which an engine may receive lubrication.

7. How is a small engine oil pump operated?

8. What is the common method of lubricating the following small engine parts; the main journal, valve stems, cam shaft journals, and timing gears?

9. How is oil pressure regulated in the small engine lubrication system?

10. What is MS engine oil?

11. What kind of operating conditions would warrant the use of an MS oil?

12. What does S.A.E. 20 designate in an engine oil?

13. What governs the number of hours that a small engine should be operated between oil changes?

14. Name the four types of lubrication systems in a small engine.

15. List four purposes that engine oil has to perform in the small engine.

16. What does the abbreviation A.P.I. mean?

17. When should the bracket on an oil slinger be replaced?

18. Where is the oil dipper located and what is its purpose in the small engine?

19. Describe, in your own words, what an oil slinger is and what its purpose is in the small engine.

20. What precautions should be taken when an oil pump has been flushed out in a small engine?

21. List the sequence in preparing and reassembling an oil pump to the sump in a Briggs and Stratton engine.

22. What is the most important fact that must be taken into consideration when dealing with lubrication?

23. When in doubt as to what oil requirement is used in a small engine, where would you find the information required?

24. Is service ML satisfactory for the Clinton four-cycle engine warant?

25. List the four methods of checking oil level in small engines.

26. How would you check the oil on a power tiller?

27. What inspections of pump parts must be made after removal of the Tecumseh Barrel Type Oil Pump?

28. What is the basic difference between the gear type oil pump and the barrel type oil pump?

29. What is the clearance between the cover and the oil pump gear on a gear type oil pump?

30. Explain, in your own words, how the barrel type lubrication pump system operates.

31. What is the actual purpose of the pressure relief valve in the barrel type pump system?

32. Explain, in a simple step procedure, the operation for replacing the oil pump on a Clinton vertical shaft Long Life engine.

33. List the different types of lubrication systems in a small engine.

34. What is the type of oil pump used on the Model 700A series Clinton engine?

35. The horizontal 300 series engines use the splash oil system. What does the vertical shaft 300 series use?

36. What precautions should be taken when an oil pump on a small engine has been flushed out?

37. List the functions that engine oil has to perform with the small engine.

38. Explain, in your own words, how engine oil removes heat from the engine.

39. Draw a small diagram showing how engine oil operates between moving surfaces.

40. What is the common method of lubrication in the small engine today?

41. What oil pressure is required on the Clinton engine?

42. How does the oil splash system work?

43. How is the oil slinger in a Briggs and Stratton engine operated?

44. What grade of oil should be used at temperature 40 degrees F., and below 40 degrees F.?

45. Is it advisable to use additive in small engine oil?

46. Where do we use soda grease?

47. What is the basic purpose of a gear lubricant?

48. What do we mean by the term E.P. lubricant?

49. How often should an engine oil be cleaned?

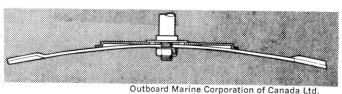
Figure 10.2c   Proper Stiffener

CHAPTER 10
LAWNMOWER SHARPENING TECHNIQUES

This chapter will cover sharpening techniques for lawnmower blades—either the rotary type, or the reel type.

ROTARY MOWER BLADE

A rotary mower blade is a straight piece of spring steel or preformed steel. The tips are usually sharpened two inches from the outside toward the centre on a 45 degree angle. Some lawnmowers require a blade stiffener to keep the blade from flexing down; other lawnmower blades are of sufficient strength that they do not require a blade stiffener.

Before the blade is removed from the lawnmower, the

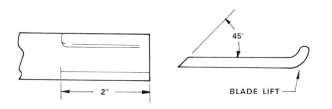

Figure 10.1   Blade Cutting Edge

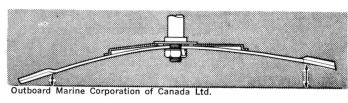

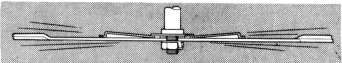

first safety precaution is to remove the high-tension lead from the spark plug. Unless this is done, if by chance the lawnmower blade is turned and if the engine happens to be on compression stroke, the engine may start. As a second precaution, a block should be put behind the rotary blade before trying to remove the bolt or nut; this block will hold the blade in place. The mower blade should be examined after it is removed.

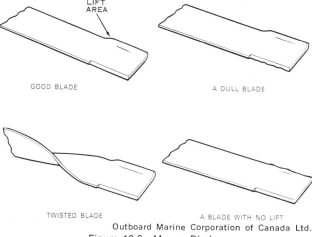
Figure 10.3   Mower Blades

A good blade has plenty of lift. A dull blade will kill the power of the engine and cut the grass raggedly. A twisted blade will cut very ragged and is also very dangerous to the person who is operating the machine. A blade with no lift will not discharge grass and will not cut grass evenly. Blades that are questionable must be replaced. Vibration from an out-of-balance blade or a bent stiffener can cause much engine damage and operator fatigue. Finally, the blade must be checked for cracks or heavy

Figure 10.2a   Bent Blade Stiffener

Figure 10.2b   Weak Stiffener

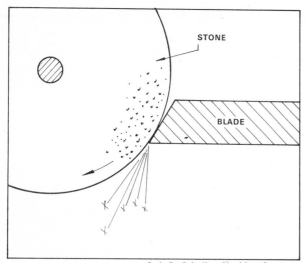

S. I. P. Grinding Machine Company

Figure 10.4 Grinding a Mower Blade

nicts that will cause metal fatigue and may endanger the operator of the mower.

Before the lawnmower blade is sharpened, it must be cleaned of grime, caked grass, or mud. A wire brush or scraper should be used to remove all particles. The blade may then be ground, as shown in Figure 10-4, being held on a 45 degree angle to the grindstone. When it is perfectly sharp, the process is repeated on the opposite side of the blade, and all burrs from the grinding are filed down.

Figure 10.5 Balance Point of a Rotary Blade

When the grinding is finished, the blade must be tested on a balancer. A blade that is out of balance will vibrate excessively and will cause severe damage to the crankshaft or to the engine itself. When the centre of the blade is poised on the balancer, the blade should be perfectly level. There are many blade balancers on the market but a simple test is to place a screwdriver in the centre hole in the blade and check the balance visually.

Before re-installing the blade, the mower housing should be cleaned thoroughly and should be checked for cracks, distortions, or breaks in the wheels. Any fault should be repaired at this time. The deck must be cleaned and the wheels lubricated; then the threads of the cap screw which will hold the blade in place must be oiled. The blade mounting bracket must be checked for possible damage.

Now the blade may be replaced. It must be tightened securely. The high-tension lead is fastened in place, and then the engine is serviced as described in the previous chapters.

When all the repairs are finished, the performance of the engine is checked. A safety shield must be used, such as hardwood frame of 2″ x 4″ or 2″ x 6″ placed around the deck, to protect against vibration or against a vibrating blade coming loose. The approximate height of the cut is checked by measuring with a straight edge across the wheels from the front left to the right rear. A typical mower cut will be approximately one and a half inches.

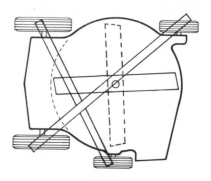

Figure 10.6 Measuring the Height of the Cut

THE PRINCIPLE OF SHARPENING A REEL TYPE MOWER

The reel type lawnmower uses the principles of a shear to cut grass. It is necessary, therefore, to have sharp cutting edges which make close enough contact to cut the grass cleanly. This is the only method of mowing that is not harmful to the lawn. Each blade of grass is supported by the bed knife, while the reel blade shears it off. This method avoids the bleeding and brown tops that are prevalent when the grass is whipped off with a rotary mower.

With a five-bladed reel mower, the bed knife does five times the work of any one reel blade, as all reel blades must shear against it. The bed knife, therefore, is the master cutting element. Although it is made of heavier and hardier steel, it is impossible to sharpen dull reel blades without sharpening the bed knife too. However, many mowers are successfully sharpened by grinding only the bed knife and restoring its shearing edge, when the shearing edges of the reel blades are in fair condition.

When the mower is brought in for servicing, it is of utmost importance to determine the cause of its faulting or its unsatisfactory operation. Often, if the mower is cutting satisfactorily in every respect but does not cut the grass cleanly, it requires only accurate adjustment of the bed knife to the reel blades. Examination of the cutting edges in the shearing corner of the reel blades and the bed knife should determine whether the mower needs a com-

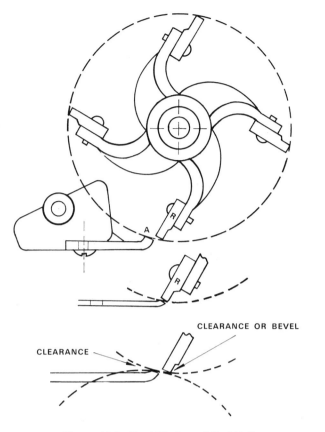

Figure 10.7   Reel Blade and Bed Knife

must first be serviced, then prepared for sharpening. These two procedures are 75 per cent of the entire operation.

In sharpening a reel type lawnmower, the cutting edge of the bed knife and the rotary reel blades must be re-sharpened by grinding. In addition, the match or pitch of the reel blades to the cutting edge of the bed knife must be restored.

For a mower to run easily and cut freely, it is important that the proper double or relief angle be ground on both the bed knife cutting edge and the reel blade cutting edges. The resulting clearance or relief behind the contacting edges reduces drag and friction. Too small a relief angle leaves too much metal in contact and causes the mower to run hard. Too much clearance or angle weakens the cutting edges, allowing them to nick easily and eventually to lose their adjustment.

Most mower manufacturers spin or cylinder grind their reels. By this method, the reel is revolved on centres or on its bearing while a large grindstone passes back and forth, grinding the reel to a true cylinder. No bevel or clearance is given to the reel blades, and the entire thickness of each blade makes a rubbing contact with the bed knife. The manufacturers do put clearance or bevel on the bed knife, however; otherwise the mower would run too hard to sell even as new.

For this reason a new lawnmower, especially a hand mower, can be improved by grinding the reel blades on a sharpener. Only when reel blades are ground one at a time can each blade be given a bevel and thus a desirable clearance behind the cutting edge. A power mower does not need as much clearance as a hand mower, as it is not

plete grinding operation. Proper adjustment of the mower, or lapping the reel end with emery compound to sharpen the blades, may restore satisfactory operation of the machine.

If a complete grinding operation is required, the mower

Figure 10.8   Parts of a Reel Mower

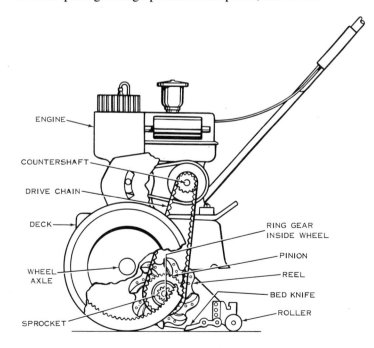

to be pushed, and the cutting edges gain extra strength from the smaller clearance angle. Because lawnmower sharpeners precisely grind a lawnmower reel to fit its bed knife, so that all the reel blades cleanly contact all points of the bed knife, it is of utmost importance that the lawnmower be properly repaired before grinding.

CHECKING AND PREPARING LAWNMOWER FOR SHARPENING

When a lawnmower is brought into a shop after winter storage, the following check should be made, in the presence of the customer if possible, and the condition of the mower recorded.

The handle should be checked for broken welds on steel handles, or splits on wooden handles. The cross arm should be checked for looseness.

The roller should be checked for splits, for worn or undersized rollers, and for loose pins. The roller hangers should be examined for excessive wear or breakage.

Pinions and pawls are checked by turning the wheels vigorously and observing whether the reel is positively driven. If there is slippage, new pawls and pinion gears may be needed.

The frame should be checked to ensure that it is steady and that the front spacer bar and the bed knife are fastened securely. If the frame is loose it may need to be realigned. The front spacing bar should be parallel to the steel axle shaft. If it is not, the alignment is corrected by loosening one end of the spacing bar and one end of the bed knife assembly and twisting the mower frame until the two units are parallel. When the spacing bar is tightened, care must be taken not to spread the frame, as this will affect the reel bearing adjustment. The side plates must be examined for cracks and the bed knife adjusting screws for stripped threads.

The bed knife may need grinding; or, if it is worn, it may need to be replaced. The general condition of the cast back and pivot points must be checked.

The reel should be checked for proper free rotation on its axis (bearing races) and the reel blades examined for bad nicks that might indicate a twisted or sprung spider. The reel blades must be securely fastened to the spiders, and the spiders must be secure on the reel shaft. A sprung reel blade can be forced back into place, and does not need to be ground excessively to restore its function.

The wheels and tires should be checked for excessive end play or wobble. Wheels may be broken or cracked, and tires may be so worn that they should be replaced.

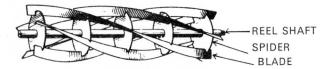

Figure 10.9 Reel Blades

Cleaning grease and grass out of the ring gear of the wheel may make the drive more noisy but should result in an easier operation. The ring gear may be cleaned during reservicing; but when new pinions are installed, the ring gear *must* be cleaned.

The reel should be checked for vertical or end play of the reel bearings, or pitted cups or cones. If the bearings are loose or worn and are of the non-adjustable type, they must be replaced.

The performance of the engine should be checked.

Lubrication of the lawnmower is very simple. When the mower is turned upside down for grinding, the crank case oil should be drained. The average engine holds one pint of oil or less.

It is not always necessary to remove the handle when sharpening a mower. However, a mower in poor condition can be worked on more easily if the handle is removed, so that it can be turned over and up on end for repairs and adjustments. Loose bearings, misalignment, sticking wheels, wire or grass tangled in the reel shaft, and excessive accumulations of grime and other particles, are a few of the faults that must be remedied before the mower can be ground.

Power mowers are generally driven by chains, which drive the reel axle; this in turn drives the wheels through the pinion gears. When repairing a mower, the drive chain should be disconnected so that the reel is free to turn. On some mowers, this chain is encased and is very difficult to remove. If the driving clutch is such that the reel will revolve fairly freely, the drag from the drive chain may not be sufficient to interfere with the sharpening operation.

Removing and Grinding Bed Knife

It is impossible to cover the exact steps and procedures necessary to sharpen every make and model of lawnmower. It will be up to the individual to use his own ability, and sometimes ingenuity, in following general instructions and applying them to the many types of mowers. Reels *must* be sharpened only with a proper sharpening machine, like the Model 900, produced by S. I. P. Grinding Co.

The first step in the sharpening procedure is to remove the bed knife (sometimes called the straight blade, cutter bar, or stationary blade) from the mower. Usually the bed knife is held in the mower by cap screws or nuts and bolts through the ends of the bed knife and the side frames of the mower. Before removing the end bolts, the pressure or tension on the bed knife adjusting screws must be relieved. If a few drops of oil are applied to all screws or bolts removed or loosened, the reassembling and adjusting will be easier and rust will be prevented. After the cap screws or bolts are removed, a large screw-

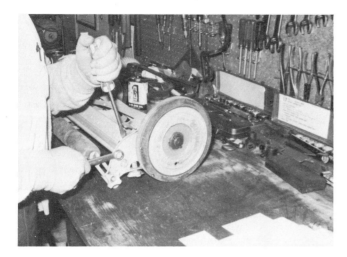

Figure 10.10   Removing Bed Knife

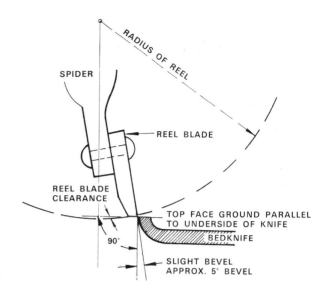

Figure 10.11   Cutting Edge Clearance

driver or pinch bar should be used to spring apart the side frames of the mower so that the bed knife can be removed.

After the bed knife assembly is removed, it should be cleaned and inspected. A screwdriver or putty knife and wire brush will effectively remove the dirt and grass that accumulates behind the lip of the bed knife. The blade must be clean before it is ground.

If the top face of the bed knife is wavy, excessive pressure of the bed knife adjustment to the reel is indicated, and, very likely, the reel bearings may be loose. The contacting area of the top face edge made by the blades also should be noted. If the mower is quite dull, this area will probably cover the entire thickness of the lip. If improperly adjusted, the bed knife may have more lip at one end than at the other. This can be corrected by removing more metal at the thick end, bringing the bed knife to an even thickness after sharpening. The roundness of the front cutting edge should be examined, as an equal amount will have to be ground away from both the front edge and the top face to arrive at a sharp shearing corner. If the edge is extremely rounded and dull, it is advisable to remove a little more metal from the front edge.

Figure 10-11 illustrates the angles and relationship of the bed knife to the ground and to the diameter of the reel blades. The front edge of the bed knife should be ground first. The wire edge left from this grind will be removed when the top face of the bed knife is ground. The front edge can be ground perfectly square, but an angle of 5 to 10 degrees is desirable. After the front edge has been ground, the top face is ready to be ground. A perfect level surface will provide clearance. When grinding a surface, the first light cut should show contact with the back of the lip, indicating clearance behind the front shearing edge when the blade is ground down to provide a new sharp front edge.

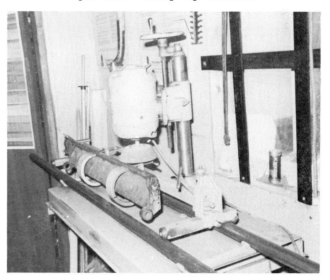

Figure 10.12   Grinding the Bed Knife Leading Edge

Figure 10.13   Grinding Bed Knife Top Edge

Removing and Grinding Bed Knife   111

REVIEW QUESTIONS

1. Name the two styles of cutting mowers.

2. Describe a rotary type mower.

3. What is the difference between the two types of mowers?

4. List the safety precautions that should be taken before working on the mower.

5. What is the cutting angle of the rotary blade?

6. What is meant by spin grinding a reel?

7. When examining a mower in for repair, what checks should be made in the presence of the customer?

8. List the steps taken for sharpening a reel mower.

9. What causes the top face of a bed knife to be wavy?

10. How is the cutting height of a rotary mower determined?

11. What is called the "master cutting element" of a reel mower?

12. List the problem that might occur on the following:
    (i)   Too small relief on cutting edge of bed knife.
    (ii) Too much relief on cutting edge of bed knife.
    (iii) Twisted rotary blade.
    (iv) Blade with no "lifts."
    (v)   Vibrating rotary blade.

CHAPTER 11
ENGINE IDENTIFICATION AND SERVICE MANUALS

This chapter will outline the fundamentals of engine identification and manual instruction and at the end of the chapter there will be some pages on trouble shooting. A service man for small engines is required to know how to read the service manual and pick out parts for repairs. It is, therefore, very important that the service man fully understand how the Master Manual operates in conjunction with the Model and Type Number of the engine. Without such knowledge of this Model and Type Number, it is virtually impossible to find parts in the Service Manuals.

BRIGGS AND STRATTON ENGINE IDENTIFICATION

The vertical crankshaft engine is one of the most popular types of motors in the small engine field. It is used mainly for rotary type lawnmowers, small generating plants and on some types of tillers.

The next engine is the horizontal type. Its crankshaft lies in a horizontal line and therefore called the horizontal-shafted engine. It is usually found in reel type lawnmowers and in pumps, in generating units and in many other applications. It is most commonly used in construction, where it is used for generating power for flood lights at night. It is also used for charging series of batteries, and for water pumps.

We have covered quite an area here, and as we discuss engines further on, these names, horizontal and vertical type, will become quite common from time to time; it is most important for engine identification.

Engine Identification

How do we identify an engine? The best way that can be followed is the chart put out by the Briggs and Stratton Corporation. It is a Numerical Model Number System. This is one of the best ways for identifying the engine of this manufacturer.

This handy chart explains their unique Numerical Model Designation System. It is possible to determine most of the important mechanical features of an engine by knowing the Model Number. This is how it works:

Figure 11.1 Briggs and Stratton Engine Identification

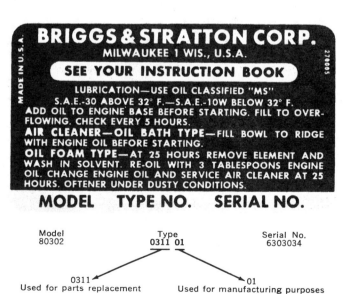

Engine Parts Lists and Engine Price Lists will show the first four digits only. As before, Model, Type, and Serial number must be known to select replacement parts or a replacement engine.

A.) The first one or two digits indicates the cubic inch displacement or size.

B.) The next digit indicates *basic design features.*

C.) The second digit after the displacement designation indicates the *position of crankshaft* and *type of carburetor.*

D.) The third digit after the displacement indicates *types of bearings* and whether or not the engine is equipped with a *reduction gear* or *auxiliary drive.*

E.) The last digit indicates the *type of starter.*

Briggs and Stratton has a handy pocket sized guide for identification of Briggs and Stratton Aluminum Engines and this can be purchased from the Briggs and Stratton Corporation by refering to form number MP-4243 (1700). It is very important that an engine service mechanic be able to follow the numerical sequence.

Choosing a Replacement Engine

The special numbers shown in the Engine Conversion list are those which have been produced in sufficient quantity that they are likely to show up for replacement. When a customer brings a mower or unit in for repair and it is found that the engine is beyond repair because of outdated parts or an outdated engine, the Service Manual, in its Conversion list, describes a replacement engine or one that is very close to it. When the Conversion lists are compiled, the production of each type number is checked and, on that basis, the number is shown or omitted. For instance, in the Conversion list covering the Model 8B, 80300, 81300 and 81400 engines, it is found that they only include those type numbers where at least 1000 engines were manufactured. In the list covering the Model 23 and the 23A engines, those type numbers for which at least 200 engines were produced are listed. Standards for these limits are low enough to be quite inclusive, yet still workable in size.

Most of the engines to be replaced will be covered in the Conversion list for that Model series. If not, there are several features on the old engine which should be checked to determine a *workable* service replacement engine.

A.) First of all, the horsepower range of the replacement engine which is needed should be determined and then, by using the Model Designation Card, the full Model Number which is needed must be established.

B.) Next, the crankshaft in the old engine must be identified by part number, using the parts' list, or by specifications, using the crankshaft identification list within the Master Manual. If the old engine is not in current production, the crankshaft identification list may be used used to find the equivalent crankshaft extension used in an aluminum bore or cast-iron bore.

C.) The engine may be checked in the price list to see if another model uses the part that is needed.

D.) Finally, the remaining external features of the old engine should be compared with the replacement which has been chosen:

type of carburetion—Standard or Choke-A-Matic; starter position; type of controls—manual or remote; and the oil fill and drain.

There are two factors which must be remembered when choosing a replacement engine:

1.) if the old engine is no longer in production (for example, many small bore cast-iron engines) there will be some general design difference found in the current production of aluminum engines;

2.) it may not be possible to find a replacement which is exact in every respect; the closest workable replacement should be used.

It is wise to keep all manuals up-to-date at all times. In the front of the manual there is a Card with the serial number of the manual on it. It is registered with the engine manufacturing company and by keeping the renewal card up-to-date (by paying the service charge) a monthly mailing will come into the service area. The manual must be brought up-to-date by putting the new sections into it. Without these new sections, current models or additions and deletions will not be known and obsolescence of parts will cause inventory problems.

Briggs and Stratton Numerical Model Number System

FIRST DIGIT
AFTER DISPLACEMENT

CUBIC INCH
DISPLACEMENT

6

8

10

14

BASIC
DESIGN FEATURE

0—Aluminum Bore

1—Sleeve Bore (under 5 H.P.)

2—Aluminum Bore

3—Sleeve Bore (over 5 H.P.)

4—Aluminum Bore-Sonoduct
(Flywheel Under Engine)

5—Sleeve Bore-Sonoduct
(Flywheel Under Engine)

SECOND DIGIT
AFTER DISPLACEMENT

CRANKSHAFT-CARBURETOR

0—

1—Horizontal
Vacu-Jet

2—Horizontal
Pulsa-Jet

3—Horizontal (Air Vane
Flo-Jet Governor)

4—Horizontal (Mechanical
Flo-Jet Governor)

5—Vertical
Vacu-Jet

6—

7—

8—

9—Vertical
Pulsa-Jet

THIRD DIGIT
AFTER DISPLACEMENT

BEARINGS,
REDUCTION GEARS
& AUXILIARY DRIVES

0—Plain Bearing

1—Flange Mounting
Plain Bearing

2—

3—Flange Mounting
Ball Bearing

4—

5—Gear Reduction

(6 to 1)

6—

7—

8—

9—Auxiliary Drive PTO

FOURTH DIGIT
AFTER DISPLACEMENT

TYPE OF STARTER

0—Without starter

1—Rope Starter

2—Rewind Starter

3—Electric—110 Volt

4—Elec. Starter-Generator
12 Volt

5—Electric Starter Only
12 Volt

6—Shock Free Windup
Starter

7—12 Volt Elec. Starter &
Power-Generator

E X A M P L E S

To identify Model 60102—First separate the displacement which is always 6, 8 or 14 cubic inches. Then refer to the tables above which describe the meaning of each successive digit following the displacement.

6	0
6 Cubic Inch	Aluminum Bore

Similarly, a Model 81796 is described as follows:

8	1
8 Cubic Inch	Sleeve Bore (Under 5 H.P.)

A Model 143337 is described this way:

14	3
14 Cubic Inch	Sleeve Bore (Over 5 H.P.)

1
Horizontal Shaft-
Vacu-Jet Carburetor

7
Vertical Shaft-
Flo-Jet Carburetor

3
Horizontal Shaft-
Flo-Jet Carburetor

0
Plain   Bearing

9
Auxiliary Drive
PTO

3
Flange Mounting
Ball Bearing

2
Rewind   Starter

6
Shock-Free Windup Starter

7
12 Volt Electric Starter &
Power Charger Generator

THE CLINTON SERVICE MANUAL

The sales-service manual is the key to servicing the Clinton engine. With the manual and a knowledge of its use, the following information is available to a mechanic: (a) replacement part numbers; (b) part and engine prices; (c) replacement engine stock numbers; (d) service procedures, specifications and tolerances.

This manual consists of nine sections.

Section I: price lists on replacement engines and parts.

Section II: complete engine part outline.

Section III: accessories and items that are not normally standard parts.

Section IV: specifications on individual crankshafts and bases which are important for installation purposes.

Section V: specifications and measurements on replacement engines.

Section VI: complete overhaul instructions and maintenance.

Section VII: interchangeability of parts from old engine models to current replacement models.

Section VIII: service bulletins covering warranty policy, short block usage, and service information.

Section IX: service letters and advance service data on new models.

How to Identify Clinton Engines

A system of identification has been established as a key for obtaining identification information. The basis of this system of identification begins with the *Name Plate* permanently attached to each Clinton engine at the factory. The reference for all *service* and *repair* on Clinton engines will be found on this Name Plate. It is very important

that the plate remain with the engine. If it ever becomes necessary to replace that part of the engine to which the Name Plate is attached, the plate must be placed on the new part.

In 1961, Clinton altered the numbering system on their engines, making the numbering system acceptable to I.B.M. equipment. To identify their engines properly, it is now necessary to understand both numbering systems.

There are three basic things that have to be taken from the engine name plate to be able to locate the parts needed in the sales-service manual:

the Model Number, the variation number and the type letter.

The Numbering System

(a) Prior to 1961.

The Model Number of the engine is found on the Name Plate, (for example, B760). By turning to Section II, Division B-700, this Model is illustrated in the Basic Parts List. In some cases, the model will be shown as B-700-2000 Series with model variations shown in the last three digits.

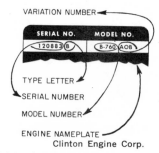

Figure 11.2   Clinton Engine I. D. Tag Plate

One thing to keep in mind when working with the Clinton manual, is that all models are set up in numerical and alphabetical sequence. The Model is further identified by the last *two* figures in the model designation number, (B-760 in this example) and is sometimes followed by additional letters or numbers. All recent models and future production will only have numbers following the basic model number. The lettering system has been discontinued. Due to varied employment of many series, there may be a large number of models. A complete list of these models, referred to as MODEL VARIATIONS, will be found following each Basic Parts List.

Under this system of assigning model variation numbers, the first variation from the standard engine will begin with "100". A typical model number might be 1200-107, for example. The model variation list following each Basic Parts List will tell what parts or assemblies are used on each variation, in addition to or in place of the standard parts found in the Basic Parts List. In the case of the name plate shown above, the Model Variation

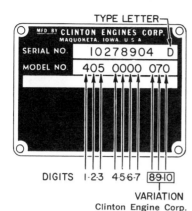

DIGITS 1·2·3 4·5·6·7 8·9·10

VARIATION

Clinton Engine Corp.

Figure 11.3 Clinton Engine Variation of Models

List following the Basic Parts List shows that the B-760-AOB has a special crankshaft, a gear reduction assembly and that the gear reducer is mounted in the 12:00 position. If, for instance, a part is needed just for the gear reducer, then one must turn to Section III (Accessories) and look up the part under the appropriate assembly number; in this case 3800. It is always advisable to check through the variations first to determine if other than standard parts were used.

The type letter is very important since it designates when a part design change has taken place and when the original part set up for this model engine will not work. Whenever a part or assembly is not used on all types, this will be noted in the basic model parts list. If no note appears, the part will be found on all types. The type in a Clinton engine is always shown as a suffix letter following the serial number (120883-B, for example).

(b) The Numbering System Since 1961.

The first digit is used to identify the type engine, (4-4-cycle and 5-2-cycle, for example).

The second and third digits complete identification of the basic series. Odd numbers will be used for vertical shaft engines and even numbers will be used for horizontal engines. 405 is a 4-cycle vertical shaft series. (406 is a horizontal shaft, 4-cycle series.)

The fourth digit identifies the starter as follows: 0 is a recoil starter; 1 is a rope starter; 2 is an impulse starter; 3 is a crankstarter; 4 is a 12-volt electric starter; 5 is a 12-volt starter generator; 6 is a 110-volt electric starter; 7 is a 12-volt generator; 8 has not been assigned to date; and 9 is a short block.

The fifth digit identifies bearing usage: -0-standard bearing; 1-aluminum or bronze sleeve bearing with flange mounting surface, and pilot diameter on engine mounting face for mounting equipment concentric to crankshaft centre line; 2-ball or roller bearing; 3-ball or roller bearing with flange mounting surface and pilot diameter on engine mounting face for mounting equipment concentric

to crankshaft centre line; 4 through 9 have not been assigned to date.

The sixth digit identifies auxiliary power takeoff and speed reducers: 0-without such equipment; 1-auxiliary PTO; 2-2:1 speed reducer; 3-not assigned to date; 4-4:1 speed reducer; 5-not assigned to date; 6-6:1 speed reducer; 7 through 9 have not been assigned to date.

The seventh digit will indicate a major design change. Model Variation numbers assigned after a seventh digit change will not correspond with variation numbers assigned before the change.

The eighth, ninth and tenth digits identify model variations.

The type letter will identify non-interchangeable part changes.

All 10 digits and the type letter must be used to identify the engine properly.

How to Order Parts and Engines:

Section I, the price list, contains descriptions of the various engine Series and up-to-date Supplements furnish the current prices for replacement engines and accessories. DIVISION B of this section is a numerical Parts Price List. The Part numbers must always be checked with the price list to make sure that this part is available on the current price list. All orders should include the part number. If the part number is not shown in the current price list, Section 1, Division C which is the Parts History, explains if the part has been depleted to another, or if it is not available.

In the price list, some parts carry a suffix letter and others have prefix letters. The prefix letter denotes the discount structure to the various steps of distribution, and the suffix letters indicates that the parts are assemblies.

IBM Numbering System

Clinton is in the process of changing the replacement part numbering system, making the numbering system acceptable to IBM equipment. This numbering system consists of three groups of numbers used in identifying the part classification, individual part identification, and the use of the part in an assembly. To clarify the numbering system refer to the example in Figure 11-4 which is broken down into three groups.

Group No. 1—Part Classification

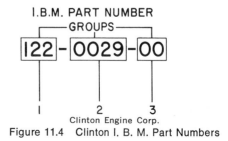

Clinton Engine Corp.

Figure 11.4 Clinton I. B. M. Part Numbers

Each group of like parts has a classification number assigned to them. All heads, for example, have a 122 for the first group of numbers.

Group No. 2

Individual part identification within the part classification is shown by these numbers.

Group No. 3

If a number 5 appears in the 3rd group of numbers, this indicates that the part is an assembly. The lack of a number would indicate that the part is not an assembly. In some cases, a 99 will appear in the 3rd group of numbers; this is for factory use, and denotes that the part is supplied by several vendors.

The three groups of numbers used in this numbering system consists of three digits for group No. 1, four digits for group No. 2, and two digits for group No. 3.

At the present time, Clinton is using both numbering systems. Most material being sent to the dealers at the present time carries both old and new part numbers. The new IBM number should only be used when there is no old number listed. The dealers will be informed when there is no old number listed. The dealers will be informed when the new IBM numbering system has been completely changed in the field. When ordering parts by IBM numbers, the group of numbers should be separated by a dash.

Section II

The first few pages of Section II contain the engines to which the new IBM numbers have been assigned. Some of the basic parts lists cover several model engines. These were set up this way since most of the parts that make up these models are alike. When parts are not interchangeable between the various models, the model they are used on will be listed. The first page of the basic parts list shows an exploded view of the parts that make up the engine. These parts have individual reference numbers, and these reference numbers can be used to find the particular part number assigned. For example, using the 400-0100-000 basic model exploded view, reference number 9, which refers to page 2 shows that the part is a part number 5735 breaker point assembly. All reference numbers listed on the exploded view of the engine are set up in numerical order on the following pages for cross-reference to part number. Once the correct terminology is known on the individual parts, the part numbers can be found without using the reference numbers, as the parts are all arranged in alphabetical sequence. For example, the breaker points would be found under the B)'s.

Some parts or assemblies are not completely described as single parts, such as the recoil starters, electric starters, fuel pump, gear reducers, and carburetors. These parts or assemblies are completely described and illustrated in Accessory Section III.

Following the basic parts list for each model are the model variations which explain the changes that have been made to the standard engine. These variations should be checked each time to make certain that the correct parts or assemblies are used on the particular model engine involved. Anytime that the variations do not show a parts change for a particular model, the part or parts would be standard as illustrated or listed in the basic parts list.

Section III

This section is set up to cover the items that are not normally considered a standard part on engines; however, there are few exceptions such as carburetors, and starters. The basic parts list or variations will direct the reader to Section III for an illustrated parts breakdown on various assemblies.

Section IV

For dimensional information on bases, crankshafts, cam gears, and breaker cams, Section IV should be consulted.

Section V

When information on exterior dimensions and horsepower is needed on service replacement stock number engines, refer to Section V.

Section VI

For information regarding the proper method of servicing, and repairing Clinton engines, refer to Section VI and the correct division.

Section VII

When information is needed in finding the current stock number of a service replacement engine needed to replace an older model Clinton, refer to Section VII. This section is set up in numerical order, listing all engines that Clinton has manufactured in past years. Clinton also has set up an interchange from competitive brands to Clinton in this section.

Section VIII

For information regarding the Clinton warranty policy, short block, and special service information not listed in Section VI, use Section VIII. Warranty and short blocks will be covered separately.

Section IX

This section is set up to keep service accounts informed on advance service information before it is finalized for the proper section of the manual.

ENGINE IDENTIFICATION
TECUMSEH ENGINE OR POWER PRODUCTS

Power Products' two-cycle engines are identified by type numbers indicated at one of a number of locations on the engine. The type number must be included in all parts orders to insure the delivery of the correct part. Early Power Products engines listed the type number as a suffix of the serial number. For example, if the indicated num-

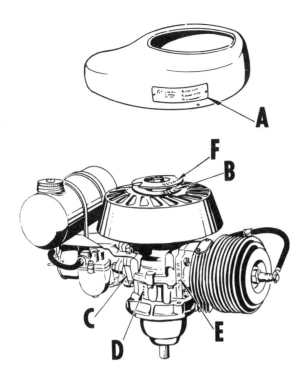

A. Name Plate on Air Shroud
B. Model and Type No. Plate
C. Metal Tab on Crankcase
D. Stamped on Crankcase
E. Stamped on Cylinder Flange
F. Stamped on Starter Pulley

The Serial Number can be found
as shown at references A, D,
and E.

Tecumseh Products Co.
Figure 11.5 Tecumseh Name Plates

ber is 365341 P 238, the 365341 is the serial number and
the 238 the type number. The letter P indicates a Phelon
magneto is used on the engine. Another example is
2616758 G 606-01A. The serial number is 2616758 and
the type number is 606-01A. The letter G designates a
model with a Phelon magneto. The important number in
in either case is the Type Number. The magneto designa-
ting letter is not important because the correct magneto
part number is listed in the part list. The type number
should be included in any correspondence concerning the
engine.

The Lauson four-cycle engines are identified by model
and type number stamped on the nameplate. The nameplate is located on the crankcase of vertical shaft models
and on the blower housing of horizontal shaft models.
Each letter or digit of the model number has a definite
meaning. The engine model and type number should be
included when parts are ordered or in any correspondence
concerning the engine.

REVIEW QUESTIONS

1. What do we mean by the terms "Vertical" and "Horizontal" engine?
2. In your own words explain how to identify a Briggs
and Stratton engine.
3. Is it always possible to match a new engine to an old
engine?
4. What are the features on the old engine that you
should check to find a usable Replacement engine?
5. Why is it important to keep the Service Manual up to
date?
6. Identify the following engines, using the Briggs and
Stratton Model Number System:
   a)   60202
   b)   81301
   c)   143452
   d)   100206
   e)   61307
7. List the nine sections and contents of the Clinton Service Manual.
8. What section of the Clinton Service Manual would
you consult if you were not sure of the repair procedure of the engine you were working on?
9. Is the Model number system in Clinton used the same
way as the Briggs and Stratton Model number system
for locating parts in the Parts Manual?
10. How is Clinton changing its parts code system?
11. Why are the Variation number and the suffix letter
important in locating part numbers for Clinton
engines?
12. What type of an engine is a Clinton engine whose
number digit is 405?
13. How does the I.B.M. Parts Number improve Identification of parts for Clinton Engines?
14. In what section of the Clinton Manual would you look
for Clinton Warranty Policy?
15. What horsepower does a Tecumseh HB 35 have?

6. If possible, leave the chain in an oil bath overnight, to ensure internal lubrication.
7. Keep the chain SHARP. Frequent light touch-ups will prevent the wear and the damage to the cutters and side links caused by operating with a dull chain.

WARNING—Do not use a reclaimed crankcase oil for bar and chain lubrication.

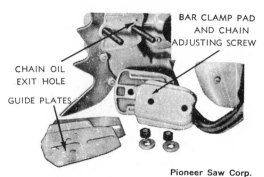

Pioneer Saw Corp.

Figure 12.2   Chain and Bar Holder

CHAPTER 12
CHAIN SAWS

To understand the terms applied to a chain saw, it is wise to follow the diagram shown in figure 12-1. There are safety hints that a person should follow and instructions which are important and will add to the efficient operation of the chain. It is wise to follow these instructions carefully:

1. Install the chain properly, with the correct chain tension.
2. Run the chain at a very slow speed for approximately 5 minutes. Use plenty of oil during break-in.
3. Switch off the motor and readjust the chain tension.
4. Recheck the chain tension often during the break-in period.
5. Keep the chain well lubricated during cutting operations.

PREVENTIVE MAINTENANCE

"Preventive Maintenance" is the elimination of potential causes of trouble before they occur. To realize the full value of an investment, to prevent unnecessary repair bills and loss of use or "down" time, preventive maintenance is a MUST. A regular schedule of inspections and tune-ups should be maintained.

Air Cleaner

The air cleaner, located on the side of the rear handle assembly, filters the air entering the carburetor. The dust and grit should be cleaned regularly from the flock screen filter element; this must be performed daily under certain extreme conditions. The air cleaner is easily serviced. By removing one centrally located 1/4-20 screw, the filter

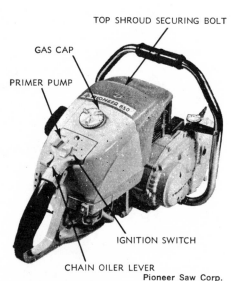

Pioneer Saw Corp.

Figure 12.1   Parts of a Chainsaw

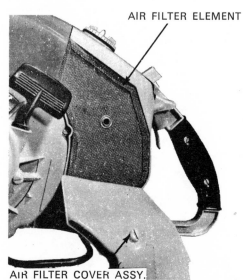

Pioneer Saw Corp.

Figure 12.3   Air Filter

element may be removed and washed in clean gasoline or solvent. This is preferable to washing in a fuel mix. The mix leaves a sticky film of oil which necessitates more frequent cleaning. The filter element may be tapped lightly to dry it. It is recommended that the area behind the filter element be wiped clean of accumulated dirt and sawdust.

Cylinder Block and Head Fins

At least once a week the outer shroud and inner shroud should be removed. This will expose the power head. Any accumulated dust and chips may be cleaned from between the fins with a thin blade type tool. Clogged fins impair the passage of cooling air from the flywheel and causes the engine to overheat.

Exhaust Ports

The exhaust muffler should be occasionally removed. The two 7/16″ nuts are taken off. The crankshaft is rotated until the piston is clear of the exposed exhaust ports. Any carbon build-up may be scraped away with a blunt edged tool from both the exhaust port openings and the muffler flange opening. The muffler gasket should be replaced if necessary.

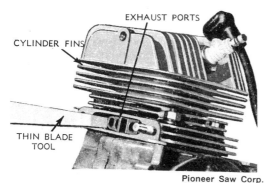

Pioneer Saw Corp.
Figure 12.4   Cleaning Exhaust Ports

Ignition

The high tension and ignition switch wires should be checked for breaks or wear.

Spark Plug

A check for carbon, fouling and porcelain cracks, should be made periodically. The spark plug should be cleaned and the proper electrode gap of .025″ maintained.

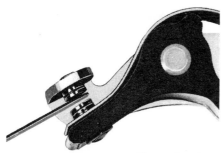

Pioneer Saw Corp.
Figure 12.5   Points

Magneto

No inspection or adjustment of the magneto should be made unless absolutely necessary. The appearance of the spark arcing from the spark plug electrode will indicate magneto condition. The breaker point gap should be .020″ when the rocker arm is riding the highest point on the cam. If the magneto is serviced, the parts must be replaced in the same location with the correct settings.

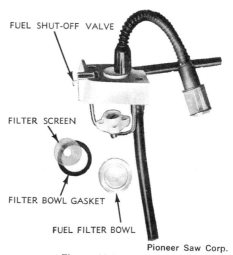

Pioneer Saw Corp.
Figure 12.6   Fuel System

Carburetor

The fuel pump valve housing is removed and the fuel pump valves cleaned of accumulated fine dust and foreign particles. A complete inspection and overhaul should be performed regularly. The carburetor adjustments must not be screwed in too tightly; a damaged needle seat can be costly to repair. When reinstalling the fuel line to the carburetor, care must be taken to ensure that the fuel line is free of all dirt and foreign particles which, if present, will immediately cause malfunction of the fuel pump valves.

Fuel Filter

Periodically, the fuel filter bowl should be removed and accumulated sediment and trapped moisture cleaned away. The filter outlet screen should also be cleaned. Care must be taken to ensure that the filter bowl gasket is correctly located before tightening the filter bowl clamp.

Clutch

The clutch is designed to engage at a specific engine speed. It is a "wet" type clutch lining and must be run in oil. The gear oil level indicated in the gearcase must be maintained. The clutch must not slip or wear from overloading. The throttle should be released immediately if the chain becomes pinched.

Gearing

The straight cut spur gear design does not require servicing under normal circumstances. The gear oil should be clean and free of foreign particles and the gear oil level topped up if necessary.

Cutter Bar

The cutter bar grooves should be clean at all times. The lubricating oil enters the grooves through the wide oil vent and is picked up by the moving chain. Inspection for cutter bar rail wear must be made at regular intervals and the bar turned over to ensure the rail wear is even on both sides. Should a sharp edge develop on the rail, it may be removed with a flat file.

Primer Pump

The primer pump requires very little servicing. However, if dirt enters the inlet valve, or exit valve, it must be removed and carefully cleaned. Dirt particles in the inlet valve will be indicated by a lack of resistance when the primer button is pressed. Dirt present in the exit valve will be indicated by a noticeably rich idle and a smoking condition caused by fuel leaking past the exit valve and entering the crankcase. A preventive measure would be to ensure a thoroughly clean fuel mix and careful refueling procedure.

SERVICING DIAGNOSIS

TROUBLE	PROBABLE CAUSE	REMEDY
Motor fails to start	Fuel tank empty.	Fill with correct fuel mixture.
	Fuel shut-off valve closed.	Open shut-off valve.
	Motor not primed.	Pump primer button 2 or 3 times after resistance is felt.
	Carburetor.	See carburetor adjustment.
	Over-priming.	Open throttle and pull starter until motor fires.
	Flooded Engine.	If the motor is continually flooding, check for plugged air filter and dirt in the carburetor inlet needle and seat.
	Dirt in primer pump inlet or outlet valve.	Remove and clean primer pump valves.
	Spark Plug.	Remove plug, clean and adjust. Re-attach wire and hold metal seat of plug against motor. Pull starter. A blue spark should jump gap between electrodes.
	Magneto.	Disconnect wire from spark plug. Hold so metal end is 1/4" from clean metal surface, (away from gas tank). Pull starter. There should be a strong blue spark across the gap. If no spark, the trouble is in breaker points, coil, condenser, shorted wire, or switch.
	*Plugged or frost covered pickup in fuel tank.	Remove and clean. Check for ice, water and dirt in fuel filter screen.
	*Plugged impulse hole in carburetor, misaligned carburetor gasket or reed valve gasket.	Remove and clean. Check for ice, water and dirt in fuel filter screen.
Chain stalls in cut.	Clutch slipping.	Check clutch shoes. If worn, replace.
	Improper filing or jointing.	Check filing and jointing instructions.
Chain moves when throttle is closed.	Cutter bar and chain pinched in log.	Use wedge if necessary to open cut wider to free bar and chain.
	Idling speed too fast.	Adjust idle speed.
Chain cuts roughly or digs in.	Top and front angles on cutters incorrectly filed. Too much joint.	Check filing jointing instructions, or see your servicing dealer.
Chain oiler stops pumping.	Dirt in pump assembly or discharge vent.	Remove and clean pump and feed line. Fill with clean oil. (S.A.E. 10 or 20).

NOTE: If motor idling is erratic or races away and then drops, it may indicate the possibility of excess air entering the crankcase. If this condition exists, the motor would continue to idle with the idle stop screw backed completely off.

Check the following points:
(1) Cocked throttle shutter.
(2) Leaking carburetor or reed valve gaskets.
(3) Loose carburetor nuts.
(4) Leaking crankshaft seals.

*Frozen gas line or ice in filter or carburetor.

Remove and clean. De-ice additive used in prescribed proportion will counteract this. (One teaspoonful to a full tank of fuel.)

*Conditions which may be experienced during cold weather operation.

Motor cuts out, leans out, or misfires.	Short circuit in ignition system.	Check all wires and connections.
	Partial stoppage in fuel system.	Clean out carefully and check carburetor.
	Fouled, wet, or damaged spark plug.	Clean and adjust, or replace.
	Magneto: faulty breaker points, coil, condenser ignition wire or connection.	Check.
	Inlet control lever sticking on the control lever hinge pin.	Remove and clean inlet lever and hinge pin, or replace.
	Improper sequence of fuel pump diaphragm and gasket.	Fuel pump gasket must be next to fuel pump valve housing.
	Dirt in fuel lines or carburetor passages.	Check and clean.
	Air leak in fuel lines.	Replace.
	**Improper inlet lever setting.	Adjust.
	Fouled spark plug.	Clean and gap, or replace.
Motor lacks power	Incorrect Fuel Mixture.	Drain tank, refill with correct mixture.
	Carburetor out of adjustment.	Adjust carburetor.
	Exhaust ports or muffler clogged.	Clean.
	Air intake filter clogged.	Clean
	Poor compression.	
Motor overheats	Cylinder fins or air system clogged.	Clean
	Incorrect fuel mixture.	Drain tank, refill with correct mixture.
	Carburetor lean.	Adjust.
	Leaking cylinder or base gaskets.	Check and replace if necessary.

Chain Sharpening

The chain must be firmly tightened on the cutter bar to hold it securely. When sharpening, a firm grip is taken on the file and a steady, even stroke used. The file must not be swung during the stroke. A constant cutting angle must be kept on all teeth, and the file must bear against the under side of the top face.

Keeping one fifth of the diameter of the file above the top cutting edge of the tooth will ensure a hollow ground cutting edge. This edge will cut fast and hold sharp longer. Only the amount of metal needed to produce a sharp edge should be filed away. A sharp file must be used since a dull file will work harden the already heat treated steel alloy and make it virtually impossible to sharpen the next time. A sharp 1/4″ full round file should be used. All the cutting teeth must be kept the same length. If the cutting

Figure 12.7 Cutter Sharpening

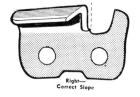
Right—
Correct Slope

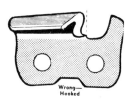
Wrong—
Hooked

Wrong—
Too Much Slope

Pioneer Saw Corp.

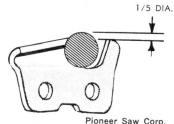

Figure 12.8   Proper Cutter Sharpening

teeth are an uneven length, the longer teeth will bite deeper and cause the saw to cut in an arc.

After sharpening the chain, it should be slacked off to the recommended tension and run with an excessive amount of oil to clear the filings from the cutter bar groove.

Chain Tension

The importance of correct chain tension cannot be over-stressed. Particular care must be used during the chain break-in period. Correct chain tension is especially important with cutter bar lengths of 32 inches and over to prevent the chain jumping off the bar and damaging the chain, cutter bar and sprocket. When the chain is correctly filed, jointed, tensioned and lubricated, it will cut smoothly and efficiently with the minimum of wear and effort.

Jointing

The chain is precision ground at the factory and has a standard joint of .030". Tests have indicated the .030" joint clearance is the best for average conditions. To suit particular cutting conditions, however, the joint can be altered, provided the joint height is kept uniform for all jointers. If the joint is changed, a Gauge No. 471135 will maintain uniform joint heights. A chain may be easily damaged or become severely worn by over-filing. When the jointer runners are filed, the round corners must be maintained. Not rounding the corners will cause rough cutting and a tendency to cut out of line.

Figure 12.9   Joint Runners

Correct Joint and Cutting Action

The recommended depth of .030" must be maintained on the depth gauge and the joint checked regularly. The chain should be jointed after every second filing. This will result in a fast cutting, smooth operating chain and less effort from the operator. The cutters are similar to a

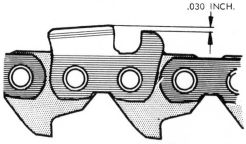

Figure 12.10   Proper Joint Cutter Height

Figure 12.11   Proper Cutting Action

properly adjusted planer blade with all depth gauges jointed evenly.

Excessive Joint

Lack of care in jointing may result in excessive or uneven joint. This will cause the cutters to bite in; the chain will grab, resulting in an overloading of attachments, poor performance and damage to both chain and bar.

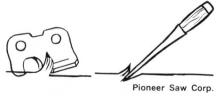

Figure 12.12   Biting Action

Insufficient Joint

Failure to check or joint regularly results in cutters that cannot bite into the wood, and a chain that will not cut efficiently or to capacity. This will require extra pressure from the operator, resulting in excessive wear to the bottom of the cutters and links, and rapid wear to the cutter bar rails.

Figure 12.13   Insufficient Jointing

Sharpening and Jointing

There are two methods in general use. In the first, a Jointing Gauge is used for simple and accurate jointing. The adjustable plate is preset, using the feeler gauge supplied, to the recommended joint. The jointing tool is put on top of the chain with the depth gauge protruding through the slot in the jointing plate and resting on the two cutters

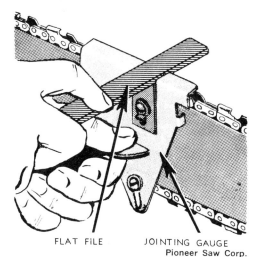

FLAT FILE   JOINTING GAUGE
                    Pioneer Saw Corp.
Figure 12.14   Jointing a Chain

near the centre of the bar. Using a flat file, the depth gauge is filed to the level of the jointing tool plate.

All work should be done near the centre of the bar, and the chain moved each time, not the tool. This is necessary because of the contour of all cutter bars. Operating the jointing tool at various positions could give an uneven joint and a rough chain.

If the above mentioned jointing tool is not available, a straight edge, long enough to cover at least six cutters, is placed on top of the chain. Next, the existing joint is measured with a standard .030″ feeler gauge. If the feeler cannot be inserted, one stroke is made with a flat file and it is re-checked. When correctly jointed, the drag between the straight edge and the top of the depth gauge should be barely noticeable. This step is repeated for each depth gauge throughout the entire chain. This method of jointing chains is much slower and less accurate than with a proper jointing tool.

Pioneer Saw Corp.
Figure 12.15a   Checking Cutters with Straight Edge

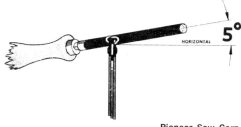

Pioneer Saw Corp.
Figure 12.15b   Angle of File

When filing, the approximate 30 degree angle from the vertical should be maintained along with approximately

Figure 12.15c   Correct Top Angle

Pioneer Saw Corp.

5 degrees from horizontal, with the handle low. As in the case of jointing, factory recommendation for general purpose calls for the 5 degrees from the horizontal when filing. Various types of wood and cutting conditions may necessitate the operator lowering the file handle an additional 5 degrees. This should only be changed after testing.

Bar and Chain Servicing

The use of the die cut corner, sheared at 35 degrees, is recommended for the maintaining of correct top angle on all cutters. This important feature on chain filing is outlined in all chain instruction pieces and the Operator's Manual.

The front end of the cutter bar tool is marked to indicate the minimum safety depth of the bar groove to avoid the chain drive lugs from riding on the bottom of the groove and from causing extensive chain and bar damage.

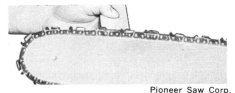

Pioneer Saw Corp.
Figure 12.16   Die Cut Corner

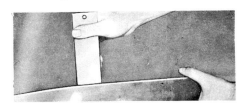

Pioneer Saw Corp.
Figure 12.17   Checking Bar Groove

By using either of the sharp corners of this tool, the bar groove can be cleaned regularly. The removal of the accumulated sawdust, old oil and chain filings will overcome the common fault of a chain riding up in the groove resulting in both chain weave and breakage.

Pioneer Saw Corp.
Figure 12.18   Cleaning Bar Groove

To carry out minor repairs such as a pinched bar, one corner of the tool is put in the groove near the pinched section, and tapped with a light hammer until the entire length of the gauge enters into the groove. While in this position, the tool is lightly tapped along the bar rail which will straighten out the pinch and give chain clearance.

A further use for the side of this tool is to close up the rails to correct groove width for proper chain performance. This overcomes chain weave and rapid deterioration of both the bar and chain.

Pioneer Saw Corp.

Figure 12.19   Straightening Rails

CHAIN DIAGNOSIS

TROUBLE	CAUSE	REMEDY
Chain stretched beyond adjustment	Dull cutters. Lack of lubrication.	Remove a side and drive link. Increase lubrication.
Chain breakage	Excessive pressure by operator. Excessive point. Lack of lubrication. Dull cutters.	Replace damaged parts. Check balance of oil. Increase lubrication. Rejoint chain. File chain.
Chain stiff, hard to tension.	Lack of lubrication. Poor maintenance.	Clean chain in solvent. Oil bath overnight. Check oil pump and vent holes.
Chain stalls in cut and/or scored drum.	Clutch slipping. Excessive pressure by operator. Clutch spring not releasing.	Check clutch shoes for wear. Check spring for tension. Apply less pressure correctly filed chain will self-feed.
Chain cuts rough or digs in.	Cutter angles incorrectly filed. Too much or uneven joint.	Check your filing instructions. Refile to correct angles. Check joint. Rejoint your chain.
Chain jumps bar.	Incorrect chain tension. Damaged cutter bar. Damaged drive links. Worn or damaged sprocket.	Correct chain tension. Check bar for damage, repair or replace. Check drive links for damage. Replace links or entire chain.
Chain cuts angle.	Cutter angles not the same on both sides. Uneven joint. Cutter bar rails uneven.	Refile cutters to same angle. Check rails. If worn, have bar serviced or replaced.
Worn drive sprockets.	Incorrect chain tension. Lack of lubrication. Dull cutters.	Rejoint. Increase lubrication. Replace sprocket. Correct chain tension. Increase lubrication. File cutters and joint chain.
Excessive wear drive links and/or side straps.	Lack of lubrication. Excessive tension. Dull chain. Worn sprocket.	Increase lubrication. Check oil pump. Extensive damage can be occasioned in a few hours. Check tension. File chain. Check sprocket.

CHAPTER 13
SERVICE FOR BRIGGS AND STRATTON STARTERS

Rewind. New and old style rewind starter assemblies are identified by the method of spring attachment on outside of blower housing.

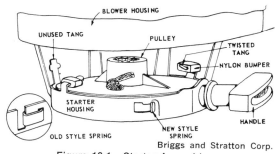

Figure 13.1   Starter Assembly

Remove spring. The knot at the starter pulley is cut to remove the rope. With the rope removed, the outer end of the starter spring is grasped with pliers and pulled out of the housing as far as possible. One of the bumper tangs is bent up and the starter pulley lifted out. The spring is disconnected. The pulley and spring are removed as a unit on the old style. The spring is disconnected by removing spring retainer. The nylon bumpers are replaced if worn.

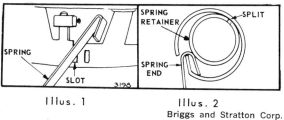

Figure 13.2   Old Style Spring

Install spring (old style). The starter spring is cleaned in a solvent, and wiped clean by pulling through a cloth. The spring is straightened to allow easier installation and to restore tension.

The end of the spring is inserted with a straight hook through the housing above the slot.

The end of the spring is hooked into the pulley slot. The spring retainer is pushed into place with a split portion of the retainer opposite spring end. A dab of grease is placed on the pulley and the pulley is set into the housing. The bumper tang is bent down.

Install spring (new style). The starter spring is cleaned in a solvent and wiped clean by pulling through a cloth. The spring is straightened to allow easier installation and to restore tension. Either end of spring is inserted into the blower housing slot and hooked into the pulley.

A dab of grease is put on the pulley and the pulley set into the housing. The bumper tang is bent down.

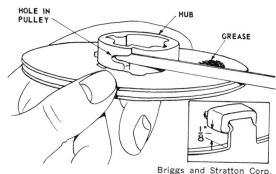

Briggs and Stratton Corp.
Figure 13.3   Install Spring Into Hub

Wind spring (new and old style). A ¾" square piece of stock is put into the centre of the pulley hub, and grasped with a wrench. The pulley is wound 13¼ turns

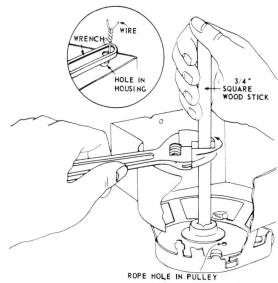

Briggs and Stratton Corp.
Figure 13.4   Winding Rewind Spring

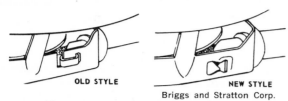

OLD STYLE   NEW STYLE

Briggs and Stratton Corp.

Figure 13.5   Locking Starter Spring

counter-clockwise, until the hole in the pulley for the rope knot and the eyelet in the blower housing are in alignment.

The spring should be securely locked in the slot in the housing, or into the smaller portion of the tapered hole.

Install rope. The rope is replaced if frayed. It is inserted through the handle and tied with a figure eight knot. A pin is put through the knot and the rope pulled tightly into the handle.

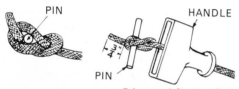

PIN   HANDLE

PIN

Briggs and Stratton Corp.

Figure 13.6   Knotting Rope

If re-using old rope, the cut end should be burned with a match and wiped with a waste cloth while it is still hot to prevent swelling and unravelling.

A stiff wire is inserted through the opposite end of the rope as near to the end as possible.

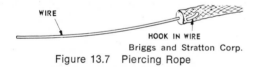

WIRE

HOOK IN WIRE

Briggs and Stratton Corp.

Figure 13.7   Piercing Rope

The wire and rope are threaded through the rope eyelet in the housing, to the inside of the guide lug and out the pulley hole. Then the wire is removed.

A knot is tied in the rope and pulled tight, while ensuring that the knot in the pulley does not contact the bumper tangs.

Install blower housing on engine. The starter clutch

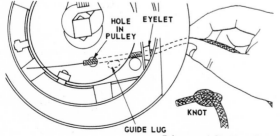

HOLE IN PULLEY   EYELET

KNOT

GUIDE LUG

Briggs and Stratton Corp.

Figure 13.8   Inserting Rope

ratchet has the word "TOP" on one side. The ratchet is turned until "Top" is nearest the cylinder head and the recoil starter assembly is installed.

Figure 13.9   Align Clutch Ratchet

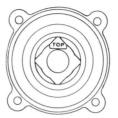

Briggs and Stratton Corp.

If wound tight, the tension is released by turning the control knob to the "Start" position. If the starter spring does not release, the control is turned to the "Crank" position. To prevent injury, the crank handle should be held with one hand while removing the Phillips head screw and handle assembly from the starter housing. This will release the spring.

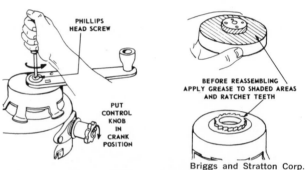

PHILLIPS HEAD SCREW

PUT CONTROL KNOB IN CRANK POSITION

BEFORE REASSEMBLING APPLY GREASE TO SHADED AREAS AND RATCHET TEETH

Briggs and Stratton Corp.

Figure 13.10   Releasing Spring

Broken Spring (windup starter). To check the starter for a broken spring, while unit is still on engine, the control knob is turned to the "Start" position and the cranking handle turned ten turns clockwise. If the engine does not turn over, either the spring is broken or the starter clutch balls are not engaged. While turning the cranking handle, the starter clutch ratchet should be watched; if it does not move, the starter spring is probably broken.

Disassemble windup. The blower housing and the screw holding the cranking handle to housing are both removed. The tangs holding the starter spring and housing assembly are bent upward and the retainer plate, spring and housing assembly lifted out of blower housing.

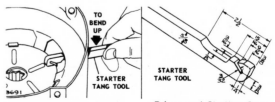

TO BEND UP

STARTER TANG TOOL

STARTER TANG TOOL

Briggs and Stratton Corp.

Figure 13.11   Removing Spring Housing

Inspect starter parts. The spring and housing assembly are inspected for spring breakage or other damage and the ratchet gear on the outside of the blower housing for wear or damage. The movement of the control knob and the handle assembly are checked for broken or worn parts.

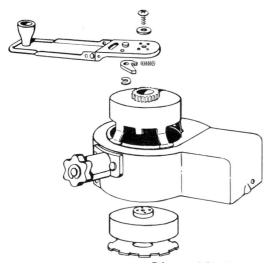

Briggs and Stratton Corp.

Figure 13.12   Inspect Parts

The control housing on the side of the blower housing is inspected for ease of operation. If binding or gritty, it is cleaned and lubricated.

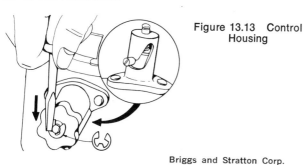

Figure 13.13   Control Housing

Briggs and Stratton Corp.

Starter clutch. The starter clutch ratchet is cleaned as indicated in Figure 13-14.

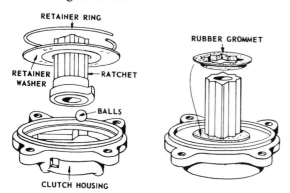

Briggs and Stratton Corp.

Figure 13.14   Inspect Starter Clutch

ELECTRIC STARTERS (110 VOLT CHAIN DRIVE)

To Remove. The three mounting screws are loosened and the chain guard removed. On horizontal shaft engines, the chain connector link and then the chain are removed. On vertical crankshaft engines, no connector link is used. The electric motor support bracket screws are loosened instead and the motor tilted to allow removal of chain.

The blower housing is then taken off and the locks that hold the heads of the two small screws inside the rope starter pulley bent open to remove the screws. The rope starter pulley, the large steel washer, and the smaller brass washer are removed. The sprocket may be taken out by turning it counterclockwise to release the spring tension and pulling it outward at the same time. The screws in the band of rotating screws are loosened to remove the screen.

The end of the adapter which is attached to the crankshaft has two flat sides and two rounded sides; the Allen set screw located in one of the rounded sides is loosened. The flywheel is held with wrench 19167 and an open end or adjustable wrench used to turn the adapter counterclockwise and to remove it. The coil spring is taken from the adapter by pushing a small screw driver into small slot. The spring must not be forced or bent.

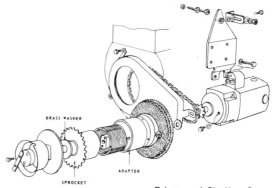

Briggs and Stratton Corp.

Figure 13.15   Chain Drive 110 Volt Starter

To install. The flywheel is installed and the clutch spring placed into the adapter so that the prong on the spring aligns with the slot in the back of the adapter. The spring is pushed into the adapter until the prong seats in the slot. The adapter is turned on crankshaft at 60 to 70 foot lbs. The flywheel is held and the Allen set screw tightened to lock the adapter to the crankshaft. The rotating screen is assembled over the adapter and the screw tightened to hold the screen in place.

The sprocket is placed inside the spring, and turned counterclockwise until it bottoms. When the parts are properly assembled, there should be a small opening between the spring and sprocket. The correct space between

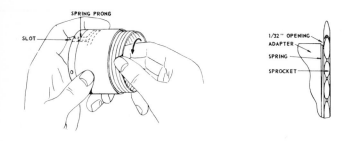

ILLUSTRATION 1   ILLUSTRATION 2
                                         Briggs and Stratton Corp.
              Figure 13.16   Install Clutch Spring

the sprocket and adapter is very important. The brass washer and the large flat steel washer which has hole with two flat sides are assembled. The rope pulley is installed and the small cup-shaped washer assembled with its hollow side toward the flywheel. The cup is fastened to the adapter with two small screws and a screw lock. The corners of the lock are bent tightly against the screw heads.

The blower housing is installed and the chain assemblied to the sprockets. The chain tension is adjusted by moving the nuts on the stud or studs at the upper end of the motor mounting bracket until the chain can be moved up and down about ¼ inch at a point midway between the sprockets. The chain guard is assembled and the three guard mounting screws tightened.

ELECTRIC STARTERS (110 VOLT BELT DRIVE)

To Remove. The mounting screws are loosened and the belt guard removed. The nuts holding the motor to the

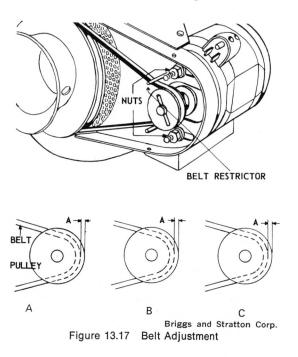

Figure 13.17   Belt Adjustment

blower housing are removed and then the motor and the belt.

The blower housing is removed. A 19167 flywheel holder is used to hold the flywheel while loosening the flywheel nut. The ½ inch nuts have a left-hand thread; the ⅝ inch nuts have a right-hand thread. The pulley is removed.

To Install. The pulley is slipped over the crankshaft and the Bellville washer is assembled with its hollow side toward the flywheel. The flywheel is held with a 19167 holder and the flywheel nut tightened to 50 to 60 ft. lbs. of torque. The blower housing, motor and belt, are installed.

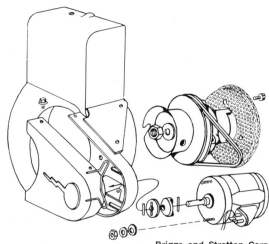

Briggs and Stratton Corp.
Figure 13.18   Belt Drive 110 Volt Starter

To Adjust the Belt. The belt must be between the prongs of the belt restrictor. The engine is cranked with the starter motor ignition "Off".

If the dimension is 3/32 inch to 1/8 inch, the belt is in its proper adjustment. If dimension "A" is less than 3/32 inch while cranking, the starter motor must be adjusted away from the engine. If more than 1/8 inch, the motor must be adjusted toward the engine.

Belt adjustment is made by loosening the two nuts and sliding the motor in the slots. Torque on nuts is 15-20 inch pounds.

The Final Check. The starting motor should be tested under maximum load. To do this, the engine is turned by hand until the compression stroke is reached and then the starter is plugged in. The belt should engage and crank the engine without slipping. When the engine starts, disconnect the plug. The belt should not circulate while the engine is running.

If a two-prong outlet is the only one available, it should be converted to a three-prong outlet.

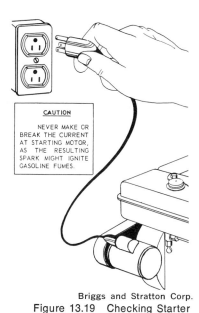

CAUTION

NEVER MAKE OR
BREAK THE CURRENT
AT STARTING MOTOR,
AS THE RESULTING
SPARK MIGHT IGNITE
GASOLINE FUMES.

Briggs and Stratton Corp.
Figure 13.19 Checking Starter

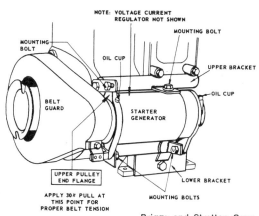

NOTE: VOLTAGE CURRENT
REGULATOR NOT SHOWN

Briggs and Stratton Corp.
Figure 13.20   12 Volt Starter Generator

12 VOLT STARTER GENERATOR, MODELS 14, 19, 23, AND 23A

To Remove. The belt guard and the screws in the slotted adjustment arms are removed and the two bolts which attach the starter motor to the starter support bracket loosened.

The starter motor is tilted toward the blower housing and the Vee belt removed. (If worn, the twin Vee belts must be replaced in a matched set of two belts.) The starter motor is tilted away from the blower housing, supporting it so that its weight does not rest on the regulator. By removing the two bolts which hold the starter motor to the bracket, the motor may be removed.

The bolts holding the starter motor support bracket to the cylinder and the strap support are then removed.

The two screws and lockwashers holding the rope starter pulley to the electric starter pulley and then the two screws and lockwashers holding the electric starter pulley to the flywheel are taken out. The pulley and flywheel nut lock is removed where used. The blower housing may now be removed.

To install. (Flywheel, fuel tank, and blower housing should be assembled to engine).

The flywheel nut lock is slipped over the flywheel nut. The electric starter pulley is assembled so that the slot in the pulley hub lines up with the locating pin into the flywheel. The pulley is locked in place with two screws in the flywheel. The rope starter pulley is assembled to the electric starter pulley.

The starter motor support bracket and the lockwashers and nuts are assembled. The slotted adjustment screw and

Figure 13.21
12 Volt Starter
Generator
Assembly

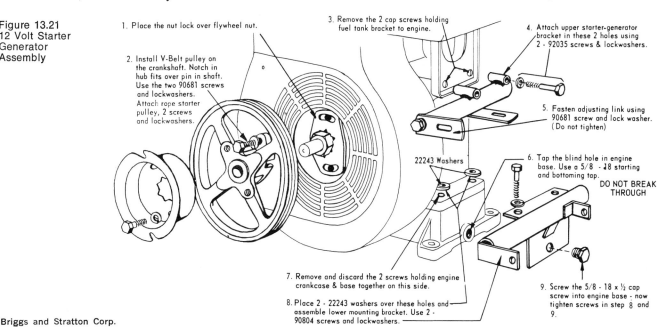

1. Place the nut lock over flywheel nut.

2. Install V-Belt pulley on the crankshaft. Notch in hub fits over pin in shaft. Use the two 90681 screws and lockwashers. Attach rope starter pulley, 2 screws and lockwashers.

3. Remove the 2 cap screws holding fuel tank bracket to engine.

4. Attach upper starter-generator bracket in these 2 holes using 2 - 92035 screws & lockwashers.

5. Fasten adjusting link using 90681 screw and lock washer. (Do not tighten)

6. Tap the blind hole in engine base. Use a 5/8 - 18 starting and bottoming tap. DO NOT BREAK THROUGH

22243 Washers

7. Remove and discard the 2 screws holding engine crankcase & base together on this side.

8. Place 2 - 22243 washers over these holes and assemble lower mounting bracket. Use 2 - 90804 screws and lockwashers.

9. Screw the 5/8 - 18 x ½ cap screw into engine base - now tighten screws in step 8 and 9.

Briggs and Stratton Corp.

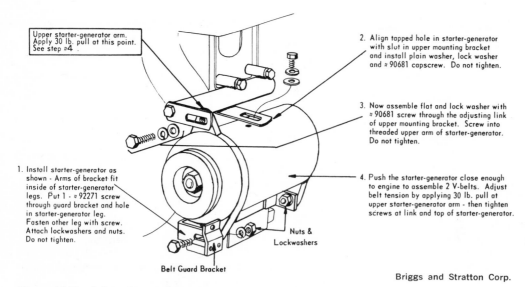

Upper starter-generator arm.
Apply 30 lb. pull at this point.
See step #4.

2. Align tapped hole in starter-generator with slot in upper mounting bracket and install plain washer, lock washer and #90681 capscrew. Do not tighten.

3. Now assemble flat and lock washer with #90681 screw through the adjusting link of upper mounting bracket. Screw into threaded upper arm of starter-generator. Do not tighten.

1. Install starter-generator as shown - Arms of bracket fit inside of starter-generator legs. Put 1 - #92271 screw through guard bracket and hole in starter-generator leg. Fasten other leg with screw. Attach lockwashers and nuts. Do not tighten.

4. Push the starter-generator close enough to engine to assemble 2 V-belts. Adjust belt tension by applying 30 lb. pull at upper starter-generator arm - then tighten screws at link and top of starter-generator.

Nuts & Lockwashers

Belt Guard Bracket

Briggs and Stratton Corp.

Figure 13.22   Adjust Starter Generator

flat washers are installed but not tightened. The starter is tilted toward the blower housing and the belts installed. If the twin belts are worn, they must be replaced in matched sets of two.

To adjust, the starter is tilted away from the blower housing until the belt moves up and down ½ inch with thumb pressure at a point midway between pulleys. The screws are tightened to hold in place and the guard installed and tightened in place.

ELECTRIC STARTER 12 VOLT (POWER CHARGER)

The Operation. The Briggs and Stratton electric starter automatically engages a belt clutch and cranks the engine when a 12-volt battery is connected between the terminal on the starter and the engine cylinder. When the engine starts, the belt clutch automatically disengages the starter motor from engine. Driven equipment should be disengaged from the engine prior to engaging an electric starter. The starting system is designed to turn over the engine only.

The Battery and Wire Size. A 12-volt battery of 20 to

24 ampere hour capacity is recommended. No. 4 size insulated wire should be used between the battery and the starter. Automotive batteries should not be used, as the starter motor may be damaged.

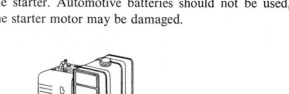

STARTER

BATTERY

Briggs and Stratton Corp.

Figure 13.24   Starter Connections

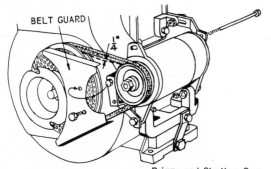

BELT GUARD

1"/4

Briggs and Stratton Corp.

Figure 13.23   12 Volt Starter Generator

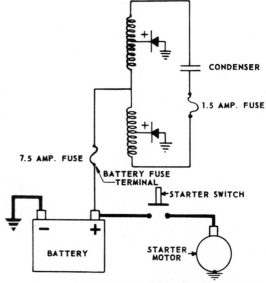

CONDENSER

1.5 AMP. FUSE

7.5 AMP. FUSE

BATTERY FUSE TERMINAL

STARTER SWITCH

BATTERY

STARTER MOTOR

Briggs and Stratton Corp.

Figure 13.25   Power Charger Wiring Diagram

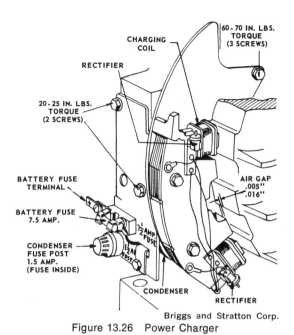

Figure 13.26   Power Charger

by a defective battery, by a defective generator or by too frequent starts per engine operation hours. To check the charge of the generator, a direct current ammeter is connected in the lead between the battery fuse terminal and the positive (+) terminal of the battery. With the engine running at 3600 rpm, the ammeter should show 2 to 3 amperes. A lower current indicates a defective generator. Partial charge can indicate any one of the following: an open condenser fuse; an excessive airgap; a defective condenser; one open rectifier; or a defective coil.

To Adjust the Belt. Nut "A" and "B" are loosened slightly so the starter motor can be barely moved by hand. The starter motor is moved away from the engine as far as possible, and the engine pulley rocked back and forth. At the same time, the starter motor is pushed slowly toward the engine until the starter motor pulley stops being driven by the Vee-belt.

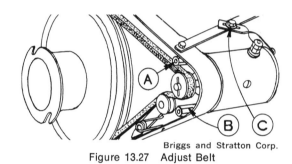

Figure 13.27   Adjust Belt

The starter motor is moved another 1/16 inch toward the engine and nuts "A: and "B" tightened.

The Proper Electric Installation. The negative (−) side of the battery must be grounded to the engine. This lead must carry the starting current, and, therefore, must be a No. 4 size wire or larger.

A No. 18 size wire or larger should be connected from the "battery fuse terminal" to the positive (+) battery terminal.

Trouble Shooting

If it is suspected that the generator is not charging, both fuses should be examined and replaced if they appear to be defective. When the 1.5 ampere fuse blows, it indicates a poor connection somewhere in the charging circuit. When the 7.5 ampere fuse blows, it indicates either that the battery is reversed (installed with improper polarity), that there is a shorted rectifier, or that there is a ground on one of the coils or coil leads.

If the battery will not stay charged, it may be caused

REWIND STARTER SERVICE
General

Several varieties of starters are used on the engines. Spring wound starters operate in much the same manner, though various means of transferring the torque from the starter pulley to the starter hub are employed. Electric starters are illustrated at the end of this chapter.

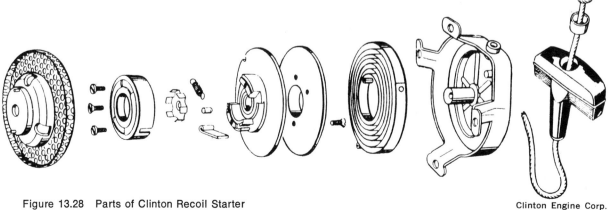

Figure 13.28   Parts of Clinton Recoil Starter

Clinton Engine Corp.

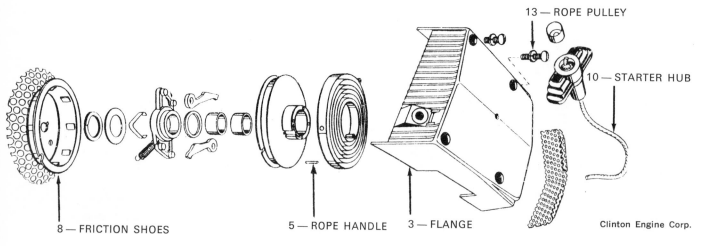

8 — FRICTION SHOES   5 — ROPE HANDLE   3 — FLANGE   Clinton Engine Corp.

Figure 13.29   Recoil Starter with Friction Shoes

As the starter rope is pulled, or cranking handle turned, a dog or friction shoes that rotate with the pulley are cammed into engagement with the starter hub. This provides the inertia to turn the engine over for starting. On Eaton starters that use a driving dog, the inside of the starter hub is notched to receive the dog. On Fairbanks-Morse starters, the inside of the hub is smooth and is engaged by the sharpened edges of the friction shoes.

As the starter rope is released for rewinding on rewind starters, the starter dog or friction shoes move out of engagement with the starter hub. The powerful clock-type spring recoils to rotate the pulley in reverse direction to rewind the rope.

Starters using a cranking handle are referred to as self starters, wind up starters, impulse starters, speedy starters or ratchet starters. Some are released by folding over the handle.

The key lock starter cannot be released until the handle is folded and a key inserted. Others employ devices for remote release.

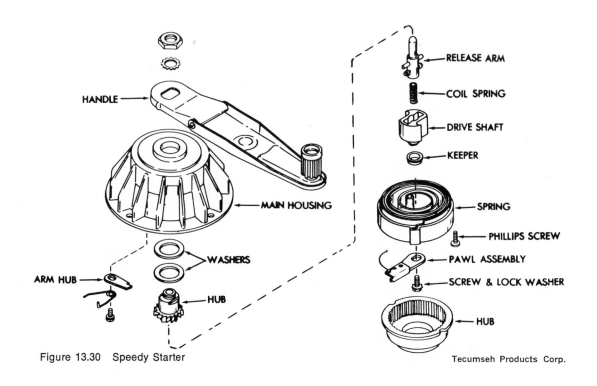

Figure 13.30   Speedy Starter   Tecumseh Products Corp.

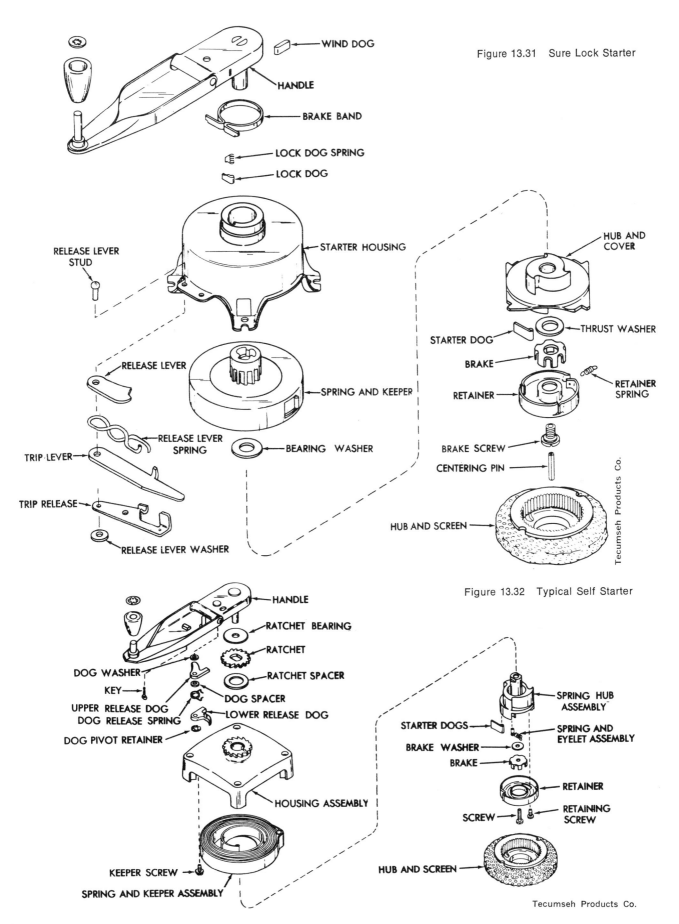

WIND DOG

HANDLE

BRAKE BAND

LOCK DOG SPRING

LOCK DOG

RELEASE LEVER STUD

STARTER HOUSING

RELEASE LEVER

SPRING AND KEEPER

RELEASE LEVER SPRING

BEARING WASHER

TRIP LEVER

TRIP RELEASE

RELEASE LEVER WASHER

Figure 13.31   Sure Lock Starter

HUB AND COVER

STARTER DOG

THRUST WASHER

BRAKE

RETAINER

RETAINER SPRING

BRAKE SCREW

CENTERING PIN

HUB AND SCREEN

Tecumseh Products Co.

Figure 13.32   Typical Self Starter

HANDLE

RATCHET BEARING

RATCHET

DOG WASHER

RATCHET SPACER

KEY

DOG SPACER

UPPER RELEASE DOG

DOG RELEASE SPRING

LOWER RELEASE DOG

DOG PIVOT RETAINER

HOUSING ASSEMBLY

KEEPER SCREW

SPRING AND KEEPER ASSEMBLY

SPRING HUB ASSEMBLY

STARTER DOGS

SPRING AND EYELET ASSEMBLY

BRAKE WASHER

BRAKE

RETAINER

SCREW

RETAINING SCREW

HUB AND SCREEN

Tecumseh Products Co.

Rewind Starter Service   135

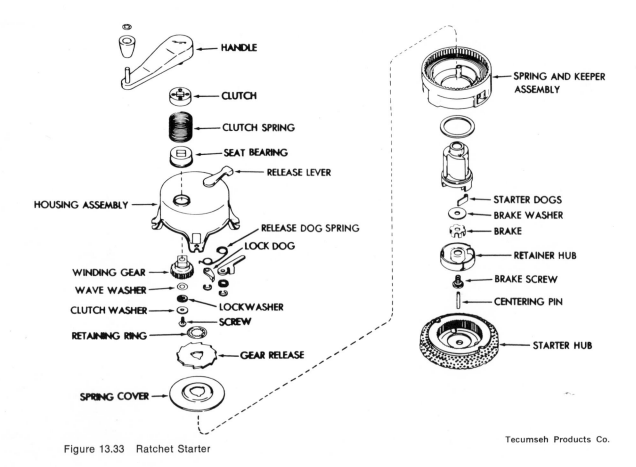

HANDLE

CLUTCH

CLUTCH SPRING

SEAT BEARING

RELEASE LEVER

HOUSING ASSEMBLY

RELEASE DOG SPRING

LOCK DOG

WINDING GEAR

WAVE WASHER

CLUTCH WASHER

LOCKWASHER

SCREW

RETAINING RING

GEAR RELEASE

SPRING COVER

SPRING AND KEEPER ASSEMBLY

STARTER DOGS

BRAKE WASHER

BRAKE

RETAINER HUB

BRAKE SCREW

CENTERING PIN

STARTER HUB

Tecumseh Products Co.

Figure 13.33   Ratchet Starter

Figure 13-33 illustrates the ratchet principle. Its handle may be turned a full radius or, if space does not permit a full turn, the ratchet action can be used.

The side mount starter is used on low silhouette vertical shaft engines. Its action differs from the rewind starters in that a gear moves up a shaft to engage a flywheel with geared teeth on its outer rim.

Figure 13-36 illustrates the starter motor used with 3½ and 5½ H.P. engine. It uses a Bendix type drive which moves the pinion gear up to contact a ring installed around the outside of the flywheel.

The 12 volt DCt and 110 volt AC starters are identical with the exception of the power source.

Rewind Starter Removal and Disassembly

The parts manual shows the exploded view drawing of the applicable rewind starter.

The four screws that hold rewind starter engine housing are removed and the rewind starter lifted off.

The tension of rewind spring must be released on Eaton starters before proceeding with disassembly. The starter assembly is held with the pulley up and the starter rope pulled until the notch in the pulley is aligned with the hole in the rope bushing. With thumb pressure on the starter pulley the pulley is kept from rotating. The rope is fed through the rope bushing in the reverse direction to obtain slack between the pulley and the rope bushing. The slack portion of rope is lifted so that it engages the notch in the pulley. Thumb pressure is slowly released to allow the spring to unwind until all tension is released.

The tension of the rewind spring of Fairbanks-Morse starters is released in the following way. The starter pulley is held securely with a thumb while the four screws that hold the two flanges to the cover are taken out and the flanges carefully removed. Thumb pressure on the pulley is slowly released and the spring allowed to rotate the pulley until it is completely unwound.

When removing the starter pulley, it must be carefully raised so that the starter spring can be disengaged from the underside of the pulley. When removing the starter pulley, extreme care should be used to keep the starter spring confined in the housing.

If the rope of an Eaton-manufactured rewind starter is damaged, the screws that join pulley halves are removed to free the rope.

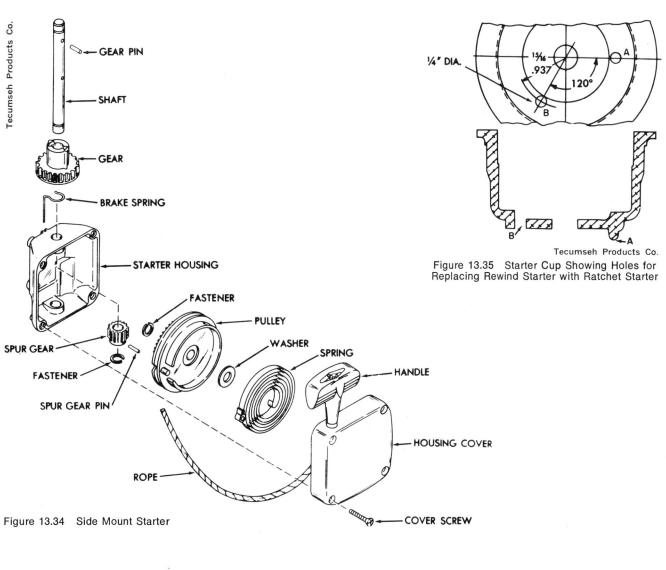

GEAR PIN

SHAFT

GEAR

BRAKE SPRING

STARTER HOUSING

FASTENER

PULLEY

WASHER

SPRING

HANDLE

SPUR GEAR

FASTENER

SPUR GEAR PIN

HOUSING COVER

ROPE

COVER SCREW

Tecumseh Products Co.

Figure 13.34   Side Mount Starter

¼" DIA.

15⁄16

.937

120°

A

B

B

A

Tecumseh Products Co.

Figure 13.35   Starter Cup Showing Holes for Replacing Rewind Starter with Ratchet Starter

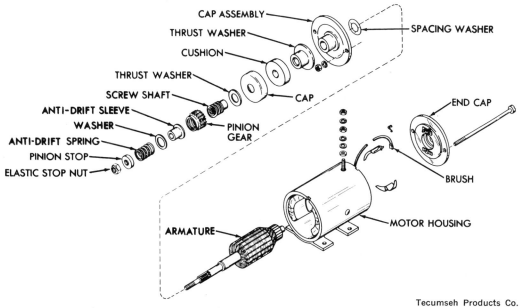

CAP ASSEMBLY

THRUST WASHER

CUSHION

THRUST WASHER

SCREW SHAFT

ANTI-DRIFT SLEEVE

WASHER

ANTI-DRIFT SPRING

PINION STOP

ELASTIC STOP NUT

SPACING WASHER

CAP

PINION GEAR

END CAP

BRUSH

MOTOR HOUSING

ARMATURE

Tecumseh Products Co.

Figure 13.36   12 Volt DC Starter Motor for 3½ to 5½ HP Engines

Rewind Starter Removal and Disassembly   137

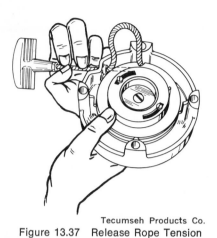

Figure 13.37   Release Rope Tension

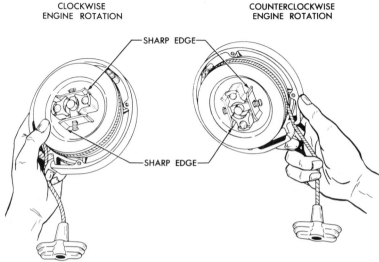

CLOCKWISE ENGINE ROTATION

COUNTERCLOCKWISE ENGINE ROTATION

SHARP EDGE

SHARP EDGE

Figure 13.39   Placement of Friction Shoes

Tecumseh Products Co.

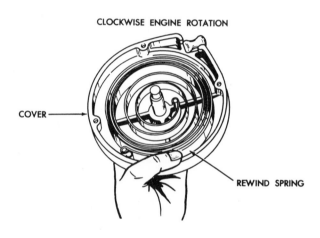

CLOCKWISE ENGINE ROTATION

COVER

REWIND SPRING

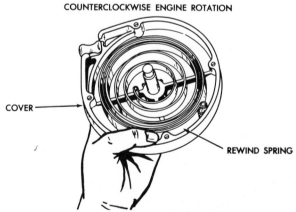

COUNTERCLOCKWISE ENGINE ROTATION

COVER

REWIND SPRING

Tecumseh Products Co.
Figure 13.38   Spring Rotation for Clockwise and Counterclockwise Rotating Engines

If the starter spring is damaged, carefully remove it from housing, noting the direction of rotation of the spring before removing.

Checking Rewind Starter Parts

The starter spring should be inspected for breaks, cracks, distortion and replaced if damaged.

The starter rope should be checked for fraying or other signs of wear; a worn or damaged starter rope should be replaced.

The rotation of the starter pulley on its pivot should be checked; the pulley should rotate freely without binding. Parts should be replaced if necessary.

Eaton Rewind Starter
Reassembly and Installation

The parts manual shows an exploded view drawing of the applicable rewind starter.

If the starter spring was removed, a new spring should be installed, with care taken to keep the new spring confined in the housing. Replacement springs are provided with holders to aid assembly. The holders slip off as the spring is inserted in the housing. The spring must be installed so that its windings are in the same direction as those of the removed spring.

If the starter rope is being replaced, the rope is crimped between the two halves of the starter pulley and the screws that join the pulley halves firmly tightened. The free end of rope is inserted through the rope bushing in the housing and through the starter handle. A double knot is tied in the end of the rope and the rope is wound onto the pulley.

To install the pulley in the housing, the notch in the pulley hub is aligned with the hook in the end of the spring. A wire bent to form a hook is used to move the spring into the correct alignment with the hub on the under-side of the pulley. When the correct alignment is achieved, the pulley is pushed down part way and the wire hook removed. The pulley is seated in the housing.

After securing the reassembled pulley to the housing, the notch in the pulley is aligned with the rope bushing in the housing. The rope is fed through the rope bushing and one finger hooked through the loop in the slack portion of the rope. The rope is pulled to engage the notch in the pulley. While the rope is held in this manner, the pulley is rotated at least two full turns in the same direction as it is pulled to pre-tension the spring properly.

After pre-tensioning the spring, the rope is pulled to its fully extended position. The spring should be pre-tensioned so that it fully rewinds the rope when the handle is released.

Fairbanks - Morse Rewind Starter
Reassembly and Installation

The parts manual shows the exploded view drawing of the applicable rewind starter.

If the starter spring was removed, the new spring is installed so that it is confined in the housing. Replacement springs are provided with holders. The holders slip off as the spring is inserted in the housing. The spring must be installed so that its windings are in the same direction as those of the removed spring.

If the starter rope is being replaced, the end of the rope is inserted through the inside pulley hole and a knot tied in the rope to secure it to the pulley. The free end of the rope is inserted through the rope bushing in the housing and through the starter handle. A double knot is tied in the end of the rope and it is wound onto the pulley.

To install the pulley in the housing, the pulley is set on the pivot stud; a screwdriver is used to engage the spring loop in the hub notch on the under-side of the pulley.

The rewind spring must be pre-tensioned to ensure full winding of starter rope. To pre-tension the spring, the pulley is rotated two full turns in the direction of the pulley rotation before installing the flanges on the cover. The pulley is held in this pre-tensioned position until the four screws that hold the flanges to the cover are tightened.

After pre-tensioning the spring, the rope is pulled to its fully extended position. The spring should be pre-tensioned so that it fully winds the rope when the rope handle is released.

The friction shoes must be assembled so that sharp angled edges engage inside of the starter hub. These edges are identified by the straight line stamped into them.

For proper operation of the starter, it is essential that parts be installed in correct sequence indicated in the applicable exploded view.

To mount the Fairbanks-Morse starter on the engine, the brass centering pin is removed from the shaft on the starter housing. The centering pin is straightened and re-inserted one-third of the way into the shaft on the starter housing. The starter is set on the engine so that the centering pin engages the hole in the end of the crankshaft. The starter is pressed into place and the mounting screws tightened.

The rope must not stop on spring tension.

Ratchet Starter
Disassembly and Reassembly

The release lever is put on "release" to remove the tension from the spring and the four screws holding the starter to the engine housing and the centering pin are removed. The retainer is removed by removing the brake screw (left-hand thread).

The brake is checked. It should be friction-tight on the retainer hub. The dogs will not release if the brake is loose and should be replaced with a new part if loose.

The brake washer and starter dogs are removed and the housing assembly picked up. It is tapped sharply to drop the spring and keeper assembly out.

The retaining ring is removed and always replaced with new ring, along with the gear release and spring cover. The spring is checked for dirt and cleaned if necessary. If the spring is broken or has been stretched and does not catch on the starter hub, it should be replaced. The spring and keeper are replaced as an assembly. The spring is not available separately.

The screw, clutch washer, wave washer and lockwasher are removed from the winding gear on the housing assembly.

The wave washer tension is checked; if flattened, it should be replaced.

The lock dog and the teeth of the winding gear are checked for wear. The tension of the release dog spring is checked; it should hold the lock dog securely against the winding gear.

The clutch spring is removed from the handle, and checked for sufficient tension. It is cleaned and wiped dry. It must not be oiled or greased. The spring bearing is turned left to seat the spring on the handle properly. The spring bearing may have sharp edges.

The winding gear is coated with a light grease. With one hand, the lock dog is help up against the release dog spring and the winding gear replaced. The lock dog should stay firmly in the teeth of the winding gear. The handle, wave washer, lock washer, clutch washer and screw are replaced.

The hub washer is put on the hub and the hub put in the spring and keeper assembly. The spring cover is replaced, and the release gear with its rounded edge upward. A new retaining ring is installed. The spring and keeper assembly are pushed into the housing assembly.

The teeth of the keeper must mesh with the teeth of the winding gear.

The brake washer is replaced and checked for a snug fit on the hub of the retainer. The starting dogs, retainer and brake screw are also replaced. Either tip of the centering pin is inserted into the centre of the starter.

With the starter release lever pointed toward the carburetor side of the engine, the tip of the centering pin is inserted into the top of the crankshaft. With the studs aligned with the starter mounting holes, the starter is pushed or gently tapped toward the engine until seated on the blower housing. The centering pin must be used with these starters to obtain the proper alignment to hub and screen.

Self Starter Disassembly and Reassembly

The tension is released from the spring and the four bolts holding the starter to the engine housing removed, along with the two screws holding the retainer to the hub. There is a hook on the retainer. When reassembling, the spring from the hub assembly is attached to this hook.

The brake screw and brake are removed and the brake inspected for tight fit on the retainer hub. If loose, it must be replaced. The dog is removed and cleaned. The hub assembly is removed by lifting straight up and is cleaned and recoated with a light grease. The spring is checked by removing the four screws holding the spring and keeper assembly to the housing assembly.

The spring and keeper assembly are lifted out. If the spring is broken or stretched, the entire assembly is replaced. Any foreign material is cleaned from the spring and keeper assembly and it is reassembled to the housing. The handle is taken from the housing and the ratchet spacer removed along with the retainer from the post on which the ratchet dogs pivot. The retainer is replaced if worn or bent during removal.

The lower dog, dog release spring, two washers, upper dog and washer are lifted off. The spring must have sufficient tension to hold the dogs against the gears. The parts are inspected for wear and cleaned and recoated with a light grease.

The ratchet and ratchet bearing are cleaned and the ratchet bearing replaced on handle. The ratchet is not replaced.

The washer, upper starter dog, washers, spring, and lower starter dog are replaced on the post. The hook on the spring must be against the lower starter dog. The retainer clip is replaced with a screwdriver or needle nose pliers. The end of the starter spring is held back with the screwdriver and the hub is replaced. The ratchet spacer is put on the end of the hub shaft which protrudes

through the housing assembly. The ratchet is positioned on top of the spacer. The teeth on the ratchet must point in the opposite direction from the teeth on gear of housing.

The handle is folded over; while the lower dog is held back with the screwdriver, the handle is reinstalled. The brake washer and brake are replaced and fastened with a screw. The retainer is set on the hub, and fastened with the two screws removed at the start of the disassembly.

The starter is remounted on the engine.

Keylock Starters

Some starters of this type have a locking device in the handle to prevent accidental release. Disassembly and reassembly instructions are the same as for the self-starter outlined above.

Speedy Starter
Disassembly and Reassembly

The tension is released from the spring and the four bolts holding the starter to the engine housing removed.

The screw and lockwasher holding the pawl assembly to spring and keeper, and the pawl assembly are taken off. The four screws holding the spring and keeper to the main housing are removed. After the spring and keeper have been removed, the drive shaft is dropped and the arm assembly released.

The handle is opened and the nut and washer holding the handle to the hub are removed with the hub and washers. The tension of the hub spring is checked.

All parts are cleaned and inspected for wear. The washers and the release assembly are coated with oil.

If the hub arm and hub spring have been removed or must be replaced, the hub arm must be against the main housing when reinstalled. The spring is positioned with the bent end against the hub arm and the long end of the spring is against the housing. The screw is fastened.

The hub and washers are replaced and the handle secured to the hub. The release arm assembly, spring and drive shaft are put back on. The spring and keeper and the pawl assembly are replaced and the starter remounted to the engine.

Later versions of the starter have a bearing between the bottom end of the drive shaft and its seat in the spring and keeper. Another change added a pawl with two arms to engage the edge of the starter cup.

Sure Lock Starter
Disassembly and Reassembly

The release lever is pulled out from the housing assembly to remove the tension from the spring.

The four screws holding the starter to the engine housing, the centering pin and the brake screw are removed. The screw has a left-hand thread.

The retainer is lifted off and the position of the spring in relation to the post on the hub and cover noted. The brake should be friction tight on the hub of the retainer. The starter dog is removed and checked for wear along with the thrust washer and bearing washer. The hub and cover are lifted off. If they do not lift off freely, they can be loosened by tapping the legs of the housing assembly on a flat surface.

The spring and keeper assembly are removed, but the spring is not taken from the keeper. The handle is removed. The spring should hold the dog firmly away from the wall of the hub. The wind dog on the post of the handle is inspected for wear. All parts are cleaned and the bearing surfaces of the keeper and the hub and cover assembly coated with light grease.

The lock dog is held with one hand and the spring and keeper assembly replaced along with the handle. The spring is held back with a screwdriver and the hub and cover dropped in. The thrust washer and bearing washer are replaced. The open end of the retainer spring is placed on the post of the hub and cover, the retainer replaced and fastened with the brake screw. The centering pin is replaced and the starter reinstalled on the engine housing.

Replacing Rewind Starter with Ratchet Starter on Lauson Engines

When replacing the Rewind Starter with a Ratchet Starter Kit, the following procedure must be followed to prevent shearing.

A $\frac{1}{4}$ inch diameter hole is drilled in the starter cup at point B, shown in Figure 13-38. The cup is fastened to the flywheel with a $\frac{1}{4}$-20x$\frac{5}{8}$ hex head screw in the puller hole, with a $\frac{1}{4}$ inch split lockwasher.

The hole must be 120 degrees from the locating pin "A" to ensure that the screw meets the flywheel puller hole. Torque screw to 50-60 inch pounds. Torque flywheel nut 25-30 foot pounds. A heavy spring ratchet starter must not be installed until the cup has been secured.

Sno-Proof Starters

Some models of the rewind starter are designated as Sno-Proof Starters. This model is serviced in the same manner as other Eaton Rewind Starters, but replacement of the starter hub and screen assembly must always be done with the special hub and screen assembly properly machined for Sno-Proof operation. Common hub and screen assemblies will not properly seal this unit.

Wind-up Starters

Difficulty may be encountered in starting an engine equip-

ped with a wind-up starter if the unit has been stored in temperatures less than 25 degrees F. for any length of time between starts.

10W oil should be used and all parastic loads such as clutches and belts disengaged. If the starter fails to turn the engine over fast enough to start, the unit must be moved to an area where the temperature is at least 25 degrees F.

If an attempt has been made to start the engine and spring tension has failed to turn over engine, the starter should be reengaged and the handle wound to one o'clock to prevent the spring tension from releasing accidentally.

Operation and Service of Top Mounted Electric Starter and Generator Unit

Mounting Starter to Engine.

The three guide post springs must be seated around the nylon bushings. The ridge on the stud caps is aligned with the slots in the nylon bushings. The starter assembly is lowered over the guide posts and the starter pressed until the stud caps project above the nylon bushings. The stud caps are twisted $\frac{1}{4}$ turn to lock the starter in place.

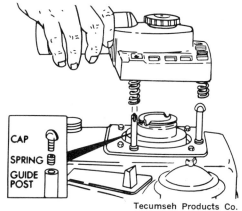

Tecumseh Products Co.

Figure 13.40 Mounting Top Mount Electric Starter

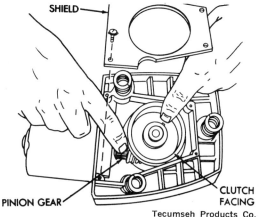

Tecumseh Products Co.

Figure 13.41 Lubricating Top Mount Electric Starter

Connection of Wires to Battery Posts and Terminal Block.
The negative wire is attached over the negative terminal block post. (The ground wire from the fuel tank is also attached to this post.) The positive wire is attached over the positive terminal block post.

Both connections are secured with lockwashers and nuts.

Other wires ends are placed over the proper battery terminals, and secured in the same manner.

The two wires that lead from the upper starter unit are each placed on the two battery terminals—on top of the wire already placed there. Either wire may be placed on either terminal. They are secured with lockwashers and nuts.

Using the Electric Starter.
The starter switch button is pressed with palm of hand just enough for the starter to run. It should reach full speed before further pressing. Then it is pressed harder until the clutch engages and cranks the engine.

An engine in correct adjustment will start in 5 seconds. The starter should never be run more than 5-6 seconds at a time. If the engine does not start in 5 or 6 tries, the information on the trouble shooting chart should aid diagnosis. When the starter unit is removed or replaced,

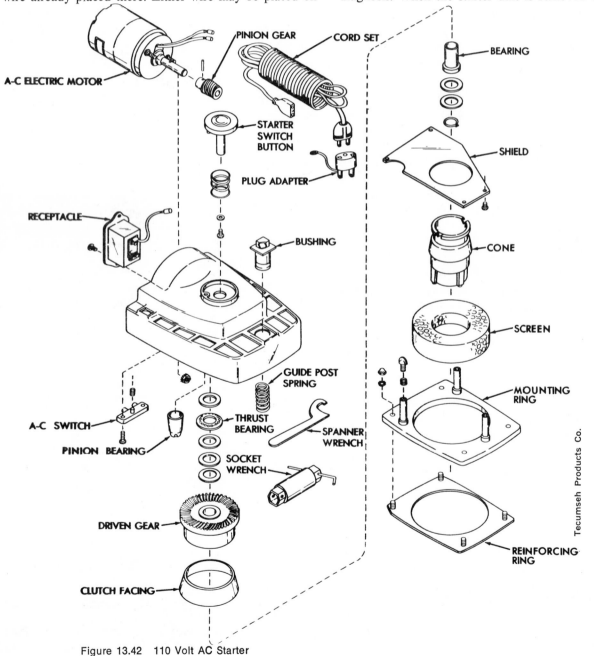

Figure 13.42 110 Volt AC Starter

Tecumseh Products Co.

pressure should be exerted on the starter-unit frame, not the starter button. The starter must not be running while it is removed or replaced. The cork cone may be damaged.

Lubrication of Electric Starters.

The electric starter should be lubricated at the beginning of each season. The starter assembly is removed, with care taken not to lay it on the starter button while connected to the battery.

The four screws and lockwashers are removed and the shield taken off. A small ball of automotive ball bearing grease is applied onto the pinion gear with a finger tip. The cork clutch facing is also coated with vaseline. The shield is then securely replaced. Whenever the clutch develops a "squeal", vaseline should be reapplied as directed above.

Operating Procedures and Service Information for 12 Volt DC Electric Starter

General.

Starter consists of an Alternator-Magneto, Rectifier Panel and 12 Volt DC Series wound motor actuating a Bendix type drive that engages an external tooth ring gear which is an integral part of the flywheel.

Preparing the Battery.

The system requires a 12 volt-20 ampere-hour battery of the automotive type. It is serviced in accordance with the manufacturer's recommendations. The battery connections should be tight and clean.

The minimum wire size of total length of both battery leads for a 2½ inch starter are:

1' to 5' — #10 wire

5' to 10' — # 8 wire

Over 10' — # 6 wire

If the engine is equipped with the new 3 inch electric starter motor SME12A2 or SME12A5, (motor number is stamped on the bottom of the end cap assembly,) use #6 wire for both battery leads and from solenoid to starter.

If wire sizes do not meet minimums, they should be replaced with the proper size.

Prolonged operation of a unit may cause battery fuming or boiling. This indicates overcharging. One of the rectifiers should be removed from the panel to cut charging rate in half.

Using the Starter

Due to size requirements, this starter has certain cold weather limitations. Under 20 degrees it may be necessary to use a recoil starter to start the engine.

The unit must be in neutral and all blades, belts and clutches disengaged to relieve the engine of extra load while cranking.

Most electric starter motors are protected from over-heating by a self re-setting cut-out switch. Continuous

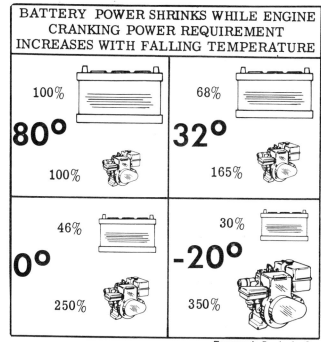

Figure 13.43   Cold Weather Effect on Battery

cranking will cause the switch to open and the starter to become inoperative. If this happens, the motor must cool until the switch closes contact.

Alternator Magneto.

This consists of the usual coil, condenser and point set for firing engines. Also incorporated are extra generating coils and flywheel magnets to generate current for the recharging of the battery. The charging rate at 3,600 rpm is approximately 3 amps.

Servicing the Alternator-Magneto.

Generating coils are supplied in pairs and can only be replaced in pairs. They should be replaced if the insulation is broken or cracked or coils are otherwise damaged.

"Burn Out" of generating coils (if the system is not protected by a 6 amp. fuse at the rectifier panel) will occur if polarity is reversed either at the rectifier panel or the battery, allowing the battery voltage to be drawn back through the system. Systems protected by a 6 amp. fuse will require fuse replacement if the polarity is reversed or the rectifier shorted out.

To test the coils, both rectifiers are removed from the rectifier panel. With the engine running, each generator terminal (as marked on the rectifier panel) is shorted momentarily to the ground with a jumper wire. If either terminal produced no spark, both coils are replaced.

Rectifiers and Rectifier Panel.

All lead connections are clearly marked on the panel and must be followed. Rectifiers are of the silicone type and are directional. One end of the rectifier is undercut to ensure proper insertion in the holding clips. Rectifiers change the generated AC current to DC for battery charging.

Servicing Rectifiers.

Running the engine with battery leads disconnected, or on a dead battery, will burn out the rectifiers unless they are removed from the panel.

If the battery shows signs of overcharging (fuming or boiling) one rectifier is removed from the panel to cut the charging rate to approximately 1.5 amps.

To test the rectifiers, the positive battery lead is removed and an ammeter placed in the circuit. One rectifier is removed and the engine started. If any reading is obtained, the defective rectifier is replaced. The second rectifier is tested in the same manner.

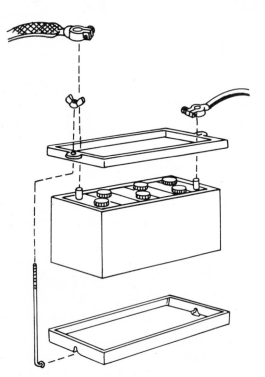

Tecumseh Products Co.

Figure 13.44   Battery Installation

NO SMOKING

Tecumseh Products Co.

Figure 13.46   Battery Safety

Tecumseh Products Co.

Figure 13.45   Servicing a Battery

WEAK
DEAD

Tecumseh Products Co.

Figure 13.47   Trouble Shooting

Coils are first tested as described above.

If the ammeter is not available, the positive battery lead is removed at the rectifier panel. One rectifier is taken from panel and the engine started. The remaining rectifier is shorted to ground momentarily with a jumper wire connected to the positive battery on the rectifier panel. If a spark results, the rectifier is good. This is repeated using the other rectifier.

All leads at the rectifier panel must be positioned to prevent any shorting between leads.

REVIEW QUESTIONS

1. When installing a new recoil spring in a recoil starter, what other parts should be checked for wear and replaced if necessary?
2. Why should you not remove the starter spring from the housing of the wind-up starter?
3. List the steps required for removing the Briggs and Stratton chain drive electric starter.
4. What type of battery is used for starting the Briggs and Stratton 12 Volt Power Charger?
5. List the steps in checking the reason for a generator not charging.
6. What would cause a generator to charge partially?
7. Describe the difference in operation between the Briggs and Stratton rewind starter and the Fairbanks-Morse rewind starter.
8. Explain how the ratchet cranking handle operates.

9. Define the following terms:
   a) Lock dog.   e) Recoil or rewind starter
   b) Hub   f) Wind-up starter
   c) Wind pulley   g) Parasitic load.
   d) Bumper tangs
10. What is the torque on the flywheel nut of a Lauson Tecumseh engine?
11. Why would you experience trouble in starting a Snow Blower engine in temperatures below 25 degrees F.?
12. When should Tecumseh Engine electric starters be lubricated?
13. List the steps required to lubricate a Tecumseh Engine electric starter.
14. What size of wire is used for battery leads on the 12 Volt electric starter?
15. If a battery starts to fume or boil, what problem is indicated?
16. What will happen if battery leads are disconnected while running the engine?
17. How can you test the rectifiers on a Tecumseh engine?
18. Explain how to test the coil on a Tecumseh engine.
19. What safety precautions should be taken before working on any starter?
20. Where would the Model 23A Briggs and Stratton 12 Volt Power Charger be used?
21. How can you tell if the starter spring is broken in the wind-up starter?
22. What is the purpose of burning the end of the recoil starter rope?

PART 2
WATER-COOLED ENGINES

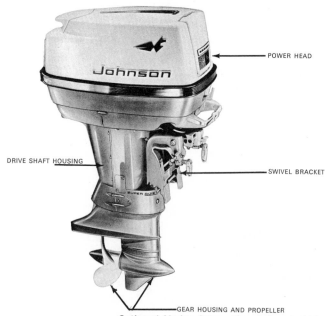

POWER HEAD

DRIVE SHAFT HOUSING

SWIVEL BRACKET

GEAR HOUSING AND PROPELLER

Outboard Marine Corporation of Canada Ltd.

Figure 14.1 Main Parts of the Outboard Engine

CHAPTER 14
OUTBOARD MOTOR FUNDAMENTALS

The outboard engine is a very interesting engine to study. It is somewhat like the air-cooled two-stroke-cycle engine; the actual difference is the method of cooling. The outboard engine is quite large for its horsepower size, because of the parts necessary for cooling. The air cooled engine is very small in size for its horsepower output, but this is because it is the prime power unit. The outboard engine contains a prime power unit (the power head), and the lower unit composed of three main sections. The main sections of the lower unit are the gear housing assembly (including the propellor), the drive shaft housing assembly, and the clamp and swivel bracket assembly.

As mentioned above, the outboard engine is like the two-stroke-cycle engine of the air cooled type. This is a true statement, but it operates differently in some cases. Let us take time to review the two-stroke cycle principle of operation.

The piston in a two-cycle engine acts as both an inlet and exhaust valve. In starting a two-cycle engine, the crankshaft turns over and the piston rises, assuming that the cylinder is filled with a mixture of air and fuel which is compressed. Then, at its high point of travel, B.T.D.C. (before top dead centre), the compressed mixture is ignited by the spark supplied by the spark plugs. The resulting explosion within the cylinder forces the piston down, exerting its working energy to the crankshaft.

During its upward stroke, the piston has drawn in a fresh charge of fuel and air through the intake valve (the reed valve) into the crankcase. This crankcase, which is airtight, contains the crankshaft and connecting rod. On the downward stroke, the charge of fuel and air, previously drawn in, is compressed in the crank case and, when the piston reaches its maximum travel (bottom), an exhaust port is uncovered on the cylinder wall. This allows the unburned gases to escape, and the cylinder pressure to fall. An instant later, the momentum created uncovers an inlet port on the opposite side of the cylinder. This allows the fresh charge of fuel and air to force its way up from the crankcase and drive the remainder of the unburned gases before it.

A projection on the piston head, on the intake side, deflects the fresh charge and prevents it from passing directly across the cylinder and out the exhaust port.

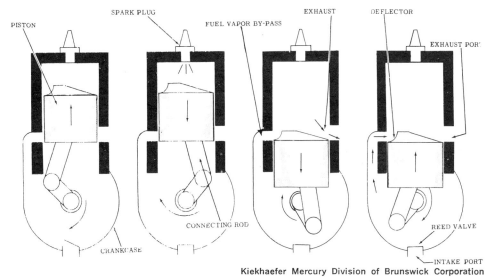

Figures 14.2 to 14.5, left to right: Compression,   Ignition Power Stroke, Exhaust, Intake

Kiekhaefer Mercury Division of Brunswick Corporation

1 Lower Cylinder Coil
2 Coil Mounting Screws
3 Breaker Arm
4 Upper Cylinder Breaker Points
5 Breaker Point Lock Screw
6 Point Adjusting Screw
7 Base Mounting Screw
8 Armature Base
9 Upper Cylinder Coil
10 Lower Cylinder Breaker Points
11 Breaker Base
12 Felt Oiler
13 Condenser Screw
14 Breaker Point Cam
15 Condenser
16 Coil Mounting and Ground Screw
17 Crankshaft

Figure 14.6   Magneto

Outboard Marine Corporation of Canada Ltd.

ALTERNATE FIRING On an alternate firing twin-cylinder outboard engine, one cylinder is delivering its power stroke while the other cylinder is on its suction stroke. The firing order of the pistons is governed by the use of a magneto which is fastened to one end of the crankshaft of the engine.

On every 180 degrees rotation of the crankshaft, an electric spark is created by the making and breaking of an electric impulse through the breaker points. This electric spark is transmitted to the spark plugs to fire the cylinders alternately. An offset cam, mounted on the crankshaft within the magneto, opens and closes the breaker points to produce this spark.

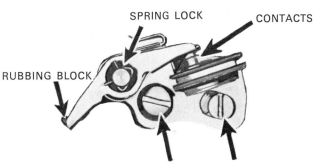

SPRING LOCK   CONTACTS

RUBBING BLOCK

HOLD DOWN SCREW   ADJUSTING SCREW
Outboard Marine Corporation of Canada Ltd.
Figure 14.7   Points

Therefore, the pistons which are connected to the crankshaft at a 90 degree angle, and a power stroke delivered at 180 degrees, produce the reciprocating motion. This reciprocating motion is, in turn, transferred to the shaft to create the rotation motion of the engine.

A simple explanation of the physics of motion of the internal combustion engine may be seen by observing the use of a brace and bit when drilling a hole. The arm and elbow move back and forth, but the bit goes around in circles. The elbow corresponds to that of the piston, and the forearm would be the connecting rod and the brace is like the throw of the crankshaft.

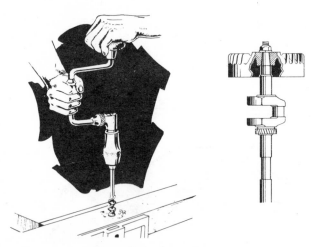

Figure 14.8   Crankshaft Action

REED VALVES   In the outboard two-cycle engine, reed inlet valves are used. They operate automatically; they do not open until the pressure in the crankcase is low enough to overcome reed tension. The rate of speed at which the motor is operating varies the crankcase pressure and regulates the rate at which the reed opens. This allows a more satisfactory performance throughout the entire speed range of the motor because the reeds only open to the demand created by the various motor speeds.

CYLINDER NUMBERING AND FIRING ORDER

The cylinder numbering is described in the example set by Mercury Engines. The six-cylinder Mercury engine fires at 60 degree intervals giving six equally spaced power impulses for each revolution of the crankshaft. Four-cylinder engines fire at 90 degree intervals, giving four equally spaced power impulses for each revolution. Two-cylinder engines fire at 180 degree intervals, giving two equally spaced impulses. Cylinders are numbered consecutively from top to bottom, the top cylinder being number one. A typical firing order chart is shown below:

6-Cylinder	1-6-4-2-5-3
Merc 800 Type 6-cyl. only	1-4-5-2-3-6
4-Cylinder	1-3-2-4
2-Cylinder	1-2

12 REED REED PLATE

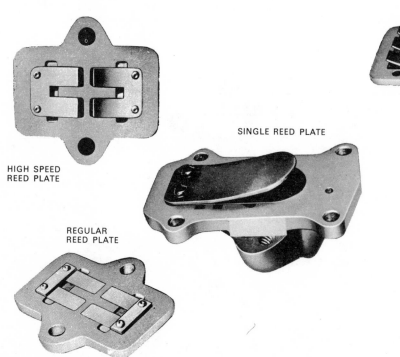

SINGLE REED PLATE

HIGH SPEED REED PLATE

REGULAR REED PLATE

6 REED REED PLATE

Outboard Marine Corporation of Canada Ltd.

Figure 14.9   Reed Plates

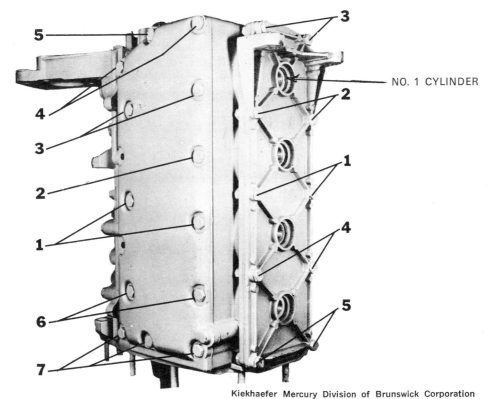

NO. 1 CYLINDER

Kiekhaefer Mercury Division of Brunswick Corporation

Figure 14.10   Four Cylinder Block

LIQUID COOLING

As was mentioned near the first of this chapter, the outboard engine is somewhat like its counterpart two-cycle air cooled engine. The outboard engine, however, is water cooled in most cases. The cooling system resembles the automotive engine's cooling system. It has water jackets, a thermostat, a water pump in the lower unit, a water inlet and a water discharge. The only item not in the outboard cooling system is the radiator that the automotive

Outboard Marine Corporation of Canada Ltd.
Figure 14.11   Intake Screen

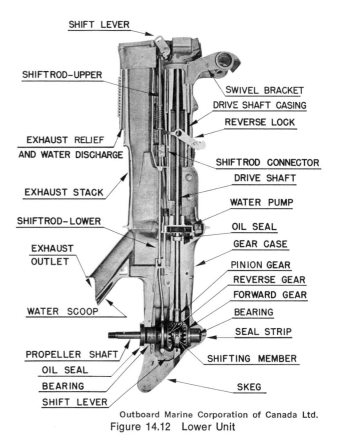

SHIFT LEVER
SHIFTROD–UPPER
EXHAUST RELIEF
AND WATER DISCHARGE
EXHAUST STACK
SHIFTROD–LOWER
EXHAUST
OUTLET
WATER SCOOP
PROPELLER SHAFT
OIL SEAL
BEARING
SHIFT LEVER

SWIVEL BRACKET
DRIVE SHAFT CASING
REVERSE LOCK
SHIFTROD CONNECTOR
DRIVE SHAFT
WATER PUMP
OIL SEAL
GEAR CASE
PINION GEAR
REVERSE GEAR
FORWARD GEAR
BEARING
SEAL STRIP
SHIFTING MEMBER
SKEG

Outboard Marine Corporation of Canada Ltd.
Figure 14.12   Lower Unit

engine needs. Obviously, a radiator is not needed in the outboard since the water that the outboard engine operates in is the source of water for the water inlet.

The flywheel of the outboard engine differs from the flywheel in the air cooled two-cycle engine because the outboard engine flywheel has no fins on it for cooling purposes.

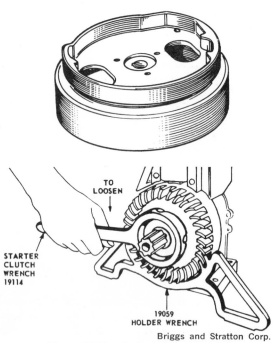

Figure 14.13   Outboard Flywheel (top)
Aircooled Flywheel (bottom)

The outboard engine is the prime source of power for many types of water surface travel: everything from a canoe to larger and heavier speed boats and pleasure type cruisers. It is impossible to say which part of the outboard engine is the most important. One must treat each part of the outboard with extreme care.

Outboard engines are divided into sections, the *powerhead* and the *lower unit*. The first section that will be covered is the powerhead.

POWERHEAD

The powerhead of the outboard engine is the source of power for the unit. The important parts of the powerhead are: bearings, pistons and piston rings, cylinder and cylinder head, connecting rod and crankshaft, starter housings and starter cords, magneto and ignition, carburetor and fuel tanks.

Bearings

The bearings in any type of engine support the revolving and reciprocating parts such as crankshafts, connecting rods and pistons. In the outboard engine, drive shafts and propellor shafts are a basic part of the unit.

Bearings are generally classified as either friction or non-friction. The friction type bearing, as employed in the outboard engine, consists of a bushing or cylindrical sleeve of bronze, machined to size. It may be of solid construction or split as required for assembly and performance of its function.

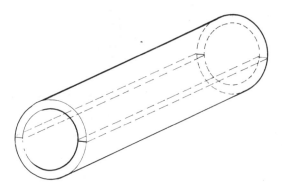

Figure 14.14   Friction Type Bearing (Bushing)

While some of the bearings or bushings in the four-cycle engine are constructed of bronze, the principle friction bearings (crankshaft mains and connecting rod) usually are of babbit (lead and tin).

Non-friction bearings are normally constructed of an inner and outer race (steel) of proper dimensions to permit installing rows of steel balls or rollers—all elements being held together by a "cage" or retainer to make up a unit assembly.

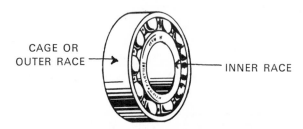

Figure 14.15   Parts of a Ballbearing

As a solid one-piece unit assembly, this type of construction is limited to installation on the top and bottom journals of the crankshaft, the driveshaft and propellor shaft. Other means are needed for non-friction bearings for the centre journal and crankpin unless tthe crankshaft is of assembled construction to permit the installation.

Where non-friction bearings are installed on the crankpin, the connecting rod is generally constructed of steel, with the crankpin end of sufficient size to accommodate the necessary rollers. The inside faces of the rod and cap are hardened and accurately ground to size. They act as the outer race, while the hardened ground crankpin functions as the inner race. The rollers are set in a split "cage" or retainer. Each half of the assembly is then placed on the crankpin. This is followed by the connecting rod and cap which, when bolted together, make up a non-friction bearing assembly.

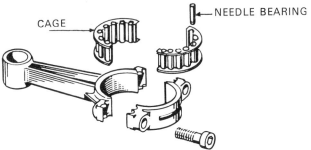

Outboard Marine Corporation of Canada Ltd.
Figure 14.16   Needle Bearing and Cage

Steel needles (needle bearings) are frequently installed on the crankpin, rather than a roller-retainer type assembly. They perform as a non-friction type of bearing—the connecting rod and crankpin acting as outer and inner races.

OIL ACCESS OPENINGS
Briggs and Stratton Corp.
Figure 14.17   Oil Access Opening

Although friction type bearings are usually provided for both the crankshaft journals and connecting rod, (especially in the smaller models) a combination of the two is frequently employed in the larger models; namely, friction on the crankshaft journals and non-friction on the crankpins.

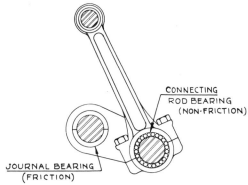

Outboard Marine Corporation of Canada Ltd.
Figure 14.18   The Common Application of Friction and Non-friction Type Bearings

Friction type bearings (bushings) are most generally used for the drive and propellor shafts in engines of low horsepower range while both friction and non-friction types are employed in the same positions in the higher powered models.

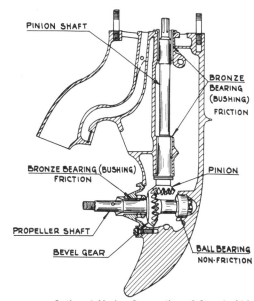

Outboard Marine Corporation of Canada Ltd.
Figure 14.19   The Combination of Friction and Non-friction Type Bearings as Frequently Employed in the Gearcase

In some motors, like the racing type, non-friction bearings are used throughout—ball or roller bearing assemblies or needles on the crankshaft journals, roller or needles on the crankpins, with ball bearings and needles

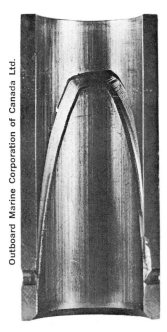

Figure 14.20   Bronze Bearing to Show Arrangement of Grooving for Oil Circulation

on the propellor shaft. The wrist pin bearings are most frequently of the friction type.

All bearings must be fitted with a certain amount of clearance (space between the bearing surface and shaft, crankpin or journal or space between tthe balls, rollers, needles, and races in the non-friction type) to provide ample *space* for lubrication and heat expansion. Grooves are cut in the bearing surface of the friction type bearings to further assist in obtaining efficient lubrication, starting or ending at the edge of the bearing or at holes drilled through the bearing wall and on through the bearing "boss" or support to the source of the lubrication supply.

The grooves are arranged to circulate the lubricant over the bearing surface. Oil enters at one end of the groove and discharges at the other end to complete the circuit. Rotation of the shaft and spiral of the groove spreads the lubricant over the bearing surfaces.

Pistons and Piston Rings

All pistons, except in some of the older type outboards, are constructed of aluminum alloy. Cast gray iron pistons were used in models of early vintage.

Since the piston, with piston rings installed, receives the force of the combustion in the cylinder head, both the piston and piston rings must be properly fitted and in

good operating conditions to seal this force or pressure above the piston head. Seepage past the piston rings and between the skirt of the piston and cylinder wall will cause a loss of power. If this seepage is excessive, it will interfere with the operation of the motor, particularly at low trolling speeds.

To retain maximum power within the cylinder above the piston head, the cylinder must be round and the piston rings correctly seated against the cylinder wall. The rings must be properly seated in the ring grooves and the gap of sufficient width to prevent "butting" and ultimate warping of the rings.

The piston rings naturally cannot be expected to retain the force of combustion if the pistons and the cylinder walls are excessively worn or otherwise scored. In this case, replacements are in order.

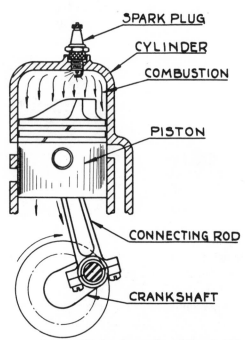

Figure 14.22   The Function of the Piston

The function of the piston in a two cycle engine is two-fold: namely, to receive tthe force of combustion which is transferred by way of the connecting rod to the crankshaft and to control the flow of fuel vapour and exhaust gases as it covers and uncovers the ports in the cylinder during its travel. The piston rings must be free in the ring grooves to expand against the walls of the cylinder. Tightness or binding in this respect, will restrict the normal activity of the ring and result in the loss of compression and power. Seepage or escape of compression through the piston rings is referred to as "blow-by" and is indicated by discolouration or carbon formation on the piston skirt.

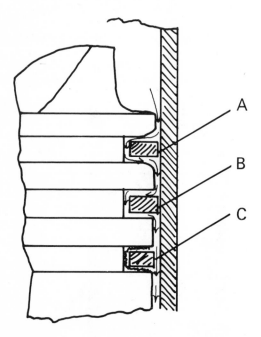

A WORN RING GROOVE (COMPRESSION LOSS)

B WORN RING (COMPRESSION LOSS AROUND RING WALL)

C INACTIVE RING (CARBON)
   CAUSING BLOW-BY

Figure 14.21   Ring Seepage

Figure 14.23   Oil Ring with Carbon

Piston rings bind or seize in the ring grooves because of carbon accumulation. The piston then operates in the cylinder without ring expansion against the cylinder wall to seal the force of compression and combustion. Naturally, the result is a loss of power, unsatisfactory, slow speed performance and hard starting, depending on the amount of restriction of ring activity.

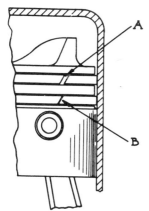

Figure 14.24   Ring Activity. A. Correct ring gap permits freedom of the ring to act against the cylinder wall, thus sealing the compression (power) above the piston. Excessive gap (clearance) results in compression (power) loss due to "blow-by". B. Insufficient ring gap causes ends of ring to "butt" to result in buckling and ultimate inactivity of the ring.

Not all rings on the piston are affected to the same extent. Usually the top ring (since the temperature is higher at the top of the piston) is the first to become carbon clogged, followed by the second ring and finally the last ring, as temperature decreases down the land area and skirt of the piston. Cooler fuel entering the crankcase absorbs a considerable amount of the heat generated by the piston as it functions throughout its cycle.

Excessively worn, scored or damaged pistons are re-

placed, and, with other corrections, this replacement restores the motor to normal operating conditions.

Piston Rings

Piston rings are constructed of high quality cast iron and in such a manner that, when installed on the piston operating in the cylinder, they expand against the cylinder wall to form a seal.

This sealing effect is accomplished by placing a slight strain in the original casting. After they are machined to the correct dimensions and severed, the ends of the ring "spring" apart. This space, created by the ends springing apart, is called "ring gap".

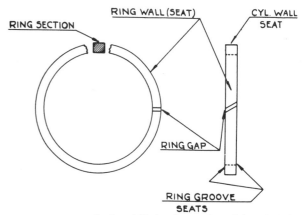

Figure 14.25   Schematic Drawing of Conventional Piston Ring

Severing or cutting of the ring is required to allow the ring seat to operate against the cylinder wall under a slight pressure. This tension must be in relation to the bore of the cylinder and to the width and depth of the ring.

Excessive pressure against the cylinder wall will cause a drag (a stiffness or friction within the cylinder), creating a high operating temperature which causes sluggish performance, abnormal ring, ring groove and cylinder wear, and possible ring scoring. Lack of ring wall tension will result in "blow-by" to cause a loss of power, overheating, carbon formation on the skirt of the piston and a general faulty performance.

There are several methods of severing the rings—(1) miter, (2) step and (3) straight.

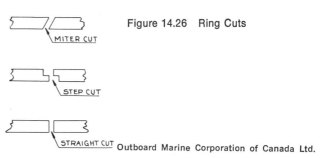

Figure 14.26   Ring Cuts

Piston rings are not true until placed in the cylinder. In the process of manufacturing, the ring is turned to a definite outside diameter, for example, a 2.5″ O.D. to fit a cylinder bore of 2.5″. Therefore, the curvature of the ring wall is identical with the curvature of the cylinder wall since both the diameter of the solid ring and cylinder bore are equal. After turning, the solid ring is slotted to obtain flexibility with the result that the ends of the ring spring apart to create a gap. The O.D. becomes greater than the one that was turned; a greater O.D. results, but not a perfect circle in contour. Although resulting variations in contour of the expanded ring could be measured only in fractions of .001 of an inch, it nevertheless is not a true circle. True contour of the ring, however, can be restored by installing it in a cylinder of like diameter.

Sufficient gap must be left between the ends of the ring prior to fitting it in the piston for installation in the cylinder. The ring must be flexible to follow the cylinder contour in the motor operation, with enough space allowed between the ends of the ring to prevent them from butting or creating the effects of a solid "lifeless" ring. Further, the ring elongates as the temperature rises during operation. Therefore, the gap must be sufficiently wide to permit a certain amount of expansion without butting to render the ring inactive. Proper ring gap depends on the diameter of the piston ring, width, depth and normal operating temperature of the engine. Before rings are installed, the manufacturer's specifications should be checked for ring clearances.

Excessive gap clearance is undesirable because it permits the seepage of compression which results in a power loss.

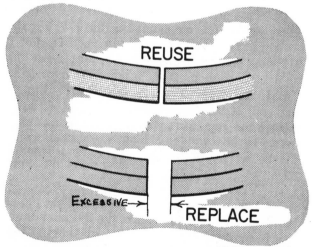

Clinton Engine Corp.

Figure 14.27   Ring End Gap

The rings should be staggered to retard as much as possible the compression loss that is always present.

The ring grooves in many outboard engine pistons are

pinned to secure the position of the ring in the ring groove. This staggers the ring and keeps it from catching on the edges of the ports (exhaust and intake). If this catching occurs in the cylinder, it causes breakage or excessive wear to the ring at this point.

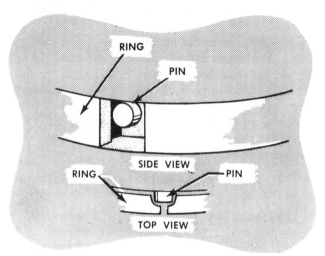

Clinton Engine Corp.

Figure 14.28   Pinned Rings

In addition to providing the proper ring gap clearance, it is equally important that clearance be provided between the ring and the ring groove to provide maximum flexibility. Like gap clearance, if excessive, the result is seepage (around the edges and the back of the ring), while if insufficient, the ring binds in the groove to affect flexibility.

When the piston rings are installed or fitted in the cylinder and in the ring groove, the piston must be fitted in the cylinder with sufficient clearance to prevent binding in the cylinder bore. This binding causes overheating and sluggish performance of the engine. On the other hand, ample clearance should be available between the piston and cylinder wall for lubrication and proper freedom of

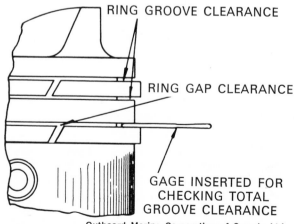

Outboard Marine Corporation of Canada Ltd.

Figure 14.29   Checking Ring Groove Clearance

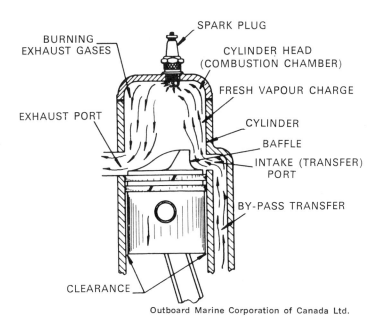

BURNING EXHAUST GASES

SPARK PLUG

CYLINDER HEAD (COMBUSTION CHAMBER)

FRESH VAPOUR CHARGE

EXHAUST PORT

CYLINDER

BAFFLE

INTAKE (TRANSFER) PORT

BY-PASS TRANSFER

CLEARANCE

Outboard Marine Corporation of Canada Ltd.

Figure 14.30   Intake and Exhaust Operation of Two-stroke Cycle Engine

the piston to function as it should. Clearance at this point depends on the diameter of the cylinder bore, the material of which the piston is constructed, the normal operating temperature of the motor and the speed at which it operates.

In those two-stroke engines where contour of the combustion chamber permits, the piston may be installed backwards by mistake. This backward installation will interfere considerably with starting and with the overall operation of the motor. The straight side of the piston baffle is placed adjacent to the intake port in the cylinder to direct the incoming fresh vapour charge from the crankcase upward along one side of the cylinder and to crowd the burning exhaust gases out the exhaust port. Since the width of the exhaust port is greater than the intake port, it is uncovered earlier by the downward moving piston. This moves the exhaust gases out the exhaust port; they are directed there by the gradual decline of the opposite side of the baffle and by the pressure in the cylinder at that moment.

Naturally, the process is not entirely efficient—not all of the spent gases are discharged from the cylinder, nor does all of the fresh vapour charge remain in the cylinder. Some of the fresh charge escapes with the exhaust gases and some of the exhaust gases remain in the cylinder to follow through in the next cycle.

Cylinder and Cylinder Head

Except for certain applications, cylinders generally (bores at least) are constructed of high quality cast iron. A more modern procedure, however, involves diecasting the cylinder assemblies, making necessary the construction of elaborate dies. These dies permit the use of cast iron cylinder bores, aluminum water jackets, bearing supports,

bronze bearing inserts, and crankcase sections where required. This construction helps to reduce the weight of the assembly, and increases production capacity and uniformity in the quality of cylinder blocks.

One of the principal factors in realizing maximum performance of any outboard motor, or for that matter, any internal combustion engine (2 or 4-stroke cycle) is the condition of its cylinder bores, pistons and piston rings.

The bore must be round and straight. The cylinder wall must be free of scores and deep scratches—smooth, but not too smooth. A minute degree of roughness is desired and required to retain the oil film for maximum compression seal between the cylinder and piston rings. In production, a cylinder block is rejected if inspection at the factory reveals that the bore is too smooth as well as too rough. The same holds true for the piston ring walls.

In the operation of the engine, both the cylinder and the

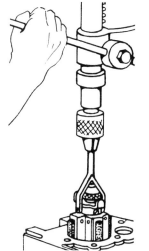

Figure 14.31   Deglazing a Cylinder

Outboard Marine Corporation of Canada Ltd.

piston ring walls become polished, which is to be expected, but only to a dull luster in appearance. If the cylinder appears to have a glazed or glossy surface, it has a reduced effectiveness on the piston rings as a compression seal. The result is sagging power.

The solution here quite frequently is merely a matter of breaking through the glaze and installing a new set of piston rings in the customary manner to restore power.

To "deglaze" a cylinder the instrument shown in figure 14-31 is pushed into the cylinder bore. A few turns with an electric drill up and down the bore breaks the glaze.

It is often possible to salvage damaged parts that are otherwise serviceable except for a stripped thread. Items damaged as a result of this condition can be rendered reuseable by the installation of a Heli-Coil in the stripped hole. Heli-Coil installation is a simple service operation that consists of drilling out the stripped hole, retapping the new hole for the Heli-Coil and installing it.

Spark plug threads that have been stripped in a cylinder head must not be repaired. This changes the heat range of the spark plug normally specified for the motor. It will hamper the transfer of combustion heat from the insulator tip of the plug to the cooling water, causing the plug to run hotter under otherwise normal conditions.

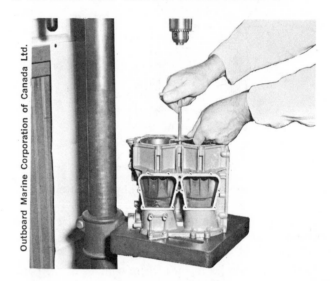

Figure 14.34   Insertion

The cylinder head, frequently referred to as the combustion chamber, is detachable. It merely consists of a cavity placed at the top end of the cylinder, above the piston, where the vapour charge transferred from the crankcase to the cylinder is compressed by the upward stroke of the piston.

The spark plug is usually installed in the cylinder head and, like the cylinder, the cylinder head is water-jacketed for cooling purposes.

Figure 14.32   Heli-coil Installation Drilling

Figure 14.33   Tapping

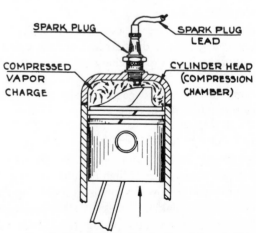

Figure 14.35   Compression in Cylinder

HOW COMPRESSION RATIO IS DETERMINED

On four-cycle engines, the piston's entire stroke (top to bottom) is used to compute piston displacement. However, on two-cycle engines that have induction and exhaust port holes in the bottom of the cylinder, piston displacement is computed by using the distance of piston travel from the top of the highest port hole to the top of the cylinder.

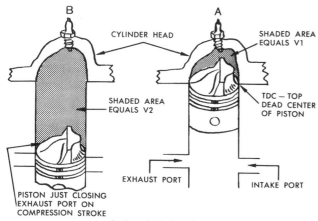

Outboard Marine Corporation of Canada Ltd.
Figure 14.36   Two-cycle Showing Volume Compression Ratio

All current production models of ported outboard engines are designed with the exhaust port located slightly higher in the cylinder than the intake port (the exhaust opens first on the power stroke and closes last on the compression stroke). Compression ratio on almost all two-cycle engines is figured by dividing the volume of the combustion chamber into the total volume existing in the cylinder when the piston reaches a point where it just closes the exhaust port. Therefore, if the volume of the combustion chamber is 20% or 1/5th, that of the sums of the combustion chamber and piston displacement volumes, the compression ratio is 5 to 1. This is the formula:

$$CR \text{ (compression ratio)} = \frac{V2 \text{ (total cylinder volume above exhause port)}}{V1 \text{ (combustion chamber volume)}}$$

SIMPLE ENGINE TERMS

At this point, it would be wise if these terms were studied and memorized for the future:

Top Dead Centre (T.D.C.):
   Top position of the piston in the cylinder.
Bottom Dead Centre (B.D.C.):
   Bottom position of the piston in the cylinder.

Clearance Volume (C.V.):
   The area or volume remaining above the piston at T.D.C.
Total Volume (T.V.):
   The area of volume remaining above the piston at B.D.C.
Piston Displacement (P.D.):
   The area or volume remaining when C.V. has been subtracted from the T.V.
Compression Ratio (C.R.):
   Area ratio calculated by dividing C.V. into T.V.

CONNECTING ROD AND CRANKSHAFT

The purpose of the connecting rod is to provide linkage between the piston and the crankshaft. The motion of the piston is reciprocative (up and down) while the crankshaft is rotative (revolves).

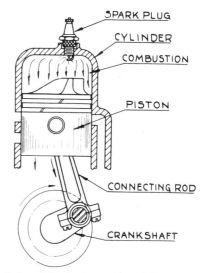

Outboard Marine Corporation of Canada Ltd.
Figure 14.37   Parts of Two-stroke Cycle Engine

The power of the combustion being applied to the head of the piston in a downward thrust is of no value for practical purposes unless it can be properly directed or gathered and applied where the resultant energy is required. This energy is required of the propellor by way of the crankshaft, driveshaft, necessary gears and propellor shaft. Therefore, energy originally directed in a straight line is converted to rotating power through the linkage between the reciprocating piston and the revolving crankshaft.

Customary practice is to design and to construct connecting rods of an "I" section with bearing bosses at either end, large at one end to accommodate the crankpin bearing and smaller at the other to support the wrist pin.

Connecting rods are usually constructed of aluminum alloy with bronze bearing inserts on the top or from steel forgings, depending on the type of bearing to be used.

Outboard Marine Corporation of Canada Ltd.
Figure 14.38   Conventional Connecting Rod Provided with Friction Type Bearing Surfaces

Aluminum is used with friction type bearings and steel inserts are used for non-friction bearings.

Wrist pin bearings on the small end of the rod are usually bronze since the amount of actual movement at this point is comparatively limited. This limited movement is governed by the angle of the connecting rod: for example a long rod in a short stroke involves a narrow angle while a short rod in a long stroke involves a wide angle. Modern practice, however, provides needles or rollers at both ends of the rod.

The crankshaft is generally made up of two or more journals, a crankpin and a cheek or web to support the crankpin at each end of it.

The cheek and the crankpin together are referred to as a throw. Where one crankpin is used, the crankshaft is classified as a single throw type.

Single throw crankshafts are employed only in one cylinder outboard motors. Some, however, are occasionally used in twin cylinder four-stroke cycle engines where two crankpins operate in the same plane.

Single throw crankshafts must be counter-balanced to offset the weight of the cheeks, crankpin and connecting rod to avoid excessive vibration.

Two-throw crankshafts are employed in the construction of the twin cylinder alternate firing motors and in four-cylinder outboard motors. There, the two crankpins are arranged in pairs and are spaced 180 degrees apart.

Crankshafts are machined from steel forgings. The crankshaft is turned to the approximate dimension of the journals and crankpins heat-treated and then given a final grind to finish size.

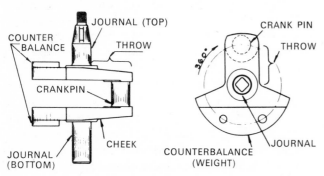

Figure 14.39   Crankshafts

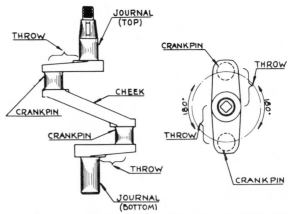

Outboard Marine Corporation of Canada Ltd.
Figure 14.40   Two-throw Crankshaft (Two Crank Pins Spaced 180° Apart) as Used in Twin Opposed Motor

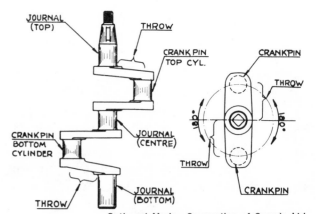

Outboard Marine Corporation of Canada Ltd.
Figure 14.41   Two-throw Crankshaft (Two Crank Pins Spaced 180° Apart) as Employed in Alternative Firing Twins

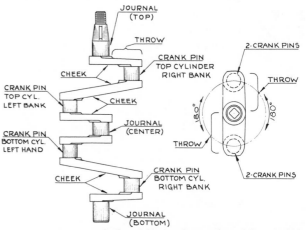

Outboard Marine Corporation of Canada Ltd.
Figure 14.42   Drawing of Two-throw Crankshaft (Two Pairs of Crank Pins Spaced 180° Apart)

In preparation for heat treating, the cheeks or webs, the threaded end of the crankshaft and a narrow area about the flywheel keyway are copperized. The crankshaft is then put to soak in a carburizing vat with a substance of high carbon content like charred bone or some other substance. Soaking is accomplished under a high temperature, during which time the carbon emitted from the carbon material soaks into the uncoppered surfaces of the journals and crankpins. The depth of penetration depends on the temperature and the length of the soaking period. At the end of the predetermined soaking period, the crankshaft is removed red hot from the vat and quenched to harden the carbon-penetrated surfaces. This heat treatment is known as case hardening.

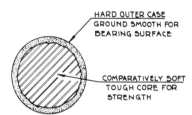

Outboard Marine Corporation of Canada Ltd.
Figure 14.43   Schematic Drawing (Cross Section) to Show Character of Case Hardened Shaft

The more modern method of case hardening, however, employs the use of a carburizing oil rather than charred bone, for better control uniformity of carburizing of the depth of penetration and for a reduced time for soaking. This time saving is a matter of importance in present day production. Carburizing in this instance is actually accomplished by soaking in vapourized carburizing oil.

As mentioned previously, only the bearing surfaces, the journals and crankpins, require case hardening to withstand bearing loads. Since there is a tendency toward brittleness in a hardened surface, the remaining portions of the crankshaft are left comparatively soft and tough to carry the full load. This includes the core of the journals and crankpins, the cheeks or webs, the threaded end of the crankshaft and a restricted area about the flywheel keyway, all of which are copper-plated prior to the carburizing. Carbon does not penetrate the copper-plated areas during the carburizing period, and they are not hardened during the procedure. They remain fairly soft and tough. This is required to withstand various degrees of distortion without cracking or breaking under power impulses and the rate of rotation.

Procedure in Removing Connecting Rod from Crankpin

When removing the piston-connecting rod assembly from the crankshaft, marks on the connecting rod and cap from either a prick punch mark or a raised line may be noted. This marking indicates the position of the original assembly and guides the repairman in reassembly of the

cap to the original position on the rod. These index marks appear only on one side of the rod.

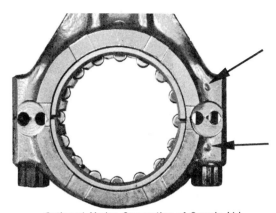

Outboard Marine Corporation of Canada Ltd.
Figure 14.44   Index Marks on Connecting Rod and Cap. When Correctly Assembled Both Marks Are in Alignment as Shown Above

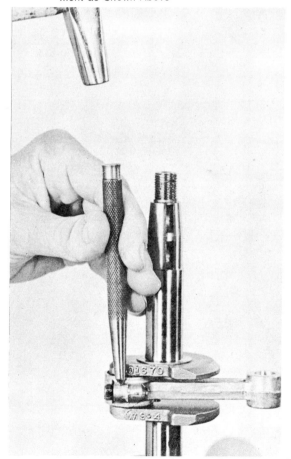

Outboard Marine Corporation of Canada Ltd.
Figure 14.45   Index Marks Being Placed on Rod

In the event that no index marks appear on the rod or cap, the indexes should be marked before removing the cap. This is important on either a new rod or on the repair of a rod assembly in the motor.

The rod and the cap are machined as a matched assembly and fit properly only when matched as an original assembly. A small prick punch may be used to mark the rod and the cap, although the punch must not be struck too hard as the rod and cap could be damaged.

Installing Connecting Rod-Piston Assembly

All parts involved in the assembly must be clean. All bearing surfaces, piston rings, ring grooves, and cylinder walls must be coated with oil to stop abrasion or scuffing until normal lubrication takes place during motor operation.

The piston must sit with the straight side of the baffle towards the intake port. The piston is placed in the cylinder accordingly, and the rings must not catch when entering the cylinder.

The piston rings, of course, must be compressed before the piston assembly can be fully inserted in the cylinder. Care must be taken to see that the rings are properly seated in the ring grooves.

The prick punch or matching marks on the connecting rod and cap are lined up and the connecting rod bolts or screws and lock plates replaced if necessary. The connecting rod is carefully placed in position on the crankpin, the cap installed with its match or index mark even with the marking on the rod.

New lock plates are put on the connecting rod screws when required, and the rod and cap bolted together. The cap is tightened snugly, but not to an overdue pressure which would result in stripping the threads. The sides of the rod and cap are hit lightly with a small hammer, if there is a slight evidence of binding, to obtain the final bearing surface. An aluminum rod must not be struck too hard. If light tapping does not free it, there are other possible causes of binding; e.g . foreign particles on the crankpin.

The bolts or screws are tightened, the two lugs bent over the edge of the bolt caps and the remaining one firmly set against the head of the bolt to prevent it from turning. (Some instances require bending only one lug up against the bolt.)

When roller bearings are used, the same procedure is followed except that the roller and retainer assemblies are installed on the crankpin prior to attaching the rod cap.

The cap is arranged in position with the match marks in alignment and new lockplates installed on the connecting rod screws. The cap is sealed on the rod and drawn up firmly on the connecting rod screws. A pencil may be drawn over the edge surface on both sides of the rod to make certain that both rod and cap align at this point. If the rod and cap are not aligned, the offset edge can be felt in the pencil point.

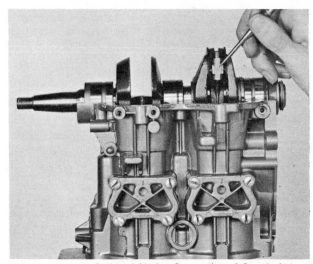

Outboard Marine Corporation of Canada Ltd.

Figure 14.47   Using Scribe to Check Alignment of Connecting Tag Plate

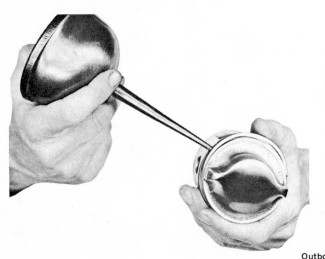

Outboard Marine Corporation of Canada Ltd.

Figure 14.46   Coat Piston Rings and Ring Grooves Liberally with Oil—Spreading Oil in Piston Ring Grooves

REVIEW QUESTIONS

1. Name the two types of bearings.
2. Give one example of use for each of the types of bearings.
3. What are the two purposes of the piston?
4. Draw a diagram of the piston and list all the important parts.
5. What does the term "deglazing" mean?
6. Draw a diagram showing the following terms:
    a) T.D.C.
    b) B.D.C.
    c) P.D.
    d) C.V.
    e) T.V.
7. Explain what "reciprocative" and "rotative" movement means in a small engine.
8. Name the two materials that connecting rods are made from.
9. In point form, describe how a connecting rod is constructed.
10. Draw a simple diagram of a crankshaft and show the major parts.
11. Explain the term "case hardening".
12. List the procedure for removing a connecting rod from a crankpin.
13. How do manufacturers index the rod and cap?
14. What precautions must be taken before the assembly of the rod to the crankpin can take place?
15. List the procedure taken in installing the connecting rod to the crankpin.
16. Name the two main sections of the outboard engine.
17. List the parts of the powerhead.
18. What are the two classifications of bearings?
19. Where is a babbit bearing located on the outboard engines, and from which material is it constructed?
20. In point form, explain how non-friction bearings are constructed.
21. List the types of non-friction bearings used in the outboard engine.
22. What are the two functions of the pistons?
23. How does carbon affect the rings of the piston after a period of operation?
24. Define the following:

    a) Blow-by   d) Piston baffle
    b) Ring end gap   e) Transfer port
    c) Ring groove clearance f) Bore

25. A "too smooth" or "too rough" cylinder bore would be rejected at the factory. What would happen to the engine if both of these cylinders where allowed to be used?
26. Explain the procedure that must be followed to remove the glossy finish in a cylinder bore.
27. How is compression ratio computed?
28. Explain the difference in finding the compression ratio on a two-cycle engine and the four-cycle engine.
29. Explain the following abbreviations:
    a) T.D.C.   d) C.V.
    b) B.D.C.   e) T.V.
    c) P.D.   f) C.R.
30. List three major differences between an air-cooled engine and the outboard water-cooled engine.
31. What are the three basic parts of the outboard engine?
32. Name the three sections of the lower unit outboard engine.
33. What acts as both inlet and exhaust valves in the two cycle engine?
34. At what piston position does the ignition of the compressed mixture take place?
35. Name the unit that acts as the intake valve in the two stroke cycle crankcase.
36. Describe the piston head of the two cycle engine and state the purpose of the design.
37. State, in your own words, how the twin cyclinder outboard engine uses alternate firing.
38. What regulates the degree of opening the reeds?
39. List firing orders for the following Mercury engines: six cylinder, Merc 800 Type six cylinder and the four cylinder.
40. Which cylinder is known as number one?
41. Name the component parts of the outboard engine cooling system.
42. Why do outboard engines not require a radiator like an automobile?
43. Give the main difference between an outboard engine's flywheel and the air cooled engine's flywheel.
44. What is the reason for the difference in the water cooled engine's flywheel?

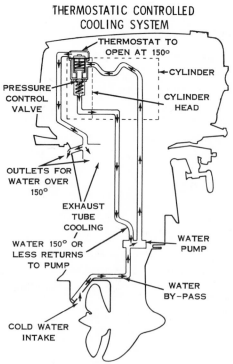

THERMOSTATIC CONTROLLED
COOLING SYSTEM

Outboard Marine Corporation of Canada Ltd.
Figure 15.1b   Outboard Cooling System

CHAPTER 15
WATER COOLING

This chapter introduces a different type of cooling system for small engines. Previously we have been discussing the air cooled engine and how it is operated, with the fins on the flywheel circling the air over the cylinder head and fins. The cylinder fins were cooled by this flow of air past the shroud which encased the engine block and directed the flow of air over the parts that needed it. Now, we shall discuss another cooling method: water cooling.

The automobile is a water cooled engine. It has a radiator, a water pump, a thermostat, and water jackets around the cylinders. It has a path in which the water travels to cool the engine and then back to the radiator again for re-circulating and cooling.

The outboard engine is somewhat similar to the automobile cooling system; however it has no radiator. Without a radiator to act as a cooling supply of water, the motor must use the water in which it travels. Therefore, extreme care must be taken in the maintenance of the circulatory system of the outboard engine to ensure a proper cooling operation.

A minute blockage in the outboard cooling system will cause serious damage to the engine, and may destroy or seriously damage it so that it becomes inoperative.

THE WATER PUMP

Cooling, of course, is provided by circulating water through the jackets surrounding the cylinders, exhaust manifold and cast in the cylinder head. Water circulation is maintained by a pump built into the gear case assembly and operated by the drive shaft.

The pump actually consists of an impeller (with flexible synthetic rubber veins or blades) rotating in an aluminum housing into which ports are cast for water discharge. The open end of housing is closed by a stainless steel plate that has an elongated slot to serve as the water pump inlet. The drive shaft is not centred in the impeller or pump housing so that the impeller is offset to one side. This causes the impeller blades to flex or bend as they

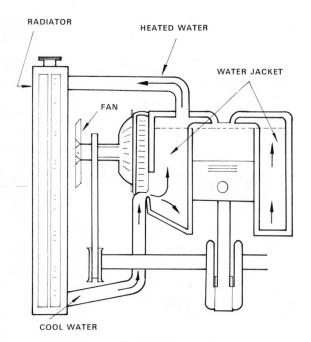

Figure 15.1a   Automotive Cooling System

WATER DISCHARGE

WATER INLET

Outboard Marine Corporation of Canada Ltd.

Figure 15.2a   Action of the Vari-volume Pump—Pump Cover
Removed to Expose the Impeller

Outboard Marine Corporation of Canada Ltd.

Figure 15.2b   Position of Impeller Blades During Operation
in Higher Speed Range

rotate in the housing; they are curved more while travel-ling through the narrow side than on the opposite, wider side that has a little curvature. The volume or space be-tween the individual blades varies with the impeller rotation, restricted on the narrow side of the impeller housing and expanded as the blades progress toward the wide side where little constriction exists.

It is this flexing or bending of the impeller blades which makes it a displacement pump at slow speeds. An inlet slot in the cover plate is so spaced as to create an opening between the impeller blades at a point just after maximum constriction occurs and when the blades commence to straighten out. The gradual increase in volume between the blades as the impeller rotates causes water to be drawn in to fill up the space thus created. At the proper moment of expansion, the top edge of the impeller blade passes the end of a slot. Water stops flowing in this par-ticular space. The water now trapped between the blades is carried around with the impeller until the blades start to flex or bend again on the narrow side. The volume between the impeller blades now constricts and creates water pressure. The tip of the leading blade, however, uncovers a slot (discharge) in the impeller housing which discharges the trapped water as the space it originally occupied constricts. Discharge continues in a proportion to diminishing volume until the tip of the following blade passes over or closes the discharge slot. Identical action takes place in the space between each of the impeller blades to provide a constant stream of water, when the motor operates at slow and intermediate speeds. Crea-tion of such suction as described permits the installation of the water pump above the water level.

At high operating speeds, water resistance within the impeller housing is sufficient to prevent the impeller blades from stretching out to maintain contact with the impeller housing. Simple impeller action results. The impeller now acts merely as a circulator, relying on pressure created by the revolving propeller and forward motion of the boat to provide sufficient water through the twin inlets in the gear case for cooling purposes.

The water discharge is through the outlet in the exhaust tube immediately below the cylinder block.

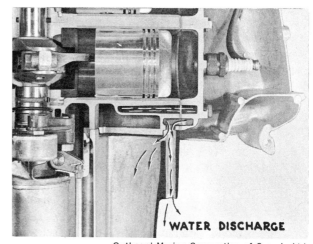

WATER DISCHARGE

Outboard Marine Corporation of Canada Ltd.

Figure 15.3   Sectional View of Power Head to Show Position
of Water Discharge

When the motor speed drops, the resistance within the impeller housing diminishes to permit the impeller blades to resume a normal position, and to function again as a displacement pump. It is the flexing or bending of the impeller blades which cause the pumping action as volume between the blades alternately diminishes and increases with the rotation. If the impeller were centred in the housing, it would simply perform as a conventional impeller and not as a displacement pump that forces water circulation at neutral, slow and intermediate speeds.

Assembly of the Water Pump

After the upper shift rod is disconnected, unscrewed and detached from the link, the gear case is disassembled by first detaching it from the upper pump housing.

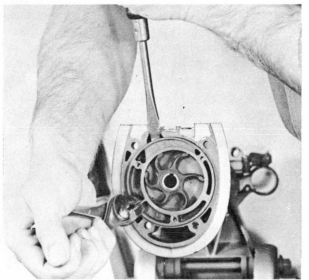

Outboard Marine Corporation of Canada Ltd.
Figure 15.4   Removing the Impeller Housing

Since the impeller, housing and drive shaft assembly are attached to the upper pump housing by three screws, the screws must be removed to detach it. The impeller is keyed to the drive shaft by a small pin. On removing the impeller plate, the drive shaft can be withdrawn from the assembly. The impeller merely lifts out. In some instances, the entire pump assembly may be removed as a unit by simply pulling on the drive shaft but most likely, the rubber "O" (seal ring) adheres sufficiently to prevent entire assembly removal in one operation. To remove the impeller housing from the upper pump housing, one of the webs in the housing is grasped with a pair of pliers and a screw driver is inserted between the impeller housing and the pump housing. The pliers are pulled and the screw driver pried carefully and evenly. It must not be forced too hard and the housing must not be cocked or uneven strain will result.

On removal of the lower pump housing, the link (offset in shifting mechanism to accommodate the exhaust valve) is detached and the screws holding the upper gear case section fast to the lower gear case are removed.

After detaching the gear case head, the lower rod and shifting yoke must be disconnected to permit the withdrawal of the propeller shaft and gear assembly. The yoke is pinned to a small shifting lever in the gear case and the pin secured with a cotter pin as shown below. This is actually the full disassembly for repairs to the water pump assembly. After visual inspection for wear, the unit can be reassembled in the reverse procedure.

THE THERMOSTAT

Some cooling systems are thermostatically controlled to achieve improved performance. A thermostat is installed in the cylinder head of each engine, conveniently located and very readily accessible.

The thermostat unit consists of a thermal element made of a powdered copper-wax compound, a rubber diaphragm and piston closed in a housing. The thermostat assembly includes a housing in which the thermostat unit is inserted and a plunger arm assembly activated by the thermostat piston, valve return and override springs.

In rising water temperatures, the copper wax compound in the thermal unit expands. The expanding thermal unit, acting against the rubber diaphragm, and at the same time against the tension of the valve returning spring, forces the piston upward to open the valve. With the valve now raised off its seat, water is permitted to circulate through the water jacket of the cylinder head assembly to maintain a pre-determined operating temperature. The thermostat unit is calibrated to open at water jacket temperature of 145 to 150 degrees F. The resulting degree of valve opening is obviously in proportion to the cooling system requirements, since the function of the cooling system is

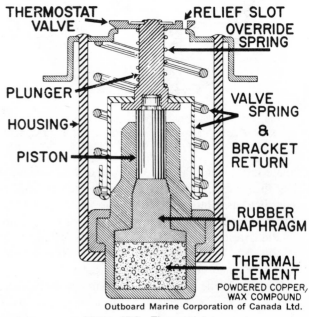

Outboard Marine Corporation of Canada Ltd.
Figure 15.6   Thermostat

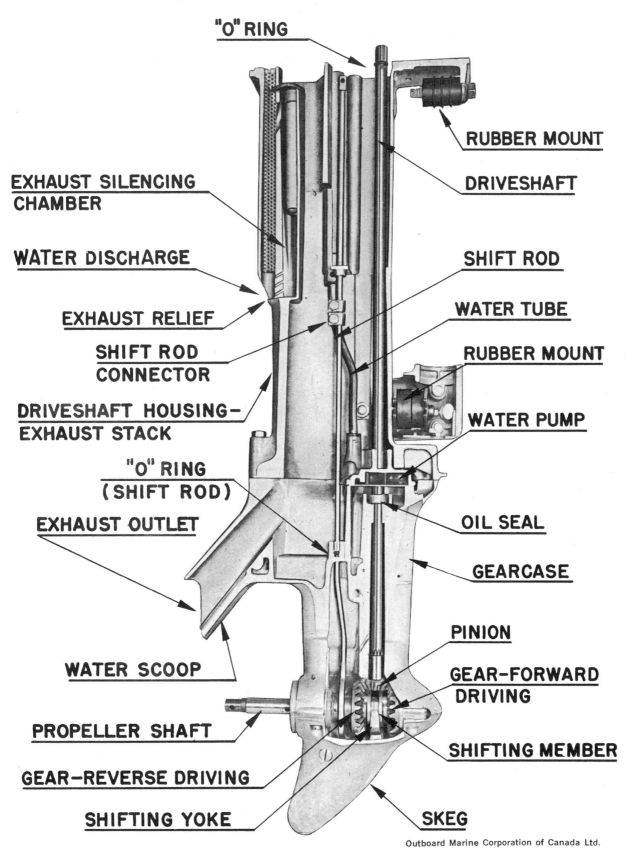

"O" RING

RUBBER MOUNT

DRIVESHAFT

EXHAUST SILENCING CHAMBER

WATER DISCHARGE

SHIFT ROD

WATER TUBE

EXHAUST RELIEF

RUBBER MOUNT

SHIFT ROD CONNECTOR

DRIVESHAFT HOUSING— EXHAUST STACK

WATER PUMP

"O" RING (SHIFT ROD)

OIL SEAL

EXHAUST OUTLET

GEARCASE

PINION

GEAR-FORWARD DRIVING

WATER SCOOP

PROPELLER SHAFT

SHIFTING MEMBER

GEAR-REVERSE DRIVING

SHIFTING YOKE

SKEG

Outboard Marine Corporation of Canada Ltd.

Figure 15.5   Lower Units Parts

to dissipate heat. Unlike the small air cooled engine which is dependent on the air current directed over the cylinder fins for cooling, the outboard engine is dependent on water to cool the cylinder head; therefore, no flywheel or cylinder head fins are required.

Outboard Marine Corporation of Canada Ltd.

Figure 15.7   Flywheel

Heat is generated by motor operations at various speeds. At high RPM's and under a full load, heat generation is at its maximum; consequently, a high rate of water cooling flow is required. When operating at a slow or intermediate speed, the heat generation is less. The thermostatically controlled valve acts to regulate its metered flow of water through the water jacket at all motor speeds to maintain as nearly as possible a constant operating temperature. The valve is particularly significant during slow

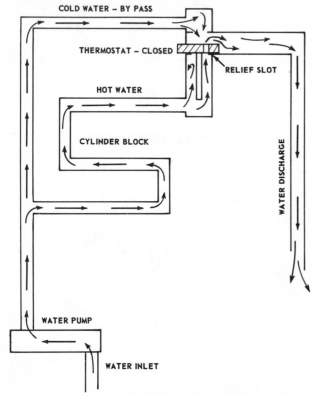

Outboard Marine Corporation of Canada Ltd.

Figure 15.8   Cooling System with Thermostat Valve Closed (Cold)

and intermediate speed operations. Activity of the thermostat is produced to some extent, naturally, by the temperature of the water in which the unit is being operated and is governed ordinarily by seasonal changes in geographical locations.

Since a rubber diaphragm, installed between the thermal element and the piston, is used to open the valve, it is returned to its closed position by the contraction of the cooling thermal element, which is accomplished by the tension of the valve return spring acting against tthe plunger bracket.

The thermostat float valve floats on the plunger shaft but is held in position by the small override spring.

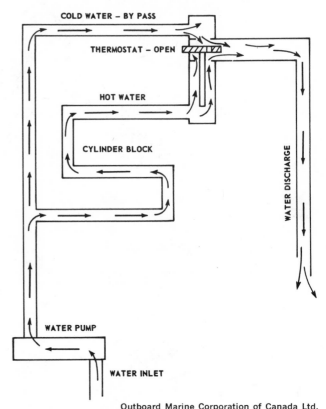

Outboard Marine Corporation of Canada Ltd.

Figure 15.9   Cooling System with Thermostat Valve Open (Normal Operating Procedure)

Starting cold, the thermosat valve is closed. The relief slot is machined into the valve plate. Water enters the pump and is directed into the cooling system; the flow separates at the junction of the water jacket in the cold water bypass channels. A major portion of the circulating water at this time is directed to the upper portion of the cylinder head, by passing the thermostat valve, and flowing on out through the discharge channel. Cold water circulation is not affected by the rising water jacket temperature. A lesser portion of the circulating water, at the same time, flows through the water jacket of the cylinder block assembly, and on to the relief slot in the thermal slot valve, eventually to enter the cold water bypass stream.

The purpose of the relief slot is to purge the cylinder water jacket of air and to permit limited circulation. Naturally, with the restricted water jacket circulation, the resulting temperature rise is very quick. Therefore, expansion of the thermal unit causes the thermostat valve to open. Circulation to the water jacket is now considerably greater, but is adjusted by the action of the thermostat in accordance with heat generated at various engines speeds. It should be noted that the circulating hot water from the water jacket and cold water bypass converge and discharge into the exhaust stream.

Normally, little if any difficulty can be expected with the thermostat unit. Adequate means have been taken to avoid damage from freezing by providing the necessary drains when the motor is stored or hung in an upright position.

THERMOSTATICALLY CONTROLLED COOLING SYSTEM ON LARGE MODELS

Circulation of water through the cylinder block and cylinder head jackets for cooling purposes is accomplished in the same way as in the smaller engine by an impeller type of water pump or circulator attached to the upper end of the gear case and driven by the drive shaft. The unit at slow speed functions as a positive displacement pump; at higher speeds it acts as a simple circulator.

The thermostat has been assembled in the water circulating system to maintain a constant operating temperature, thereby achieving greater flexibility and more efficient operation throughout the entire rage of operation. The maintenance of pre-determined operating temperature particularly at slow speeds and intermediate ranges results

in a more complete combustion of fuel vapours and a clean burning charge. This minimizes sludgy carbon deposits and the accumulation of petroleum gum or varnish which interferes with the performance of the engine. In like manner, an active spark plug life is considerably extended.

The assembly of the thermostat consists of a pressure release valve and a thermostatically controlled element enclosed in the cylinder head.

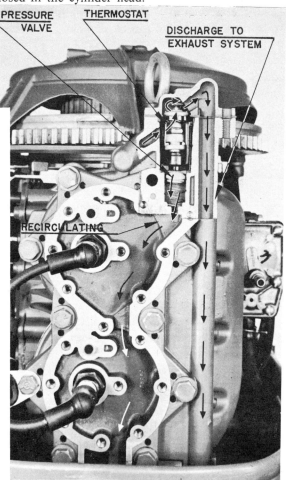

Outboard Marine Corporation of Canada Ltd.
Figure 15.11   Position of Thermostat

When the motor is started, water is pumped into the water jacket system until a pressure of approximately 1 pound has been established. Then, since the spring tension acting against the pressure valve is preset to break at 1 pound, the pressure valve is forced off its seat to commence water circulation. Water thus released by this pressure valve is directed by means of a second water tube to the water pump to be re-circulated. Re-circulation continues in this manner until the water jacket temperature has reached 130 to 150 degrees F. when the thermostatic valve is opened by the action of the thermostat. The resulting overflow is conducted into the exhaust assembly

Outboard Marine Corporation of Canada Ltd.
Figure 15.10   Impeller Installed in the Pump Housing

where it circulates to cool the exhaust stack. After that a portion is discharged immediately below the power head assembly (above the water line) with the remainder of the water jacket discharge overflowing into the exhaust stream and out through the underwater exhaust.

A "V" slot is formed in the thermostatic valve face, allowing air to escape and later, water to rinse the valve assembly free of salt crystals or other impurities.

When the pre-determined operating temperature is reached, the thermostat valve opens. A sudden spurt of water will eject from the discharge outlet. A failure to spurt at the discharge after motor operation for a reasonable length of time indicates possible pump failure. The motor should be immediately stopped and an investigation of the cooling system conducted. Under some circumstances, little water will be seen to emit from the water discharge because of the suction created in the exhaust stack when the engine is operating at a comparatively high boat speed.

To check the functioning of the thermostat, a thermometer is placed into the water discharge outlet after the motor has reached a running temperature. The reading should not exceed 170 degrees F.

WARNING

Under no circumstances should the motor be run out of water. It may be rather tempting, after completing an installation of a motor on a boat, to start and run the motor dry for the purpose of checking an electrical hook-up. It is urged that such a practice be restricted, to avoid permanent damage to the water pump impeller. All trial checks must be performed with the motor in the water.

CHECKING OPERATION OF COOLING ON JOHNSON MOTORS

After the gear case has been reinstalled, operation of the cooling system should be checked to determine if water circulation is adequate, since there may be instances when the water tube has not been properly fitted into the water pump grommet.

One method commonly used to check for water circulation is that of running the engine in a test tank to observe whether or not water spray is being discharged at the exhaust relief openings in the rear section of the exhaust housing. Water spray will not be noted, however, until the engine is turning at least 1000 RPM's ,throttle quadrant approximately in start position) .

A better method for checking water circulation, however, would involve the use of Thermal Melt Stiks. These stiks are available through Stevens Experimental Company, 2015 Grand Avenue, Waukegan, Illinois.

The engine is started and run in a test tank. (The engine must be fitted with the appropriate test wheel) .

Outboard Marine Corporation of Canada Ltd.

Figure 15.12a   Thermal Melt Sticks on Thermostat Housing

Outboard Marine Corporation of Canada Ltd.

Figure 15.12b   Thermal Melt Sticks on Cylinder Wall

The engine is set to run at a fairly fast idle until normal operating temperature is reached.

A 165 degree Thermal Melt Stik is placed against the side of the cylinder, preferably on the serial plug. This stick should not melt, indicating that the engine operating temperature is not exceeding 165 degrees.

Thermal Melt Stiks must not be set against the cylinder head of a 3 H.P. engine, since the centre of the head will run slightly hotter than 165 degrees F.

If, in concluding the above test, the results indicate that proper circulation throughout the power head is doubtful, the gear case is removed to determine whether the water tube has been properly located in the impeller housing grommet. In most instances of inadequate water circulation after gear case removal, the problem can be traced to an improperly located water tube.

REVIEW QUESTIONS

1. Why is the radiator not required on the outboard engine?
2. What are some of the causes that would make the impeller stop operating?

3. Explain why the impeller is off centre.

4. The description of the removal of the water pump in Fig. 15-4 is not a common procedure. Why is this procedure not a common practise?

5. What is the purpose of the copper-wax compound in the thermostat?

6. How is the impeller pump driven on the outboard engine?

7. Where would you look to see if the outboard engine was pumping water?

8. Make a list of engine parts that could be damaged or worn through lack of water circulation.

9. Draw a diagram of the thermostat and explain how it operates.

10. After examining an outboard lower unit, make a list of precautions that should be taken to ensure water circulation.

11. Will water appear at the water discharge immediately after starting the motor?

12. What is the purpose of the relief slot in the thermostat?

13. Explain the meaning of the following terms:
    a) Water Jacket
    b) Impeller
    c) Displacement Pump
    d) Circulatory Pump
    e) Exhaust Stack
    f) Relief Slot

14. What is the main purpose of the Thermostat?

15. Draw a diagram showing the water circulation system and label it.

16. Can the outboard engine be started and operated out of the water?

17. Explain, in your words, the difference between an automobile cooling system and that of an outboard engine.

18. Name three basic cooling systems.

19. Explain, in your own words, what a displacement pump is used for in the outboard engine.

20. How does the pump act at high speed?

21. How may the temperature of an outboard engine be determined without removing the thermostat?

22. Draw two diagrams showing the difference in water circulation systems when they are hot and cold.

23. Why do you feel it is important to study the disassembly and reassembly of older type outboard engines?

With the exception of a common flywheel and breaker cam, it will be noted that two separate systems are really involved, one for each of the cylinders. From the diagrams, it can readily be seen that each comprise two separate wiring circuits.

The primary circuit

Several hundred turns of fairly heavy wire (copper insulated) are wound around a laminated steel core of special alloy for the purpose extended and shaped to form the poles that are more frequently referred to as the coil heels.

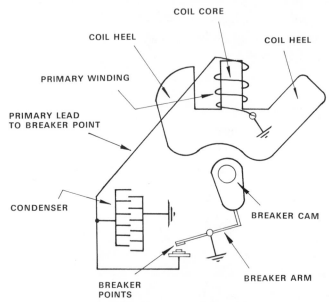

Figure 16.2   Primary Circuit

CHAPTER 16
IGNITION SYSTEMS

THE MAGNETO

The magneto consists chiefly of an armature plate or base, upon which are mounted two ignition and coil heel assemblies, two condensors and two sets of primary breaker points, a permanent magnet cast into the rim of the engine flywheel and an eccentric cam properly assembled to the upper crank shaft journal, or a *flat* milled into the journal, to activate the breaker points.

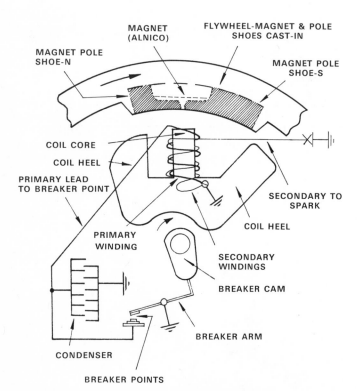

Figure 16.1   Magneto Layout

There is a set of breaker points; one is insulated and attached to the primary by means of an insulated copper wire lead. The other point, not being insulated, is connected through to the armature base to the ground terminal of the primary winding to complete the primary circuit.

Since the purpose of the breaker point assembly is to make and to break the primary circuit, the insulated point is obviously made stationary, while the other uninsulated one, which actually makes and breaks the circuit, is riveted to the rocking arm and actuated by the revolving breaker cam.

A condensor completes the circuit. It has one side insulated and wired to the stationary insulated breaker point; this is the lead. The other is attached to the armature base to shunt the assembly across the breaker points; this is the ground.

The secondary circuit

Several thousand turns of fine gauge insulated copper wire are wound into a coil and placed in position in the primary winding. Each is insulated from the other. One end of the secondary winding leads to the ground, running

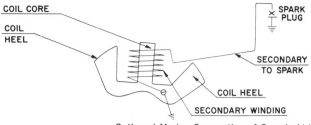
Outboard Marine Corporation of Canada Ltd.
Figure 16.3 The Secondary Circuit

from the coil or heel assembly to the armature base. The other end is attached to a heavily insulated stranded wire which leads to the spark plug terminal to complete the circuit after arcing the point gap.

The operation of the magneto assembly basically should not be too difficult to understand. As the magnet pole pieces, cast into the revolving flywheel, pass over the area of the coil heels, a current flows into the primary winding circuit, followed subsequently by a magnetic field build-up about the coil.

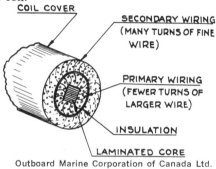
Outboard Marine Corporation of Canada Ltd.
Figure 16.4 Cross Sectional View of Conventional Ignition Coil

At the appropriate time, predetermined in design, a breaker point, one set at a time, is separated by the action of the revolving cam; thus, the primary circuit is broken. The primary circuit then suddenly ceases to flow and since the magnetic field now established about the coil is, for the moment, no longer supported by the primary current flow it collapses instantly. During the period of instant field collapse, a current of exceptionally high voltage intensity is induced in the many fine wire turns of the secondary winding. This is conducted through an ignition lead to the spark plug where it arcs the gap between the points to ignite the compressed fuel vapour in the combustion chamber above the piston and, therefore, develops the power impulse.

Magneto Breaker Points and Condensor

Since the efficiency and intensity of the spark is dependent to some considerable extent on the condition of the breaker point contact surfaces and gap setting, faulty or irregular operation of the motor may be often caused by a de-

ficiency in the breaker action. All contact surfaces must be clean, free of pitting and corrosion, in alignment and adjusted to the specified .020 inches of gap. The breaker arm must rock freely on its pivot post to realize the maximum breaker point performance.

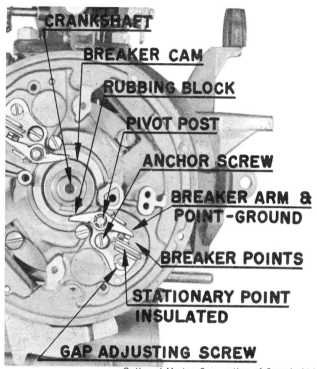
Outboard Marine Corporation of Canada Ltd.
Figure 16.5 Operation of Points

Other factors, of course, enter into the picture of a badly acting magneto, such as a faulty coil, condensor, spark plugs, wiring and partially "loose" or corroded electrical connections.

Pitting, discoloration (oxidation) and misadjustment of the gap eventually appear during the normal operation of the motor. Oxidation occurs during periods of inactivity, such as storage, and, therefore, affect the starting. Excessive pitting is frequently associated with a faulty condensor, loose or corroded terminal leads at point of attachment, and faulty wiring. Abnormal reoccurence of breaker gap misadjustment may be attributed to a "rough" or cracked breaker cam surface that causes rapid wear of the rubbing block rivetted to the breaker arm, resulting in a lessening of the gap and of the throw of the spark timing. It is of extreme importance that the specified .020 inch gap setting be constantly maintained. New breaker cam and breaker arm, in this event, should be installed if the condition of the rubbing block reveals too much wear.

It is economical and more practical to install new point assemblies rather than to attempt to recondition them except in an emergency. An ordinary point dresser will do as a temporary measure in this event but, when the magneto is available for shop repair, it is advisable to remove the flywheel for a better and more thorough service job. At the same time this servicing provides an excellent opportunity for inspection of other details in the assembly. Tungsten point faces have usually been employed; however, in recent years, platinum point faces have been used exclusively. It is important that no time be wasted in servicing the breaker points when there is evidence of excessive pitting.

The breaker cam surface must be smooth. Roughness acts to wear excessively on the breaker arm rubbing block to rapidly alter the gap setting. Cracks in the cam face contribute to like results.

The breaker points must be set, as instructed, to .020 inches gap full open; that is, with the breaker arm rubbing block riding on the high side of cam. This gap is important to obtain the desired results. After having installed and adjusted the new points, the motor should be run for several minutes in the tank and the gap setting then rechecked. A slight roughness in the face of the rubbing blocks, perhaps minute burrs, wears down quickly to cause a decrease in the gap setting until the rubbing surface eventually smooths up. The gap should be reset if necessary.

Breaker Points and
Their Direct Relation for Spark Efficiency

Fundamentally, the performance of an electric ignition (sparking) system is dependent on current intensity that is induced or built up first in the primary and subsequently in the secondary winding of the coil during normal functioning of the magneto assembly.

Because of the nature of the magneto's construction and its principle of operation, current gathered to cause the sparking is not maintained at a constant level but fluctuates between points of high and low voltage. It is readily understood, therefore, that current for maximum sparking strength must be picked up at the peak of the current intensity. The breaker points simply function then as a trigger to fire the spark.

Greater voltage is required to cause a spark across a gap that is under compression in an engine cylinder than one that is in normal air, under atmospheric pressure. Thus a spark plug may fire weakly outside a cylinder, but fail entirely in the cylinder.

Actually, in the magneto, with the separating or opening of the breaker points, the primary circuit is broken to interrupt the flow of current through the primary winding. The attendant magnetic field set up about the coil assembly at this time suddenly collapses to start a current flow of high voltage to the fine windings of the secondary coil which, when conducted to the spark plug terminal, fires across the gap to ignite the compressed fuel charge. Since sparking occurs at the instant of breaker point separation, to gain the utmost efficiency of the coil for greater sparking strength, the magneto points are timed to break at the precise time when the peak range or maximum current flow through the primary winding is reached. Timing in this respect is predetermined in design but maintained in service by adjusting the breaker gap to .020 inches full open for best average setting. Basically, gap setting of greater than specified .020 inches results in a proportionately earlier spark occurring on the build up of current intensity in the primary circuit and, therefore, weaker sparking. A gap setting of less than .020 inches causes a proportionately later spark which takes place at the falling side of current intensity with a similarly weaker sparking.

Minor variations in magneto characteristics normally exist during the process of overall production. Occasionally an individual motor starts more readily with the breaker point gap adjusted to slightly above or below the specified .020 inches. In this instance, there is evidence of variation or tolerance affecting the time at which current intensity in the primary circuit reaches its maximum.

Beyond adjusting the breaker point gap setting, however, other conditions may enter to affect sparking efficiency merely as a result of normal operation—like pitting, corrosion or erosion of the breaker point faces. Breaker points wear out in time because of the constant pounding received during ordinary performance. Pitting and erosion, the result of arcing across the points during normal operation or exaggerated because of deficiencies in the condensor or primary wiring system, all these contribute to a faulty spark. The corrosive effect of salt air deteriorates breaker points and performance. Circulating oil vapour within the magneto assembly is similarly conducive to breaker point deterioration and even to an eventual failure.

Breaker point faces ordinarily are finished with an extremely smooth surface but with a slight curvature to ensure a clean contact and a minimum of arcing in action; they produce a clean break with just enough arc to assure clean contact surfaces.

Since it is a characteristic of the primary current to continue to flow as a result of primary induction by jumping or bridging across the gap created on the instant of point breaking, some steps must be taken to minimize this tendency towards arcing if maximum sparking intensity is to be expected at the spark plug gap. Therefore, a condensor is used to shunt the breaker point gap.

The condensor consists of alternative layers of tin or aluminum foil and wax paper of the proper area as specified for the particular ignition unit. This is rolled com-

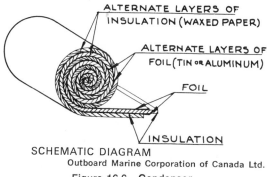

ALTERNATE LAYERS OF INSULATION (WAXED PAPER)

ALTERNATE LAYERS OF FOIL (TIN OR ALUMINUM)

FOIL

INSULATION

SCHEMATIC DIAGRAM
Outboard Marine Corporation of Canada Ltd.

Figure 16.6   Condensor

pactly. Each layer of foil is then insulated from the other and one side is attached to the insulated breaker points by a copper wire lead; the other is attached to a ground.

Fundamentally, the function of the condensor is two-fold. It momentarily absorbs the primary current which otherwise would proceed to bridge the gap on the instant of the point opening and, in this way, avoids contact arcing.

When the condensor is loaded to capacity, the charge is suddenly expelled to start a current flowing in the opposite direction, which gives added force to the collapsing magnetic field about the coil as it produces sparking efficiency at the plug. By this time, however, the breaker gap has been increased by the cam action beyond the ability of the current flow to overcome the resistance of the wider gap. The establishment of an arc or bridge is thereby avoided. Surging currents created by the action of the condensor continue as long as the breaker points remain open but progressively diminish as the induced current dissipates itself.

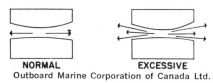

NORMAL   EXCESSIVE
Outboard Marine Corporation of Canada Ltd.

Figure 16.7   Normal and Excessive Breaker Point "Arcing"

Any interference with the condensor's capacity, such as seepage or short circuiting between the insulated layers of foil, loose or faulty terminal connectors, affects efficiency. As a consequence, a weak or faulty sparking at the plug results. Minor seepage between the foil plates causes a proportionate increase of breaking across the breaker point gap and is identified by flashing. A com-

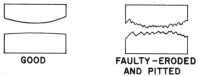

GOOD   FAULTY—ERODED
                    AND PITTED
Outboard Marine Corporation of Canada Ltd.

Figure 16.8   Good and Faulty Breaker Point Faces

plete or full short circuit across the condensor plates renders ineffective the action of the breaker points and a dead ignition system.

Erosion or pitting of the breaker point faces follows in line with the arcing to cause a faulty spark. A flash of the arc actually consists of incandenscent particles of materials vapourized or eroded from the face of the points. This frequently causes a cavity to form on one face and a corresponding pinnacle or dome to build up on the other as the material transfers from one face of one point to the other.

Maximum sparking intensity at the plug depends on the rate or suddenness of the magnetic field collapse and demands a clean break between the points on the instant of separation. A minimum or slight amount of arcing is desired to maintain a clean, active contact area; otherwise oxidized or faulty contact faces retard the build up of the primary current in the coil and proportionately affects the sparking strength. The introduction of incandescent metal particles which partially bridge the gap because of arcing causes a retarded or gradual interruption of the primary current flow and a corresponding laziness in the magnetic field collapse. A weak or faulty spark is induced. The maximum sparking intensity depends on a condensor that is in good condition, on a clean break of the contact faces at the time of primary current interruption and on clean, solid, primary terminal connections.

Oil and other foreign material accumulating on the faces of the breaker points contribute to arcing as do rough contact faces which similarly affect sparking efficiency. Redressing of the contact faces may be performed only as a temporary measure unless special equipment for reconditioning them is available. No attempt should be made to redress any platinum contacts in the ordinary manner.

MAGNETO DIAGNOSIS

Proper diagnosis of magneto difficulty is most important when an attempt is made to correct a faulty spark. It is not too mysterious if it is remembered that, for practical purposes, electricity flows much the same as water; high pressure (or voltage) seeks a level of low pressure and moves in a circuit. Water flows through a pipe; electricity flows or is conducted generally through a copper wire. A broken water pipe is comparable to a broken wire; the water stops flowing in its circuit and, similarly, electricity stops flowing if the wire is broken or the circuit otherwise interrupted. A water system does not function as it should if the conductors (pipes) leak nor does an electrical system properly function if the conductors leak (faulty insulation).

Naturally, any fault in the ignition system makes its presence known by a faulty spark at the plug and results in non-starting, hard starting, misfiring or an otherwise irregular operation of the motor. The object is, therefore, to locate the source of the difficulty and to arrange corrective measures.

Diagnosis should be carefully conducted in an orderly manner. The spark plug, since it is the most readily accessible, is the starting point. The entire ignition system is checked until the source of the difficulty is brought to light. A checklist is given below:

(1.) *Spark plug*: (a) loose connections; (b) fouled; (c) wrong type for model motor; (d) residue on porcelain (salt water areas).

(2.) *Spark plug leads*: (a) loose; (b) faulty insulation (shorting to the motor).

(3.) *Wiring on armature plate*: (a) loose or broken connection; (b) corroded connections (particularly in salt water areas); (c) fault insulation (short circuits); (d) faulty connections in ground or cut out switch.

(4.) *Breaker points*: (a) improperly adjusted; (b) pitted or corroded; (c) breaker arm binding on pivot post or breaker push rod binding in bracket.

(5.) *Condensor*: (a) loose connections; (b) faulty.

(6.) *Coil heels*: (a) improperly adjusted to magnetic pole shoes; (b) rubbing on magnetic pole shoes.

(7.) *Coil*: (a) loose connections; (b) faulty.

Servicing the Magneto

The magneto is designed and constructed so that it can be depended upon to perform efficiently over extremely prolonged periods of normal operation. Otherwise, irregular motor performance may be caused by a faulty ignition, the already familiar procedure for checking the ignition components should be carried out. An inspection includes:

(1.) Ignition point sparking quality.

(2.) Spark plugs.

(3.) Spark plug leads.

(4.) Drive belt and timing.

(5.) Breaker point action.

(6.) Condensor.

(7.) Distributor cap and rotor.

(8.) Ignition coil.

After the spark plugs are removed, a quick check for overall sparking quality may be accomplished in a few moments with the aid of the device shown in Figure 16-9. Ordinarily, if a strong spark is revealed at each of the four plug terminal gaps, further probing of the ignition system may not be necessary. The terminal gaps of the check units should be adjusted to a .250 inches for best results. The possibility of surface seepage or a breakdown of the distributor cap, however, should not be overlooked at this time.

The condition of the spark plug should be observed in

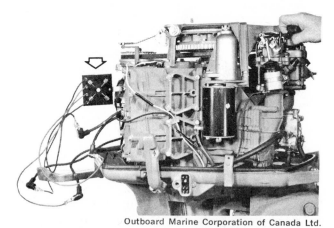

Outboard Marine Corporation of Canada Ltd.
Figure 16.9   A Preliminary Check of Magneto Sparking

the usual manner in a spark plug checking device if available. It should be discarded if its condition appears to be in doubt. The correct spark plug gap is .030 inches.

Both ends of the spark plug are inspected to ensure good contact, and to ensure that the screw type magneto at the terminal end is securely attached to the stranded core and that the prong of the spark plug cover terminal pierces the centre of the stranded core. The surface of the spark plug lead is wiped with a dry cloth to remove possible traces of objectionable residue while simultaneously a check is made for breaks or nicks in the insulating cover.

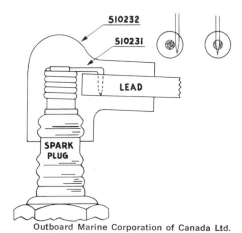

Outboard Marine Corporation of Canada Ltd.
Figure 16.10   Spark Plug Cover Installation and Clip

It is possible to encounter ignition difficulty though all familiar details of magneto and spark plug fitness have been checked and found in order. These are often revealed as weak sparking at one of the plugs, as resultant uneven running at slow and intermediate speeds or in starting qualities of the motor.

Wiring naturally becomes a significant matter to be thoroughly inspected in a situation of this sort; checking is carried out for faulty wiring, loose terminal leads, corroded connections and faulty insulation, and, beyond this, for a poor assembly of the spark plug cover installation.

The terminal lead, when properly installed, should pierce the stranded core of the spark plug lead. Unless some precaution is taken during assembly, the piercing end may miss the stranded core entirely or make only a slight contact; the core must be pierced for satisfactory contact.

During any probing for fringe irregularities in the ignition system, a check should be made to see if the spark plug is properly seated with a good gasket and gasket faces. Compression seepage between the spark plug and the cylinder head causes irregular performance and alters the characteristics of the plug. Plug temperatures rise excessively with gasket seepage.

The magneto belt and timing in the magneto should be examined.

The condensor and breaker point assemblies and their direct relation to sparking efficiency are along with the breaker point contact in the continuity tester as shown in Figure 16-11. While contact surfaces of the breaker points may appear to be in good condition on casual observation, there may, in fact, be a thin coating of oxidation, oil, foreign particles or acids from human touch, all of which affect contact resistance and prevent the proper action of the breaker points. Should a further check reveal poor contact, a careful or light swabbing with alcohol will frequently restore good contact; carbon tetrachloride must not be used. Excessive wear and the resultant errosion contribute to faulty breaker point action, and except in an emergency the contact surfaces should not be redressed; it is a better and more economical practice to replace doubtful breaker point assemblies. The condensor is tested on a unit designed and built for that purpose for the following items: (a) leakage or shorts; (b) series resistance; (c) capacity.

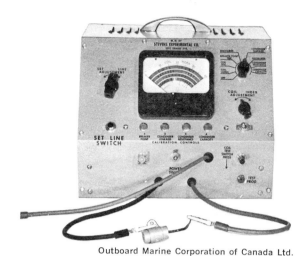

Figure 16.12   Testing the Condenser with Stevens Testing Unit

The ignition coil is tested in the similar manner but, under no circumstances, is this check done without first having removed the coil from the magneto housing. Installed as it is in the housing (bridging the magnetic pole shoes), a current sent through the primary winding for test purposes will result in an intermittent magnetic charge induced by some types of testing equipment and this charge will have its effect on the original charge of the magnet in the field housing.

Another step to further eliminate the occurrence of coil failure is the addition of two insulator plates, one on each end of the coil. Because of the proximity of the coil ends to the wall of the magneto housing, the secondary voltage will eventually burn a new path through the relatively thin area of the coil end insulation and discharge to the ground through the magneto housing. Instead of following the desired path from the high tension lead to the spark plug gap to the ground, secondary voltage in this instance does not reach the spark plug and causes erratic running or a dead engine.

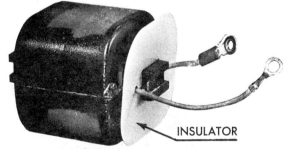

INSULATOR

Figure 16.13   Magneto Coil with Insulator Plate Installed

The figures on this page show coil insulators that have been designed to provide additional insulations at the coil ends to prevent the coil from breaking through their end insulation. To assemble the insulator on the coil, both

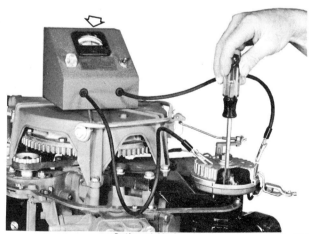

Figure 16.11   Checking Breaker Point Contact with Continuity Meter

coil wires are passed through the rectangular opening in the insulator, and slipped through the slits to the small holes on each side. The insulator is slid against the end of the coil. One insulator is required on each end, (two per coil).

The insulator was installed on all of the first few 1962 V-75 engines of Outboard Marine and it is suggested that these insulator plates be installed on any engine (50 or 75 h.p.) brought in for service that does not already have them. The coil is removed from its housing by disconnecting the primary leads, removing screws that secure the spring clips at each end of the coil core. The clips are withdrawn with long nose pliers and the coil lifted out of the magneto housing. The coil is tested on the instrument available for the purpose in accordance with the manufacturer's instructions. The distributor cap on the larger engines is tested for electrical breakdown as result of cracks, fractures and the accumulation of surface residue that causes seepage, which collectively have their effects on alternate sparking at the spark plug gap.

Because of its sturdy construction, it is doubtful that a magneto will need to be disassembled beyond that described above for normal observation and corrective measures, except when the motor has fallen overboard and there is reason to suspect that water, particularly salt water, has found its way into the rotor bearing area.

Outboard Marine Corporation of Canada Ltd.

Figure 16.14   Driving Rotor Assembly Out of the Magneto Housing

The ball bearing assemblies are otherwise sealed and half packed with a special high melting point grease (340 degrees) and ordinarily they require little if any attention. If it is necessary to repack them, each bearing assembly must be washed thoroughly with clean gasoline and then repacked with a high melting point grease.

During the reassembly caution should be exercised against the temptation to drive the rotor shaft assembly in or out of the magneto housing with a hammer blow, thereby avoiding damage to the balls and race surfaces in the bearing assembly. Steady pressure is applied by a small arbour press for this purpose. As a further precaution against damage to the ball bearing assemblies, pressure is only exerted against the inner race. This may be easily accomplished by a parallel bar or mandrel of proper design.

THE SPARK PLUG AND ITS PERFORMANCE

It is well known that all reciprocating internal combustion engines, exclusive of the diesel, are fired by an electric spark. An electric arc between points is inserted into the combustion chamber of each cylinder for that purpose. No ignition system can be more proficient than the performance qualities (determined by the design and construction) of the spark plug that is installed.

The modern spark plug, while appearing extremely simple in its construction, is the result of extensive engineering and long research. It is able to withstand the rigorous activity expected of it.

The spark plug consists of:

(1.) A hard core or insulator, usually a specially treated aluminum oxide compound fabricated to meet the demands of intermittent periods of high shock pressures and correspondingly high temperatures, and the strength of high voltage and chemical attack during the process of combustion.

(2.) The electrodes, centre and side are of special alloy to resist the rigours of high combustion temperatures, the ever present corrosive effects of chemical action and sparking erosion.

(3.) A shell in which the core assembly is contained and which has a threaded area for cylinder head installation and an all important gasket.

It will be seen, and it should be noted from the assembly drawing, that the side electrode of the outboard spark plug does not extend over the entire width of the centre electrode as it ordinarily does in the automotive spark plug. The two stroke outboard engine does not scavenge as effectively as the four stroke automotive engine with the result that bits of loose carbon are apt to be left floating in the cylinder and combustion chamber to lodge or wedge between the points and to short circuit the plug.

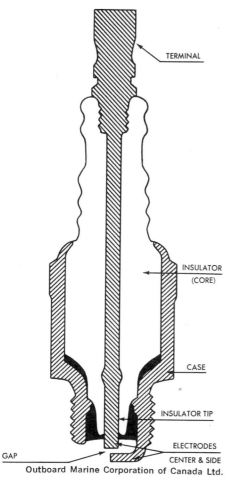

Figure 16.15   Spark Plug—Sectional View—Spark Cut Away

The shorter side electrode in this event presents less area for carbon wedging.

Beyond this, all spark plugs, regardless of usage, are classified to perform in certain heat ranges—each classification depending upon temperature characteristics developed in the combustion chamber in the respective engine. Obviously, not all engines are, by nature of their

Figure 16.16   Two-stroke Cycle Spark Plug

Outboard Marine Corporation of Canada Ltd.

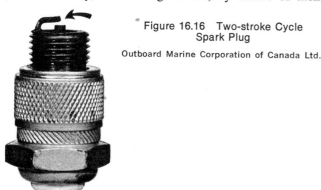

Note clipped side electrode — recommended for 2-stroke outboard motor installation. Spark gap normally adjusted to .030″ for best performance.

design, constructed to operate under like conditions. Specifying the heat range qualities of the plug to be installed in the given engine then becomes the co-operative effort of the spark plug manufacturers and the motor manufacturer's engineering department.

The heat range ultimately established for any spark plug is determined fundamentally in design by the amount of coil or insulator exposed to the burning fuel charge within the combustion chamber and this depends upon the rate of the absorption and heat flow from the region of the spark gap electrode and the insulator tip to be dissipated through the cooling system. For most effective sparking throughout any desired RPM range and conditions of operation, the degree of electrode and insulator tip temperature should be maintained at a level sufficiently high to vapourize or burn off all particles of fuel mix having collected in the area. Low level operating plug temperatures obviously result in wet fouling due to the progressive accumulation of unused fuel particles, carbon bits, sludge; excessively high temperatures are responsible for premature firing (pre-ignition) when the insulator tip and electrodes have reached a stage of incandescence. The compressed fuel vapour charge is fired prior to the time of sparking pre-determined for normal ignition.

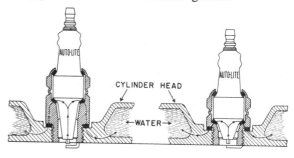

Figure 16.17   Hot and Cold Spark Plugs

Spark plugs are, therefore, classified as hot or cold with intermediate designations in accordance with the nature of service expected. The hot plug may be easily recognized by the comparatively large insulating section exposed to a flame. Conversely, a cold plug may be pointed out by the relatively small insulators exposed.

The low compression engine, running at a moderate RPM, operates naturally at low combustion temperatures and, therefore, requires a spark plug on the hot end of the operating temperature scale. The high compression, high speed engine needs spark plugs classified in the cold end of the scale for best performance. Basically, a cold running engine requires a hot plug and a hot running engine demands a cold plug. By the same token, a cold plug in a cold running engine would wet-foul during the short running time while a hot plug performing in a hot engine

The Spark Plug and Its Performance   177

would pre-ignite. It is for this fact that spark plugs are designed and classified to function efficiently in engines developing various performance characteristics—each to the temperature range requirements for the particular installation.

Since an engine running at idle or at a low RPM does not develop the power nor the combustion temperatures that it does at a high RPM under load conditions, the operating temperature range of the plug must be wide enough to permit effective firing at both ends of the performance range without fouling at idle or intermediate RPM nor pre-igniting at top RPM under full load.

Due to design and performance characteristics of the high RPM two stroke engine, the heat range selected for the best results would lean more towards the cold end of the operating temperature range than a plug performing under like conditions in a four stroke engine of equal piston displacement; and still colder for like use in the air cooled engine of either two or four stroke design. There are no sharply drawn lines of distinction between the heat range classifications of cold and hot running plugs.

Assuming the ignition system and engine assembly are up to standard for good performance qualities, observation of insulator tip coloration of the spark plug after a reasonable period of use will aid in determining whether the heat range selected for the installation is correct. Fundamentally, if the heat range is correct or acceptable, the insulator tip will have taken a cocoa tannish color. If it is an exceptionally light tan or whitish, the heat range may be too hot. A dark, black or sootish coloration or a wet appearance ordinarily reveals the heat range as too cold. During extreme high temperature pre-ignition, a gradual and characteristic drop in the engine RPM will follow and be maintained until the plugs have cooled to a correspondingly low combustion temperature.

Cocoa or tannish colouration of the insulator tip above reveals generally that the established heat range of the plug selected for the installation is meeting its requirements. However, prolonged periods of slow or intermediate speed running results in a darker or sootish colouration. Conversely, with high speed (RPM) running, the hotter tip shades toward lighter appearance.

Outboard Marine Corporation of Canada Ltd.

Figure 16.18   Normal Spark Plug Wear

Whitish colouration of the insulator tip shown here indicates perhaps incorrect heat range (spark plug) for the application — too hot. If otherwise black, gummy or oil wet — too cold.

Outboard Marine Corporation of Canada Ltd.

Figure 16.19   Incorrect Heat Range

On reaching this state, normal sparking and RPM would be restored only until the sparks have again reached their high level of temperature when the cycle repeats itself and continues to repeat itself until corrected.

Performance of this sort should not, however, be confused with such engine assembly problems as misalignment of the functioning parts, or improper bearing, piston or piston ring fits. These create a similar situation because of binding or dragging as expansion and contraction occurs with alternate rising and falling temperatures.

Whether the difficulty lies with the spark plug or engine assembly, in this instance, is not easily determined by removal and inspection of the plugs. Indications of excessively high plug temperatures or pre-ignition are ordinarily revealed by a very light (sometimes nearly white) coloration of the insulator tip. If of extended duration, they may involve a severely blistered, cracked or broken insulator tip that is customarily accompanied by burned or eroded electrodes. Otherwise, a normal appearance on the insulator tip and electrodes would suggest a search of the assembly for the disturbing factors. Attention

Outboard Marine Corporation of Canada Ltd.

Figure 16.20   Eroded or Burned Centre Electrode to Affect Spark Gap and Sparking Performance

should be directed to other possible malfunctions leading to overheating and attendant pre-ignition.

In the manually operated spark synchronized control system, the degree of spark advance and the carburetor throttle shutter opening are fixed in relation to each other, whether the engine is running at idle, intermediate or full RPM. At full throttle, the spark is adjusted to full advance and the carburetor shutter to open for the top performance and the horsepower of which the unit is capable. The spark is advanced to fire the plug at approximately 35-38 degrees before piston top dead centre on compression with the desired RPM at 4400-4800.

The time required to develop combustion fully for maximum effect after the sparking ignition is basically calculated at the given RPM range to be consumed or on the interim of time of piston travel from its position in the cylinder at the instant of spark introduction to top dead centre.

Destructive pre-ignition, or premature sparking, sometimes occurs when the engine RPM is retarded or falls below the recommended RPM while operating under full throttle conditions because of overloading due to an excessively large propeller for the specific installation and kind of service. There is simply too much pitch and blade area to permit the engine to run in the desired RPM range.

During a situation of this kind, ignition of the compressing fuel charge is introduced at precisely the same time regardless of piston travel—at 35 or 38 degrees before top dead centre. Combustion develops normally but the time of piston travel from the point of ignition to top dead centre has now been correspondingly increased because of the lower RPM rate. As a consequence, the possible time element available to develop combustion fully has been lengthened and the combustion is actually completed before the slower moving piston has had time to reach its top dead centre position. The subsequent opposing forces prevailing under these circumstances create a sudden shock wave or impulse as the approaching piston and pressure of combustion clash.

The destructive effects of pre-ignition due to propeller overloading are varied and contribute to—

(1.) Intense temperature rise in the combustion chamber area—spark plugs.
(2.) Burned or eroded spark plug electrodes.
(3.) Carbon caked or blistered insulator core section.
(4.) Insulator erosion.
(5.) Cracking or breakage of insulator.
(6.) Overall malfunction of the unit assembly.
(7.) The persistent telegraphing of damaging shock waves through the entire assembly of functional parts—pistons, connecting rods, crank shaft, drive

shaft, gear assembly—to result eventually in major and expensive corrective measures.
(8.) Burned or eroded piston heads.

All of these may be avoided by strict adherence to the factory recommended RPM range under any and all conditions for top performance at full open throttle.

The spark plug heat range specified by the manufacturer for the outboard motor does not, in any manner, include the pre-ignition caused by lower than recommended RPM at full throttle as result of an overloading with too much propeller for the installation.

Spark plugs foul because of the following:

(1.) Malfunction of the magneto.
(2.) Excessive oil content in the fuel mix and over-rich settings of either the high or slow speed needles; the slow speed needle adjustment affects them only when a fixed high speed jet is provided.
(3.) Malfunction of the thermostat (where installed) particularly in the slow and intermediate RPM ranges; in addition, running cold under stress circumstances or hot when the thermostat control is closed.
(4.) Pre-ignition as described above.
(5.) Improper heat range installation for the service or the failure to adhere to the manufacturer's spark plug recommendations.
(6.) Faulty spark plug installation.
(7.) Moisture seepage into the motor assembly.
(8.) Cracked and broken insulator.
(9.) Burned or eroded electrodes.
(10.) Faulty spark plug terminal connection.
(11.) Repeated carbon wedging from excessive carbon accumulation.

Misfiring when rapidly accelerating frequently reveals a deficiency in the fuel system.

Spark plug installation is the most important factor for good performance of the plug.

Suggestions for proper installation:

(1) A check of the spark plug threads in the cylinder head to ensure that all are clean, intact and have no indication of a cross thread or stripping.

(2) A check of the spark plug gasket and gasket face machined into the cylinder head. The gasket ought to be new but otherwise in good condition. The gasket face should be cleaned and inspected for the possibility of burrs, chips, or excessive pitting and corrected if required.

(3) On installation, the plug to be installed should be in the correct heat range specification.

Installation:
(1.) Install gasket on the plug.
(2.) Insert plug and draw to finger tightness.

(3.) Apply torque wrench with appropriate deep socket attached and draw up to 20-20½ foot pounds as specified for the aluminum cylinder head.

All the details above, relating to installation of the spark plug, should be followed explicitly to avoid possible compression or combustion seepage. Seepage by way of the threads or gaskets affects the original heat range characteristic built into the plug to a significant extent. An abnormal heat rise follows, often leading to pre-ignition and irregular engine performance sometimes difficult to diagnose.

Heat from the spark plug is dissipated through the cooling system by way of the threads, plug body, gasket and cylinder head casting; the importance of proper torque tension applied during installation cannot be over emphasized. Unless sufficient tension is applied, a heat barrier is established between the spark plug body, gasket and cylinder head casting and interferes with the expected rate of heat transfer from the plug to the cooling system.

The end result is obvious—higher plug operating temperatures than normal and pre-ignition. The gasket must be tightly compressed between the spark plug and the cylinder head casting to avoid possible seepage and to assure the proper rate of heat transfer but not to the point of excessively straining or perhaps stripping the threads, particularly in the aluminum cylinder head.

Outboard Marine Corporation of Canada Ltd.
Figure 16.21   Torque Spark Plug 20 to 20½ Ft.-Lbs.

TUNE UP: CHRYSLER OUTBOARDS

This section of the ignition chapter describes the procedure to be followed to adjust the ignition system and to check the performance of starting and charging the system of Chrysler Outboards.

Aligning Timing Pointer

Align the timing pointer as follows:
(A.) Remove the spark plug from the top cylinder and install the barrel of the timing tool in the spark plug hole.
(B.) Insert the rod portion of the timing tool into the barrel.
(C.) Hold the rod tightly against the piston, rotate the crank shaft and locate top dead centre.
(D.) The zero degree mark on the flywheel in the index

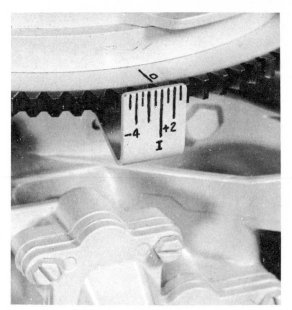

Chrysler Canada Outboard Ltd.
Figure 16.22   Flywheel Timing Marks

line (I) on the timing pointer should be in alignment; if not, shift the timing pointer and align these two points.

Breaker Point Adjustment or Replacement

Adjust and replace breaker points as follows:
(A.) Remove the distributor cap and the two bolts which secure the distributor housing to the power head.
(B.) Remove the distributor belt.
(C.) Inspect the breaker points; replace or clean if necessary.
(D.) Use a feeler guage and set the breaker point gap at .014 inches (75 HP) or .010 inches (105 HP).
(E.) Install the distributor loosely to the power head.
(F.) Turn the flywheel to align the zero degree mark to the flywheel with the pointer index line (I). Turn the distributor pulley to match the index mark on the distributor pulley with the outside diameter of flywheel.
(G.) Install the distributor belt over the distributor pulley and adjust the distributor to obtain a slight deflection. The deflection is ¼ inch with one pound pressure exerted on the belt. Fasten the distributor bracket securely in place. The tower shaft linkage will bind if the belt is too tight.
(H.) Set controls at cruise throttle position (maximum spark advance).
(I.) Turn the flywheel to line up the 36 degree mark on flywheel with the index line (I) on the timing pointer.
(J.) Turn the tower shaft to line up the upper tower shaft arm and the distributor swivel screw in a straight line, as viewed from the right side.
(K.) Connect the circuit light special tool between the distributor primary white wire and the ground wire.
(L.) Adjust the distributor control rod by turning it

Figure 16.23 Tower Shaft

counterclockwise until the breaker point closes as indicated by the circuit light coming on. Turn the control rod clockwise until the breaker point just opens as indicated by the circuit light dimming. Lock the control rod in this position with the lock nut. Breaker points must be properly gapped before performing step (L.).

(M.) Advance the controls to a wide open throttle position.

(N.) Turn the flywheel to line up the 36 degree mark with the minus 4 degree line on the timing pointer.

(O.) Adjust the wide open throttle stop adjusting screw on the throttle stop until the breaker point just begins to open as indicated by dimming of circuit light.

Figure 16.24 Adjusting Throttle Stop

Adjust the Neutral Interlock Switch

To adjust the neutral interlock switch proceed as follows:

(A.) Place the engine gear shift control in a neutral position.

(B.) Connect the circuit light to the terminals of the interlock switch.

(C.) Advance the tower shaft to the neutral stop.

(D.) Adjust the neutral interlock cam until the light just comes on.

(E.) Tighten the cam screws securely.

Figure 16.25 Neutral Stop

TO CHECK ALTERNATOR OUTPUT

(A.) To check the electrical output of an alternator, an ammeter is connected, while the engine is running, (10 amp or more, full scale reading) between the battery cable and battery terminal.

(B.) Run the motor at about 2500 RPM's and the ammeter should read approximately 8 amps.

(C.) Disconnect the two gray leads from the rectifier terminal. Connect the ohmmeter or circuit light between the two gray leads. Check for the continuity reading or light illuminating. Remove the remaining red and purple leads connected to the rectifier, and mark the terminal and leads with identifying tags for re-assembling and test tube purposes.

(D.) Using an ohmmeter or circuit light, put the black probe on the terminal wire where the red lead was secured. Place the red probe on each of the remaining terminals of the rectifier, and the ohmmeter should indicate a low resistance or, if using the circuit light, it should illuminate.

(E.) Again using the ohmmeter or a circuit light, put the red probe on the terminal where the red lead was secured. Place the black probe on each of the remaining terminals, The ohmmeter should indicate a very high resistance or, if using a circuit light it should not illuminate.

(F.) A final check of the rectifier is performed by placing

the red test probe on the rectifier mounting stud or the power head ground (it may be necessary to remove the point on the power head). Then place the black test probe on each of the terminals where the two gray leads where secured. The ohmmeter should read a low resistance or, if using the circuit light, it should illuminate.

(G.) Re-assemble all leads to the rectifier.

Magnapower Ignition System

The basic principal of operation of the magnapower ignition system can be best explained by comparison with the conventional coil—condensor—breaker point system.

CONVENTIONAL IGNITION SYSTEM

The conventional ignition system stores electrical energy in the iron core of an ignition coil by passing the battery current through a primary winding of a relatively heavy copper wire, thereby building up a magnetic field about the primary coil. At the same time as the spark plugs fire, a set of breaker points opens the primary circuit and stops the current flow through the coil primary windings. This causes the magnetic field to collapse and induces voltage into the coil secondary winding. This steps the voltage up from the 12 volts supplied by the battery to approximately 16,000 volts. The high voltage is sent to the spark plug to ignite the fuel air mixture in the engine cylinder.

MAGNAPOWER SYSTEM

The Chrysler capacitive discharge system (Magnapower

system) stores electrical energy in a capacitor rather than in the magnetic field surrounding the coil primary. This method of electrical energy storage differs from the conventional system.

The amount of energy available is limited only by the amount of energy needed. No electrical power is used to maintain the charge. In a conventional system, the current must flow to the primary coil all the time that the points are closed in order to maintain a magnetic field. The capacitive discharge, or C-D system, draws power only while placing the initial charge on the capacitor. Almost all of the energy stored is converted to the spark energy.

SEQUENCE OF OPERATION

A definite sequence of events takes place during the C-D system operation. These events occur in the six basic stages of the system and these basic stages are as follows:

(1.) Trip regulator.
(2.) Convertor.
(3.) Storage capacitor.
(4.) Breaker points.
(5.) Electronic switch.
(6.) Ignition coil.

Trip Regulator

The trip regulator essentially is an electronic switch connected between the alternator rectifier (which changes the A.C. alternator output to D.C.) and the electrical system

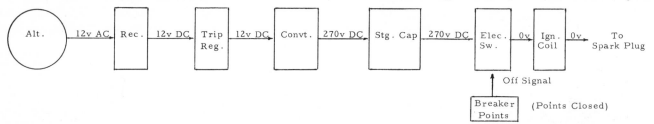

PLUGS NOT FIRING

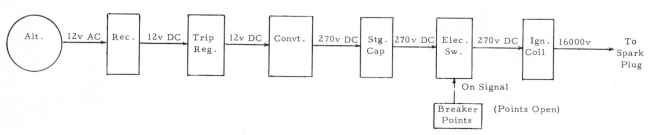

PLUGS FIRING

Figure 16.26   Block Diagram of Magnapower Ignition System

Chrysler Canada Outboard Ltd.

of the engine. Its primary function is to protect the electrical system, particularly the electronic components of the C-D unit, if the alternator output should rise to a destructively high level. Under normal conditions the trip regulator acts as a closed switch, conducting the alternator output from the rectifier to the engines electrical system. When the alternator output reaches 27 volts (plus or minus 1 volt), the trip regulator electronically switches the output to ground, thereby preventing damage to the electrical system. When the alternator output drops to a safe level the trip regulator electronically switches the power back to the engine's electrical system.

Converter and Storage Capacitor

The converter changes the 12-volt direct current to 270 volts direct current.

The 12-volt D.C. is passed through a compact, highly efficient transformer where it is stepped up approximately twenty times. The storage capacitor then stores D.C. voltage for energizing the coil to fire the spark plugs.

Breaker Points in the Electronic Switch

The breaker points, located in the distributor, act as the tiny trigger for the electronic switch. The opening and closing of the breaker points is controlled by the distributor which is mechanically linked to the engine crank shaft. This is what determines the engine timing, for example, the relationship between the position of the piston in its cylinder bore and the time when the spark plug fires. When the points are closed a signal is supplied to the electronic switch, holding it in the off position; consequently, no power is supplied to the spark plug. When the breaker points open, a signal is supplied to the electronic switch, turning it to the on position; thereby, D.C. voltage passes from the storage capacitor to the ignition coil.

Ignition Coil

The ignition coil acts, in part, as a step-up transformer. The inductive reactance (a factor that limits or resists the amount of A.C. in a coil) of the coil, in conjunction with the storage capacitor, forms a resonant circuit, which is a circuit that develops its maximum power at a specific frequency. This, along with the step-up property of the coil, converts the D.C. voltage, supplied to the coil to a high frequency 16,000 volts A.C. This high frequency burst of energy is sent to the spark plug, causing a spark inside the cylinder.

Trouble Shooting
Magnapower Ignition System

The C-D ignition unit can be field tested for proper operation without removing the system from the engine. To isolate suspected malfunctions in the ignition proceed as follows:

(1.) Turn the ignition switch to the *on* position and listen for a high pitched singing noise from the C-D unit. Its tone should be smooth and steady. Check that 12 volts D.C. are being supplied to the blue washer terminal on the C-D unit. If no voltage is present, with the ignition switch in the *on* position, the fault is in the engine electrical system rather than the C-D unit.

(2.) Turn the ignition switch to the *off* position. Set the engine controls at wide open throttle. Rotate the flywheel until the 36° mark on the flywheel aligns with the minus 6° mark on the timer pointer. Connect the circuit light between the terminal on the distributor and the ground. The circuit light should go on and off when the distributor belt is depressed and released. Note if the circuit light will not go on and off; the breaker point gap and engine timing need to be re-checked.

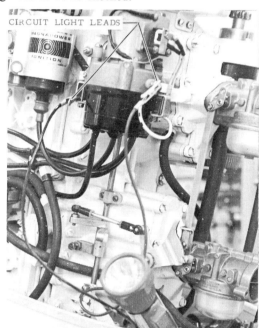

Chrysler Canada Outboard Ltd.

Figure 16.27   Connecting Circuit Light to Distributor

Turn the ignition switch to the *off* position. Remove the circuit light leads from the distributor. Remove the number one spark plug from the cylinder. Use insulated tongs to hold the spark plug.

Connect the spark plug lead wire to the number one spark plug. Hold the spark plug against an unpainted portion of the cylinder head next to the spark plug hole. Turn the ignition switch to the *on* position and depress and release the distributor belt. The spark plug should fire momentarily when the belt is depressed and released.

(3.) If no spark is observed in step 2, replace the ignition coil.

(4.) If a continuous spark is observed in step 2, replace the C-D unit.

Trip Regulator

Connect the negative lead of the circuit light to the yellow washer terminal of the trip regulator. Connect the positive lead of the circuit light to the red washer terminal of the trip regulator. The light should illuminate. If no light is observed, the trip regulator must be replaced.

The Storage Battery

The storage battery, as we know it, is classified as a secondary chemical generator. The electrical current is temporarily produced by a chemical action on two dissimilar methods when submerged in an acid solution; it is capable of being revitalized by reversal of the current through it from an outside source.

The battery's construction basically consists of a series of skeleton or grids composed on an alloy of lead and antimony on which are pressed and treated, masses of lead oxide. These, after initial charging, become sponge lead, gray in color, on the negative plate in the lead peroxide and brownish in color on the positive plate. Several of each are grouped and placed in a cell of hard rubber; the number of positive plates is determined by the capacity specified for the particular assembly with one additional negative plate. The plates are assembled in an alternative row: negative, positive, negative, positive. They are separated with sheets of corrugated wood or a special rubber construction. All positive plates are bridged to a common connector with a strap of lead across their projections for this purpose. The negative plates are similarly bridged together and the entire assembly is installed and sealed in a hard rubber container.

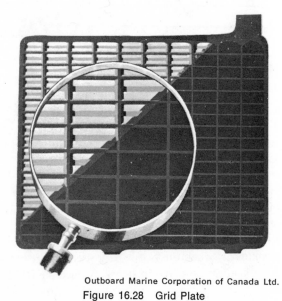

Outboard Marine Corporation of Canada Ltd.
Figure 16.28   Grid Plate

This is followed by assembling three similar assemblies in a master rubber case connected in a series (positive to negative); it is sealed and finally filled with the electrolyte (sulphuric acid and water) to make up a 6 volt chemical generator, after they are charged from an outside source. Six cells are employed in the assembly of a 12 volt battery. The voltage is pre-determined by the potential difference naturally existing between the chemical composition in the sponge lead negative and peroxide of lead in the positive and established in average storage battery assembly at about 2.1 volts per cell. Voltage is multiplied by the number of connecting individual cells in a series such as positive to negative. Therefore three cells make up approximately six volts.

Amperage is determined by the battery plate area, the size of the plates, the number included in the assembly, and the nature of the acid condition acting upon them.

Electrolyte solution acting upon the battery plates is balanced at a specific of 1.260 or 1.280 as specified by the battery manufacturer. It is a mixture of water and sulphuric acid. The density or weight of water is established as 1.000; sulphuric acid for battery use as 1.400; the weight or density of sulphuric acid is 1.4 times that of the equal volume of water. The density of a carefully prepared electrolyte is either 1.26 or 1.28 times the weight or density of water it is observed by floating a battery hydrometer bulb in a quantity of the solution.

On discharge of the battery, during the starts of the outboard engine, for example, current flows to turn the starting motor because of a chemical action of the electrolyte acting on the positive or red side and the negative gray plates. During this process, the SO_4 of the electrolyte ($H_2 SO_4$) unites with the lead element of the negative plates, and with the lead element of the positive plate to form a lead sulphate on the faces of both. The oxygen of the positive plate unites with the hydrogen liberated during the procedure of discharging to form water (H_2O). When lead sulphate accumulates on both plates to the extent that further acid penetration or contact with the lead in the lead peroxide of either plate can no longer be maintained, the battery is said to be discharged or dead. Obviously there are various degrees of discharge to be considered.

Re-charging of a normal battery activity as a chemical generator is accomplished by causing a specified current from an outside source to flow through it in an opposite direction. This outside source could be an alternator or an electrical generator run by the engine itself.

Two methods of charging mentioned above are in general use; the generator and regulator, and the alternator. The generator and regulator combination is mounted on the engine and the slow charger usually plugged into a 110 volt A.C. light supply. The engine generator produces

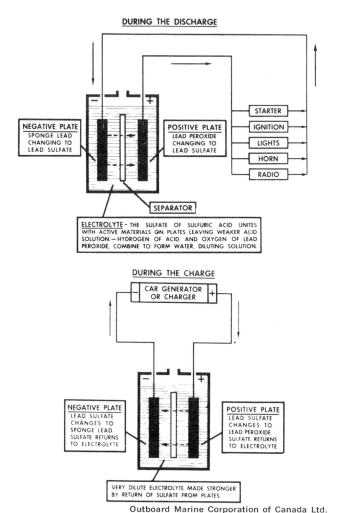

DURING THE DISCHARGE

NEGATIVE PLATE
SPONGE LEAD
CHANGING TO
LEAD SULFATE

POSITIVE PLATE
LEAD PEROXIDE
CHANGING TO
LEAD SULFATE

STARTER
IGNITION
LIGHTS
HORN
RADIO

SEPARATOR

ELECTROLYTE – THE SULFATE OF SULFURIC ACID UNITES
WITH ACTIVE MATERIALS ON PLATES LEAVING WEAKER ACID
SOLUTION. – HYDROGEN OF ACID, AND OXYGEN OF LEAD
PEROXIDE, COMBINE TO FORM WATER, DILUTING SOLUTION.

DURING THE CHARGE

CAR GENERATOR
OR CHARGER

NEGATIVE PLATE
LEAD SULFATE
CHANGES TO
SPONGE LEAD.
SULFATE RETURNS
TO ELECTROLYTE

POSITIVE PLATE
LEAD SULFATE
CHANGES TO
LEAD PEROXIDE
SULFATE RETURNS
TO ELECTROLYTE

VERY DILUTE ELECTROLYTE MADE STRONGER
BY RETURN OF SULFATE FROM PLATES.

Outboard Marine Corporation of Canada Ltd.

Figure 16.29   Condition of Battery in a Fully Charged State
Showing Current Flow on Discharge

direct current which is controlled by the regulator so that the maximum generator capacity is produced when the battery is discharged.

As the battery becomes charged, the regulator reduces the output to prevent overcharging and possible damage to the battery.

The slow charger, or external charger, converts the A.C. power supply into direct current and a rheostat is used to control the voltage and current output. An accepted practice is to start charging at a current equal to the number of positive plates per cell, and then to reduce the output when the battery is nearly charged and its temperature is rising. It is possible that damage to the battery will result if its internal temperature is allowed to rise above 125 degrees F.

With both methods of charging, it is very important that the proper polarity be maintained in the battery. When the battery is connected to an engine having a generator and a regulator, it must be connected with the nega-

tive terminal grounded; otherwise, the regulator will be damaged. A slow charger must also be properly connected or the charger will reverse the charge to the battery which will result in severe damage to the battery.

The function of re-charging, basically, is to restore the original battery by converting the positive plates from lead sulphate to peroxide of lead and the negative plates from lead sulphate to sponge lead and to restore the specific gravity of the electrolyte.

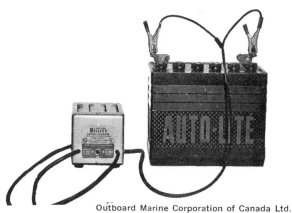

Outboard Marine Corporation of Canada Ltd.

Figure 16.30   Charging Storage Battery with One of the
Chargers Available for the Purpose

During the charging, the water in the electrolyte is split by electrolosis into hydrogen and oxygen gas, the components of its structure; the radical leaves the lead sulphate accumulated on the surface of both the positive and negative plates and unites with the liberated hydrogen to form sulphuric acid. The liberated oxygen unites with the lead of the positive plate to form peroxide of lead. The SO_4, having being liberated from the sulphated negative plate, returns to the electrolyte and leaves its sponge lead. The original state of the battery is restored.

When charging the battery, it is advisable to follow the instructions of the battery manufacturer and the manufacturer of the charging unit.

Battery Installation

Since the voltage regulator unit must be operated with the negative battery terminal connected to ground, care should be used when making the installation. After first installation the lights or the accessories are turned on and the ammeter measured, (but not a radio, if the boat is supplied with one, as the transistors will be damaged by incorrect polarity). If the ammeter indicates *charge,* either the battery or ammeter is reversed. If it indicates *discharge,* the installation is either correct or both the ammeter and battery have been reversed. If the ammeter is known by previous tests to have been properly connected, this test will quickly check the battery installations. The battery should not sit loosely in a cradle or box. The vibration will shake the heavy load plates and cause them to become notched, or it will break the connectors, as well as accelerate the normal shedding of the active materials within the battery. A hold-down clamp should be very tight to hold the battery firmly in place but should not cause distortion of the battery case itself.

The cable should be of sufficient size to carry the starting load and it should not be frayed or the cable strands broken. The terminals should be clean, tightened securely, and coated with vaseline or a mineral grease to keep corrosion to a minimum.

Occasionally when making battery or charging circuit connections the generator will become reversed-polarized. After the above ammeter check for correct battery polarity, the engine is started and operated at a fairly high speed with all accessories turned off. The ammeter should show *charge* if the engine speed is sufficient to operate the generator. If it remains at a slight discharge or vibrates excessively, it may indicate that the generator is incorrectly polarized. To polarize the generator, the engine is stopped. One end of a piece of wire is touched to the regulator terminal marked "arm" and then, momentarily, the other end touched to the regulator battery terminal. Extreme care should be taken that no connection is made between the battery and the field terminal at either the generator or regulator. Even a momentary connection will ground the battery through the regulator contacts, thereby damaging it beyond all use.

FACTS ABOUT STORAGE BATTERIES

The battery liquid level should be retained at approximately ⅜ of an inch above the top edge of the cell plates to avoid damage caused by exposure and to retain the originally specified ratio of sulphuric acid and water in the electrolyte. Distilled water is added if necessary (but never acid) to obtain the desired liquid level. In the event that the battery solution spills by accident, a local battery dealer or distributor will restore the normal acid-water balance.

The specific gravity reading by the hydrometer will be low if taken immediately after adding water. The charging should proceed for an hour to achieve a thorough circulation to the battery solution prior to taking a hydrometer reading.

Specific gravity readings vary with the existing temperature of the electrolyte. When it is relatively high, the gravity readings will be low on the hydrometer scale because of the proportionate expansion of the liquid and, therefore, high with falling temperature as a result of constant contraction. It is an accepted practice, therefore, to correct specific gravity readings to 80 degrees F. The correction factor being .004, or 4 points specific gravity

added to or subtracted from the reading taken for each 10 degrees F. above or below the established 80 degrees F.

EXAMPLE A
HYDROMETER READING	1.255
BATTERY SOLUTION	
TEMPERATURE	100 degrees F.
CORRECTION—ADD	.008
CORRECTED SPECIFIC	
GRAVITY IS	1.263

Battery solution density or specific gravity should not be permitted to fall below 1.220 when the battery is not in use to avoid the harmful effects of an excessive cell plate sulphation. It should be placed on charge before reaching a low state of discharge.

Original specific gravity specifications vary under certain conditions and as established by battery manufacturers.

			Voltage Reading Per Cell	
	Specific Gravity		1.260 Gravity	1.280 Gravity
*FULL CHARGE	1.260	1.280	2.10	2.12
¾ CHARGE	1.220	1.250	2.08	2.10
½ CHARGE	1.170	1.200	2.05	2.07
¼ CHARGE	1.120	1.150	2.02	2.04
DISCHARGED	1.070	1.100	1.98	2.00

Current trends in battery construction deviate from the familiar 1.280 specific gravity in favour of the 1.260 gravity specification for better quality batteries.

A fully charged battery is known to withstand temperatures as low as minus 90 degrees F.; a dead battery will freeze at about 10 degrees F. and may burst both the cell and battery case.

FREEZE CHART
Specific Gravity (Corrected to 80°F.)	*Freeze At*
1.280	—90°F.
1.250	—60°F.
1.200	—16°F.
1.150	+5°F.
1.100	+19°F.

Hydrometer readings should be taken of the solution in each cell every 30 days throughout the life of the battery whether it is in use or not. An open circuit volt meter may be used to test the condition of each cell with a fully re-charged battery; it should indicate 2.10 volts per cell. The battery should be placed on a charge when the specific gravity reading falls to 1.220. A hydrometer reading should not be taken immediately after adding water but only after the charging has continued for an hour to permit circulation throughout the electrolyte solution. If an

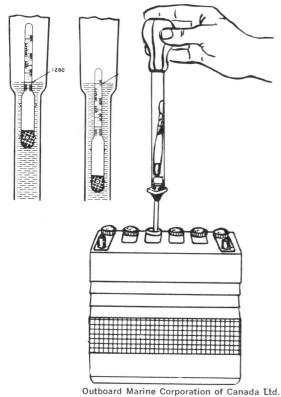

Outboard Marine Corporation of Canada Ltd.

Figure 16.31 "Taking" Specific Gravity Reading of the Battery Solution (Electrolyte) to Determine State of Charge

ed to the ratio of 1 tablespoon of baking soda to a quart of water). The posts should be scrubbed with a stiff bristle brush if necessary, and the clean surfaces smeared with vaseline to prevent further corrosion. The cell covers should be in place when using the soda solution to avoid the possibility of spilling any of it into the battery electrolyte. The soda solution should not be splashed around during this cleaning procedure. There should be a final rinse with fresh water. When replacing the battery in the spring, it should be fully charged, all terminal connections clean and a coat of vaseline applied to the exposed areas on the battery posts and clamp connectors to retard the accumulation of sulphation.

It would be wise, at this time, to check all electrical wiring harness for corrosion or breaks for necessary replacement.

Removing evidence of corrosion from battery posts and connectors with wire brush.

Swabbing battery posts and connectors with a solution of household baking soda and water to neutralize possible acid condition existing in the area. Rinse later with fresh water. Be careful not to "spill" soda solution into battery cells.

Outboard Marine Corporation of Canada Ltd.

Figure 16.32 Battery Care

open circuit volt meter is used, the battery should be recharged when the voltage of each cell falls to 2.07 volts or less.

Overcharging causes excessive gases, harmfully high shredding of the lead peroxide active material in the cell plate, and damage to the supporting grids.

A hydrogen gas is liberated from the battery cells on charge and, to a considerably lesser degree, when it is idle. This gas is very explosive and dangerous. Charging batteries should be kept away from flame, sparks and cigarettes, and there should be ample circulation of air around batteries that are in storage. If they are in a room, it is essential that ventilation be provided for sufficient circulation to guard against mishap or explosion.

If the battery is to be removed from a boat and stored, it should be placed in a room where the average temperature is not likely to fall below 32 degrees F. or to rise above 80 degrees F; preferably it should be stored in a cool temperature. Batteries in storage should never be placed near a steam pipe boiler or other heating devices, on cement floors, or in direct rays of sunlight.

It is wise to remove all evidence of corrosion from the battery posts and connectors by swabbing or scrubbing with a solution of household baking soda and water (mix-

REVIEW QUESTIONS

1. How are the points adjusted on the larger Chrysler outboard engines?
2. Why should the distributor belt not be too tight on the Chrysler outboard engine?
3. How can the output of an alternator be checked?
4. Explain how the Chrysler magnapower ignition system operates.
5. What is the purpose of the trip regulator on the magnapower ignition system?
6. How is electrical current produced in a storage battery?
7. What is an electrolyte?
8. What are the two methods of charging the storage battery?
9. How is "Polarity" insured on a charging system?
10. Explain how a battery is recharged.
11. What is the proper installation procedure for a storage battery?
12. List at least three steps that should be taken to ensure long battery life.
13. What is the specific gravity reading of a fully charged battery?
14. When should a battery be recharged?
15. How many volts should be indicated on a voltmeter when checking each battery cell?
16. Explain how a battery should be prepared for storage.
17. Why should the soda solution not mix with electrolyte when cleaning a battery?
18. How can corrosion on battery terminals be kept to a minimum?
19. What is the purpose of the coil in the magneto system?
20. Which of the two circuits contain the points and condenser?
21. List the parts that make up the magneto system assembly.
22. Name the two wiring circuits that are in the magneto assembly.
23. List the parts that make the heavy wire circuit.
24. What are the two purposes of the condenser in the ignition circuit?
25. In a paragraph, explain how the magneto system operates.
26. What could be the cause of excessive point pitting?
27. Why is it advisable to replace the condenser when replacing the the points?
28. How does the electrical circuit flow resemble the flow of water in a water system?
29. List the steps that should be taken for diagnosis of the following:
    a) Spark plugs.
    b) Spark plug leads.
    c) Breaker points.
    d) Coil.
    e) Coil heels.
    f) Wiring on the armature plate.
30. What problem could cause a weak spark if the ignition was checked and found to be in good working order?
31. Why is it not a good practice to re-dress breaker points?
32. Draw a diagram of the spark plug and label all of the parts.
33. In what way is the two-stroke spark plug different from the four-stroke spark plug?
34. Draw a diagram to show the two heat ranges of spark plugs.
35. List some of the problems that could cause pre-ignition and prepare a list of corrective repairs for these problems.
36. List reasons why a spark plug should foul.

CHAPTER 17
CARBURETION
AND FUEL SYSTEMS

To understand fully the basic carburetion of an outboard motor, we must first review the two-stroke theory.

The two-stroke engine is common to all outboard motors and differs considerably in construction and design from the familiar four-stroke engine used almost universally in all air cooled appliance installations and automotive engines.

The differences in design are due to the method of conducting fuel vapour and exhaust gases through the cycle-intake, through the compression, power, and exhaust strokes. In the two-stroke cycle engine, an automatic reed valve system and ports machined into the cylinder wall are used instead of mechanically operated poppet valves and the steps of the cycle are accomplished in the two strokes of the piston or one revolution of the crankshaft, rather than four strokes or two revolutions. The two-stroke fires each revolution and the four-stroke once every second revolution.

During the first upward stroke of the piston, negative pressure or suction is created in the crankcase, and to equalize the atmospheric and crankcase pressures, the reed valve is lifted from its seat. During the process, fuel vapour is drawn in from or through the carburetor to charge the crankcase.

As the reed automatically closes on the downward stroke, the crankcase charge is compressed, until the by-pass or intake port is uncovered by the head of the moving piston, thereby releasing the fuel charge to the bypass into the upper cylinder region. Thus the charge is directed upward to the combustion chamber by the contour of the piston deflector.

Since the bypass port is covered or closed by the piston moving upward on the succeeding stroke, the trapped fuel vapour charge, released from the crankcase during the proceed stroke, is now compressed above the piston in preparation for ignition. A second fuel vapour charge enters the crankcase at the same time.

Near the end of the compression stroke, a spark created by the magneto arcs the gap between the spark plug points, igniting the compressed fuel vapour charge. Rapid expansion of the burning vapour following ignition, forces the piston downward to develop the power impulse. The full length of the power stroke, is not, however, consumed in the developing of the power impulse. It is sometimes required to rid the cylinder of the resulting

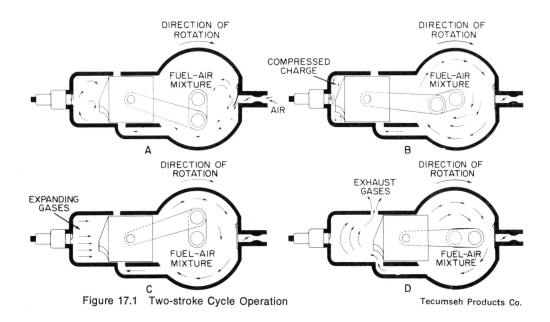

Figure 17.1   Two-stroke Cycle Operation   Tecumseh Products Co.

spent or burning gases and to receive a fresh charge from the crankcase to the next power impulse.

A close observation of the Figures above reveals that the width of the exhaust port is somewhat greater than that of the bypass port and, as such, the time of its opening significantly proceeds opening of the bypass port by the downward motion moving piston. Relatively high pressure exists within the cylinder at this time; consequently, at partial uncovering or opening of the exhaust port, the spent exhaust gases commence to flow out through the exhaust port, being directed in that direction by the gradual sloping of the piston deflecter.

Further downward progress of the piston uncovers or opens the bypass port which instantly releases the compressed fuel vapour charge now contained in the crankcase and proceeds to crowd the burning gases out of the cylinder and into the atmosphere to complete the cycle.

LUBRICATION AND FUEL BLENDING

Lubrication for outboard motors is achieved primarily through the mixing or blending of oil and gasoline at certain proportions according to the manufacturer's specifications. As such, the oil for lubrication and the gasoline for combustion flow at the same time to the carburetor. There, they are appropriately mixed with air into the crankcase in a vapour, thereafter to be compressed and transferred to the combustion chamber. The oil content performs its chore of lubricating internal moving parts after which it is dissipated by the combustion and discharge to the exhaust system.

Lubrication, to be most effective in the two stroke engine, requires just so much oil content in the fuel mix, a definite ratio of oil to gasoline. The use of too little oil obviously leads to premature wear and early breakdown. On the other hand, fuel richer in oil than recommended or demanded is not only wasteful and costly but contributes to faulty performance and, in time, to expensive corrective measures because of the disturbing effects of excessive carbon accumulation which follow. A frequent occurrence of spark plug changes may similarly be traced to too much oil in the fuel mixture.

Most outboard engineering departments have, after long research and evaluation, developed a ratio by volume of one part of oil to twenty-four parts of gasoline best suited for the efficient lubrication of outboard motors and economy of the operation. The ratio of 1:24 is equivalent to 1/3 of a pint to 1 gallon or 1 quart in each 6 gallons of fuel.

The operator's best assurance of maintaining a correct fuel mix ratio is through the use of a 1:24 premix from dealers dispensing a high quality outboard oil (SAE 30) and non-premium gasoline.

Instructions relating to the mixing of fuel as otherwise published in the operator's manual and provided with each new motor shipped from the outboard factories are clear, recommending a mix of 1/3 of a pint of high quality outboard oil SAE 30 to each gallon of gasoline or one quart to each 6 gallons, the ratio in which either event is 1:24. Care, nevertheless, should be exercised during each refill to make certain that the recommended 1:24 ratio spread is being constantly maintained at all times for the best results. There is an exception to this rule; some of the newest motors now use a ratio of 1:50.

It is of utmost importance that oil grade and amounts specified be thoroughly mixed with gasoline to assure efficient lubrication and operation of the motor throughout its operating RPM range. In a proper mix or blend, approximately a gallon of gasoline is poured in the tank with the required amount of oil and the tank shaken briskly for a minute or two to ensure complete blending and then the remaining gasoline poured to fill the container or tank. The tank is again rocked back and forth several times for a full blend.

Unless the oil and gasoline are properly mixed, it is possible to operate first in an excessively oil rich blend which causes smoking and sluggish performance. The oil is heavier and tends to linger near the lower part of the tank, to be first used. The remaining fuel mix is obviously not rich enough in oil to achieve ample lubrication. Overheating, perhaps seizure and premature wear follows.

Many ills costly to the operator can be laid to careless blending of fuel mix during seasonal operation. Every possible effort should accordingly be made to avoid them by adhering strictly to the desired recommendations of the outboard engine manufacturer. These factory recommendations provide for the best performance, uninterrupted boating, prolonged spark life and economy in operation.

Every tune up or repair should among other things include: draining the operator's fuel tank of its old fuel; replacing these with a new 1:24 fuel mix (or as the manufacturer's specifications outline); a word of advice to the operator recommending the use of a reliable 1:24 premix during future refills where and whenever available and caution in obtaining manually blended refills; encouragement to use a precise 1:24 or 1:50 ratio of high quality outboard oil and premium gasoline. The compression ratio is not high enough to warrant the use of gasoline containing a lead coloured ethyl to overcome certain combustion characteristics, common to high compression, high speed engines. However, most gasolines now on the market contain a type of ethyl lead in various quantities; it can be used, but it is advisable to adhere to gasoline with minimum lead content.

Due to atmospheric conditions and temperature changes, moisture condensation is more or less continually taking place within the gas tank. This results in water droplets accumulating in the tank, gas line and carburetor which, if excessive, are sufficient to interfere with the performance of the engine, causing it to act in many instances as though it were starving for gasoline. Water will not pass through the fine screens and the small carburetor jets. The fuel system must be free of moisture. All fuel should be poured into the tank through a fine filter if possible.

BASIC CARBURETION

All gasoline-operated engines are of the internal combustion type; that is, the fuel mixture is ignited and burned within the cylinder.

The fuel, gasoline and air must be prepared or mixed for combustion by an outside device. This simple device is merely a mixing valve or carburetor. Air and gasoline must be mixed in certain proportions to provide a combustible vapour, roughly one part of gasoline to eight or eleven parts of air. Too much or too little of either gasoline or air affects the combustible quality of the vapourized fuel, and the performance of the engine. An arrangement is thus required to meter the amount of gasoline flowing into a stream of air that is created by the suction in the cylinder of the engine, as the piston progresses in its downward stroke.

This is carried out in a somewhat different manner, however, in a two stroke engine. The suction is created in the *crankcase* in the upward stroke of the piston. The air must be in motion to vapourize the gasoline.

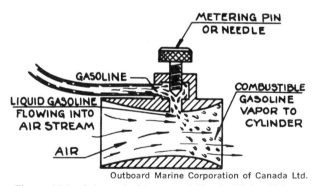

Outboard Marine Corporation of Canada Ltd.

Figure 17.2   Schematic Diagram of Simple Mixing Valve

The simple mixing valve consists of a venturi to which is attached a metering pin which is threaded to permit variations in metering the flow of gasoline into the air stream. It can be readily seen from the above figure that the more the metering idle is open, the more will be the amount of liquid gasoline flowing into the air stream to be vapourized. The vapour thus becomes rich in gasoline. If excessively rich, partial combustion results in the cylinder from the insufficient supply of air and this produces a sluggish operation of the engine. On the other hand, the

more the metering needle is turned down, the less the amount of liquid gasoline flowing into the air stream. The vapour then becomes lean in gasoline and this results in a slow burning fuel charge, evident by the loss of power and faulty operation of the engine.

The mixing valve is the simplest form of carburetion for practical purposes. While suitable under certain conditions, it is not adaptable to variable speed engines as in the case of an outboard motor. Some arrangements must be made to maintain constant fuel level in proportion to the speed at which the engine is running to realize the proper fuel-air ratio at the various speeds once the metering needle is correctly set. This is accomplished by the addition of the float chamber.

The float chamber, or float bowl as it is sometimes called, consists of a bowl or cavity large enough to contain a float, usually a cork or a hollow cylinder constructed of thin brass sheet. It is closed at both ends to permit it to float in a liquid (gasoline in the case of the carburetor). The purpose of the float is to maintain a pre-determined level of gasoline in the carburetor by operating a valve (float valve) in the float chamber. Where a cork float is used, operation of the float valve is by direct connection or, more frequently, by a lever arrangement.

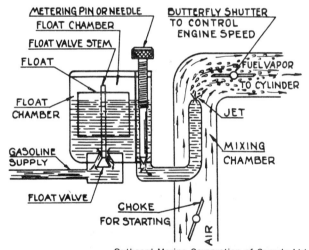

Outboard Marine Corporation of Canada Ltd.

Figure 17.3   Simple Float Feed Carburetor

Naturally, with no gasoline in the float bowl, the float comes to rest at the bottom of the bowl, and opens the float valve to permit the flow of gasoline. As gasoline flows into the bowl, the float rises to decrease gradually the flow of gasoline by closing the float valve to a point where the maximum level is reached when the float valve closes entirely to shut off the flow of gasoline. As gasoline is used, the float settles to permit an additional flow of gasoline into the float chamber. This is in proportion to the rate of consumption by the running engine. The faster the engine runs, the greater is the fuel consumption;

therefore, the float settles deeper in the bowl to increase the flow of gasoline through the greater opening of the float valve. As the engine speed is decreased, fuel consumption is lessened and the float will rise to decrease the flow of gasoline. When the engine is stopped, there is no fuel consumption. The float rises to the maximum level and closes the float valve to stop the flow of gasoline.

To obtain variable speed performance from any gasoline-operated engine, some means must be provided to control the charge admitted into the cylinder. The larger the charge, the faster the engine runs. Conversely, the lesser the charge, the slower the engine runs. Spark timing naturally must be considered at this point since the degree of spark advance is in relation to the fuel charge and engine speed. Engine speed, as far as the carburetor is concerned, is controlled by a damper or shutter plate built into the mixing chamber in such a manner that it can be manually opened or closed at will to increase or decrease speed as desired. A full open shutter prevents maximum vapour charge from being drawn into the cylinder, thus maximum engine power for top speed performance. Various degrees of opening of the shutter plate results in various engine speeds since the degree of opening governs the charge to the cylinder.

Since a comparatively rich fuel mixture is required for starting a cold engine, a second shutter (a choke) is built into the mixing chamber forward of the gasoline jet to restrict the flow of air to the mixing chamber. This creates a high suction at the jet, causing proportionally more liquid gasoline to flow into the air stream as required for starting. On the starting of the engine, the choke is gradually opened as the engine temperature rises until the opened position is reached for normal operation. The en-

gine runs at its proper ratio of gasoline and air for maximum efficient performance.

To obtain greater flexibility of engine speed, a second jet is inserted into the mixing chamber to provide more efficient carburetion at slow and intermediate speeds. This jet is usually placed slightly forward of the closing position of the shutter plate and arranged to function at the near closed position of the shutter when the air velocity over the high speed jet is not sufficient to properly vapourize the gasoline. Comparatively high velocity of air over the slow speed jet at the near closed position of the shutter plate causes the gasoline to be vapourized for slow speed performance. As the shutter is opened, the engine picks up speed with the result that the slow speed jet becomes proportionally less effective since the velocity of air through the mixing chamber becomes great enough for gasoline at the high speed jet to vapourize. Vapourization at the slow speed jet gradually diminishes as the shutter plate opens for maximum power but becomes effective again as the shutter plate closes and the engine speed decreases. In this simple arrangement the engine operates entirely on vapourization at the slow speed jet when the shutter is set for slow engine speed.

CARBURETOR ADJUSTMENTS JOHNSON MOTORS

Carburetor Model JW

The carburetor on the Model JW is similar to that employed on other Models in that it is a float feed two-jet type, consisting of a mixing chamber and conventional float chamber. Two adjustments are provided; namely, for high and slow speed performance.

Induction to the crankcase similarly is by means of an

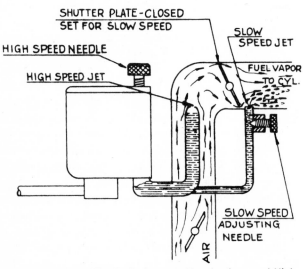

Figure 17.4 Simple Carburetor Showing Low and High Speed Operation

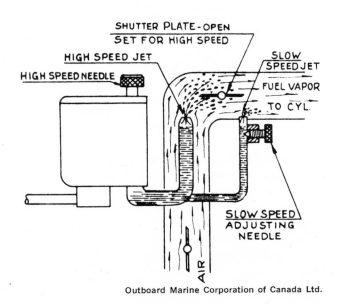

Outboard Marine Corporation of Canada Ltd.

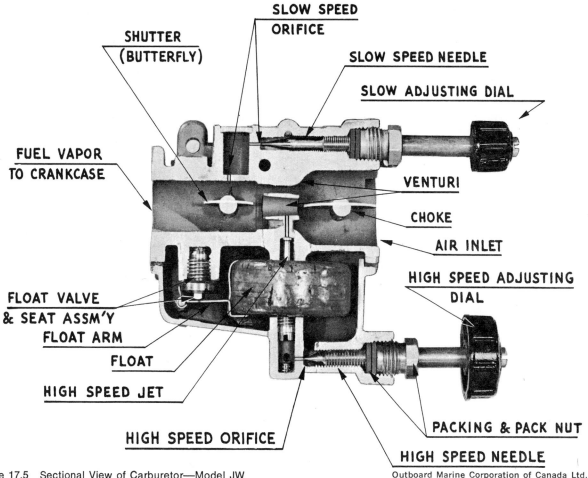

SLOW SPEED
ORIFICE

SHUTTER
(BUTTERFLY)

SLOW SPEED NEEDLE

SLOW ADJUSTING DIAL

FUEL VAPOR
TO CRANKCASE

VENTURI

CHOKE

AIR INLET

HIGH SPEED ADJUSTING
DIAL

FLOAT VALVE
& SEAT ASSM'Y
FLOAT ARM

FLOAT

HIGH SPEED JET

HIGH SPEED ORIFICE

PACKING & PACK NUT

HIGH SPEED NEEDLE

Figure 17.5   Sectional View of Carburetor—Model JW

Outboard Marine Corporation of Canada Ltd.

automatic intake valve situated between the carburetor and crankcase which functions in accordance with the changes in the crankcase pressure as the pistons travel up and down to complete the cycle.

A

C

B

Illustrating the Model JW Automatic Valve Assembly
Including (a) Valve Plate, (b) Automatic Valve,
and (c) Automatic Valve Back-up Plate.

Outboard Marine Corporation of Canada Ltd.

Figure 17.6   Reed Plate

The automatic intake valve is not made up of several segments, as in the case of Models QD and RD, but of a single strip—one for each crankcase chamber.

CARBURETOR CONTROL (SPEED) ADJUSTMENT

Since the gas and spark are synchronized to permit a consistent performance throughout the entire speed range of the motor by correctly proportioning the volume of the fuel charge with respect to the degree of spark advance, some adjustment is required to gain end results.

Synchronizing is accomplished by means of a cam, cam follower and linkage arrangement. The cam is attached to the armature plate and moves with it as the spark is advanced. At retard spark, the cam follower rides on the low end of the cam to result in a partial opening of the carburetor shutter. With an advance of the spark, the follower progresses toward the high end of the cam—a greater opening of the carburetor shutter to permit a larger charge of fuel vapour and a subsequent increase in power and speed.

Some adjustment is required to properly synchronize the carburetor. A checklist is provided below.

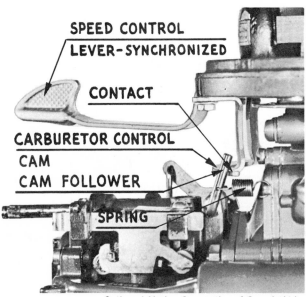

SPEED CONTROL
LEVER-SYNCHRONIZED

CONTACT

CARBURETOR CONTROL
CAM
CAM FOLLOWER

SPRING

Outboard Marine Corporation of Canada Ltd.
Figure 17.7   Speed Control Synchronizing

(1.) Loosen screws slightly at both ends of the speed control cam (on the underside of the armature plate).

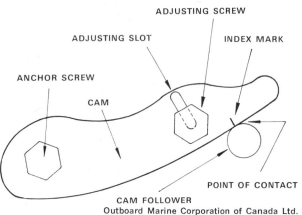

ADJUSTING SCREW

ADJUSTING SLOT   INDEX MARK

ANCHOR SCREW

CAM

POINT OF CONTACT

CAM FOLLOWER
Outboard Marine Corporation of Canada Ltd.
Figure 17.8   Cam Follower Parts

(2.) Move the speed control lever to a position between the embossings on the gas tank bracket as indicated by the dotted line in the illustration.

(3.) Note line stamped on top side of the control cam. With the speed control lever set in the position described above, move the free end of the cam out until it makes contact with the cam follower (but only after slack in the linkage has been taken up) at the point of index mark.

(4.) Draw up on both screws holding the cam to the armature plate to secure them in this position.

CARBURETOR ADJUSTMENT

The carburetor, the two-jet (float feed) type, is designed for maximum efficient carburetion at all speeds. Two adjustments are thus required; namely, high and slow speed. Both high and slow speed needles are adjusted at the fac-

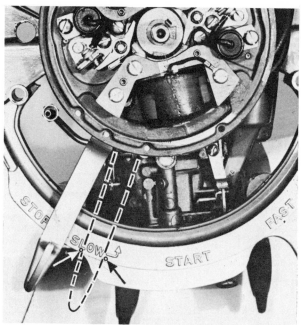

Outboard Marine Corporation of Canada Ltd.
Figure 17.9   Speed Control Lever

tory with provisions for limited variations to compensate for atmospheric conditions. However, if ultimate adjustment does not fall within the limited range or in case of repairs, proceed as follows:

(1) Loosen, but do not remove, screws in the centre of the slow and high speed dials. (Dials are held firmly in position on their respective adjusting needle shaft by the expansion of the slotted serrated ends as a result of drawing up on the counter-sunk head screws.)

(2) Pull the dials out until the limiting stops on dial (back side) clear the stop cast onto the motor cover. The dial is now free to be turned beyond the normal limited range: tighten the centre screws to secure to the needle shafts.

(3) Carefully turn both dials to the right, to the position where the adjusting needles come to rest gently on their seats. Be careful not to injure the seats by turning them down too tightly. Then back off (turn left) the slow speed dial approximately one full turn and the high speed dial about ¾ of a turn.

SLOW SPEED ADJUSTMENT

The motor is started as instructed and run at fast speed until the normal operating temperature has been reached. The throttle is set down to the slow speed range. The dial is turned right or left as required to obtain the best setting for slow speed.

Turning needles to the left enriches the fuel mixture. It increases the proportion of fuel to air to result in a rich mixture. An excessively rich mixture is indicated by rough running of the motor. Spitting or coughing in the carburetor is indicative of a lean mixture, caused by turning the needle too far to the right.

The centre screw is loosened to arrange the dial properly, without disturbing the position of the slow speed needle. Should the dial tend towards binding on the needle shaft, it may become necessary to pull it free entirely to permit rearranging of its position withot affecting the adjustment of the needle at this time. The dial is set to the position where the pointer is directed to numeral 4, and pushed back onto the shaft to clear the motor cover by approximately 3/32″, which should be sufficient to engage the limitation stop on the cover. The centre screw is firmly tightened to secure the dial. Atmospheric conditions may necessitate slight variations from time to time. The limited range now available should be sufficient.

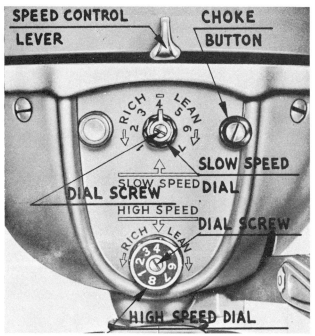

Outboard Marine Corporation of Canada Ltd.
Figure 17.10   Carburetor Control Panel

HIGH SPEED ADJUSTMENT
This must be performed only after the final slow speed adjustment has been made. The dial is turned left or right as required to obtain the best setting for top speed performance and the dial numbers rearranged as described above. Number 4 should be directed up.

Carburetor - Models CD and AD
Carburetion built into the Model CD and AD assembly is identical in principle to that used in the JW, QD and RD. Except for minor details in construction, their functioning is similar. They employ two carburetor adjustments to achieve efficient carburetion throughout the entire speed range of the motor (high and slow speed), a reed type of fuel vapour intake valve to the crankcase, a synchronized shutter control, a manually operated choke and a fuel filter attached as an integral part of the carburetor float

body casting. Fuel is supplied by means of pressurizing the tank.

CARBURETOR INSTALLATION
Illustrated in Fig. 17-12 is a back view of the intake manifold showing oil return channels leading into the manifold proper. Here, oil returning from the upper and centre bearings enters the fuel-vapour stream to be conducted into the crankcase chambers.

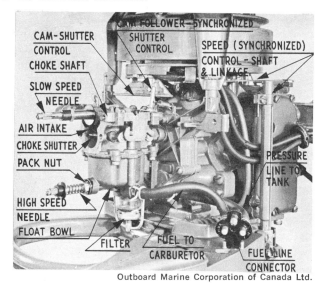

Outboard Marine Corporation of Canada Ltd.
Figure 17.11   Fuel Throttle Operation

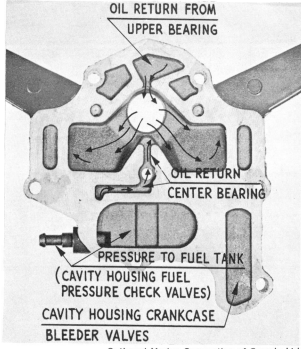

Outboard Marine Corporation of Canada Ltd.
Figure 17.12   Crankcase Bleeder Valve

Shown also are cavities that house the fuel pressure check valves and crankcase bleeder valves.

Shown here are the carburetor and intake manifold (de-

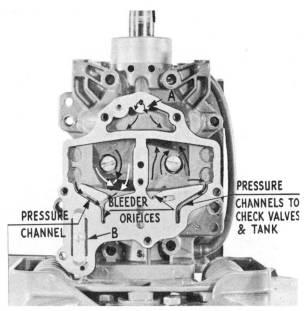

Outboard Marine Corporation of Canada Ltd.

Figure 17.13   Bleeder Operation

tached to expose the valve plate). The reed (automatic intake) valves and check valves release crankcase pressure to the tank and the crankcase bleeder valve arrangement is employed for escape of heavy fuel vapour ends which settle out during slow speed running of the motor.

The small arrows, A, indicate the oil return from the upper journal bearing where it flows through a corresponding hole in the valve plate to enter the fuel-vapor stream flowing through the intake manifold, re-entering the crankcase for further use.

The spark and gas are synchronized by means of a cam

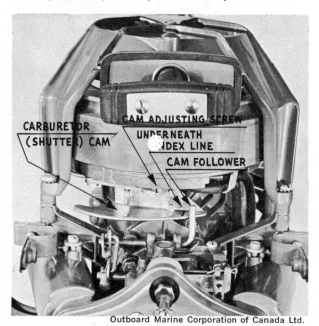

Outboard Marine Corporation of Canada Ltd.

Figure 17.14   Throttle and Cam Follower

and linkage arrangement for best motor performance. Some adjustment may be required. There is an index line cast onto the cam and spring loaded cam follower. When properly adjusted the cam follower should contact the contour of the cam at the point of the index line, but only after the slack in the linkage has been taken up with the carburetor shutter just on the verge of opening. In any adjustments, the adjusting screw under the armature plate is slightly loosened and the hole in the cam is elongated. The low end of the cam is moved in or out as required to achieve the correct indexing or contact of the cam follower, and the adjusting screw retightened. The carburetor shutter is closed when the follower rides on the low end of the cam and open at the high end for maximum speed.

Maintaining the correct fuel level in the float bowl is important to proper functioning of the carburetor throughout the speed range of the motor. Since the fuel level is controlled by the cork float acting on the float valve, some adjustment may be required on the cork float. The fuel level is correct when the top face of the float comes to rest flush with the face of the carburetor body when it is turned upside-down.

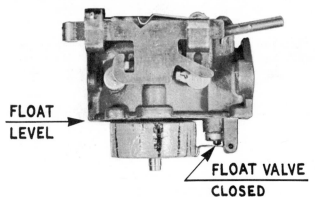

Outboard Marine Corporation of Canada Ltd.

Figure 17.15   Float Operation

If the float is too high or too low, the float arm is carefully bent up or down as required to obtain the position indicated by the arrow. A float level set too high causes overflowing, dripping of the carburetor or a sluggish motor operation; a level set too low results in faulty operation and, in extreme instances, spitting back through the carburetor.

In either case, the carburetor needle adjustment has little effect.

The filter assembly is attached to the carburetor float bowl. To clean it, nut A is loosened and the supporting bracket swung aside to permit removal of the filter bowl, B. The screw C is removed to free filter element D for cleaning which is then washed with clean gasoline of foreign accumulation in its vessel. The assembly is re-

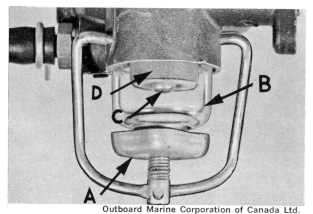

Outboard Marine Corporation of Canada Ltd.
Figure 17.16   Fuel Filter

placed in the reverse order and the condition of the filter bowl gasket checked at this time to ensure against fuel seepage later. A new gasket is installed if necessary.

CARBURETOR ADJUSTMENT—SLOW AND HIGH SPEEDS

Both high and slow speed needles are adjusted at the factory on final assembly and testing, with a limited range provided for further adjustment to compensate for local operating conditions such as temperature, atmospheric pressure and humidity. These conditions frequently require slight variations in needle settings. A boss or stop is cast on the carburetor panel and a similar arrangement cast on the back or inside of the slow speed adjusting knob. These permit somewhat more than a half turn of the knob as required to achieve the best performance. There is a pointer on the knob and numbers 1 to 7 on the control panel.

Similar provisions are made for compensating the adjustment of the high speed needle, except that the limiting stops for the high speed adjusting lever are built into the cover. It has numerals 1 to 7 and any adjusting is limited to less than a half turn.

If the carburetor has been taken apart for cleaning or repairs, a primary or initial adjustment will be required for both high and slow speed needles. This is best accomplished with the motor cover removed. A checklist is outlined below:

(1.) The slow speed knob and high speed lever are made fast to their respective needles by means of serrations on the slotted end of the needle which are expanded when the taper headed screw is drawn up. Remove both screws to gain access to the slot at the extreme end of each needle.

(2.) Insert a screw driver bit into the slotted end of the high speed needle and turn it right to close it until the face of the pointed needle rests gently on its seat in the carburetor body. Do not turn it down tightly or the face of the needle will score and the seat will expand or distort after which further adjustment becomes impossible. Then turn left or unscrew it approximately $\frac{1}{2}$ turn for high speed.

(3.) Perform the same function on the slow speed needle but open or unscrew it about $1\frac{1}{8}$ turn.

(4.) Attach the test wheel and start and run the motor in a test tank until the normal running temperature has been attained.

(5.) Turn the high speed needle right or left as required to obtain the best setting for maximum performance.

(6.) Reduce the motor speed toward an idling position.

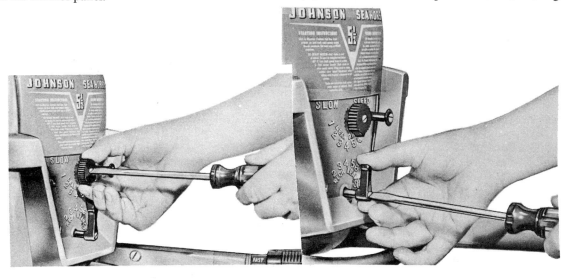

ILLUSTRATION 1   ILLUSTRATION 2

Figure 17.17   (1) Adjusting Position of Slow Speed Dial
(2) Adjusting Position of High Speed Lever

Outboard Marine Corporation of Canada Ltd.

Turn the slow speed needle right or left as required to obtain a smooth operation in the lower speed range. Further retard the motor speed. Adjust its position in a similar manner for best performance. Repeat the operation until the best setting for maximum slow speed running has been accomplished.

NOTE—a rough or jumpy running of the motor denotes an excessively rich carburetor mixture. Turning the needle adjusting valve to the right reduces the flow of liquid fuel into the carburetor air stream and leans the fuel vapor mixture. Turning it left increases the flow of liquid fuel to a correspondingly richer mixture.

(7.) Re-check both needle settings to ensure the best performance.

(8.) Without disturbing the position of the slow speed needle, install the slow speed knob over the protruding serrated end with its pointer directed toward number 5. Insert and draw up snugly on the taper headed screw provided for the purpose.

(9.) Locate the position of the high speed needle lever as described above with the lever directed toward number 4.

(10.) Make certain the taper headed screws are drawn up securely to hold the knob and lever on their respective needles.

Carburetion - Basic Models QD and FD

The Model QD is a two port, two-stroke engine, relying on the use of an automatic leaf valve for crankcase induction. As suction is created by upward movement of the piston to result in low crankcase pressure, the leaf valve is forced off its seat due to higher pressure without and comparatively low pressure within the crankcase. This causes an air stream to flow through the carburetor mixing chamber and the resultant fuel vapor to flow into the crankcase, thus charging the crankcase. Crankcase suction diminishes as the piston reaches the top of its stroke. The leaf valve then springs back against its seat to seal the crankcase. The charge in the crankcase is compressed on the following downward movement of the piston. Crankcase pressure builds up until the head of the piston uncovers the transfer or intake port in the wall of the cylinder when the compressed vapour charge in the crankcase discharges into the cylinder.

Actually, the automatic leaf valve consists of several leaves or segments arranged in daisy petal fashion anchored in the centre position to a plate drilled with corresponding holes to complete the valve assembly. There is one assembly for each crankcase chamber. The plate, of course, must be flat and true to maintain a tight seal with the surface of the leaf. A guide is attached to the assembly to limit the movement of each segment. Naturally, all leaves or segments lift from their respective seats simultaneously to admit fuel vapor into the crankcase

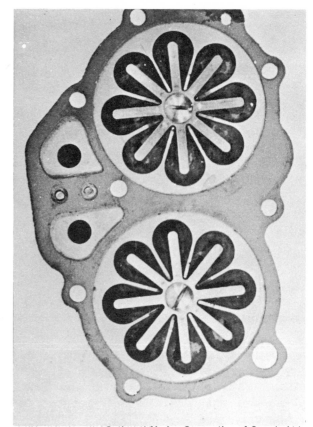

Outboard Marine Corporation of Canada Ltd.

Figure 17.18   Leaf Plate Assembly—Side Opening Into Crankcase

when there is sufficient suction and close together as suction diminishes. The leaves open into the crankcase. Leaf plate is constructed of specially heat-treated beryllium copper or plated steel. Under no circumstances, should the leaves be bent or flexed by hand. In such an event, they are rendered unfit for use and should be discarded.

The automatic leaf valve, in this case, replaces the third port or rotary valve employed in older models. It is automatic in that it does not open until sufficient low pressure is built up in the crankcase to overcome the leaf tension pre-established by special heat treatment of the material of which it is constructed. The degree of leaf opening depends upon the crankcase pressure which varies with the rate of speed at which the motor is operating. Such action results in a more satisfactory performance throughout the entire speed range of the motor. Both the third port and rotary valve open to the same degree regardless of motor speed, while the automatic leaf valve opens only in proportion to the demand at various motor speeds, thus acting more efficiently.

The carburetor is of the float feed two-jet type consisting of a mixing chamber with an integral intake manifold and conventional float chamber to which are added synchro and speed limitation control mechanisms as re-

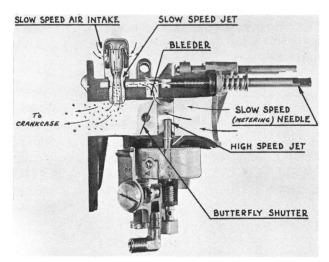

Figure 17.19 Mixing Chamber—Slow Speed

quired for gear shift. Two adjustments are provided; namely, the high and slow speed performance.

The Figure above illustrates the action of the carburetor during slow speed performance of the motor. The butterfly shutter is closed to permit very little air to flow through the mixing chamber except for a small stream entering the bleeder opening. The high suction created in the crankcase at this time causes the air to enter through the slow speed jet at a high velocity. The area of the jet is comparatively small. Air velocity is further increased by the venturi as can be seen in the sectional view. This subsequently results in partly vapourised fuel flowing through the several small holes in the slow stream jet to mix with the high velocity air stream for the fuel vapour essential to combustion.

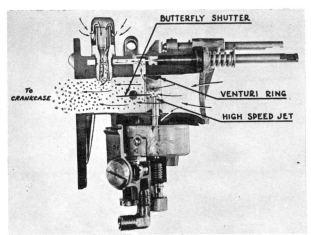

Figure 17.20 Mixing Chamber—High Speed

The sectional view in Figure 17-20 shows the action of a carburetor during top speed performance of the motor. The butterfly is full open to permit a maximum flow of air through the mixing chamber. The velocity through the

mixing chamber at this time is comparatively high but proportionally diminishes with the closing of the butterfly shutter as motor speed reduces. To obtain the maximum air velocity required for maximum fuel vaporization in the area of the high speed jet, a venturi ring has been installed. A cross section of the venturi indicates a rather abrupt but curving constriction on the leading side, gradually tapering to full diameter on the trailing side to result in maximum air velocity in the jet area, and in maximum fuel vapourization.

High and slow speed jets do not function independently of one another; however, maximum vapourization occurs only at the slow speed jet when the butterfly shutter is closed for slow speed motor operation. Vapourization at the slow speed jet decreases in proportion to the butterfly shutter opening. Conversely, vapourization at the high speed jet proportionately increases until the open position of the butterfly shutter has been reached and results in maximum vapourization. The slow speed jet then functions in various degrees throughout the entire speed range of the motor. The high speed jet remains idle when the butterfly shutter is closed for slow speed motor performance.

TO ADJUST HIGH SPEED NEEDLE: A CHECKLIST

The high speed needle is initially adjusted at the factory, but provisions are made for limited adjustment to compensate for variations apt to be encountered during normal operation of the motor. If the restricted range of adjustment is not sufficient to obtain proper high speed needle setting, proceed as follows:

(1) Start the motor, set the shift lever to the forward position and allow it to run at top speed until normal operating temperatures reached. Turn the high speed

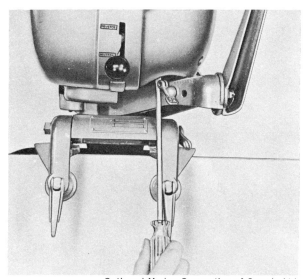

Figure 17.21 Adjusting High Speed Needle

needle knob to the right or left as required to obtain maximum performance. This adjustment should be performed only with the control speed lever set for top speed.

(2) Loosen the screw holding the bell crank fast to the high speed needle.

(3) The end of the high speed needle is slotted to accommodate screw driver bit.

(4) Start and operate the motor on fast speed until normal temperature is obtained. Set the high speed adjusting knob to centre position with the arrow down, and hold in this position.

(5) Insert a screwdriver through the port in the side cover to engage the high speed needle.

(6) Turn the high speed needle left or right as required to obtain the maximum speed or the best running position (left, to enrich mixture—right, to lean it out).

(7) While still holding the high speed needle, adjust the adjusting knob in the centre position and tighten the screw in the bell crank to secure it.

TO ADJUST SLOW SPEED NEEDLE: A CHECKLIST

(1) Move the control speed lever to a slow range position.

(2) While operating it in the slow speed range, turn the slow speed needle right or left as required to obtain satisfactory slow speed performance. Move the control lever farther left to retard the motor speed further.

(3) Reset the slow speed needle as required to obtain a smooth operation left to enrich the fuel mixture—right for a lean mixture .

(4) An excessively rich mixture is indicated by a rough running of the motor. Spitting or coughing in a carburetor is indicative of a lean mixture.

The high speed needle may require further attention on the final adjustment of the slow speed needle. Proceed as above in this event.

TO ADJUST FLOAT LEVEL

It may become necessary to adjust the float level, a possibility that might result from an attempt to install the float bowl which has thrown it slightly out of adjustment. The float bowl assembly is turned upside down and a straight edge placed across the edge of the bowl. The float level is correct when the top face of the cork float comes to rest flush with the edge of the bowl. If it falls below the level edge of the bowl when in an upside down position, the fuel level is too high and the float bowl overflows and drips. Dripping from the float bowl may also be caused by a loose fitting or otherwise impaired float valves and seat assembly. This assembly must be secure in the float bowl.

If the top surface of the float fails to reach a position flush with the straight edge, the fuel level will be too low and the carburetor is starving, particularly at high speed.

To correct the float level the float arm is carefully bent as required to obtain a proper setting. There must be no binding; the float must function freely to obtain maximum carburetor performance.

SPEED CONTROL

Since the spark and carburetor shutter control are synchronized, the motor speed is controlled by the movement of the speed control lever—slow at the left and progressively faster as the lever is moved to the right.

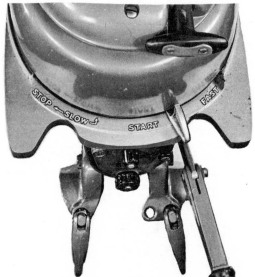

Outboard Marine Corporation of Canada Ltd.
Figure 17.23   Speed Control Lever on Panel

Model QD 15 Carburetor

The carburetor employed in the assembly of the Model QD 15 differs somewhat in design and construction from those of earlier models in that the familar primer has been omitted and replaced with a spring loaded hand choke for simplification and ease of starting. Otherwise the principles of operation are very similar, embodying slow and high speed carburetion.

Since a motor running in the slower speed range ope-

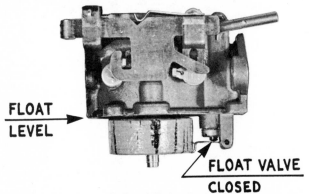

FLOAT LEVEL →

FLOAT VALVE CLOSED

Outboard Marine Corporation of Canada Ltd.
Figure 17.22   Position of Float when Properly Adjusted

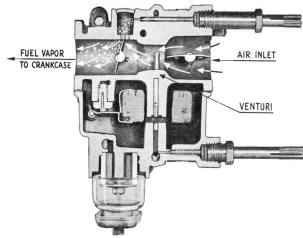

Outboard Marine Corporation of Canada Ltd.

Figure 17.24 Mixing Chamber Slow Speed

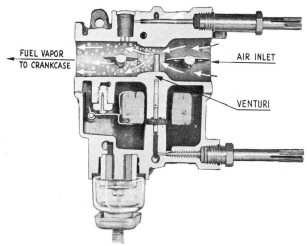

Outboard Marine Corporation of Canada Ltd.

Figure 17.25 Mixing Chamber High Speed

At this stage vaporization at the slow speed orifices diminishes since manifold suction is not great enough to maintain the high fuel level required for vaporization in the slow speed range. However, the velocity of air flowing through the carburetor at this time is considerably increased by the choking or restricting effect of the venturi into which the high speed jet is inserted.

The resultant high velocity air stream flowing or passing over the high speed jet in the venturi causes the liquid fuel to raise to a point of overflow when it mixes or vaporizes in the rapidly moving air.

Since the rate of liquid fuel flow from the high speed jet increases out of proportion with the increase of air velocity through the carburetor as the motor speed increases, some provisions must be taken to equalize or proportion the rate of liquid flow with the velocity of the air stream. This is usually accomplished by bleeding—that is, by interjecting air into the high speed jet at desired levels to reduce progressively the liquid flow as air velocity increases. A decrease in motor speed obviously produces lower air velocity through the carburetor and subsequently lowers the effect of air bleeding to increase proportionately the flow of liquid fuel and, therefore, to maintain a more favourable balance in fuel-air ratio.

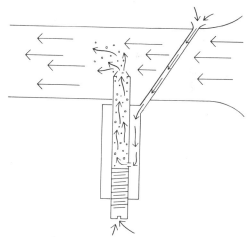

Outboard Marine Corporation of Canada Ltd.

Figure 17.26 Carburetor Operation

As the motor speed drops, the shutter is closed to build up high suction in the manifold while simultaneously diminishing the air velocity through the carburetor. This increased suction or low pressure in the manifold causes fuel vaporization to be resumed in the slow speed vaporizing area while vaporization at the high speed jet proportionately disappears.

Both slow and high speed metering needles must be adjusted separately to realize maximum performance.

The choke is spring loaded to avoid choking or flooding during the initial period of starting. The choke remains

rates with the carburetor shutter closed or nearly closed, suction at the intake manifold side is sufficient to lift liquid higher than normally maintained. With the float in the float bowl, it reaches the slow speed mixing or vapourization area at the top side of the carburetor. Here, the liquid fuel is metered by adjustment of the slow speed needle to obtain a combustible vapour mixture as it enters the air stream.

With low pressure suction in the manifold during the periods of slow operation, the velocity of the air rushing through the small gap on the top side of the shutter is considerably increased. Thus the liquid fuel flowing from the small orifices in the immediate area is thoroughly vapourized.

As the motor speeds up, the degree of shutter opening suction in the manifold is progressively reduced while the velocity and volume of the air flowing through the carburetor's throat is increased.

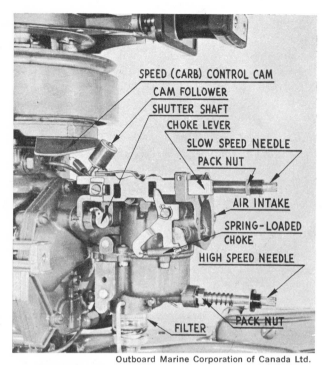

SPEED (CARB) CONTROL CAM
CAM FOLLOWER
SHUTTER SHAFT
CHOKE LEVER
SLOW SPEED NEEDLE
PACK NUT
AIR INTAKE
SPRING-LOADED CHOKE
HIGH SPEED NEEDLE
PACK NUT
FILTER

Outboard Marine Corporation of Canada Ltd.

Figure 17.27   Carburetor Mounted on Power Head

closed for starting but, as running commences, the choke opens against the tension of the spring applied to it, thus admitting sufficient air to maintain a combustionable vapour mixture in the crankcase. Choking naturally ought to be released from its gross position.

Ordinarily, the carburetor does not require a great deal of attention except for periodic cleaning and removel of gum deposits. Obviously, all sludge or foreign matter should be removed and all channels, jets, and orifices freed of it. If there is gum or varnish accumulation, it may be removed by emersion in one of the commercial solvents available for the purpose. However, before the gum is removed, the cork float is removed to avoid dissolving the coating applied to it and to ensure its buoyancy.

Constant flooding or overflowing can be traced to an improperly adjusted float level, a faulty float, a faulty float valve and seat, and a float valve seat not made properly secured in the carburetor body. Seepage goes past the threads in this case to by-pass the float valve assembly.

Under no circumstances should either the slow or high speed needles ever be turned hard against the respective needle point seats. In this event, not only the pointed metering end of the needle becomes ringed or grooved but its seat in the carburetor becomes distorted or expanded after which further adjustment is impossible. Adjusting needles can be replaced at very little cost but ruined needle seats in the carburetor body must be replaced and are very expensive.

Naturally, all screws should be tight, gaskets in a good

condition and the carburetor securely mounted to the crankcase.

In extreme instances, an inspection should be made for excessive wear about the carburetor shutter shaft to permit unwanted air from entering the vapour stream.

CARBURETOR ADJUSTMENT—SLOW AND HIGH SPEEDS

Both high and slow speed needles are adjusted at the factory on final assembly and testing, with a limited range for further adjustment provided to compensate for local atmospheric conditions such as temperature atmospheric pressure, and humidity. These frequently require slight variations in needle settings.

A boss or stop is cast on the carburetor panel and a

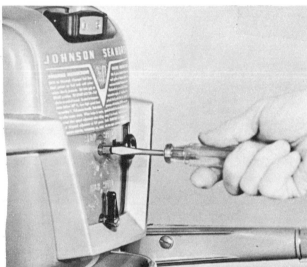

Outboard Marine Corporation of Canada Ltd.

Figure 17.28a   Adjusting Needle Setting with Screwdriver Prior to Final Placing of the Slow Speed Dial and High Speed Lever

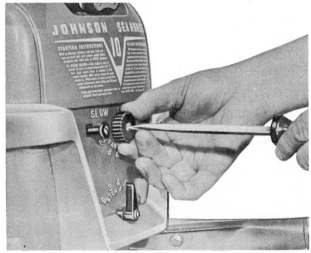

Outboard Marine Corporation of Canada Ltd.

Figure 17.28b   Locating Position of Knob on the Slow Speed Needle

similar arrangement cast on the back or inside of the slow speed adjusting knob which permits somewhat more than a half a turn of the knob as required to achieve the best performance. There is a pointer on the knob and the numbers 1 to 7 on the control panel.

Similar provisions are made for a compensating adjustment of the high speed needle except that the limiting stops for the high speed adjusting lever are built into the cover with numerals 1 to 7 on it which limit adjusting to less than half a turn.

If the carburetor has been taken down for cleaning and repairs, primary or initial adjustment may be required for both high and slow speed needles. This is best accomplished with the motor cover removed.

A checklist is provided below.

(1.) The slow speed knob and high speed lever are fastened to the respective needles by the serrations on the slotted end of the needle. Remove both screws to gain access to the slot at the extreme end of each needle.

(2.) Insert a screw driver bit into the slotted end of the high speed needle. Turn right to close it until the face of the pointed needle rests gently on its seat in the carburetor body. Then turn it left or unscrew it approximately one-half of a turn for high speed.

(3.) Perform the same operation on the slow speed needles but open or unscrew about $1\frac{1}{8}$ of a turn.

(4.) Attach the test wheel. Start and operate the motor in a test tank until a normal running temperature has been obtained.

(5.) Turn the high speed to an idling position and turn the slow speed needle right or left as required to obtain a smooth operation in the lower speed range. Further retard the motor speed and adjust the position for best performance. Repeat the operation until the best setting for maximum slow speed running has been accomplished. Rough running of the motor denotes an excessively rich carburetor mixture (too much fuel or too little air) and is evidenced by a smoky exhaust. Turning the needle adjusting valve to the right reduces the flow of liquid fuel into the carburetor air stream and leans the fuel vapour mixture; turning it to the left increases the flow of the liquid fuel to a correspondingly richer mixture.

(6.) Recheck both needle settings to assure the best performance.

(7.) Without disturbing the position of the slow speed needle, install the slow speed knob over the protruding serrated end with its pointer directed toward number 4. Insert and draw it snugly on the taper headed screw provided for this purpose.

(8.) Locate the position of the high speed needle lever as described above the lever should be directed toward numbers 4.

(9.) Make sure that the taper headed screws are drawn

up securely to hold the knob and lever in the respective needles.

FUEL PRESSURE SYSTEM

Since fuel is supplied to the carburetor by a pressurized gas tank, a device is built into the motor assembly to permit a portion of pressure built up in the crankcase during the operation to escape through a flexible rubber tube into the tank. The fuel mixture then under pressure is conducted to the carburetor through a second flexible rubber tube. Both tubes, however, are molded together and provided with the necessary connectors and terminal fittings for convenient handling.

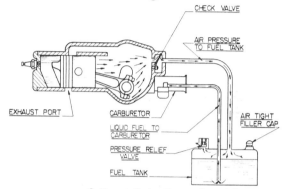

Outboard Marine Corporation of Canada Ltd.

Figure 17.29a Carburetor and Fuel Pressure System

Attached to the aluminum valve or leaf plate, but not associated with the functioning of the automatic intake, is the fuel pressure check valve assembly. This assembly consists of two small brackets connected to the rubber disks and held in position over two corresponding holes drilled into the plate, a flat spring of predetermined tension which comprises a check for each crankcase chamber.

When pressure in the crankcase reaches a point determined by the tension of the spring, the disk is momentarily forced off the seat, permitting the escaping pressure to be conducted through an air line to the fuel tank.

The checks function alternately as the cylinders fire. First one opens, then the other, to build up and maintain sufficient pressure in the tank to feed the carburetor. When pressure in the tank equals the pressure in the crankcase, there is obviously no valve action. The degree of valve action depends on the volume of fuel in the tank. As the fuel level in the tank lowers, the resulting increase in air space causes proportionately greater check valve activity. Normal fuel tank pressure is from two to five pounds, depending on the motor speed and fuel level. An automatic pressure release is installed to relieve any pressure above eight pounds.

When the filter element is cleaned, the wing screw is loosened, the bracket holding the filter in position and the filter bowl are removed and rinsed out and cleaned

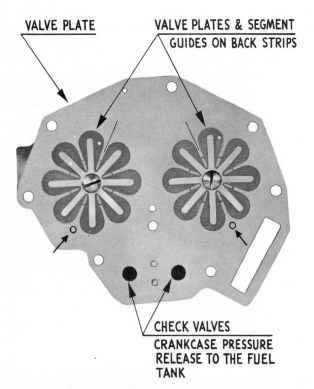

VALVE PLATE   VALVE PLATES & SEGMENT GUIDES ON BACK STRIPS

CHECK VALVES

CRANKCASE PRESSURE RELEASE TO THE FUEL TANK

Back View of the Automatic Valve Plate Showing Valves and Back Plates (to Guide Each Segment) when Installing New Valve Plates, Include New Back Plates. Note "Ink" Dot on One of the Valve Segments which Should be Visible when Properly Installed — Also the Fine "Scratch" Line or Circular Embossing Equidistant Between Two of the Holes in the Valve Plate. On Securing Position of the Valve Plate, this Line Should Fall Midway Between Edges of the Corresponding Segments to Correctly Center.

Outboard Marine Corporation of Canada Ltd.

Figure 17.29b   Reed Plate

with gasoline. The screw holding the filter element in place is removed and the element lifted free, and rinsed in a container of gasoline. It is replaced if necessary. The elements frequently clog with a gummy substance after long periods of idleness and are a barrier to a consistent flow of liquid fuel. The filter bowl is replaced and its gasket must be in good order to permit the proper seating of the bowl. The bracket is replaced and the wing screw secured.

THE HIGH SPEED JET RD CARBURETOR

The screws holding the float bowl fast to the carburetor are removed and the bowl worked carefully off to make the float, float valve and seat assembly at high speed jet accessible for inspection or replacement. The high speed needle is easily removed with a screw driver. After the inspection, it can be similarly reinstalled or replaced. It must be properly seated.

TO CHECK FLOAT FLOAT LEVEL AND FLOAT VALVE ASSEMBLY.

(1) Remove the small pin and the float and arm assembly from their position on the brackets provided on the carburetor body.

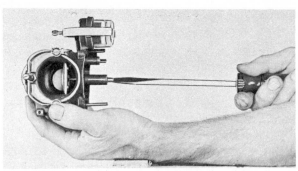

Outboard Marine Corporation of Canada Ltd.

Figure 17.30   Removing High Speed Needle

(2) Lift the float free and remove the float valve seat with a screw driver. Check the float for defects and replace them if necessary.

(3) Be sure to rinse the float valve and seat in clean gasoline and look for sticky gum coating on the seat in the valve point. The float action becomes sluggish after long periods of idleness.

(4) Replace the float valve in the seat assembly. If the tapered face or float valve appears badly ringed or grooved, turn the float valve seat in the carburetor body with a screw driver, tightening it securely.

(5) Insert the float valve, replace the float and check for the float level. The top face of the float should come to rest flush with the face of the carburetor body. Otherwise bend the float arm up or down to gain the proper level. The float action should be free. Check for binding. Replace the carburetor body and install new gaskets if required.

Carburetor Adjustment — Slow and High Speeds

(1) To adjust high and slow speed needles after repairs, proceed with the operation prior to installing the motor covers as it is more easily accomplished in this manner.

(2) On removing the carburetor needle dials, note stops or ribs on the inside smooth surfaces of both corresponding stops cast on the motor covers. These permit approximately one turn of each needle after their initial setting to compensate for variations frequently encountered during normal operation of the motor.

(3) Dials are held fast in their respective needles by slotting and knurling a short distance on the end of each and by installing a countersunk head screw which, when screwed into the end of the needle, are expanded or bound to hold the dial fast. When the dial is removed, it is simply a matter of loosening the centre screw, and pulling it free of the needle as required.

(4) Gently and carefully close both needles against their respective seats. Do not, under any circumstances, screw them tightly since doing so will only result in ringing the needle point face and distorting the needle seat in the carburetor body. Later needle settings will then be im-

possible. Damaged needle points and needle valve seats cannot be properly adjusted for satisfactory performance.

(5) After having loosened both needles, open the slow speed needle approximately one turn and the high speed needle about three quarters of a turn.

(6) Start the motor and let it run until a normal operating temperature is reached. Adjust both needles to their best running position by first setting the speed control grip to the fast position and by adjusting the high speed needle to a lower setting for best running. Then set the speed control grip to slow and adjust the low speed needle higher for best running.

(7) Assemble both dials in their respective positions with number 4 in each case directed up without disturbing either needle setting.

(8) Allow sufficient room between the dial and the covers to prevent rubbing and secure in this position by drawing up on the screw on each end of each needle. It is advisable to check each needle packing nut to make sure that sufficient drag is present to prevent any creeping during the operation of the motor. (Don't overdo it, though.)

Any variations required in the needle valve settings after the motor has been turned over to its operator can easily be performed by the individual without the danger of throwing the carburetor too far out of adjustment. The dials can always be turned up and the motor made to perform, providing of course, that all other mechanical details function as they should.

Speed Limitation Control

Speed limitation control is accomplished by means of a lever acting against a stop attached to the underside of the magneto armature plate. Thus, there is no limit to the motor speed when in forward or reverse. Caution is necessary when operating in reverse. The reverse speed is limited in later models. For changes in the RD 12 carburetor spring choke lever tensions springs, the Johnson service manual tells of changes in construction.

Cam follower "A" rides a contour of cam "B" attached to the armature plate through the linkage. The carburetor shutter shaft acts to control the speed of the motor as it advances towards the high end of the cam. Spark gas is, therefore, synchronized to proportion the opening of the shutter with the degree of spark advance. When the spark is set at full advance, the carburetor shutter is full open for maximum speed. The shutter closes to reduce motor speed and the retard spark cam follower rides the low end of cam "B".

Cam "B" is adjustable for proper synchronization through a slotted hole at the low end. The low end of the cam can be shifted in or out to accomplish this adjustment. When correctly adjusted, the follower should make contact with the contour edge of the cam when aligned with the index mark "C".

Outboard Marine Corporation of Canada Ltd.
Figure 17.32   Method of Spark and Carburetor Control Installed on Models RD-12 and 13

Models RD 12 and 13 make use of a similar arrangement to synchronize spark and gas. The index mark has been omitted from the cam in this case but a depression has been provided at the extreme end of "A". The depression completely closes the carburetor shutter as the cam follower drops into position when the maximum spark retard and speed control lever are set to stop.

Outboard Marine Corporation of Canada Ltd.
Figure 17.31   Carburetor Control Cam

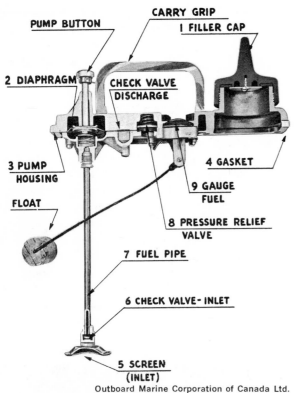

PUMP BUTTON

CARRY GRIP

1 FILLER CAP

2 DIAPHRAGM

CHECK VALVE
DISCHARGE

3 PUMP
HOUSING

FLOAT

4 GASKET

9 GAUGE
FUEL

8 PRESSURE RELIEF
VALVE

7 FUEL PIPE

6 CHECK VALVE - INLET

5 SCREEN
(INLET)

Outboard Marine Corporation of Canada Ltd.

Figure 17.33   Pump Mechanism and Gauge as Attached
to the Fuel Tank

Pressurized Fuel Tanks

The fuel tank is a simple but rugged construction with a capacity of five gallons. It contains the pump for filling the carburetor bowl, the fuel level float and gauge, the pressure relief valve, connections for fuel and air lines, a bracket arrangement around which the fuel line is coiled when not in use, and a carry grip.

The pump uses a diaphragm that flexes in a small housing to force the fuel to the carburetor for starting purposes. It is necessary only when pressure has been released from the tank for re-filling or when it has been idle for some time. Two check valves are required, one for intake and the other for discharge like any other conventional pump. A screen is installed to prevent the entrance of foreign matter.

The failure to pump in most cases is a result of a clogged screen or a fractured or improperly installed diaphragm. This is easily replaced. Like all service operations on the power head or the gear case, they must be carefully performed.

Essentially the mechanic observes assembly prior to doing the job, then dismantles and reassembles it in reverse order. New parts are installed and sections of the pump housing are checked to ensure flatness, if necessary.

When the diaphragm is replaced, a thin coat of hard drying cement is applied around the hole in both cuptic washers, and the diaphragm contact side. This eliminates

possible seepage. When assembled, the holes in the diaphragm and the corresponding holes in the pump housing must be lined up. This is important. The discharge check valve disk, when replaced, must not be tilted off its seat on the assembly. The intake disk is installed above the screen at the lower end of the suction pipe. The diaphragm must not be wrinkled when the sections of the housing are bolted together; the bolt holes must be lined up and the diaphragm must not overlap or the pump will fail to operate and leakage will interfere with the tank operations. Similarly, the gasket between the pump assembly and the tank must be in place and in good condition to avoid the possibility of air leaks.

The pump should be used only when the carburetor bowl is empty. This will be indicated by little or no resistance when the pump button is pressed, except from that tension produced by the spring in the assembly.

The float valve in the carburetor closes as the bowl fills to build up resistance to pumping progressively. Under no circumstances should the pump be forced; depressing the primer pump button four or five times should be sufficient to fill the bowl or the diaphragm might otherwise be fractured.

Leaks in the assembly are indicated by a failure of the pump and often by fuel seepage around the tank cover. In some instances, the motor cannot be operated without constantly pumping fuel; in others, seepage may be slight, requiring manual pumping only at higher speeds. Seepage of the fuel mixture around the pump shaft is evidence of an improperly installed or faulty diaphragm.

Checklist for Fuel Tank

Since the fuel tank plays such an important part in overall performance of the motor, it is imperative that it be checked for fitness when the motor is being repaired. The motor cannot perform with a faulty fuel tank, and it must always be considered as part of the motor assembly.

Major tank difficulties involve principally air or pressure leaks.

Check the following items and faults when diagnosing fuel tank irregularities or performing repairs on the tank.
1. Filler cap and gasket: (a) loose or cracked; (b) faulty or improperly seated; (c) gasket faces damaged.
2. Diaphragm: (a) punctured; (b) leaking at the end of the pump shaft and allowing fuel to escape under the pump button nuts, because the end of the pump shaft is loose or the area around the cup washers is not properly cemented; (c) not properly seated between pump housings.
3. Pump housings: (a) surfaces not flat and causing air seepages and resultant pressure drop; (b) not bolted together securely.
4. Gasket: (a) damaged; (b) not secure against pressure loss between the pump assembly and the tank.

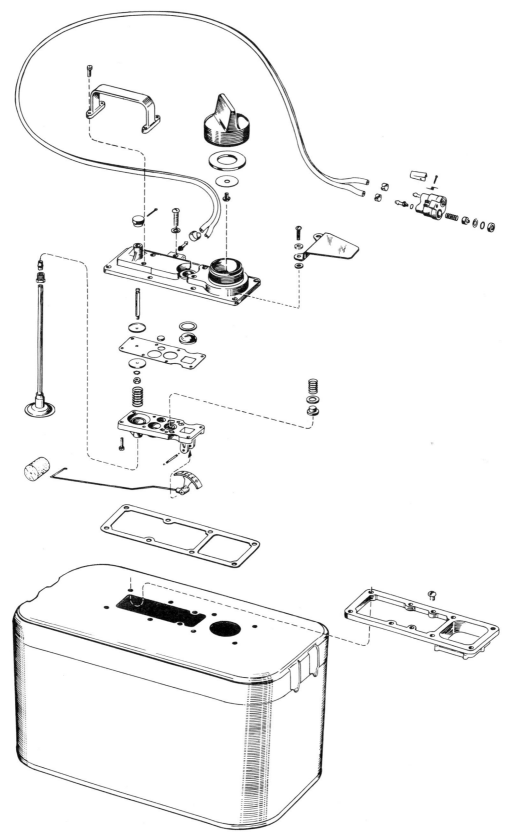

Figure 17.34 Assembly Layout—Mile-master Fuel Tank—Pressurized   Outboard Marine Corporation of Canada Ltd.

5. Screen: clogged with foreign matter.
6. Disc valves: (a) sticking; (b) improperly seated.
7. Fuel pipe: loose in the pump housing, causing a pressure leak.
8. Pressure release valve: (a) improperly seated to cause pressure leak; (b) sticking.
9. Fuel gauge glass: (a) cracked; (b) improperly scaled.
10. Fuel tank: punctured, causing pressure leaks.
11. Fuel line and connectors: (a) faulty, permitting loss of pressure; (b) clogged.
(For tank breakdown, see Figure 17-34.)

CARBURETOR AND FUEL SYSTEM: CHRYSLER CANADA OUTBOARDS

Fuel System Introduction

In the Chrysler outboard the fuel is transferred from the fuel tank to the engine by means of either a prime pump in the fuel line, which charges the fuel line and carburetor prior to starting the engine, or a fuel pump which delivers fuel to the carburetor when the engine is running. The latter is used on all 6 and 9.2 HP models.

Servicing the Fuel Line

If the engine does not prime properly, make the following checks:

1. Check the fuel supply in the tank. The fuel must cover the lower end of the filter in the pick up tube in the tank, which is approximately half an inch from the bottom.
2. Make sure that the fuel tank vent cap screw or guage is open.
3. Check the fuel line, prime pump, and connections for leaks.
4. Check the entire fuel line for kinks or restrictions.
5. Check the fuel line coupler to make sure that it is functioning properly and that it is fully engaged with the bushing on the fuel tank and engine.

After prolonged use the rubber seals in the fuel line couplers sometimes become distorted, cracked, or swollen, prohibiting sufficient fuel flow. These seals are available as a service replacement part. Refer to the appropriate parts book for the correct number and description.

6. Check the fuel line tank adapter at the fuel tank. On models which do not have the fuel line check valve in the prime bulb, the check valve is located in the fuel tank adaptor. In some cases, small deposits of sealant accumulate on the check valve and cause it to stick in an open or closed position. A sticking check valve will cause difficult priming, hard starting on models which start manually, and starter motor failure on electric start models as a result of prolonged cranking. If adaptors are faulty, the complete adaptor must be replaced. The fuel line components are replaceable as individual parts. Refer to the

appropriate parts book for the correct part number and description.

Fuel Pump

The fuel pump operates on a two stage principal. The two stage, vacuum operated, diaphragm type pump is mounted on the rear starboard side of the lower power head. Refer to the parts book for the correct part number and description of the component parts. The heart of the fuel pump, the diaphragm, is divided into two separate sections, each operating as an individual pump.

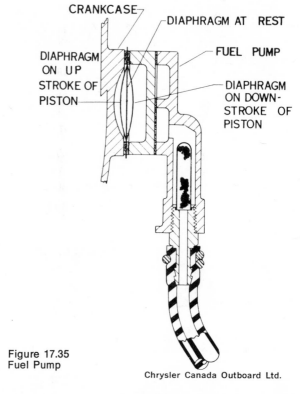

Figure 17.35
Fuel Pump

Chrysler Canada Outboard Ltd.

The first stage, the larger diaphragm area, draws fuel from the fuel tank and pumps it into the second stage, which in turn pumps fuel to the carburetor. The first stage consists of a fuel sediment bowl, screen, gasket, diaphragm, and two valves: an inlet valve, which prevents fuel from backing up into the inlet fuel line, and an outlet valve, which serves to keep the fuel from flowing back into the pump. The second stage consists of a diaphragm and a single valve, which operates as an outlet valve. The inlet valve for the second stage is the outlet for the first stage. At the outlet of the second stage, there is an elbow which distributes the fuel to the carburetor.

The pump operates as follows. When the number two piston travels up on compression, a vacuum is created in the number two crankcase. This vacuum is relayed to the top of the first stage diaphragm by a pressure hose, which runs from the fitting on the upper transfer port cover to the fitting in the top centre of the first stage. The vacuum lifts the first stage diaphragm, drawing fuel from the tank through the sediment bowl and through a one-way disc type valve into the first stage compression chamber and into the fuel pump. When the number two piston travels down on the power stroke, the crankcase bottom in the number two cylinder decreases, and there is a sharp rise in pressure. This pressure exerts force from the top of the first stage diaphragm, forcing the fuel through a one-way disc type valve into the compression chamber of the second stage. The second stage (which operates in the same manner as the first, except that it is controlled by the number one cylinder, which lags 180 degrees behind number two cylinder) picks up fuel and forces it through the disc type valve to the carburetor. This stage assists the first stage in delivering fuel to the compression chamber of the second stage.

Because of the simplicity of its construction and operation, the fuel pump requires very little maintenance other than replacement of the diaphragm and valves, because of normal wear.

Inspecting the Fuel Pump

Because of the relatively small volume displaced by the flexing of the diaphragm, there must be no leaks in the fuel system and there must be no restriction in the flow of fuel.

These are important points to look for when servicing a fuel pump:

1. The diaphragm must be free from holes or breaks of any kind and must completely cover the surface of the crankcase gasket.
2. When assembling the diaphragm to the crankcase, be sure that it is not wrinkled and that it extends beyond the gaskets and cover; it must be properly indexed to fit the crankcase boss. Tighten all screws before squeezing the bulb. Do not use gasket cement.
3. Examine all gaskets, connections, and fuel lines for leaks.
4. Check the tension of the fuel pump reeds. The reeds should be flat and should cover the hole in the reed plate. Check the reeds for flatness; maximum warpage at the centre must not exceed .0015 inches. Straighten if necessary. When the reeds are assembled to the plate, they must seat flush with no initial tension to a maximum of .003 inches open. The reeds should not stand open, and should not be warped, bent, or bowed.

Disassembly

To remove a fuel pump from the engine, proceed as follows:

1. Remove the fuel lines from the inlet, outlet, and air pressure fittings on the fuel pump.

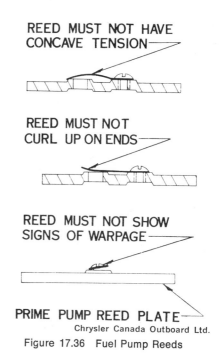

REED MUST NOT HAVE CONCAVE TENSION

REED MUST NOT CURL UP ON ENDS

REED MUST NOT SHOW SIGNS OF WARPAGE

PRIME PUMP REED PLATE

Chrysler Canada Outboard Ltd.
Figure 17.36 Fuel Pump Reeds

2. Remove the screws which retain the fuel pump bracket assembly to the cylinder, and then remove the pump.

Servicing the Fuel Pump

Under normal conditions, it is not necessary to remove the fuel pump from the engine to perform maintenance repair. To service, proceed as follows:

1. Disconnect the two air pressure hoses from the top of the front cover.
2. Remove the six body half retaining screws, and separate the body halves as illustrated in Figure 17-37.

Chrysler Canada Outboard Ltd.
Figure 17.37 Separating Fuel Pump Body Valves

3. Carefully remove the fuel pump diaphragm, and inspect it for punctures or tears. Replace the diaphragm if it is excessively distorted or shows evidence of leakage.
4. Remove the centre fuel pump valve, retaining the screws, and lift out the valve as shown in Figure 17-38.

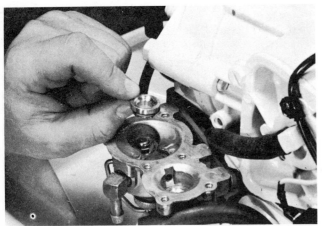

Figure 17.38   Inspecting Fuel Pump Body Valves

Chrysler Canada Outboard Ltd.

Inspect the valve and replace it if it shows evidence of excessive wear, or if the disc is cracked or distorted. The fuel pump valve replacement should be made with the latest valve — identified by the body, which is made of brass.

5. Remove the fuel sediment bowl, and clean the bowl and filter screens with fresh gasoline.

6. Visually inspect the first stage inlet valve (located on the left side of the pump, as viewed in Figure 17-38). Do not attempt to remove this valve unless it has to be replaced. If inspection shows that replacement is necessary, proceed as follows:

A. Using a half-inch diameter punch, drive the first stage inlet valve out from the bottom of the pump.

B. Using a new gasket and valve, with a light hammer and punch tap the new valve into place. Use extreme care to prevent damage when installing the valve.

7. Inspect the outlet valve of the second stage. This valve *cannot* be removed without damaging it completely. If inspection indicates that it has to be replaced proceed as follows:

A. Remove the fuel pump from the engine.

B. Remove the outlet fuel elbow from the bottom of the second stage.

C. Drive the second stage valve out from bottom of the pump using a punch.

D. Using a new gasket and valve, with a light hammer and 11/16 diameter punch, tap the new valve into place. Use extreme care when installing the valve to prevent damage.

E. Re-install the elbow to the bottom of the second stage.

8. Re-install the sediment bowl to the pump, using a new gasket. Tighten the thumb screw finger.

9. Using a new gasket, assemble the first stage outlet valve to the pump body, installing the retaining screws, and tighten securely.

10. Place the fuel pump gasket, diaphragm, and pump cover in position on the pump body. Install the six body half retaining screws, and tighten securely.

11. Install the pump to the engine and tighten the screws securely. Install the outlet fuel line and pressure hoses (the pressure hose from the first stage is connected to the elbow at the top of the transfer port cover, and the pressure hose from the second stage is connected to the elbow on the lower transfer port cover).

Adjusting Carburetor

The initial setting of the carburetor used on Chrysler outboard motors incorporates the use of a non-adjustable high speed jet. The idle adjustment needle should be adjusted as follows:

1. Turn the idle adjustment needle in (clockwise) until it seats lightly. *Do not* overtighten, as the needle and seat may be damaged. Back the idle adjustment needle out one full turn.

2. Start the engine and run until it is fully warmed up.

3. Move the control lever to a neutral position.

4. Turn the idle adjustment needle counterclockwise (open), until the engine loses power and begins to "roll" or "gallop" as a result of an over-rich mixture. Slowly turn the needle clockwise (closed), until the cyclinders fire unevenly and the motor picks up speed. Continue turning clockwise until the engine "pops" or "stalls" because of too lean a mixture. Set the adjustment screw half-way between these two points.

5. Do not adjust the carburetor to a mixture that is leaner than necessary to obtain smooth idling. It is better to have the idle settings a little rich rather than too lean.

Point of Throttle Opening

The amount of throttle opening is synchronized with the degree of spark advance through the throttle cam and related linkage. This adjustment varies with the different models and should be checked when servicing a motor.

1. Unsnap the ball joint connector from the throttle tower shaft.

2. With the throttle shutter in the carburetor closed, adjust the eccentric screw holding the throttle roller to the throttle shaft so that the pick up line on the lower end of the throttle cam is exactly centred on the throttle roller.

3. Advance the throttle tower shaft and throttle cam to full advance position (throttle shutter horizontal).

4. Adjust the ball joint connectors until the spacing is identical to the spacing between the connector stud on the throttle cam and the throttle tower shaft.

5. Snap the ball joint connector in place in the throttle tower shaft. The point of throttle opening will have to be re-adjusted if the correct high speed neutral warm-up

RPM cannot be reached. The correct high-speed neutral warm up is 1,800 to 2,500 RPM.

OPTIONAL SIZE MAIN FUEL JETS
(Use Only at Altitudes Indicated)

HP	Jet Size	Part No.	Altitude Use
35	.089*	013367	Sea level - 1,250 ft.
35	.080	013194	1,250 - 3,750 ft.
35	.076	013191	3,750 - 6,250 ft.
35	.070	013430	6,250 - 8,250 ft.
45-50	.096*	012947	Sea level - 2,500 ft.
45-50	.008	013193	2,500 - 5,000 ft.
45-50	.080	013194	5,000 - 7,500 ft.
45-50	.076	013191	7,500 - 10,000 ft.

*Standard equipment on models indicated.

Removing Carburetor

When disconnecting the throttle link from the carburetor, exercise caution, as the link must not be bent out of shape. If the link is bent, it is recommended that it be replaced with a new one, as it is extremely important that the correct geometry be maintained for this setting.

For removal, proceed as follows:

1. Remove the fuel line from the carburetor.
2. Disconnect the choke wire from the choke shaft.
3. Remove the two hexagon nuts which retain the carburetor to the adaptor flange.
4. Pull the carburetor forward and off the studs.

Checking Inlet Needle, Seat and Float Adjustment

The inlet needle, seat, and float are located in the top half of the carburetor. To inspect, disassemble the carburetor as follows:

1. Separate the body halves by removing the four body half retaining screws.
2. Remove the float lever pin from the top half of the carburetor and lift out the float.
3. Remove the inlet needle and check for excessive wear on the points. If the needle point is notched or pitted, replace both the inlet needle and seat.
4. Re-assemble the float to the carburetor and install the float lever pin.

Checking Float Level

Tip the top half upside down and note the position of the float. The float should be perfectly level and the edge

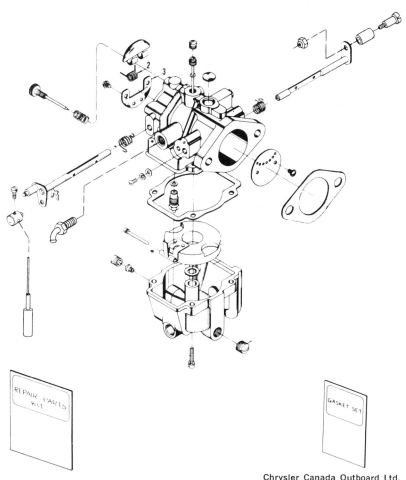

Chrysler Canada Outboard Ltd.

Figure 17.39   Carburetor Parts

Figure 17.40   Checking Float Level

should extend 13/32 inch plus 1/64 inch above the edge of the body casting, as illustrated in Figure 17-40.

To adjust the float to the 13/32 plus 1/64 dimension, bend the short curved activating arm on the float in the direction desired. Do not press down on the float when it is assembled to the carburetor, as the inlet needle is made of neoprene and may be damaged.

Checking Float Drop

When checking the float adjustment, the float drop should be checked. The correct float drop dimension is 13/16 inch plus 1/32 inch, as indicated in Figure 17-41. This setting controls the amount of fuel supplied at high speed operation.

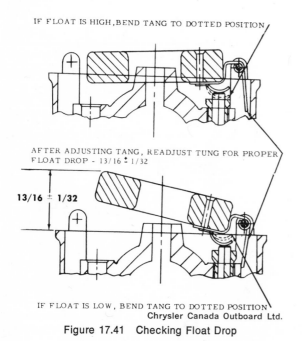

IF FLOAT IS HIGH, BEND TANG TO DOTTED POSITION

AFTER ADJUSTING TANG, READJUST TUNG FOR PROPER FLOAT DROP - 13/16 ± 1/32

13/16 ± 1/32

IF FLOAT IS LOW, BEND TANG TO DOTTED POSITION
Figure 17.41   Checking Float Drop

Cleaning Idle Tube

The idle tube, used on all 35 through to 50 HP models equipped with Tillotson carburetors, is located on the upper half of the carburetor. It is replaceable, and can be serviced as follows:

1. Remove the idle adjustment needle from the top half of the carburetor.
2. Remove the plug screw located in the centre top half of the carburetor. This will allow access to the idle tube screw.
3. Using a slim screwdriver, remove the idle tube from the bore from which the plug screw in step two above was removed.
4. Soak the idle tube in fresh gasoline or a carburetor cleaning solution, and blow out the compressed air to remove dirt and foreign particles.
5. Re-assemble, reversing the steps listed above.

When reassembling the carburetor body halves, be sure the main nozzle boss gasket is in place, as shown in Figure 17-42. If this gasket should fall out during re-assembly, the engine will show all indications of an excessively rich fuel mixture.

Figure 17.42   Main Nozzle Gasket

Throttle Shutter

If the throttle shutter is removed for any reason, care must be exercised when it is re-installed to the carburetor, as the edges of the shutter are bevelled to fit the contour of the carburetor throat.

When replacing the throttle shutters, or any carburetor repair parts, refer to the parts book for the parts breakdown and description for the specific carburetor model.

Using parts which are not interchangeable will result in poor operation throughout the entire operating range.

The throttle shutter on these models is attached to the needle shaft by two screws which automatically align the shutter. The throttle shutters are not interchangeable between horsepower classes. If the incorrect throttle shutter is installed, poor operation throughout the operating range will be the result.

Carburetor Service Hints

To disassemble for cleaning and repair, remove parts in the following order:

Bowl casting
1. Bowl retaining screws.
2. Drain valve channel plug screw.
3. Drain valve spring and drain valve.
4. Main fuel adjustment.

Body casting
5. Main nozzle gasket.
6. Body gasket.
7. Float fulcrum pin, float, inlet seat, and needle.
8. Idle adjustment and spring.
9. Idle channel plug screw.

For cleaning purposes, it is not necessary to disassemble the carburetor beyond this point. However, excessive wear may make it necessary to remove and replace the following parts:
1. Throttle shutter and shaft assembly.
2. Choke shutter and shaft assembly.
3. Welch plug covering the idle discharge ports.

After the carburetor has been disassembled and all parts thoroughly washed in clean gasoline, the following channels should be blown out with clean compressed air:
1. Main nozzle and main air bleed tube.
2. Idle supply tube, idle mixture passage and idle discharge holes.
3. Fuel supply channel.
4. Main fuel adjustment orifice and channels.
5. Drain valve channels.

After cleaning, the carburetor should be reassembled in the reverse order of the above instructions. It is recommended that a new carburetor and flange be installed whenever the carburetor is removed from the engine and disassembled. Exercise caution when installing the bowl gasket. If it is not installed properly, it can interfere with the carburetor flow, which in turn will cause the engine to run "rich" or cut off the fuel supply, depending on the position of the float.

Reed Valves

The reed valves of the two-cycle engine perform a very important function. They open to permit fuel to enter the crankcase on the up-stroke of the piston; and they close to seal the crankcase and prevent the escape of fuel on the downward stroke of the piston. Motors of 35 to 50 HP have two "V" type reed blocks with two sets of four reeds in each block. One reed block serves the upper cylinder, and one the lower. All reeds are treated to prevent corrosion. A reed stop limits the amount of reed opening.

If a reed cracks or breaks off, it can always be detected by a blow-back through the carburetor, and by an engine that blubbers and misses on one cylinder. Blow-back will occur when the piston or the cylinder that has the broken reeds is on the downstroke. The pressure created by this reduced crankcase volume will escape through the hole left by the broken reed and will pass to the outside through the carburetor.

Checking Reeds

To visually inspect or replace the intake reed valves, proceed as follows:
1. On hand start models, remove the starter rope handle and tie a knot in the rope to prevent it from rewinding on the spool.

On electric start models, remove the electric starter mounting brackets, upper and lower, from crankcase in the adapter flange. Remove the lead wire from the terminal on the lower front of the starter motor.
2. Remove the carburetor and linkage as outlined above.
3. Remove the carburetor flange attaching screws.
4. Inspect the reeds. Replace any that are cracked, broken, or warped. A reed must seat lightly against the reed plate along the entire reed length and should completely cover the hole in the reed plate.
5. Inspect the reed stop spacing. The reed stop is to be set at 9/32 inch opening. Assembled reeds may stand open a maximum of .010 inches. The reed stop must be pushed ahead, and the reed back as far as the mounting holes

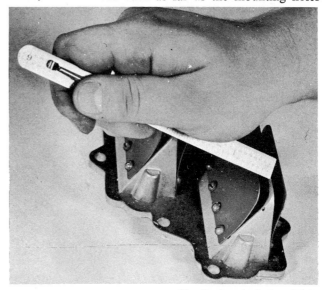

Chrysler Canada Outboard Ltd.
Figure 17.43   Reed Stop Spacing

allow, to give reed stops maximum overlap. When replacing reeds, the reed stop shoud also be checked. The only reed stops that should be used are part number 88161-2. These reed stops are substantially longer than the old style stop. Measure the reed stop spacing as shown in Figure 17-43. If reeds are broken, check the reed stop spacing, as this is one of the contributing causes of reed failure.

Recovery of Broken Reeds
Should a reed breakage occur, the pieces may be removed without disassembly of the power head. Perform the following steps to recover the broken portion of the reed to prevent it from entering and damaging the engine.
1. Remove the reed plate and examine the crankcase.
2. Remove the transfer port cover or covers and look for the broken reed.
3. Remove the cylinder head and examine the combustion chamber. Rotate the flywheel slowly during examination.
4. Replace the cylinder head and transfer port covers, using new gaskets.

It is not necessary to disassemble the power head further than outlined above, even though the broken portion of the reed is not found. Larger pieces of the broken reed will be found either in the crankcase or in the transfer port passage. Smaller pieces will probably pass through the combustion chamber and be discharged with the exhaust.

Any time the reed plate or carburetor is removed, when reinstalling, new gaskets should be used.

Puddle Drain System
The puddle drain system on a two-cycle engine performs a very important role. The puddle drain keeps the crankcase free of excess raw fuel which normally accumulates in the lower portions of the crankcase cavities. These puddles of raw fuel are formed by the condensation of the fuel mixture on the cylinder walls while the fuel charge is in the crankcase. The severity of the puddle accumulation is greatest in lower RPM, or when the engine is operated at low speeds for any length of time, because the fuel charge is delayed in the crankcase for longer periods of time and has more opportunity to condense on the cylinder walls.

If raw fuel were allowed to remain in the crankcase, the puddles of it would tend to enrich the fuel mixture within the crankcase, and the engine would tend to load up and display characteristics of an over-rich fuel mixture. An engine which has a faulty puddle drain system will stutter and falter during acceleration and will generally run rough. The fuel which accumulates in the crankcase is drained out through a metering cup and reed valves, pass-

ing down to the motor leg, and is discharged along with exhaust gases.

The puddle drain system is located just forward of the transfer port cover on the starboard side of the engine. (See Figure 17-44.)

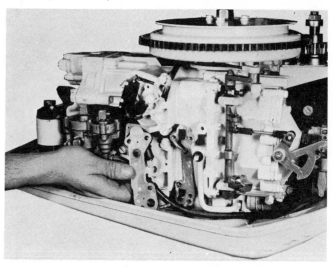

Chrysler Canada Outboard Ltd.
Figure 17.44   Puddle Drain

Puddle Drain Reed Adjustment
On all 35 to 50 HP models, the puddle drain reeds must not stand open and the reed stop must be set so that they are open .017 inches to .023 inches at the tip.

When installing the cylinder drain reed plate, make sure the screens are in place.

Because the puddle drain system serves such an important function, it is important that it be kept clear of foreign objects.

The puddle drain system can be cleaned by blowing the passages and valves clear with compressed air and by cleaning the screen in clean gasoline. If compressed air is not available, a wire of correct size may be pushed through the passages to clear the system. When installing the cylinder drain cover and gaskets, apply Permapex No. 1 to both sides of the lower half of the gasket *immediately* prior to assembly of the cylinder.

REVIEW QUESTIONS
1. What is the basic difference in the operation of two-stroke cycle engine and the four-stroke cycle engine?
2. How is the fuel vapour transferred from the carburetor to the combustion chamber of the two-stroke cycle engine?
3. How is the two-stroke cycle engine lubricated?
4. What is the proper fuel ratio mix for most outboard engines?
5. Draw the simple carburetor diagram and label it.
6. What is the venturi?

7. What is the purpose of the carburetor float?
8. Explain the operation of the carburetor by using fully labelled diagrams, showing the throttle and float system.
9. How are the gas and spark "synchronized" on a Johnson JW outboard engine?
10. Explain how the carburetor adjustment dials are reset on the Johnson JW engine?
11. List the steps necessary to adjust the slow speed on the Johnson JW carburetor.
12. Name the basic differences in construction of the Johnson CD and the Johnson JW carburetor controls.
13. In step form, explain how the Johnson CD carburetor operates.
14. Why are test wheels used for testing outboard engines?
15. Describe the design of the reed plate assembly of the Johnson QD engine.
16. What part of the carburetor must be removed first when removing the Johnson QD carburetor?
17. What part has been changed on the QD 15 Basic carburetor?
18. Name the four factors that can contribute to carburetor flooding.
19. Draw a diagram of the fuel pressure system and explain how it operates.
20. How are the carburetor dials on the Johnson RD held in place? Explain how they are reset.
21. What is a "Speed Limiting Control"? Explain its operation.
22. Name the basic parts of the pressurized fuel tank?
23. Explain the operation of the Chrysler outboard fuel pump.
24. What is the difference between the operation of the fuel pump on the outboard engine and that of the fuel pump on the automobile?
25. List the important parts to check when inspecting the outboard fuel pump.
26. List the items that should be checked when servicing the fuel lines of the outboard engine.
27. What is the maximum allowance of reed valve opening with no tension for a Chrysler outboard?
28. Can the Chrysler fuel pump be serviced without removal from the engine?
29. How is the Chrysler fuel pump's first stage inlet valve removed from the pump body?
30. Can the first stage inlet valve be removed from the pump when the body is fastened to the engine?
31. Can the high speed jet be adjusted on the Chrysler outboard?
32. How is the point of throttle opening checked on the Chrysler outboard engine?
33. How can the high speed jet of the Chrysler outboard engine be repaired?
34. What main fuel jet is required for a Chrysler 45 HP outboard engine to be used at 5,000 feet above sea level?
35. What are the dimensions required for setting the float level of the Chrysler outboard engine?
36. List the steps necessary for servicing the Chrysler outboard idle tube.
37. Name the two basic parts of the Chrysler O.M. series carburetor.
38. List the parts contained in each of the two basic carburetor parts named in question 37 above.
39. How can a broken reed in an outboard engine be detected?
40. List the steps required to remove a broken reed from the crankcase.
41. What is the purpose of the puddle drain system of the outboard engine?
42. Where is the puddle drain system located on the Chrysler 50 HP outboard engine?
43. Where is this drain system located on the Johnson QD 15 outboard engine?

CHAPTER 18
THE LOWER UNIT

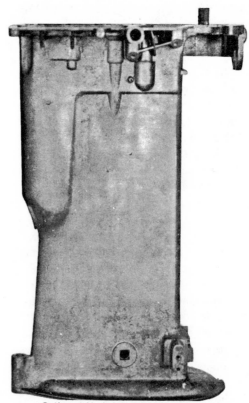

Outboard Marine Corporation of Canada Ltd.

Figure 18.1   Die Cast Aluminum Exhaust Housing

The lower unit is that part of the outboard motor assembly comprising the stern brackets, drive shaft casing, or exhaust housing, gear case, and, of course, necessary shafting required to deliver the power generated (by the power head) to the propeller which drives the boat. It also contains the water pump and the water scoop, shift linkage and piping for circulation, and in some instances a system for recirculation of water to the cooling system. The lower unit is one of the most important units of the outboard motor, for it comprises the propulsion unit and without this the engine would be of little use.

The drive shaft casing may be of tubular construction or of cast aluminum, while the exhaust housing is constructed of die cast aluminum only. Both are provided with flanges at either end for mounting to the power head and the upper part of the gear case. A drive shaft casing of tubular construction generally has some form of clamping arrangement provided for attaching to the gear case and these two parts make up a solid assembly. The drive shaft casing or exhaust housing also contains the water tube or cast in channels which conducts water to and from the power head for cooling purposes.

Where they are used in cast aluminum drive shaft casings, the water tubes are either spun in or secured by means of a jam nut. In engines which have exhaust housings, the water tubes are secured at either end by means of a rubber grommet. In either event, the connections must be water-tight. The water tubes are usually assembled inside the drive shaft casing or exhaust housing; however, on many early models they were installed outside the tubing, with means provided to permit full pivot steering.

The drive shaft casing is of simple but rugged construc-

tion. The water tubes must be tightly mounted inside it; the flanges at either or both ends must be flat to guard against air seepage into the cooling system; and, of course, the casing must be straight and true.

The exhaust tube or exhaust housing also is a simple unit. Again, the water tubes must be properly inserted into the grommets at either end of the exhaust housing, and at the top of the water pump housing. Exhaust housings are always found on larger model motors, because they are capable of handling higher horse power. They are large enough to contain the drive shaft, water tube or tubes, and shift mechanism.

Leaky water tube connections or cast in water channels permit the inside of the drive shaft casing or exhaust housing to fill with water. This eventually finds its way into the crankcase of the motor by way of the lower journal bearing and interferes with motor performance, injuring the functional parts. It may also find its way into the gear case and wash out the lubricant. Water seepage may not necessarily be caused by leaking water tubes or water tube connections, but may result from a faulty gasket or warped gasket faces. Therefore, gaskets and gasket faces must be checked carefully and new ones installed if necessary. On assembly, holes or openings in the gaskets must be aligned with corresponding holes in the drive shaft casing or exhaust housing flange, the base of the

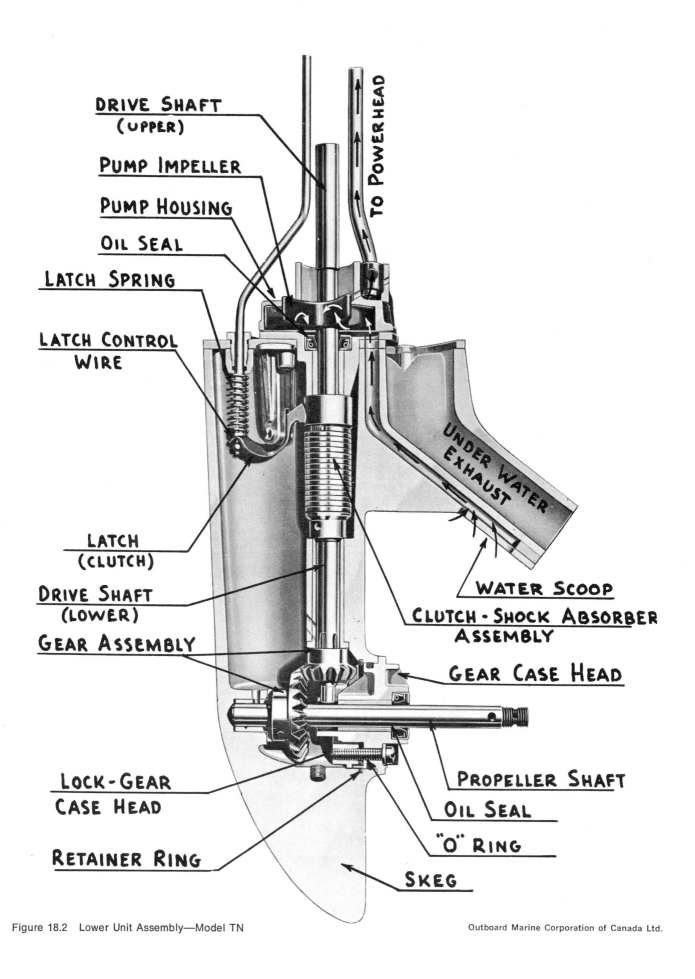

DRIVE SHAFT (UPPER)

PUMP IMPELLER

PUMP HOUSING

OIL SEAL

LATCH SPRING

LATCH CONTROL WIRE

LATCH (CLUTCH)

DRIVE SHAFT (LOWER)

GEAR ASSEMBLY

LOCK-GEAR CASE HEAD

RETAINER RING

TO POWERHEAD

UNDER WATER EXHAUST

WATER SCOOP

CLUTCH-SHOCK ABSORBER ASSEMBLY

GEAR CASE HEAD

PROPELLER SHAFT

OIL SEAL

"O" RING

SKEG

Figure 18.2   Lower Unit Assembly—Model TN

Outboard Marine Corporation of Canada Ltd.

cylinder, or the top of the gear case. Improper installation of a gasket may cause obstruction of the flow of water through the cooling system.

The drive shaft casing or exhaust housing must be straight and true—if it is bent or sprung, excessive drive shaft coupling wear may result, and there will be an added load on the bearings on both the power head (lower) and gear case, causing abnormal wear.

Except on some of the earlier models of outboard motors, the gearcase is constructed of aluminum casting (die or sand cast, the former being of bronze to better withstand the corrosive effect of salt water). Brass construction, however, makes a motor heavy and cumbersome, reducing its portability. Recent developments and improvements in aluminum castings, coupled with advanced manufacturing processes, have made the aluminum gearcase practical and well adapted for salt water service. For durability gearcase castings are given what is known as "treatment"; they are subjected to a chemical process, called lyfinite, which retards the action of salt water on aluminum. In addition, the castings are sprayed with salt water resistant prime coat, followed by an enamel coat that is highly resistant to salt water. The enamel coat is then baked dry, giving the case an even, durable finish.

Most gearcase housing assemblies are made up of the gearcase proper and a gearcase head, while some include a separate bottom and top gearcase section, as well as the gearcase head which contains the required bearings, shafting, and gears.

In addition to containing final drive gears, the gearcase housing on many early models included a slip clutch or shock absorber, installed in the driveshaft. This was designed to reduce the possibility of shearing a propeller pin and to avoid possible injury to motor parts if an underwater obstruction was struck. A slip clutch is incorporated into the propeller.

CHECKING EXHAUST HOUSING AND UPPER GEARCASE ALIGNMENT

Sometimes an outboard motor develops a broken drive shaft, worn or stripped driveshaft and crankshaft splines, and premature gear failure for no apparent reason.

In most cases, these failures or breakages are caused by misalignment of either the gearcase or exhaust housing as result of an accident or perhaps the striking of an underwater object. Figures 18-3 and 18-4 show two methods of checking for housing alignment.

When checking for alignment with a drill press, as illustrated, use the following procedure.

Set the housing on the drill press table and lower the chuck, with the jaws closed, until very light contact is made on the flat machine surface of the housing. Lock the drill arbor in this position, so that the chuck cannot move

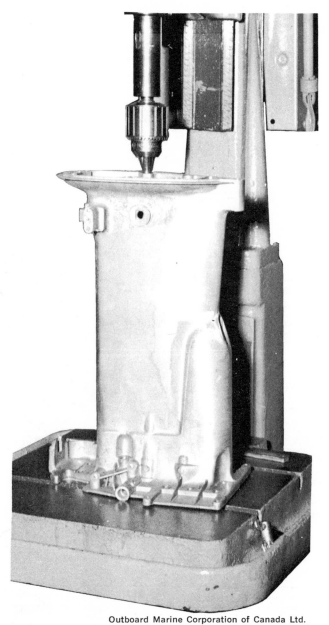

Outboard Marine Corporation of Canada Ltd.
Figure 18.3   Using Drill Press to Check Exhaust Housing for Sprung Condition

up or down. Move the flat surface of the housing under the jaws, and follow the surface around to the starting point. If the housing is in perfect alignment, the clearance between the chuck and jaws in the housing flat surface will be the same at all points. If there is any difference in the clearance between the chuck jaws and the housing at any point, the housing is out of alignment and should be discarded. NOTE: Both top and bottom housing surfaces must be parallel to one another for a perfectly aligned casting.

If a drill press is not available, a flat surface plate and dial indicator may be used as indicated in Figure 18-4.

The amount of gear oil that is used in the lower unit

Figure 18.4   Using Surface Plate and Dial Indicator to Check Alignment of Upper Gear Housing

should be watched carefully. A drop or two of gear oil may escape on removal of the fill spout as the gearcase cavity becomes air bound, with the vent screw in position (see Figure 18-5).

To drain the gearcase of oil, simply remove the vent screw at the top end of the gearcase and then the lower fill screw. Allow the case to drain until empty.

To refill, insert the spout of the lubricant tube into the lower fill opening. Fill to the overflow point (top vent). Replace the vent screw. Remove the fill spout and replace the fill screw. Make certain that the fill screw is clean and that it is securely installed.

A small cylindrical screen is assembled in the water scoop (intake) of gearcase models CD, AD, QD, FD, and RD. It must be kept clean; for if the mesh is obstructed or clogged, the circulation will be impeded and overheating of the motor will result. Occasionally marine growth (greenish in colour) will clog the screen, cutting off the water supply for cooling. It can be cleaned off with a wire brush and the mesh blown out with an air stream.

LOWER UNIT MODEL CD JOHNSON

The model CD lower unit is of simple but sturdy construction. It is built along conventional lines, except that the cushion mounting and an exhaust expansion or silence chamber is attached to the exhaust stack, to reduce audible operating noises to a minimum. Cushion mounting minimizes the sounding board effect of the transom to which the motor is attached, while the exhaust silencer reacts to reduce the staccato effect of exhaust discharge.

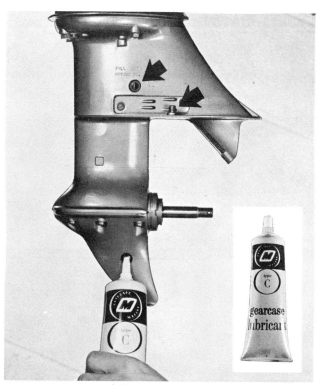

Figure 18.5   Inserting Oil Gear with Tube

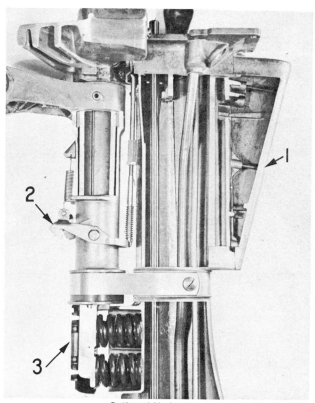

Figure 18.6   Upper Section (Sectional of the Lower Unit)
1. Muffler Silencer. 2. Reverse Lock. 3. Cushion Mount Springs.

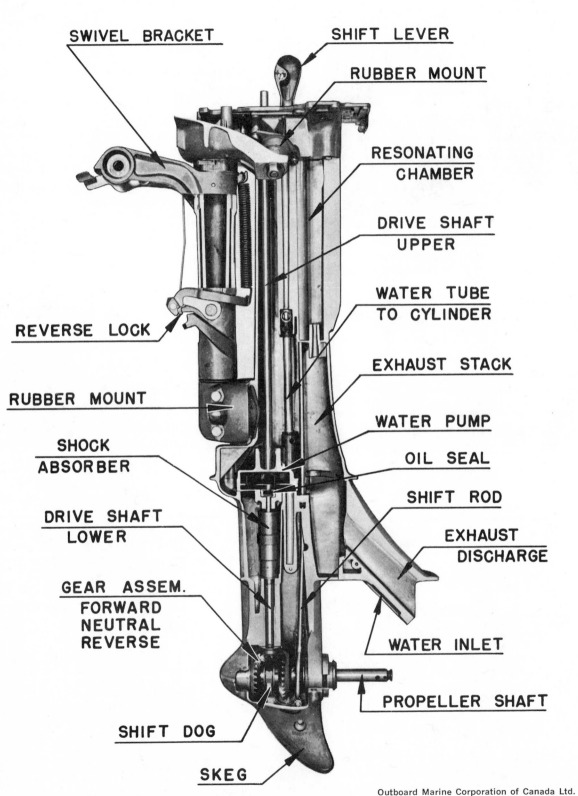

SWIVEL BRACKET

SHIFT LEVER

RUBBER MOUNT

RESONATING CHAMBER

DRIVE SHAFT UPPER

WATER TUBE TO CYLINDER

EXHAUST STACK

WATER PUMP

OIL SEAL

SHIFT ROD

EXHAUST DISCHARGE

WATER INLET

PROPELLER SHAFT

REVERSE LOCK

RUBBER MOUNT

SHOCK ABSORBER

DRIVE SHAFT LOWER

GEAR ASSEM. FORWARD NEUTRAL REVERSE

SHIFT DOG

SKEG

Figure 18.7   Sectional View—Lower Unit Models CD-13 UP and AD Series

A gear shifting arrangement—forward, neutral, and reverse—is provided, and a variable pump for cooling purposes. A propeller shock absorber is built into the driveshaft assembly. Maintenance and assembly are not difficult on this model.

The shock absorber consists of two sleeves "riding" together: one keyed to the upper drive shaft, the other keyed to the lower drive shaft. As will be seen in the illustration, a spring of pre-determined tension is inserted within the sleeves with tension bearing against the inner walls. Under normal operating conditions, the assembly turns as a unit to drive the propeller. However, if the propeller strikes an underwater obstruction, the spring is caused to coil slightly; this reduces the outside diameter just enough to permit slippage between the spring and the sleeves. On release of the obstruction the spring returns to normal diameter and drives against the inner wall of both sleeves to resume turning as a unit. The shock absorber requires no servicing, but only replacement in the event of failure.

Figure 18.8 Sectional View of the Shock Absorber Assembly

All but one of the bearings used in the QD Johnson outboard motor are of non-friction type, and the only bronze bushings employed are "cast-in" and machined to size. Thus no reaming operations are required. Ball and lower bearings are replaced as units and rest on properly machined seats. Clearances are established in original manufacture. Bronze bushings can be replaced only by the installation of a new lower pump housing. Possibly a new driveshaft may be required if bronze bearing wear is excessive. An oil seal is installed on the driveshaft on the bronze bearing and another one on the propeller shaft immediately behind the propeller. Ball bearings are installed to support the propeller shaft, with a taper roller bearing supporting the pinion and the bottom end of the driveshaft, in this case to carry the load of gear thrust.

The gearcase housing assembly on this model is comprised of several sections: the upper pump housing, the lower pump housing, the upper gearcase and lower gearcase, the water pump, driveshaft, propeller shaft, required gears, and gear shifting mechanism.

Outboard Marine Corporation of Canada Ltd.

Figure 18.9   Shifter Dog Engaging Forward Driving Gear— Reverse Gear Floats on the Propeller Shaft

Outboard Marine Corporation of Canada Ltd.

Figure 18.10   Shifter Dog in Neutral Position—Engaging Neither Gear, Both of Which Now Float on the Propeller Shaft

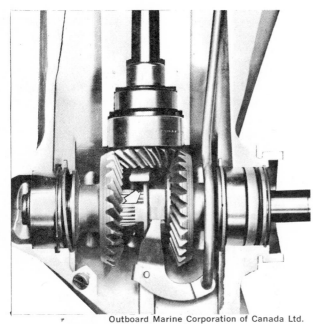

Outboard Marine Corporation of Canada Ltd.

Figure 18.11　Shifter Dog Engaging Reverse Driving Gear—
Forward Driving Gear Now Floats on the Propeller Shaft

Gear Shift

The three gears of "forward", "neutral", and "reverse" operate by means of a sliding member and a shifting mechanism. The pinion (gear) is splined to the driveshaft and rotates constantly with the operation of the motor. The bevel gears (one forward and one aft) float on the propeller shaft and like the pinion, rotate with the operation of the motor, one in one direction and one in the other. A sliding member is keyed or splined to the propeller shaft and remains motionless, as does the propeller shaft and propeller (neutral) during the operation of the motor, until the "dogs" of the sliding member engage corresponding "dogs" on either gear (forward or reverse, depending on which gear is engaged).

THE ELECTRAMATIC GEAR SHIFT

The electramatic gear shift employed in the models RK, 40 HP series, and the gear shift in other models function in a similar manner, except that the clutch engagement in the former is achieved through an electrically activated rather than mechanical arrangement.

Both the forward and reverse driving gear assemblies float on the propeller shaft until engaged or coupled to the propeller shaft, forward and reverse. The electramatic gear shift assembly consists of:

1. The pinion attached to the driveshaft
2. A forward driving gear
3. The reverse driving gear
4. The propeller shaft
5. Two clutch hubs, splined to the propeller shaft
6. Two clutch drive coils, each anchored respectively to

the forward and reverse driving gears (both assemblies float on the clutch hub splined to the propeller shaft)
7. Two electro-magnets, energized by a battery current. A lead from each is directed to a powerful switch in the control box and appropriately attached to the forward and reverse sides.

When shifting to forward, the toggle switch is actuated by the control lever and establishes a forward driving circuit. The energized electro-magnet then attracts and anchors the free end of the clutch drive coil to the clutch hub. As a result, the revolving coil is caused to drag and wrap itself tightly around the hub to establish a direct coupling with the propeller shaft. Thus, the path energy supplied to drive the propeller is through the pinion, forward driving gear, clutch drive coil, clutch hub, the propeller shaft, and finally the propeller.

Forward drive is thus retained until the control lever is returned to the neutral position, at which time the circuit is automatically broken. The electro-magnet instantly de-energizes. The clutch coil releases its grasp on the clutch hub and resumes its normal position. The assembly now floats on the clutch hub and neutral is restored. Similar action occurs in reverse gear.

Power transmitted from the power head to the propeller head follows basically the same path through the

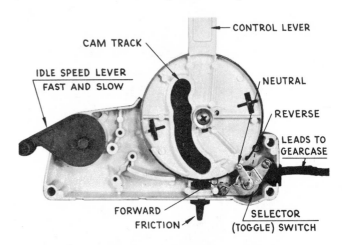

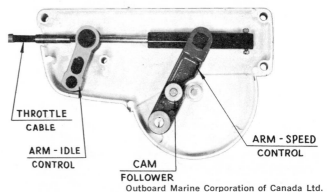

Outboard Marine Corporation of Canada Ltd.

Figure 18.13　Remote Control Housing

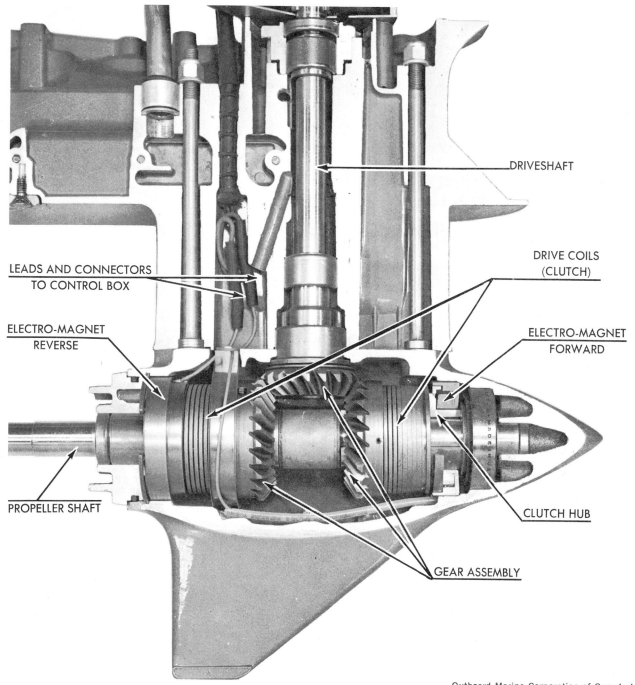

DRIVESHAFT

LEADS AND CONNECTORS
TO CONTROL BOX

DRIVE COILS
(CLUTCH)

ELECTRO-MAGNET
REVERSE

ELECTRO-MAGNET
FORWARD

PROPELLER SHAFT

CLUTCH HUB

GEAR ASSEMBLY

Figure 18.12 The "Electramatic" Gearshift

gear shift train and shafting as employed in the manual shift levers, but the fundamental difference is in the manner in which the downward and reverse gears are engaged or disengaged. The following text and illustrations (Figures 18-14, 18-15, and 18-16) have been planned in a definite sequence and accordingly arranged to avoid the possibility of damage to the components during the process of disassembly, restoration, or re-assembly. Extreme caution

must be exercised during the assembly procedure to avoid damage to the unit.

The upper and lower gearcases are held together by two studs which also serve to align the two gearcase sections. Alignment is accomplished by means of close tolerance shoulder immediately above the bottom threaded section of each stud, which fits into a similarly machined recess in the upper gearcase. Two self-locking nuts are used at

Figure 18.14   Small Cover Plate Removed from Front Exhaust Housing Covering Exposing Gearcase Cable

Figure 18.15   Removing Electrical Wiring

Figure 18.16   Exhaust Housing Cover

the top end of the gearcase studs to draw the gearcase sections together; the nuts are torqued to 18 to 20 foot pounds.

The self-locking nuts must not be re-used. New nuts should be installed on each occasion to ensure future security of the assembly.

It is important to prevent possible damage to the rear electro-magnet lead by removing the small screw, washer, and nylon holding block retaining the electro-magnet lead immediately after separating the upper and lower gearcase. Any attempt to remove the rear electro-magnets without first removing the retaining screw could result in the lead being torn from the electro-magnet.

Since the rear electro-magnet is fairly snugly slip-fitted into the gearcase, no pullers or drivers are required to re-move or install it. A small punch is inserted into the drive pin hole of the propeller shaft, and a few sharp pulls outward will remove the electro-magnet. Again, the lead must be free before the rear electro-magnet is removed. As the propeller shaft is pulled from the gearcase, the rear electro-magnet and the reverse gear assembly are brought out with it.

The pinion gear can now be extracted through the rear gearcase opening, by removing the forward gear assembly.

The manner in which the forward electro-magnet lead is secured should be noted. A quick glance will reveal the small channel at the bottom of the gearcase provided for the lead, and also will show how the lead is captured between the metal lead guard and the side of the gearcase.

The stiff nylon covering near the electro-magnet end of the lead conforms to the contour of the gearcase. Both this nylon covering and the metal guard prevent the lead from becoming entangled in the revolving gears.

NOTE: Caution must be exercised when installing the metal guard over the lead. If part of the lead is left protruding from the guard, the insulation may fray, exposing the bare wire and eventually shorting out the electro-magnet.

The electric shift cable can be removed only from the lower end of the upper gearcase. The cables used on standard and long length motors leads are identified as follows: green, forward; blue, reverse.

During disassembly of the electramatic shift gearcase, several important items should be noted:

1. The forward clutch hub is knurled.

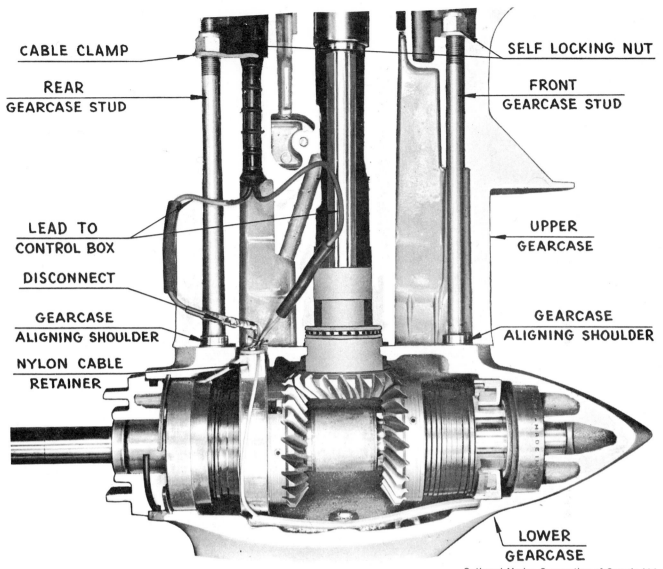

CABLE CLAMP

REAR
GEARCASE STUD

LEAD TO
CONTROL BOX

DISCONNECT

GEARCASE
ALIGNING SHOULDER

NYLON CABLE
RETAINER

SELF LOCKING NUT

FRONT
GEARCASE STUD

UPPER
GEARCASE

GEARCASE
ALIGNING SHOULDER

LOWER
GEARCASE

Outboard Marine Corporation of Canada Ltd.

Figure 18.17   Leads to Control Box and Disconnects

Figure 18.18   Remove Metal Lead Guard

Outboard Marine Corporation of Canada Ltd.

2. A bushing is used with the forward gear assembly.
3. A needle bearing is used with the reverse gear assembly.

The knurled clutch hub provides a more immediate drive coil engagement when used with the forward gear assembly. It is not recommended that the knurled clutch hub be used with the reverse gear assembly, since the greater percentage of motor operation is in forward gear, and also since the reverse gear and the reverse clutch hub are turning in opposite directions.

Similarly, the forward gear bushing should not be interchanged with the reverse gear needle bearing assembly. Again with the majority of motor operation in forward gear, and with both the forward gear and the forward clutch hub turning in the same direction, the use of a needle bearing assembly between the two eventually would result in the needles being flattened by normal vibration.

Cleanliness and caution are emphasized during assembly or disassembly of all gearcase components, particularly the forward gear and clutch hub. A metal chip, a speck of grit, or a hurried repair technician are frequently contributing factors leading to premature failure of electramatic gearcases.

Disassembling forward gear and clutch hub is accomplished by:
1. Removing the small snap ring from the clutch hub.
2. Carefully slipping the forward gear from the clutch hub.

If the bushing between the forward gear and the clutch hub starts to bind when the two parts are being separated, the operation should be stopped, the two parts carefully slipped back together, and the edges of the snap ring groove cleaned with crocus cloth, removing all traces of grit. Then disassembly can be resumed. The slightest scuffing or binding of the bushing render it useless, so that it must be replaced.

The nylon spacer, installed as shown between the drive coil and the gear, maintains a parallel relationship between the two. With the omission of this spacer, the drive coil is apt to fall out of line and to miss the coupling with the gear clutch hub.

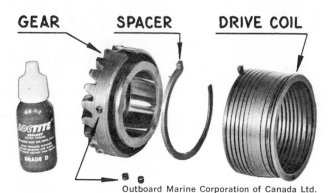

GEAR   SPACER   DRIVE COIL

Outboard Marine Corporation of Canada Ltd.
Figure 18.19   Gear, Drive, Coil, and Spacer

A recess is provided in the gear for the tabs of the spacer and drive coil. These tabs prevent the drive coil from turning in the gear and they locate the spacer.

The unit is held together by three Allen setscrews. The drive coil, spacer, and gear must be held together firmly while the three Allen setscrews are tightened, to eliminate the possibility of misalignment.

The Allen setscrews, size 8-32 thread by 5/32 inch long, are torqued to 15 to 20 inch pounds. It is strongly recommended that a drop of lock tight or similar fluid be applied to the threads of each setscrew during assembly to secure its position.

The electro-magnet has a rated current draw of 1.7 amperes, plus or minus .2 amperes. This current draw can be checked on the low ohm scale of the ohmmeter, as follows:
1. Set right hand dial of low ohm scale.

2. Tabulate scale (red) to infinity with low ohm dial.
3. Attach lead to electro-magnet as shown.
4. Scale reading should be approximately 8 ohms.

Outboard Marine Corporation of Canada Ltd.
Figure 18.20   Checking Electro-magnet with Stevens VOHM Meter

The electro-magnet is made up of many fine strands of copper wire coiled into a loop and contained within a steel casing. One end of the coil is attached to a lead, green or blue, the other to a ground. As the toggle switch in the control box is activated, the shift circuit is closed allowing the current to flow from either the forward or the reverse electro-magnet.

A magnetic field is then set up about the electro-magnet, and it is this magnetic field that accordingly draws the free end of the drive coil. Once this has been accomplished, the drive chain is electrically coupled for operation in either forward or reverse gear, whichever has been selected.

As the operator shifts from in-gear to neutral, the current flowing from the electro-magnet is broken by the toggle switch, causing the magnetic field about the electro-magnet to collapse. This in turn automatically releases the forward or the reverse drive.

Converting Engine from Long Shaft to Standard Lengths

Engines are converted from long (L) length to standard length in the manner outlined below. Naturally a standard length drive shaft must be used. Also, since engines which were shipped from the factory (new) are assembled with a long shift rod in the lower case, it is necessary to install the standard length gearcase shift rod to complete conversion.

The following items will be removed:
1. A gearcase extension.
2. Drive shaft extension.

It is not necessary to replace the two long water tubes with standard length tubes, since this necessitates removing the power head. Five inches should be cut off the bottom of each tube and the sharp edges left from the cutting carefully removed with emery cloth or sandpaper. All metal chips and sanding grit must be wiped off tubes prior to assembly.

The final assembly should be torqued as set up by the manufacturer of the specific motor.

Gear and Shifter Clutch Dog Wear

Gear and shifter clutch dogs may appear to be prematurely worn because the top edges of the ears are slightly rounded. This rounded condition is normal and is not indicative of, nor should be confused with, severely worn parts.

Outboard Marine Corporation of Canada Ltd.
Figure 18.21   Normal Gear Wear

Rounding or wear of ear edges on gears and clutch dogs is normal, even though the operator shifting practice is ideal. Gear and clutch dog wear can be much accelerated, however, by gentle shifting (easing into gear). Gears and clutch dogs removed for inspection from engines operated in this manner for prolonged periods are usually chipped or otherwise gently chewed up. Where the shifter clutch dog or gears are chipped, damaged parts should be replaced. For correct shifting practice to be understood, however, gear shift linkage adjustment of the engine must first be described, as illustrated in the next 10 figures.

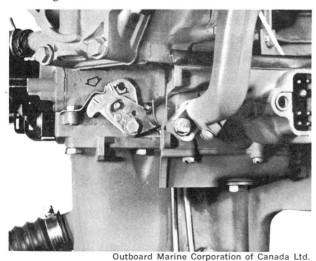

Outboard Marine Corporation of Canada Ltd.
Figure 18.22   Position of Shift Adjustment Bracket

Outboard Marine Corporation of Canada Ltd.
Figure 18.23   Securing Shift Adjustment Bracket

Outboard Marine Corporation of Canada Ltd.
Figure 18.24   Position of Shift Lever

Outboard Marine Corporation of Canada Ltd.
Figure 18.25   Position of Detent Plate

Outboard Marine Corporation of Canada Ltd.
Figure 18.26   Position of Detent Plate in Relation to Spring When Clutch Dog Should Disengage the Reverse Driving Gear

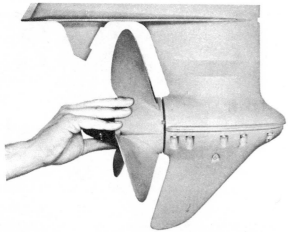

Outboard Marine Corporation of Canada Ltd.

Figure 18.27   Checking Engagement of Shifter Dog

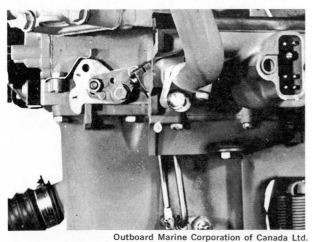

Outboard Marine Corporation of Canada Ltd.

Figure 18.28a   Position of Detent Plate When in Reverse

Outboard Marine Corporation of Canada Ltd.

Figure 18.28b   Position of Detent Plate When in Forward

Outboard Marine Corporation of Canada Ltd.

Figure 18.29   Position of Detent Plate When in Neutral

Outboard Marine Corporation of Canada Ltd.

Figure 18.30   Sectional View of Propeller Hub

It is of the utmost importance that the gear shift linkage in the lower unit be correctly adjusted, to minimize wear and possible damage to the engaging surfaces of the gear and shifter dog assembly. Once a gear shift procedure has been adopted, it should be continued; and it should be remembered that when in neutral, both forward and reverse driving gears should be completely disengaged and free to "float" on the propeller shaft. When in "forward", the forward driving gear should be fully engaged by the shifter clutch dog: when in "reverse", the reverse driving gear similarly should be fully engaged.

A detent plate and corresponding spring are attached to the motor assembly. A centred detent, engaging the spring, denotes neutral position, and linkage must be to this position. To adjust gear shifting linkage, proceed as follows:

1. Place the detent plate in position to engage the "fix" detent spring. Loosen the detent adjusting nut. Adjust the position of the linkage control plate so that the detent adjusting screw falls mid-way in the slot.

2. Tighten the detent adjusting screw in the neutral position.

3. Loosen the shift lever adjusting screw. Adjust to a position where the distance from (A) - (B) is 6.5 inches. (See Figure 18-24). Tighten the adjusting screw to secure the shift lever, an important adjustment required to accommodate the remote control shifting cable assembly.

4. Score marks on the detent plate when it is in line with the detent spring as shown in Figure 18-26, indicate the position of the shifter clutch at the time of breaking the engagement with the forward or reverse driving gears. As a possible check of linkage adjustment, set to forward position.

5. Turn the propeller by hand as shown, to check.

6. Repeat the process to check the reverse gear engagement.

7. Slight variations, if any, may be corrected by further adjustments of the detent plate.

After the linkage check, be certain also to check the adjustment of the knurled nut on the remote shift cable, if used, so that the cables lock and the plug aligns with the hole in the shifting lever when in neutral position. Double check this lock plug alignment in forward and reverse gears also, to be certain of full and complete gear engagement with remote operation.

The final step in reducing accelerated gear and clutch dog wear, is to advise the owner of the rules of shifting Johnson outboard engines:

1. Shift only at recommended idle speeds (600 RPM plus or minus a 100).

2. Smartly snap shift (a quick snappy movement of the gear shift lever to its full limit of travel).

3. Don't shift above recommended idle speeds.

4. Don't ease into gear.

5. Don't slam into gear.

Use only the type of gear lubricant that is recommended by the motor manufacturers, otherwise bearing and gear wear will result. The recommended lubricant is custom designed specifically for all use in the manufacturer's outboard gearcase.

CHRYSLER OUTBOARD ENGINES INSTRUCTIONS FOR REPLACE OR REPAIRING LOWER UNITS

Shock Mount Lower Thrust

The shock mount covers and shock mounts used on all models can be serviced and replaced without removing any other components or disrupting any settings.

Drive Shaft Removal

1. Disassemble the gear housing upper from the motor leg, and remove the water pump.

2. Pull the drive shaft up and out of the gear housing upper, being careful not to damage the drive shaft seal.

3. Inspect the drive shaft seal, replacing it if it is worn or damaged.

Assembly

4. Install the drive shaft from the top side of the gear housing upper. Dip the lower end of the drive shaft in oil and assemble carefully to prevent damage to the drive shaft seal.

5. Assemble the water pump to the gear housing, and the gear housing to motor leg, and adjust the gear shift linkage.

Stern Bracket Disassembly

1. Remove the angle adjusting bar from the hole in the lower end of the stern brackets.

2. Remove the hex nuts and/or safety chain ring from the stern bracket pivot bolt, and remove the pivot bolt. Remove the stern brackets. NOTE: Before the stern brackets can be removed, the tilt stop screws must be unscrewed from the swivel bracket. Make a note of the assembly method to facilitate reinstallation later.

Assembly

3. Install the tilt stops, port and starboard, to the stern brackets as follows:

A. Insert the tilt stop pivot through the hole in the top of the brackets.

B. Assemble the wavy washer and the spacer over the pivot screws.

C. Start the pivot screws in the stern bracket and tighten securely. Exercise caution when tightening to avoid burring the screw head, as this will cause the tilt mechanism to bind.

4. Re-install the stern brackets in the reverse order of disassembly, making sure to install the stern bracket friction cones between the stern brackets and the swivel bracket with the small end in the swivel bracket. Torque the pivot bolt nut to 110-130 inch pounds.

5. Install the free ends of the tilt stops to the swivel bracket, using a spacer only between the swivel bracket and the tilt stop brackets. Apply Loctite "D", Part No. T-2963, to the threads of the pivot screws in the swivel bracket only. Use caution when tightening pivot screws. NOTE: Assemble the spring to the stern bracket lock bar with the small end of the spring against the lock bar tabs.

Models Using Tilt Lock Plunger Only

6. If the tilt lock plunger and body have been removed from the stern bracket, install as follows:

A. Assemble the tilt lock plunger housing to the port stern bracket.

B. Install the spring over the plunger and insert the assembly into the hole in the upper-rear portion of the stern bracket from the inside. Apply Loctite "D" to the threads on the plunger.

C. Holding the large end of the plunger with pliers, push

it through the stern bracket and install the knob to the plunger. Tighten securely.

7. If the tilt stop pin has been removed, install to the top-rear hole in the starboard stern bracket, using a lock washer between the head of the pin and the stern bracket. Install the pin so that the unthreaded end protrudes through the inside surface of the stern bracket.

Swivel Bracket Removal

1. Remove the set screw from the upper-starboard side of the swivel bracket.

2. Remove the shock mount lower thrust as outlined in this section.

3. Pull the swivel bracket down and off the kingpin.

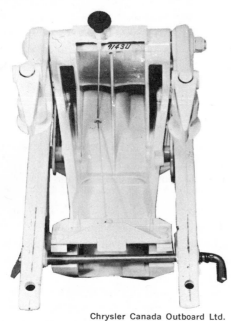

Chrysler Canada Outboard Ltd.

Figure 18.31   Stern-swivel Bracket and Reverse Lock Detail

Disassembly

REVERSE LOCK MECHANISM—It is not necessary to remove the swivel bracket to service the reverse lock.

4. Remove the reverse lock release cable from the reverse lock.

5. Remove the reverse lock pins from both sides of the lower end of the swivel bracket. Note the position of the reverse lock springs to facilitate reassembly. Remove the reverse lock mechanism. Replace the damaged parts as necessary.

Assembly

7. If the swivel bracket has been removed from the engine, proceed as follows:

A.   Coat the swivel bracket washer with grease and install on the kingpin.

B.   Coat the swivel bracket bearings in the top and bottom of the swivel bracket with grease and install the swivel bracket to the kingpin.

C.   Install the shock mount lower thrust and covers to the motor leg and kingpin.

D.   Install the set screw to the hole in the upper starboard side of the swivel bracket.

8. Install the reverse lock springs to the slots in the swivel bracket so that the hooked end of the springs will hook over the flange on the reverse lock.

9. Place the reverse lock into position and install the reverse lock pins. Apply Loctite "D" (T-2963) to the threads of the pins when installing.

10. Route the reverse lock cable through the hole in the top front of the swivel bracket, and down through the cable guide.

11. Install the reverse lock cable clip, screw and washer to the top of the reverse lock.

12. Route the reverse lock cable through the hole in the reverse lock, through the hole in the cable clip, under the washer on the screw, and through the other hole in the cable clip. Adjust the reverse lock cable so that there is no slack in it when the cable knob is "down", in the locked position (reverse lock engaged). Tighten the screw securely. Pull the release knob out to release the reverse lock. When tilting the engine, the reverse lock should just clear the lock bar in the stern brackets.

Friction Adjustments

Steering Friction

Steering handle models are controlled by a friction plate attached to the swivel bracket. Adjust the nut to obtain the steering friction desired.

Remote Control Models

Steering friction on remote control operated models is

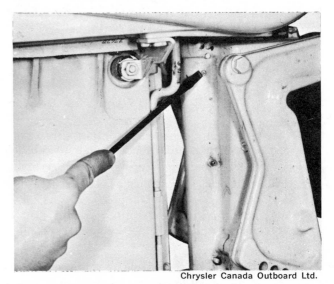

Chrysler Canada Outboard Ltd.

Figure 18.32   Adjusting Steering Friction

controlled by a friction screw in the top starboard side of the swivel bracket. This screw exerts pressure on the upper nylon swivel bracket bearing and in turn, applies pressure on the kingpin.

Motor Leg Covers

When installing motor leg covers, a procedure has been established which will greatly facilitate their installation.

1. Coat the grooves in the leg covers with a silicone rubber adhesive sealant and install rubber packing. Tape in place as shown in Figure 18-33. Make sure the motor leg covers are oriented correctly when installing. If they are not installed in the correct position, the covers will ground out and make a noise, or "sing".

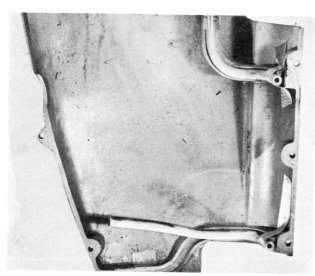

Chrysler Canada Outboard Ltd.

Figure 18.33   Installing Steering Friction

2. Place both cover halves into position around the motor leg.

3. Install one standard size mounting screw to the centre

Chrysler Canada Outboard Ltd.

Figure 18.34   Installing Leg Covers

hole in the forward set of mounting holes. Tighten securely.

4. Install one long screw (2") to the centre hole in the rear of mounting holes. Tighten securely.

5. Install the rest of the standard size screws to the leg covers and tighten securely.

6. Remove the long screw installed in Step 4 above, and install a standard size screw.

NOTE: When tilting or releasing, make sure that the engine is pointing straight ahead. If tilted with the engine turned, damage to the tilt mechanism and motor leg covers can occur as a result of the tilt mechanism striking the motor leg covers.

Trailering

The engine may be trailered with the engine held in the tilted position by the tilt hole mechanism. However, it is recommended that a block of wood be wedged into the open area between the stern and swivel bracket for added protection.

Water Pump

The water pump used on Models 35 through 50 H.P. acts as a positive displacement type at low engine speeds and a centrifugal type pump at higher engine speeds. It is located at the top of the gear housing upper, and consists of a water pump body, impeller, and a top and back plate of stainless steel. The impeller is driven by the drive shaft which passes through the centre of the water pump body.

Operation

The water pump impeller, keyed to the drive shaft, turns within a cam-shaped cavity in the water pump body. As the impeller turns, water is picked up from the intake, forced through the pump body and up the water inlet line to the power head. A thermostat is used on 35 through 50 HP models to control the water temperature in the power head. When the engine is cold, and the thermostat is closed, water flows through the by-pass line located between the cylinder head and exhaust port cover. After the engine has reached operating temperature, approximately 165°, the thermostat is fully open. The flow through the by-pass line is now restricted. If the thermostat is removed for operation, water will continue to flow through the by-pass line, and overheating of the engine will result.

Removing Gear Housing from Motor Leg

1. Disconnect the coupler between the shift rod intermediate and the shift rod upper, as shown in Figure 18-35. On models using the acoustical leg cover, it will be necessary to remove the covers for accessibility to the coupler.

2. Remove the four screws that attach the gear housing to the motor leg, and remove the gear housing.

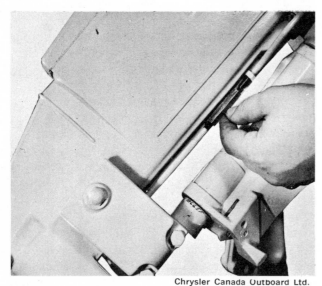

Figure 18.35   Shift Rod Coupler

Disassembly of Water Pump

1. Remove three screws that attach the water pump body to the gear housing.
2. Slide the water pump body and impeller off the drive shaft.
3. Remove the impeller drive pin and the water pump back plate.

Re-assembly of Water Pump

1. Install the water pump back plate to the gear housing upper.
2. Install the water pump drive pin and slide the impeller down over the drive shaft.
3. Place the water pump top plate in the pump body. Use a small amount of grease on the back of the top plate to retain it to the pump body.
4. Slide the pump body down over the drive shaft. Rotate the drive shaft and push the pump body over the impeller. Install three pump body retaining screws.

Assembly of Shift Linkage

1. Slide the shift handle and shaft into the boss on the motor leg. Place the spacer inside the motor leg and insert the shaft through the spacer and into the gear shift lever arm. Hold the shift handle tight against the boss and the gear shift lever arm tight against the spacer. Tighten the screw and locknut.
NOTE: The shift handle should be in a vertical position when gears in gear housing are in neutral. Adjustment of the handle may be accomplished by removing the shift handle and shaft, and turning the gear shift arm and coupling clockwise or counterclockwise, whichever is necessary to align the handle in a vertical position.

2. Install a new cylinder exhaust gasket with correct side up.
3. Install the power head and connecting linkages.

Installing Gear Housing to Motor Leg

1. Install the drive shaft upper spline seal to the drive shaft.
2. Apply a coating of grease to the end of the water line so that it will engage easily into the water pump body boss. Apply a generous amount of grease to the spline on the drive shaft.
3. Assemble the gear housing to the motor leg, guiding the shift rod and driveshaft into place.
4. Be sure the inlet water line is engaged properly to the water pump body boss, and then install four screws and nuts, retaining the gear housing to the motor leg, and torque to 256-275 inch pounds.
5. Assemble the gear shift rod coupling between the shift rod upper and lower. Be sure the right hand thread in the coupler is to the top.

Adjusting the Gear Shift Linkage

1. Shift the gear housing to forward by moving the shift arm or handle into the forward position.
2. Scribe a mark on the gear shift rod where it emerges from the motor leg. (See "A", Figure 18-36).
3. Shift the engine into neutral. Again, scribe a mark on the gear shift rod. (See "B", Figure 18-36).

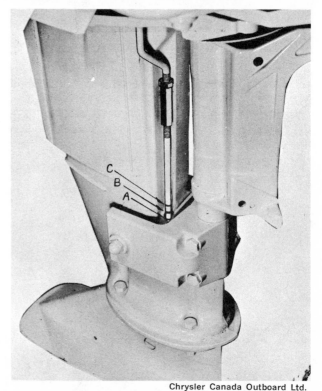

Figure 18.36   Scribing Gear Shift Rod

4. Shift the engine into reverse and again scribe a mark on the gear shift rod. (See "C", Figure 18-36). The distance between the marks should be equal.

5. Adjust the gear shift rod coupling clockwise or counter-clockwise, or whichever is necessary to align the marks an equal distance apart.

Motor Leg Covers

On models using motor leg covers, to facilitate this installation, the following procedure should be followed:

1. Place both cover halves into position around the motor leg.

2. Install one standard size mounting screw to the centre hole in the forward set of mounting holes. Tighten securely.

3. Install one long screw (2″) to the centre hole in the rear set of mounting holes. Tighten securely.

4. Install the rest of the standard size screws to the leg covers and tighten securely.

5. Remove the long screw installed in Step 3 above, and install a standard size screw. If the long screw described in Step 3 above is not used, installation of the leg covers can prove very difficult and cumbersome.

Disassembly of Gear Housing

1. Remove the gear housing from the motor leg as outlined under "Water Pump Servicing".

2. Drain the lubricant from the gear housing.

3. Remove the water pump and drive shaft.

4. Disconnect the gear shift rod intermediate and lower coupling, and remove the nut from the front stud, as shown in Figure 18-37.

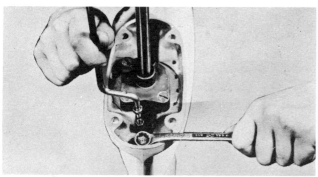

Chrysler Canada Outboard Ltd.
Figure 18.37   Removing Lower Coupling and Nut

5. Remove two Allen head screws retaining the propeller shaft bearing cage, and turn the cage 90 degrees.

6. Install two 3/16″ x 1½″ screws and nuts in the propeller shaft bearing cage, and remove the cage using Special Tool #T-1904.

NOTE: Before removing the bearing cage, be sure to remove all burrs on the propeller shaft with a file.

7. Remove the nut from the rear stud, shown in Figure 18-37, and separate the gear housing lower from the upper.

8. Remove the bevel pinion gear bearing cup and bevel pinion gear and bearing assembly from the gear housing lower.

9. Pull the propeller shaft assembly from the gear housing, as shown in Figure 18-38(a), 18-38(b) and remove the front and rear bevel gears.

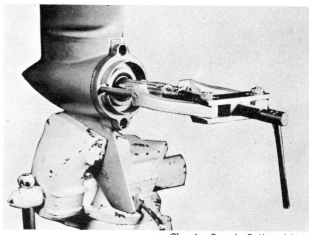

Chrysler Canada Outboard Ltd.
Figure 18.38a   Removing Propeller Shaft Bearing Case

Chrysler Canada Outboard Ltd.
Figure 18.38b   Gear Housing Stud Nut

Chrysler Canada Outboard Ltd.
Figure 18.39   Removing Propeller Shaft

10. Remove the clutch pin retaining ring from the clutch.
NOTE: When removing the retaining ring, be careful not

to lose the clutch detent ball and spring. (See Figure 18-40.)

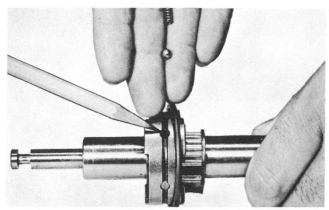

Figure 18.40   Clutch Detent Ball and Spring

11. Use a drift punch to drive the spring out of the clutch.
12. Remove the clutch and shift pin from the propeller shaft.

Removing Front Bevel Gear Housing Cup From Lower Gear Housing

13. Remove the gear shift rod lower assembly from the gear housing.
14. Place the bearing cup remover, Special Tool #J21328, behind the bearing cup.
15. Using the bushing guide set, Special Tool #J9385-3, remove the bearing cup, as shown in Figure 18-41, 18-42, 18-43, 18-44.

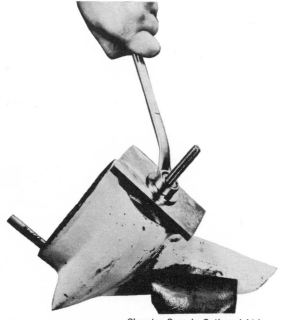

Figure 18.41   Removing Bearing Cup

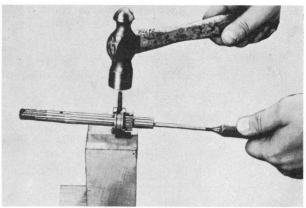

Figure 18.42   Installing Clutch

Figure 18.43   Installing Bevel Gear Bearing

Figure 18.44   Installing Bevel Gear Bearing

Assembly of Gear Housing

Installing Front Bevel Gear Bearing Cup

1. Use Special Tools, #J21838 Adapter, #J-8592 Driving Handle and #J9385-3 Bushing Guide to drive the front bevel gear bearing into place, as shown in Figure 18-45.

Figure 18.45 Installing Bearing Cup

The bottom of the bearing cup must settle in the gear housing.

NOTE: A light coating of oil should be applied on the outside of the bearing cup before it is driven into place. Be sure to use a block wood under the gear housing when driving the bearing cup in place.

Assembly of Clutch to Propeller Shaft

2. Assemble the clutch to the splined portion of the propeller shaft, making sure that the detents for the clutch detent ball in the propeller shaft are aligned with the hole in the clutch.

3. Insert the gear shift pin into the end of the propeller shaft, and drive the spring through the clutch and through the hole in shift pin. Use a drift punch to align the shift pin, as shown in Figure 18-46. Do not drive the spring pin all the way down. Allow the end to protrude 3/32", or the thickness of the retaining ring. This will serve to prevent the retaining ring from turning and releasing the detent ball and spring.

4. Insert the detent ball and spring into the hole in the clutch and slide the retaining ring into place.

NOTE: The protruding portion of the spring pin must be between the ends of the retaining ring.

5. Install the gear shift rod lower assembly to the gear housing.

6. Install the thrust washer and front bevel gear and bear-

Figure 18.46 Installing Shift Pin

ing assembly and the thrust washer and rear gear and bearing assembly to the propeller shaft. Assemble the gear shift yoke to the shift pin in the propeller shaft with the open end down. Use a small amount of grease to hold the yoke in position.

Installing Propeller Shaft Assembly to Gear Housing

7. Install the propeller shaft assembly to the gear housing lower, as shown in Figure 18-43. Make sure the pins on either side of the gear shift arm yoke engage with the slots in the gear shift arm.

8. Install the bevel pinion gear, pinion gear bearing and bearing cup to the gear housing lower.

Replacement of Drive Shaft Seal

9. If the drive shaft seal, located in gear housing upper, is in need of replacement, proceed as follows:

A. Use a screwdriver to pry the seal out from the top. Caution: Do not damage the machined surface of the gear housing.

B. Install the new seal with the spring on the sealing lip to the top (garter spring toward the water side).

C. Apply a generous amount of grease to the area between the lips of the seal.

D. Use a socket or pipe of proper size to drive the seal in place.

Replacement of Shift Rod Seal

10. If the shift rod seal, located on bottom of gear housing upper, is in need of replacement, proceed as follows:

A. Use a screwdriver to pry out the seal retainer, and remove the seal retainer, seal and spacer.

B. Install the spacer, new seal, small seal retainer, and new large seal retainer, in that order.

C. Flatten the seal retainer with a large ball peen hammer.

Assembly of Lower Gear Housing to Upper Gear Housing

11. Coat both sides of a new gear housing gasket with Permatex #1 or Gasoila Varnish Sealer and install to the lower gear housing.

NOTE: If the gear housing stud front has been removed, apply Loctite "D" (T-2963) to ¾″ of threads when re-installing. If the rear stud in the gear housing upper has been removed, install to a height of 1-7/32″.

12. Assemble the lower gear housing to the upper and tighten the stud nuts securely.

13. Install the coupler to the gear shift rod lower. Turn the coupler all the way down.

A. With the lower unit in forward gear (the gear shift rod lower pushed all the way down), turn the gear shift rod intermediate into the coupling until the bend in the rod clears the water pump body by approximately 1/16 inch.

B. Turn the gear shift rod intermediate approximately 28 degrees from the centre to the starboard side, and tighten the locknut to retain this position. (See Figure 18-47.)

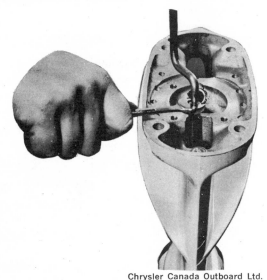

Chrysler Canada Outboard Ltd.

Figure 18.47 Installing Gear Shift Rod

14. Install the drive shaft and water pump assembly as previously outlined under "Water Pump Servicing".

NOTE: When re-installing the gear housing assembly to the motor leg, torque the bolts to 265-275 inch pounds.

Replacement of Propeller Shaft Seal

15. If the propeller shaft seal, located in the propeller bearing cage, is in need of replacement, proceed as follows:

A. Use a screwdriver to pry the old seal out of the bearing cage.

B. Install the new seal with the garter spring on the sealing lip to the outside.

C. Apply a generous amount of grease to the area between the lips of the seal.

D. Use a socket or pipe of proper size to drive the seal in place.

Installing Propeller Shaft Bearing

16. Place the propeller shaft seal protector, Special Tool #T-3617, over the end of the propeller shaft and install the propeller shaft bearing cage to the lower gear housing. A coating of grease on bearing cage outer "O" ring seal will help facilitate this operation.

Installing Gear Housing and Motor Leg Extension to Motor Leg

1. Install the screw, locknut, and square nut to the gear shift lever arm on end of the shift rod.

2. Install the drive shaft upper spline seal to the drive shaft.

3. Position the nylon gear shift rod guide with the "V" pointing to the drive shaft. The notches on the guide must be to the top.

4. Apply a coating of grease to end of the water line so that it will engage easily into the water line extension. Apply a generous coating of grease to the spline on the drive shaft.

5. Attach a piece of wire or string to the arm on the end of the shift rod. Feed the wire up through the motor leg.

6. Pull on the wire to guide the shift rod lever arm up through the motor leg while assembling the gear housing to the motor leg.

7. Be sure the water line and water line extension are properly engaged and then proceed to install and tighten four screws and nuts which secure the motor leg extension to the motor leg.

Models Using Two Piece Shift Rod

1. Remove the water pump body, impeller and drive shaft.

2. Install the new long drive shaft and re-assemble the water pump. Be sure the water pump impeller drive pin is properly engaged through the drive shaft and impeller.

3. Remove the shift rod lower from the gear housing and re-assemble to the new gear shift rod extension.

4. Install the gear shift rod and extension to the gear housing. The gear shift rod and extension should be turned all the way down and then backed out to the correct position.

5. Apply a small amount of grease to the end of the water line extension and insert in the water pump body seal.

6. Assemble the motor leg extension to the gear housing and tighten securely.

NOTE: The motor leg extension must be installed with the "Spray Plate" pointing forward and toward the skeg of the lower gear housing.

Installing Gear Housing and Motor Leg Extension to Motor Leg

1. Install the upper drive shaft spline seal to shaft and apply a generous coating of grease on the spline.

2. Apply a light coat of grease to the end of the water line to enable it to fit easily into the water line extension.

3. Assemble the gear housing and motor leg extension to the motor leg. Install two screws which retain the gear shift rod lower to the upper.

4. Be sure the water line and water line extension are properly engaged and then proceed to install and tighten four screws and nuts which secure the motor leg extension to the motor leg.

Lubricating Lower Gear Housing

The grease in the lower gear housing should be checked after every 30 hours of operation and replaced every 100 hours, at least, each season with a Non-Corrosive Leaded Outboard Gear Oil—EP90, such as Texaco Outboard Gear Oil—EP90 or equivalent. DO NOT USE A CORROSIVE HYPOID OIL UNDER ANY CIRCUMSTANCES.

To Drain:
With the engine in an upright position, remove both the upper and lower plug screws and allow the grease to drain completely.

To Refill:
1. When all the water and diluted grease has drained, insert the nozzle of the gear lubricant into the lower screw hole.

2. Add lubricant until it appears at the top hole.

3. Re-install the top plug screw and washer.

4. Re-install the lower plug screw and washer. Tighten securely.

5. Allow the engine to stand in an upright position for at least half an hour to permit the gear lubricant to completely fill all cavities in the gear housing.

6. Remove the top plug screw and washer and recheck the gear lubricant level. Add grease as outlined below if necessary to bring the lubricant level up to top hole. Re-install the top screw and washer, and tighten securely.

To Add Grease:
1. Remove the lower plug screw and washer, and insert the nozzle of the gear lubricant into the lower screw hole.

2. Remove the upper plug screw and washer.

3. Add the lubricant until it appears at the upper hole.

4. Re-install the upper plug screw and washer, and tighten securely.

5. Re-install the lower plug screw and washer, and tighten securely.

REVIEW QUESTIONS

1. What is the purpose of the outboard lower unit?
2. How many basic parts make up the lower unit?
3. Name the chemical process which retards salt water action on the aluminum lower units.
4. The slip clutch was formerly used on the drive shaft. Where is it now located on outboard motors?
5. If the drive shaft breaks for no apparent reason what might be the cause?
6. Name the two methods for checking housing alignment.
7. List the steps necessary to drain and refill a lower unit gear case.
8. What damage should one look for when examining seal seats of a lower unit?
9. Explain the operation of the Johnson CD drive shaft shock absorber.
10. What type of bearings are used in the Johnson QD outboard engine lower unit?
11. Draw a diagram of how the shifter system operates.
12. What is the outboard motor "skeg"?
13. Describe the method for disassembly and reassembly of the gearcase assembly.
14. List the parts of the electramatic gear shift assembly.
15. How does the electramatic shift operate?
16. Can the forward gear bushing be interchanged with the gear needle bearing assembly?
17. What is the correct way to shift gears on an outboard motor?
18. Where is the friction screw located on the lower unit of the Chrysler outboard engine?
19. How is the gear shift linkage adjusted on the Chrysler outboard?
20. List the steps necessary to replace the propeller shaft seal on the Chrysler outboard engine.
21. How often should the lower gear housing grease be checked?
22. How often should the lower gear housing grease be changed?
23. List the steps necessary to dismantle the water pump of the Chrysler outboard.
24. How does the Chrysler outboard water pump operate?
25. What added precaution should be taken when "trailering" an outboard engine?
26. On the Johnson outboard engine, what will increase the wear on the clutch dogs and gear edges?

27. What steps should be taken to convert a long shaft engine to a short shaft engine?

28. What is the "current draw" of a electro-magnet of the electramatic shift system?

29. How is the alignment of the upper and lower gear case accomplished in the Johnson electramatic gear shift?

30. Why is it advisable to remove the strip plate above the cavitation plate when tank testing an outboard engine?

CHAPTER 19
SERVICING
OUTBOARD MOTORS

In this chapter we discuss some important items in servicing outboard engines: nomenclature of the outboard, trouble shooting, propellers, and rpm performance.

OUTBOARD MOTOR NOMENCLATURE

Sometimes the words "right" and "left" are very confusing in reference to an outboard motor, and so the terms "starboard" and "port" are used instead. Starboard means on

the right hand while facing the bow (front) of the boat; port means on left hand.

Service required for the Johnson 9½ HP motor is generally one of three kinds:

1. Normal care and maintenance. This includes putting a new motor into operation, storing motors, lubrication, and care under special operating conditions, such as in salt water and in cold weather.

2. Operating malfunction due to improper motor mounting, propeller condition, or the malfunction of some part of the motor. This includes motor tune-up procedures to keep the motor in prime operating condition.

3. Complete disassembly and overhaul, such as inspecting a motor that has been submerged, or rebuilding trade-in units.

The service man must be able to determine before disassembly just what the trouble is, and how to correct it quickly at minimum expense to the owner. The Trouble Check Chart below helps in diagnosing motor malfunctions.

JOHNSON CHECK CHART

TROUBLE	POSSIBLE CAUSE
1. Motor	A. Fuel system
will	Fuel line improperly connected
not	Engine not primed
start	Speed control not advanced (throttle closed)

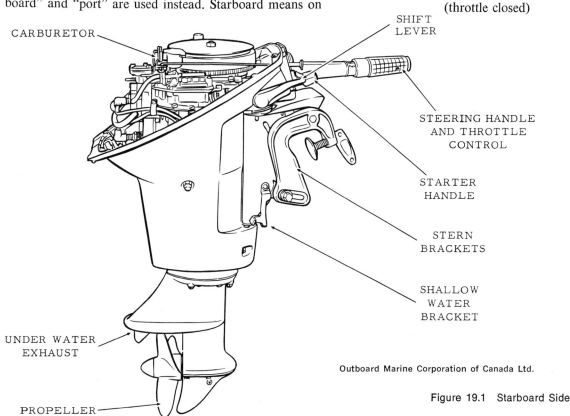

CARBURETOR

SHIFT LEVER

STEERING HANDLE AND THROTTLE CONTROL

STARTER HANDLE

STERN BRACKETS

SHALLOW WATER BRACKET

UNDER WATER EXHAUST

PROPELLER

Outboard Marine Corporation of Canada Ltd.

Figure 19.1 Starboard Side

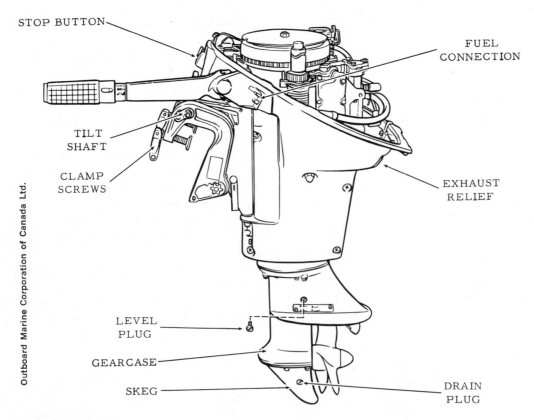

STOP BUTTON

FUEL CONNECTION

TILT SHAFT

CLAMP SCREWS

EXHAUST RELIEF

LEVEL PLUG

GEARCASE

SKEG

DRAIN PLUG

Outboard Marine Corporation of Canada Ltd.

Engine flooded
Old fuel
Clogged fuel filter
Choke not closing completely
Fuel system faulty

B. Ignition system
   Timing, cam, or linkage improperly
      adjusted
   Inverted breaker cam
   Sheared flywheel key
   Safety switch screws loose
   Ignition system faulty

2. Loss of A. Power head
   power   Carburetor and magneto not synchronized
   (assum-   Throttle control won't advance
   ing   Air leak at manifold gaskets—warped
   ignition   manifold (backfires)
   is not   Broken leaf valves (backfires)
   faulty)   Excessive carbon on pistons and cylinder
                  head
              Stuck piston, rings, or scored cylinder
   B. Carburetor
      Poor fuel mix—too much oil
      Carburetor adjustment (too lean—
         (backfires; too rich—excessive fuel)
      Choke not operating

Air leaks at packing nuts
Inlet needle and seat worn or sticky
Incorrect carburetor float setting
Incorrect orifice plug

C. Fuel pump and tank
   Faulty fuel hose (poor clamps or seals)
      (kinked)
   Fuel tank or pump filter plugged
   Fuel filter restricted
   Fuel and vent valves not opening
   Valves not operating
   Operating hose passage restricted
   Diaphragm leaking or damaged
   Fuel system hoses plugged

D. Exhaust gas entering carburetor
   Exhaust cover screws leaking
   Cover plate gasket damaged
   Damaged exhaust housing seal
   Exhaust relief boot cut
   Adapter gaskets leaking
   Cracked exhaust housing
   Exhaust tube to cylinder screws
      loose or missing

E. Overheating power head
   Exhaust cover gasket leaking
   Inner exhaust cover leaking
   Thermostat housing broken

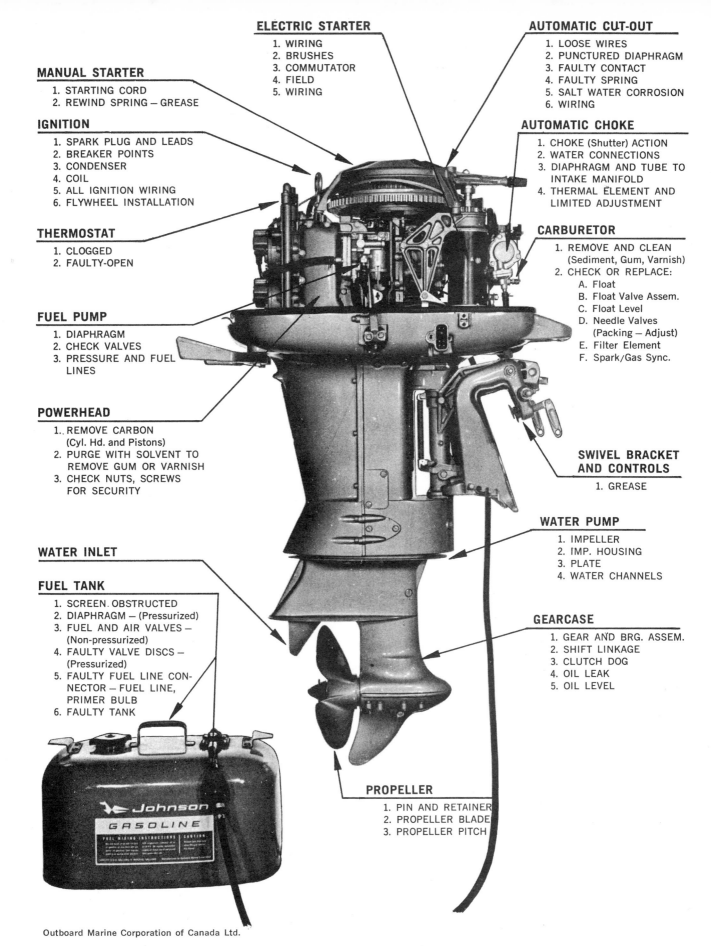

MANUAL STARTER

1. STARTING CORD
2. REWIND SPRING – GREASE

IGNITION

1. SPARK PLUG AND LEADS
2. BREAKER POINTS
3. CONDENSER
4. COIL
5. ALL IGNITION WIRING
6. FLYWHEEL INSTALLATION

THERMOSTAT

1. CLOGGED
2. FAULTY-OPEN

FUEL PUMP

1. DIAPHRAGM
2. CHECK VALVES
3. PRESSURE AND FUEL LINES

POWERHEAD

1. REMOVE CARBON (Cyl. Hd. and Pistons)
2. PURGE WITH SOLVENT TO REMOVE GUM OR VARNISH
3. CHECK NUTS, SCREWS FOR SECURITY

WATER INLET

FUEL TANK

1. SCREEN. OBSTRUCTED
2. DIAPHRAGM – (Pressurized)
3. FUEL AND AIR VALVES – (Non-pressurized)
4. FAULTY VALVE DISCS – (Pressurized)
5. FAULTY FUEL LINE CONNECTOR – FUEL LINE, PRIMER BULB
6. FAULTY TANK

ELECTRIC STARTER

1. WIRING
2. BRUSHES
3. COMMUTATOR
4. FIELD
5. WIRING

AUTOMATIC CUT-OUT

1. LOOSE WIRES
2. PUNCTURED DIAPHRAGM
3. FAULTY CONTACT
4. FAULTY SPRING
5. SALT WATER CORROSION
6. WIRING

AUTOMATIC CHOKE

1. CHOKE (Shutter) ACTION
2. WATER CONNECTIONS
3. DIAPHRAGM AND TUBE TO INTAKE MANIFOLD
4. THERMAL ELEMENT AND LIMITED ADJUSTMENT

CARBURETOR

1. REMOVE AND CLEAN (Sediment, Gum, Varnish)
2. CHECK OR REPLACE:
   A. Float
   B. Float Valve Assem.
   C. Float Level
   D. Needle Valves (Packing – Adjust)
   E. Filter Element
   F. Spark/Gas Sync.

SWIVEL BRACKET AND CONTROLS

1. GREASE

WATER PUMP

1. IMPELLER
2. IMP. HOUSING
3. PLATE
4. WATER CHANNELS

GEARCASE

1. GEAR AND BRG. ASSEM.
2. SHIFT LINKAGE
3. CLUTCH DOG
4. OIL LEAK
5. OIL LEVEL

PROPELLER

1. PIN AND RETAINER
2. PROPELLER BLADE
3. PROPELLER PITCH

Outboard Marine Corporation of Canada Ltd.

Figure 19.3   Suggested Tune-up Chart

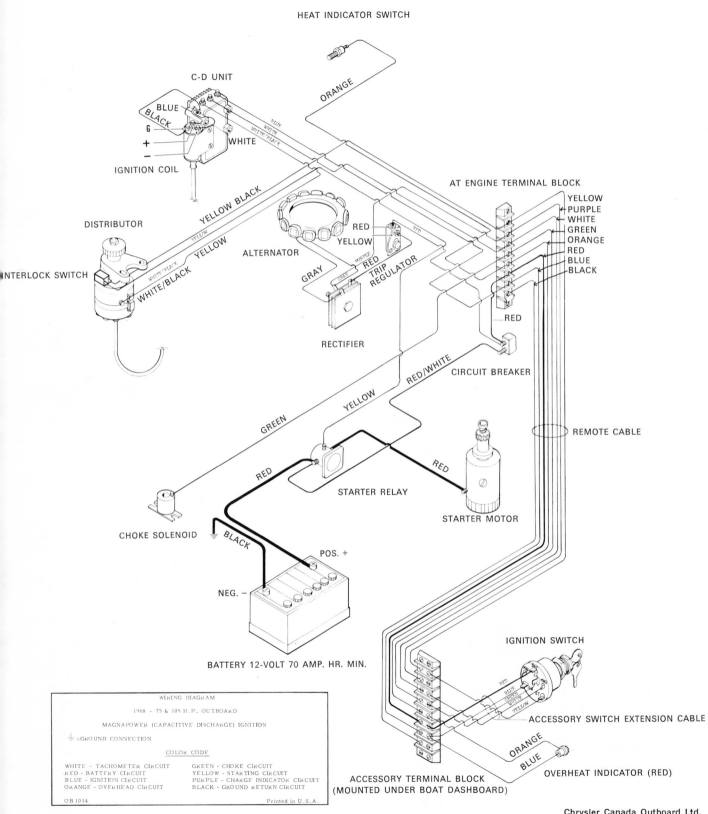

HEAT INDICATOR SWITCH

ORANGE

C-D UNIT

BLUE
BLACK
G
+
−
WHITE

IGNITION COIL

WHITE
WHITE/BLACK

AT ENGINE TERMINAL BLOCK

YELLOW
PURPLE
WHITE
GREEN
ORANGE
RED
BLUE
BLACK

YELLOW BLACK

DISTRIBUTOR

YELLOW

ALTERNATOR

RED
YELLOW

RED
YELLOW

INTERLOCK SWITCH

WHITE/BLACK

YELLOW

GRAY

GRAY

PURPLE

RED

RED
TRI/P
REGULATOR

RED

RECTIFIER

RED/WHITE

CIRCUIT BREAKER

REMOTE CABLE

GREEN

YELLOW

RED

STARTER RELAY

RED

STARTER MOTOR

CHOKE SOLENOID

BLACK

POS. +

NEG. −

BATTERY 12-VOLT 70 AMP. HR. MIN.

IGNITION SWITCH

RED
BLUE
GREEN
WHITE
YELLOW

ACCESSORY SWITCH EXTENSION CABLE

ORANGE
BLUE

ACCESSORY TERMINAL BLOCK
(MOUNTED UNDER BOAT DASHBOARD)

OVERHEAT INDICATOR (RED)

WIRING DIAGRAM

1968 - 75 & 105 H.P. OUTBOARD

MAGNAPOWER (CAPACITIVE DISCHARGE) IGNITION

= GROUND CONNECTION

COLOR CODE

WHITE - TACHOMETER CIRCUIT   GREEN - CHOKE CIRCUIT
RED - BATTERY CIRCUIT   YELLOW - STARTING CIRCUIT
BLUE - IGNITION CIRCUIT   PURPLE - CHARGE INDICATOR CIRCUIT
ORANGE - OVERHEAD CIRCUIT   BLACK - GROUND RETURN CIRCUIT

OB 1034   Printed in U.S.A.

Chrysler Canada Outboard Ltd.

Figure 19.4   Typical Wiring Diagram

Power head gasket improperly installed
   or damaged
Head gasket leaking (warped head—
   water in cylinders)

F. Lower unit
  Water intakes obstructed
  Pump plate not sealing (bottom)
  Pump impeller damaged
  Pump housing or plate worn
  Pump housing seal worn (driveshaft
    grooved)
  Water tube bushing loose

G. Exhaust gases entering cooling system
  Pump impeller plate not sealing (bottom)
  Damaged water tube grommets or
    "O" rings
  Pump housing seal damaged

3. Motor misfires (assuming fuel system and carburetor are not faulty)

A. Spark plugs
  Crossed or reversed leads
  Cover or inner terminal damaged
    (spark plug point out of H.T. lead)
  Faulty leads
  Loose—low torque
  Incorrect heat range
  Defective (cracked insulator)

B. Magneto
  Incorrectly adjusted points (vibration)
  Loose wiring
  Coil or condenser damaged (loose)
  Fibre breaker block worn
  Points dirty or pitted
  Defective breaker cam

4. Poor performance on boat

A. Incorrect propeller
  Incorrect tilt angle (smoking)
  Poor fuel mix—too much oil (smoking)
  Propeller hub slipping
  Bent or worn propeller
  Exhaust outlet damaged
  Bent gear housing or exhaust housing
    (broken driveshafts)
  Altitude horsepower loss
  Exhaust leaks
  Overheating

B. Cavitation
  Protruding hull attachments
  Keel too long
  Bent propeller (vibration)
  Transom too high

C. Boat
  Improper load distribution
  Marine growth on bottom
  Added weight (water absorption)
  Hook in bottom

CHECKING FIELD COILS

Since one end of the field coil winding is grounded to the frame of the starter motor (see Figure 19-5), it is difficult to make a resistance test on the windings of this circuit. However, a stall-torque test can be used to determine field coil condition.

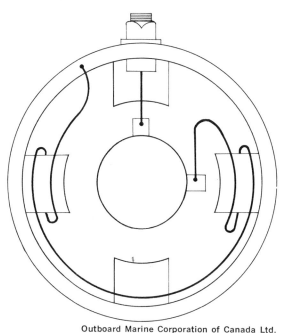

Outboard Marine Corporation of Canada Ltd.

Figure 19.5 Field Coil Viewed from Commutator End

Since field coils are serviced only in an assembly with the starter frame, it is not necessary to weld the field coil ground strap to the starter frame in the service shop.

STARTER TESTING - NO-LOAD TEST

The no-load test will determine whether or not a starter motor is capable of developing maximum power (RPM in this instance) under free-running conditions. This test can be made by merely removing the starter from the engine, installing two 1/4-20 nuts to the starter thru-bolts to hold the motor together, clamping the starter in a vise, and making an electrical hookup with the necessary equipment. If the starter is in satisfactory condition, the amperage draw during no-load running should be approximately 43 amperes. Armature shaft speed during this test should be 6,000 rpm minimum; and the voltmeter hooked in this circuit should indicate 6 volts. If the starter motor turns slowly, smokes after a very few seconds of running, or gets hot instantly, *stop testing.*

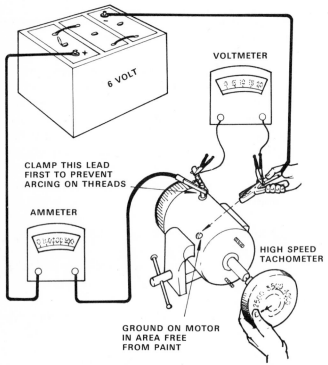

Figure 19.6 Starter Test

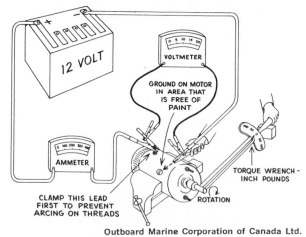

Outboard Marine Corporation of Canada Ltd.

Figure 19.7 Starter Test—Stall Torque

Starter should be disassembled and checked for shorts. If the armature checks as sound in this instance, the field coils can be assumed defective.

CAUTION: Use only a 6 volt battery (fully charged) when making no-load tests to avoid excessive free-running and subsequent overheating. Allow sufficient time for the starter to return to normal room temperature if it is necessary to repeat the no-load test.

It is recommended that a no-load test be made following internal starter motor repairs to determine whether or not the starter is operating at maximum efficiency. Excessive amperage readings during no-load testing usually point up conditions of faulty brushes (high resistance) and/or armature shaft bind. Generally speaking, if the armature turns freely by hand, yet an excessive amperage or low rpm reading is recorded during testing, the brushes may require replacing, the commutator may require turning and undercutting, or both.

STARTER TESTING - STALL TORQUE

Stall-torque testing is used to determine whether or not the starter has sufficient turning power to crank the engine for fast starting. For a stall-torque test, the starter motor must be removed, and the same basic hook-up made as is utilized for no-load testing. The inside of a $1\frac{1}{8}$ inch brass or steel nut can be grooved with a three-corner file to fit over the spur gear so that a socket and

torque wrench can be adapted to the armature for this test.

With the nut, socket, and torque wrench attached to the armature gear, momentary closing of the electrical circuit should be ample to note stall torque which will be indicated on the torque wrench dial (minimum 48 inch-pounds or 4 foot-pounds), and maximum amperage draw (330 amperes). The voltmeter reading during this test should be approximately 9.0 volts. If the motor smokes or gets hot instantly, *stop testing*. The starter should be disassembled and checked for shorts. If the brushes and armature do not prove faulty, the field coils are no doubt shorted.

CAUTION: Use only a fully charged 12 volt battery when making a stall-torque test. Obtain readings as rapidly as possible to prevent starter overheating. Allow sufficient time for the starter to return to room temperature if it is necessary to repeat stall-torque test.

Stall-torque testing should always follow internal starter motor repairs. If a low stall-torque and excessive amperage draw is noted, and the armature and brushes can be proven satisfactory, the trouble can generally be traced to the field coils.

Each armature coil can also be checked for an open circuit during the stall-torque test, merely by rotating the torque wrench handle through a 180 degree arc after the initial torque reading is noted. This must be done quickly. The torque should be uniform throughout this arc, although the reading will decrease slightly each time the brushes move from one commutator segment to another. However, if an appreciably wide area is found in which very little torque is noted, the starter should be disassembled and the commutator examined carefully. If two commutator segments which are located approximately 180 degrees apart from each other appear excessively burnt, the armature has an open-circuited coil. If this condition is caused by a loose wire, the wire can be re-soldered and the commutator turned and undercut, providing the burning is not excessive. Otherwise the armature must be replaced.

STARTER CIRCUIT TESTING

NOTE: All starter circuit testing must be done with a fully charged 12 volt battery.

Starting circuit testing is a quick means of pinpointing probable causes of hard starting that may result from a faulty electrical component. The following series of tests can be made without having to remove any components from the engine—merely by hooking test meters to the various components in the circuit as indicated by the accompanying illustrations.

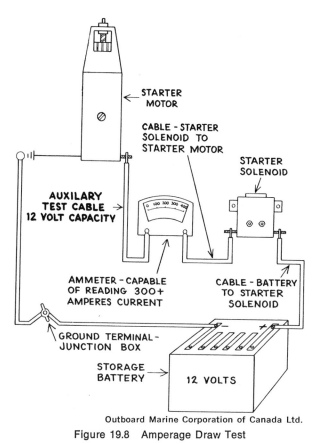

Figure 19.8   Amperage Draw Test

STARTER MOTOR AMPERAGE DRAW TEST

The red battery cable is removed from the starter motor and attached to an ammeter that is capable of reading several hundred amperes. Another short piece of 12 volt battery cable (auxiliary test cable) is used to hook the other ammeter post to the starter motor terminal. The ignition switch starting circuit is closed and the amperage read with the engine cranking (high tension lead from coil grounded to engine to prevent starting). The amperage draw should be between the minimum and maximum amounts specified as follows if the starter motor is in good condition (minimum 110 amperes, maximum 140 amperes).

CAUTION: Avoid operating starter motor continuously for more than 30 seconds to prevent overheating.

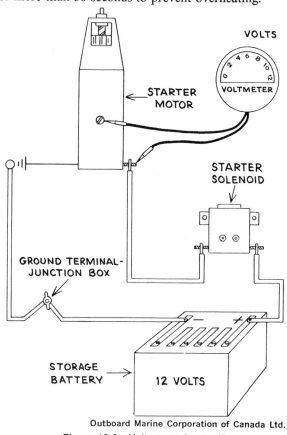

Figure 19.9   Voltage at Starter Test

Compare the reading obtained with each of the following headings to pinpoint trouble area if the amperage draw is not within specified limits.

TEST READINGS	AREA OF TROUBLE	REMEDY
High amperage reading	Indicates trouble in starter motor	Remove starter and perform no-load and stall-torque tests

TEST READINGS	AREA OF TROUBLE	REMEDY
High amperage reading, yet starter motor checks as sound	Bind in engine—i.e., powerhead, driveshaft, gears or improperly meshed starter-armature and reduction-shaft spur gears	Check all possible areas for binding
Low amperage reading	Excessive voltage drop (resistance) in starting circuit	Proceed with available voltage at starter motor test
Amperage reading within specified minimum and maximum limits	Problem may not be in starting circuit	Check engine (ignition, carburetion, and compression) for causes of hard starting
High voltage reading	Excessive resistance in starter motor	Remove starter motor and perform no-load and stall-torque tests
Low voltage reading	Excessive resistance in starter motor circuit—i.e., corroded battery terminals, loose connections, faulty starter solenoid, lengthy and/or undersized battery cables and poor ground circuits	Proceed with starting circuit voltage-drop test
Voltage reading within specified minimum and maximum limits	Problem may not be in starting circuit	Check engine (ignition, carburetion, and compression) for causes of hard starting

AVAILABLE VOLTAGE AT STARTER MOTOR TEST

A voltmeter is placed across the starter motor as shown in Figure 19-10 (one lead to starter motor terminal, the other to ground on starter frame). The starter switch is closed and the available voltage read with the engine cranking (high-tension lead from coil grounded to engine to prevent starting). With no excessive resistance in starting circuit, the available voltage reading should be 9.5 volts minimum, 10.5 volts maximum.

CAUTION: Avoid running starter motor continuously for more than 30 seconds during this test to prevent overheating. Allow ample time between each test for starter motor temperature to normalize. Voltmeter readings will change as starter temperature increases.

If the available voltage reading at the starter motor is low, review the following chart for probable causes and remedies.

Outboard Marine Corporation of Canada Ltd.

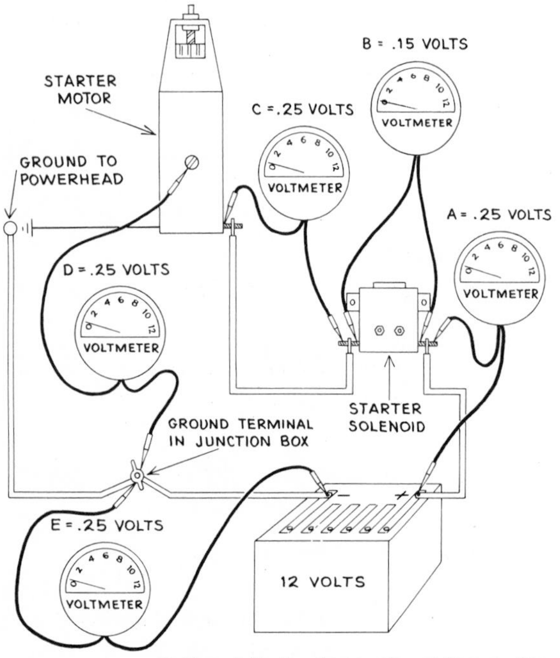

Figure 19.10 Starting Circuit Voltage—Drop (Resistance) Test

Outboard Marine Corporation of Canada Ltd.

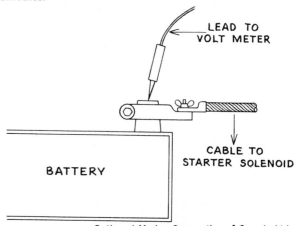

Figure 19.11 Voltage Drop

TROUBLE SHOOTING AND TESTING

START ALL MAJOR DIAGNOSIS WITH A COMPRESSION TEST AND A TEST WHEEL RPM CHECK

Engine Reaction	Check Points

1. Electric starter inoperative
   - A. Loose or corroded connections
   - B. Safety switch open or out of adjustment
   - C. Weak battery (corroded battery terminals)
   - D. Faulty starter solenoid
   - E. Moisture in electric starter motor
   - F. Broken or worn brushes in starter motor
   - G. Faulty fields
   - H. Faulty armature
   - I. Broken wire in harness or connector
   - J. Faulty ignition switch
   - K. Worn or frayed insulation

2. Electric starter does not engage but solenoid clicks
   - A. Loose or corroded connections
   - B. Weak battery
   - C. Faulty starter solenoid
   - D. Broken wire in electric harness
   - E. Loose or stripped post on starter motor
   - F. See steps in number 1
   - G. Sticky Bendix drive

3. Hard to start or will not start
   - A. Empty gas tank
   - B. Gas tank air vent not open
   - C. Fuel lines kinked or severely pinched
   - D. Water or dirt in fuel system
   - E. Clogged fuel filter
   - F. Motor not being choked to start
   - G. Engine not primed — pump up hose
   - H. Carburetor adjustments too lean (not allowing enough fuel to start engine)
   - I. Timing and synchronizing out of adjustment
   - J. Automatic choke out of adjustment
   - K. Spark plugs improperly gapped, dirty, or broken
   - L. Ignition points improperly gapped, burned, or dirty
   - M. Loose, broken wire or frayed insulation in electrical system
   - N. Reed valves not seating or preloaded shut
   - O. Weak coil or condenser
   - P. Faulty gaskets
   - Q. Cracked distributor cap or rotor
   - R. Loose fuel connector

4. Low-speed miss or motor will not idle smoothly and slowly
   - A. Too much oil or too little oil
   - B. Timing and synchronizing out of adjustment
   - C. Carburetor idle adjustment — mixture lean or rich
   - D. Ignition points improper — gapped, worn, or fouled
   - E. Weak coil or condenser
   - F. Loose or broken ignition wires
   - G. Broken crankshaft seal ring
   - H. Spark plugs improperly gapped, or dirty
   - I. Head gasket, reed plate gasket, blown or leaking
   - J. Reed valve standing open or preloaded shut
   - K. Plugged crankcase oil drain system
   - L. Leaking crankcase halves
   - M. Leaking crankcase seals, top or bottom
   - N. Exhaust gases returning through intake manifold
   - O. Heat exchanger cracked
   - P. Loose distributor drive pulley

5. High-speed miss or intermittent spark
   - A. Spark plugs improperly gapped or dirty
   - B. Loose, leaking, or broken ignition wires
   - C. Breaker points improper — gapped or dirty
   - D. Weak coil or condenser
   - E. Water in fuel
   - F. Leaking head gasket or exhaust cover gasket
   - G. Spark plug heat range incorrect
   - H. Engine improperly timed
   - I. Carbon or fouled combustion chambers
   - J. Distributor poorly grounded
   - K. Oiler wick bad

6. Coughs, spits, slows
   - A. Idle needles set too lean
   - B. Carburetor not synchronized
   - C. Leaking gaskets in induction system
   - D. Obstructed fuel passages

E. Float level set too low
F. Improperly seated or broken reeds
G. Fuel pump — punctured diaphragm, check valves stuck open or closed, fuel lines leaking

E. Faulty coil or condenser
F. Loose, leaking, or broken ignition wires
G. Reed valve not properly seated, or broken
H. Blown head or exhaust cover gasket
I. Weeds on lower unit or prop
J. Incorrect propeller
K. Insufficient oil in gas
L. Insufficient oil in lower unit
M. Fuel restrictions
N. Scored cylinder, stuck rings
O. Marine growth, hooks, rockers, or change in load of boat
P. Carbon build-up on piston head at deflector

7. Vibrates excessively or runs rough and smokes
A. Idle needles set too rich
B. Too much oil mixed with gas
C. Carburetor not synchronized
D. Choke not opening properly
E. Float level too high
F. Air vent passage in carburetor obstructed
G. Crankcase drain passages plugged
H. Transom bracket clamps loose on transom
I. Propeller out of balance
J. Broken motor mount
K. Exhaust gases getting inside motor cover
L. Poor ignition — see steps in number 5
M. Heat exchanger cracked

8. Runs well, idles well for a short period, then slows down and stops
A. Weeds or other debris on lower unit or prop
B. Insufficient cooling water
C. Carburetor, fuel pump, or filter dirty
D. Crankcase drain passages plugged
E. Lower unit binding because of lack of lubrication
F. Gas tank air vent not open
G. Not enough oil in gas
H. Combustion chambers and spark plugs fouled, causing pre-ignition
I. Spark plug heat range too high or too low
J. Wrong propeller (pre-ignition)
K. Slow-speed adjustment too rich or too lean

9. Will not start, kicks back, backfires into lower unit
A. Spark plug wires reversed
B. Flywheel key sheared
C. Belt timing off
D. Timing and synchronizing
E. Reed valves not seating, or broken

10. No acceleration, low top rpm
A. Improper carburetor adjustments
B. Improper timing and synchronization
C. Spark plugs improperly gapped or dirty
D. Ignition points improperly gapped or faulty

11. No acceleration, idles well but when put to full power dies down
A. Slow-speed needle set too lean
B. Dirt behind needles and seats
C. High-speed nozzle obstructed
D. Float level too low
E. Choke partly closed
F. Improper timing and synchronization
G. Fuel lines or passages obstructed
H. Fuel filter obstructed, fuel pump not supplying enough fuel
I. Not enough oil in gas
J. Breaker points improperly gapped or dirty
K. Bent gearcase

12. Engine runs at high speed only by using hand primer
A. Wrong carburetor adjustments
B. Dirt behind needles and seat
C. Fuel lines or passages obstructed
D. Fuel line leaks
E. Fuel pump not supplying enough fuel
F. Float level too low
G. Fuel filter obstructed
H. Fuel tank or connector at fault
I. Ruptured fuel pump diaphragm

13. No power under heavy load
A. Wrong propeller
B. Weeds or other debris on lower unit or propeller
C. Breaker points improperly gapped or dirty
D. Ignition timing over-advanced or late
E. Faulty carburetion and/or faulty ignition
F. Propeller hub slips

G. Fuel filter obstructed
H. Fuel tank or connector at fault
I. Ruptured fuel pump diaphragm

14. Cranks over extremely easy on one or more cylinders

Low compression:
A. Worn rings
B. Scored cylinder or pistons
C. Blown head gasket
D. Loose spark plugs
E. Loose head bolts
F. Crankcase halves improperly sealed

15. Engine will not crank over

A. Safety switch adjustment
B. Pistons rusted to cylinder wall
C. Lower unit gears, propeller shaft rusted or broken
D. Broken connecting rod, crankshaft
E. Engine improperly assembled after repair

16. Motor over-heats

A. Motor not deep enough in water
B. Not enough oil in gas or improperly mixed
C. Faulty water pump parts
D. Seals or gaskets burned, cracked, or broken
E. Impeller key not in place, or broken
F. Plugged water inlet, outlet, or cavity
G. Obstruction in water passages
H. Broken or leaking water lines
I. Advanced ignition timing
J. Motor not assembled properly during repair
K. Shorted heat light wiring
L. Faulty impeller, plate, or housing

17. Motor stops suddenly, freezes up

A. No oil in gas, or no gas
B. Insufficient cooling water
C. No lubricant in gearcase
D. Rusted cylinder or crankshaft
E. Bent or broken rod, crankshaft, propeller shaft, or stuck piston
F. Gas tank air vent closed
G. Faulty water pump or plugged water passages
H. Faulty fuel connector

18. Motor knocks excessively

A. Too much or not enough oil in gas
B. Worn or loose bearings, pistons, rods, or wrist pins
C. Advanced ignition timing

D. Carbon in combustion chambers and exhaust ports
E. Flywheel nut loose
F. Loose assemblies, bolts, or screws

19. A.C. generator will not charge

A. Battery condition
B. Connections loose
C. Connections dirty
D. 60 amp. fuse blown
E. Faulty regulator
F. Faulty rectifier diodes
G. Faulty generator
H. Faulty ammeter

20. Excess fuel consumption

A. Hole in fuel pump diaphragm
B. Deteriorated carburetor gaskets
C. Altered or wrong fixed jets
D. Slow-speed needles improperly adjusted
E. Carburetor casting porous
F. Float level too high
G. Loose distributor pulley
H. Plugged air bleeds in slow and high-speed carburetor circuits

21. Electra-matic slips

A. Improper remote control installation
B. Faulty coils
C. Faulty springs
D. Faulty clutch and gear
E. Faulty bearings
F. Wrong lubricant
G. Loose gearcase
H. Shorted wiring
I. Sprung gearcase

HELI-COIL INSTALLATION TO SALVAGE PARTS WITH STRIPPED THREADS

Overtightening screws and bolts in aluminum castings generally results in damaged or stripped threads. This is why we insist upon the use of a torque wrench for applying proper torque specifications to each screw, bolt, and nut during all repair work. Parts that are damaged as a result of stripped threads can be repaired through installation of a HELI-COIL in the damaged hole. HELI-COILS are easily installed and completely suitable for use in aluminum castings. Kits are available through HELI-COIL CORPORATION in DANBURY, CONNECTICUT, which provide a "rethread" of all thread sizes for outboard use.

Installation of HELI-COILS is quite easy. Follow the instructions supplied with the kit, describing how to drill, tap, and insert a HELI-COIL.

The following chart indicates the various drill sizes that

are required for HELI-COIL installation in the outboard repair shop:

NATIONAL COARSE

National Thread Size	Drill Size	Drill Depth Minimum
10-24	13/64 (.2031)	31/64
1/4-20	17/64 (.2656)	39/64
5/16-18	Q (.3320)	23/32
3/8-16	X (.3970)	27/32

GROUND PLATE INSTALLATION

The problem of electrolysis on engine gearcases can be very serious where electronic equipment is used, such as radios, depth sounders, direction finders, and telephones. The identical problem also exists when other electric equipment is installed. Electric motors used to operate bait wells, bilge pumps, and so on are examples of the second type of electrical equipment which can cause electrolysis, resulting in gearcase corrosion.

In most instances that electrolysis is caused by improper hook-up of ground plates or the failure to use them at all. Although electrolysis occurs in both fresh and salt water, electrolytic action occurs more rapidly in salt water and also has a much more severe effect. Figure 19-12 shows our recommendations for proper grounding of any external hull fittings.

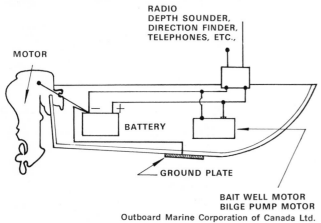

Figure 19.12 Boat Electrical Equipment

Ground plates are available through most marine hardware and radio dealers and should provide a minimum rated area equal to 12 square feet of exposed area. This does not mean the ground plate must actually cover an area of 12 square feet; only that the plate's rated area must provide the equivalent of 12 square feet minimum for efficient grounding purposes. Such grounding plates are available in sizes as small as 3¾ inches in diameter and ¼ inch thick, yet still provide the minimum rated area of 12 square feet. Ground plates may, of course, be

of other sizes and shapes; they may be of various compositions and have higher ratings.

When hooking up a ground plate, it is imperative the plate be connected directly to the negative side of the battery and not directly to ground of the electrical equipment being used. This connection procedure prevents voltage drop between the engine and ground plate.

A voltage drop between the ground plate and engine can be checked by using a sensitive D-C voltmeter with a scale reading from zero (O) to one (1) volt. Such voltmeters are available through most radio parts stores on special order.

GENERATOR CHARGING CIRCUIT
Maintenance and Checks

The charging system supplies electric power for the electrical accessories and keeps the battery charged. It includes the battery, ammeter, generator, regulator, and the wiring which connects these units.

The regulator controls the amount of electricity produced by the generator. It contains three electromagnetic devices. First, it automatically connects the generator to the battery when the generator is operating fast enough to charge the battery, and disconnects the generator from the battery when the generator slows or stops, thus preventing discharge of the battery through the generator. Second, it limits the maximum current output of the generator to a value that is safe for the generator. Third, it limits the voltage output of the generator to a value that will be safe for the battery, radio, and other accessories.

The charging system requires no periodic maintenance except to see that all connections are clean and tight. All wiring and connections should be inspected frequently for looseness and corrosion. This inspection should include cleaning of terminals in the cable connector plug as well as the pins on the mating receptacle. Use care not to over-tighten the terminal nuts at the generator and ammeter, since too much force will twist off the terminals. All terminal nuts and screws should have lockwashers and be snug. The connections at the terminal block in the junction box should be tight and clean. The ground connections in the terminal box, the terminal box cover, and the cable connector also should be checked.

The generator mounting bolt nuts should be checked for tightness (70 to 80 pounds).

Voltmeter Checks

These tests are needed only if there is some indication that the generator and regulator are not operating properly. If the ammeter does not show the proper charge rate, the battery is consistently run-down. If it requires an excessive amount of water, a voltmeter may be used to isolate the cause of trouble. (Use 20 volt scale or higher.)

Outboard Marine Corporation of Canada Ltd.
Figure 19.13   Checking Junction Box

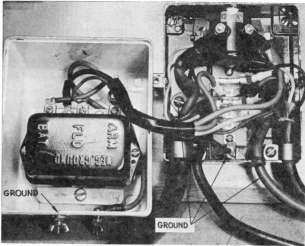

Outboard Marine Corporation of Canada Ltd.

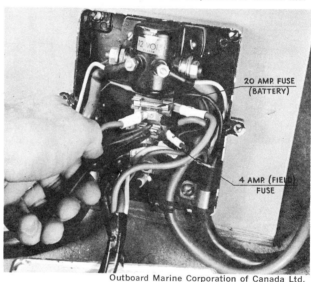

First, battery must be checked for correct connection.

Then all accessories must be disconnected from the power take-off terminals on the junction box and the voltmeter connected to the terminals.

The accompanying charts show voltages and check points, should any corrective measures be necessary.

Figure 19.14   (Upper Right) Check Ground Connections

Figure 19.15   (Lower Right) Check Fuse Clips

Outboard Marine Corporation of Canada Ltd.

READING	INDICATION	CHECK OR CORRECTION
Approximately 12.5 volts	Fully charged battery	Proceed with tests
Slightly below 12.5 volts	Partially discharged battery or bad connection in battery circuit	Check wiring and connections. Fully charged battery may be installed to reduce checking time
No reading	Open battery circuit	Check 20 amp. fuse in junction box. Clean fuse clips. Replace fuse if needed (See Figure 19-15)
Still no reading	Open battery circuit	Check wiring and connections from battery to starter solenoid, at ammeter terminals and back to junction box
Still no reading	Open in ground side of battery circuit	Check ground connections at battery and at two points in junction box and one in cover (See Figure 19-14)

The engine is started and operated at 3,500 rpm or above, approximately ¾ throttle. If the motor is mounted on the boat, the propeller should be removed, a test propeller installed, and the motor operated in gear.

READING	INDICATION	CHECK OR CORRECTION
Voltmeter reads above battery voltage, but not over 15.0 volts. Panel ammeter reads near 10 amps and decreases as voltage climbs	Normal operation	After 15 minutes' operation, voltage should hold steady at 14.5 to 15.2 volts and ammeter reading should have fallen off to less than 10 amps.
Voltage above 15.2 volts. Ammeter reading high	Grounded field circuit or improperly operating regulator	Disconnect field lead at regulator "FLD" terminal. Voltage should drop to 12.5
If voltage drops to 12.5 with lead disconnected at regulator	Improperly operating regulator	Regulator should be replaced or repaired by qualified electrical service station
If voltage still remains high with field lead disconnected at regulator	Ground in generator field or field lead between generator and regulator	Disconnect field lead at generator "F" terminal
If voltage still remains high with field lead disconnected at generator	Grounded generator field	Refer generator to qualified electrical service station for repairs
If voltage drops to 12.5 with field lead disconnected at generator	Grounded in field lead between generator and regulator	Locate ground and retape or replace lead. Reconnect lead to generator and regulator "FLD" terminals
If voltmeter reading is correct and ammeter shows discharge	Reversed terminal connections at ammeter	Be sure battery is installed for negative ground and reverse ammeter leads, if necessary*
If voltmeter remains at battery voltage and ammeter remains at zero	No generator output	Remove 4 amp. fuse, clean slips, install new fuse and recheck (See Figure 19-15) CAUTION: Disconnect battery while removing or replacing fuse as any contact between fuse clips (field) and adjacent terminal (battery) will permanently damage regulator

Outboard Marine Corporation of Canada Ltd.

Figure 19.16   Grounding Field Terminal

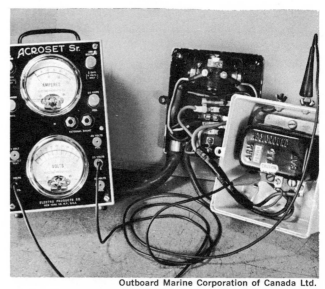

Outboard Marine Corporation of Canada Ltd.

Figure 19.17   Check for Defective Wiring

READING	INDICATION	CHECK OR CORRECTION
If voltmeter still remains at battery voltage and ammeter at zero	No generator output	Check wiring for correct hookup and poor connections. Then carefully ground regulator "FLD" terminal to regulator base with screwdriver (see Figures 19-16 and 19-17)
If voltage climbs to a high value with "FLD" terminal grounded (remove screwdriver immediately.)	Inoperative regulator (this operation bypasses voltage and current regulators)	Regulator should be replaced or repaired by a qualified electrical service station
If voltage remains low with field grounded	Inoperative generator circuit breaker or defective wiring	Move voltmeter lead from positive take-off terminal to regulator "ARM" terminal. Repair grounding
If voltage now increases to a high value with field grounded	Inoperative circuit breaker in regulator	Regulator should be replaced or repaired by a qualified electrical service station

If the battery connections were incorrect and are changed, it will be necessary to pinpoint the generator. To polarize, with a short piece of wire touch one end to the regulator "ARM" terminal, then momentarily touch the other end to the regulator "BAT" terminal. (See Figure 19-18.)

*CAUTION: Use extreme care that the centre terminal (marked "FLD") is not touched, as battery voltage applied to any point in the field circuit will damage the regulator.

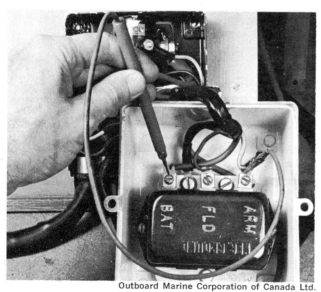

Outboard Marine Corporation of Canada Ltd.
Figure 19.18   Polarize the Battery

Outboard Marine Corporation of Canada Ltd.
Figure 19.19   Fuel Tank Pump

FUEL AND FUEL TANKS

Figure 19-19 shows a substantially constructed and practical fuel tank pump. This unit will drain every last drop of fuel mixture from the tank in a few minutes. This operation should be performed prior to off-season storage.

The tank is too often neglected during tune-up and/or preparation for storage. While the motor may be in excellent mechanical and operating condition, faulty performance at the beginning of the season can frequently be traced to a quantity of "last year's gas" still remaining in the tank.

Petroleum gum and varnish characteristically accumulate with aging fuel mixture. They clog the screen and small orifices, and also interfere with starting and normal running until the contents of the tank are eventually consumed.

Permanently installed tanks also should be drained thoroughly to avoid this problem.

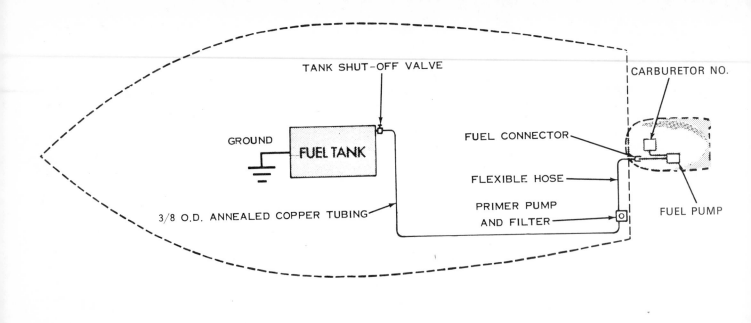

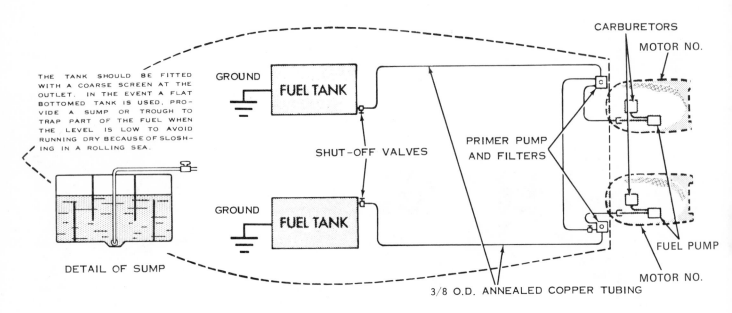

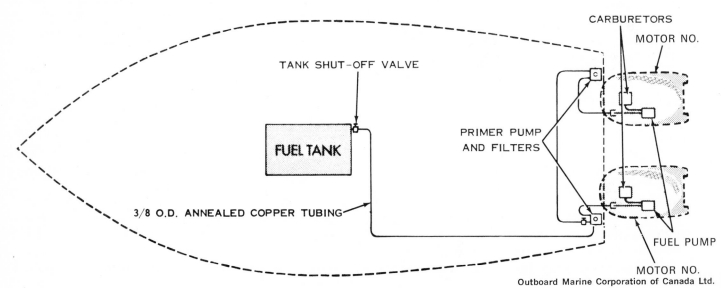

Figure 19.20 (top) Single Tank—Single Motor Installation, (middle) Twin Tank—Twin Motor Installation, (bottom) Single Tank—
Twin Motor Installation

This procedure should be followed in draining the fuel tank:

1. Clamp all flexible hose connections securely.
2. The entire fuel line should be inclined upward from the tank to the motor. Avoid loops and humps as much as possible.
3. Place the tank shut-off valve at the top of the tank for easy accessibility and to minimize any leakage through a faulty or worn valve.
4. Ground the fuel tank to a metal strip fastened on the keel, to an unpainted copper ground plate of about 48 square inches in area, or to a sintered bronze plate of equivalent area attached to the bottom of the boat below water level, adjacent to the keel.
5. The fuel tank must be vented outside the boat.
6. Locate the fuel tank, filling the spout above the deck (not inside the cabin). If the filler spout is connected to the fuel tank by means of a rubber or other non-metal tubing, the filler spout must be grounded to the fuel tank. Use a heavy flexible ground lead.

MIXING FUEL IN LARGER QUANTITIES

For large capacity fuel tanks, these mixing instructions should be followed carefully to make sure that the motor receives proper lubrication. These recommendations apply to outboard marine engines.

Suppose the tank capacity is 24 gallons. At a ratio of 1 to 24, the quantity of oil needed is four quarts. Adding four quarts of oil to the tank before or after the gasoline, however, would result in improperly mixed fuel. Therefore, a portion of the fuel should be pre-mixed before it is put into the tank.

Sometimes it is convenient to carry pre-mixed fuel on board; therefore, the smallest can that will do the job efficiently should be used. A two-gallon pre-mix can will usually be large enough, since when fuel is added in the fuel tank normally it will be a quantity less than 20 gallons. First, four quarts of oil and one gallon of gas are poured into the pre-mix can. These are mixed thoroughly, and poured into the fuel tank. Then 22 gallons of gas are added to the fuel tank.

NOTE: Oil that has been pre-mixed by using equal parts of oil and gasoline, or less oil than gasoline, will mix uniformly when more gasoline is added. However, oil that has been pre-mixed in a ratio of more oil than gasoline will not readily mix and disperse uniformly. Therefore, never pre-mix in a ratio of more oil than gasoline—for example, never pre-mix three quarts of oil and two quarts of gasoline.

CHECK LIST
Poor Performance, Lack of Power, Loss of Speed

1. Were the engine, test tank, and boat checked before delivery?
2. Have you verified the complaint? (Rpm at full throttle.)
3. What have you done to correct the problem?
4. Have you checked the following:
    (a) Engine rpm's using a tachometer and test wheel?
    (b) Rpm reading, full throttle?
    (c) Timing, synchronizing, and full throttle opening?
    (d) High and low-speed needle valve adjustment?
    (e) Cooling system, automatic choke?
    (f) Correct fuel and oil ratio?
    (g) Spark plugs, magneto, high tension leads?
    (h) (Removing intake bypass covers) pistons, rings, and cylinder?
    (i) All reed valves for proper clearance and operation?
    (j) Condition of propeller, correct propeller application?
    (k) Boat bottom for marine growth, hooks, or rocker?
    (l) Remote control for full speed range?

Make of boat ....

Total hours used .... Weight loaded ....

Length .... Beam ....

Transom height ....

Primary use ....

Every tune-up and/or repair should include:
1. Draining the operator's fuel tank or existing contents.
2. Replacing with a correct fuel mix.
3. Advising the operator that he should use a reliable pre-mix during future refills where and whenever available, or exercise caution when obtaining manually blended refills—insisting on a correct mix of high quality outboard oil and non-premium gasoline.

THE TACHOMETER - RPM COUNTER

The importance and necessity of a tachometer as an instrument of service equipment cannot be stressed too emphatically.

In the test room, by counting the rpm under full throttle running conditions, the tachometer indicates whether or not the engine (motor), with appropriate test wheel installed, is measuring up to the performance characteristics established for it. Should it fall short, further diagnosis and corrective steps are required.

On boat installation the tachometer indicates whether or not the propeller selected is correct for the purpose, again by simply counting the rpm at full throttle position for maximum performance. Should the motor fall short of, or exceed, the required rpm, the tachometer indicates the

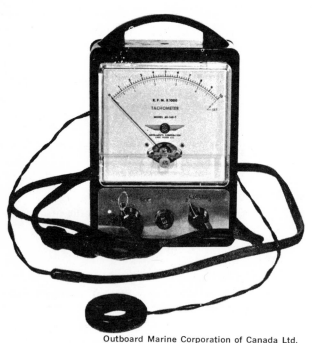

Outboard Marine Corporation of Canada Ltd.
Figure 19.21   Tachometer—RPM Counter

appropriate propeller adjustment—down pitch or up—assuming that the installation is correct.

Any attempt to finalize carburetor needle adjustments and/or tune-up is wasted effort if the rpm as measured by the tachometer does not fall within the factory-recommended operating range for top performance.

PROPELLER AND PERFORMANCE

For a number of years, the propeller provided as standard equipment with outboard motors, in the 25 and 35 HP group particularly, performed quite effectively for average overall service; consequently, installation was not considered crucial. But with the advent of increased horsepower and the ever-widening scope of outboard use, from light runabouts to heavier loaded cruisers and use for water skiing, the selection of a propeller best suited for a specific unit and type of service became a predominant factor in realizing the maximum capacity of the motor and overall performance.

Since the load applied to the motor is governed largely by the pitch and diameter of the propeller, specifications of the propeller selected for a given unit to achieve maximum performance should permit it, at full open throttle and under normal load, to operate within the peak rpm range recommended for the model.

Rpm normally tends to fall off with additional load and to increase with lessening of the load carried. Excessive pitch for the installation holds the motor rpm down, below that recommended. A propeller of less pitch than required conversely permits rpm exceeding that recommended. The recommended rpm range for peak per-

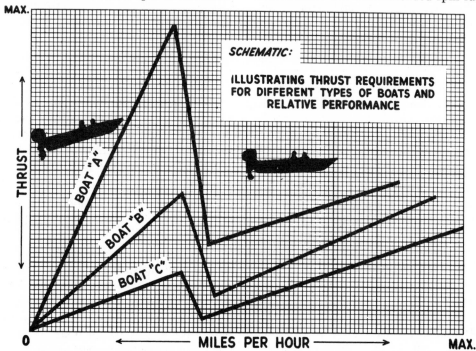

Boat A – Large runabout, Boat B – Medium runabout, Boat C – Light runabout.

Outboard Marine Corporation of Canada Ltd.
Figure 19.22   Performance Chart

formance for Johnson's model RD-40 and model V4-75 is 4,400 to 4,800.)

On a dynamometer test, it is found that the horsepower developed by a reciprocating internal combustion engine progressively increases (though not in direct proportion) with increasing rpm, but only up to a certain critical point (known as peak horsepower range). Beyond this point, horsepower falls off rapidly.

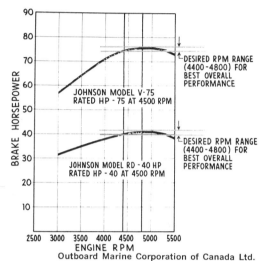

Figure 19.23   Brake Horsepower Chart

It does not necessarily hold that an engine (motor) capable of developing, say, 40 HP at its established rpm range for best performance will develop 20 HP at half engine speed or 30 HP at three-fourths engine speed. "Fall off" in this respect is not directly proportionate to falling rpm. Thus, the significance of maintaining as nearly as possible (by correct propeller installation) recommended rpm for the model is clear.

Various conditions of operation, boats, and boat loads also affect rpm performance.

Characteristically, a given engine develops zero horsepower at zero rpm but commences to deliver the instant it starts running and continues doing so progressively until its rated horsepower has been attained at a range (rpm) established by characteristics of its design and construction for best performance. This presents us with two questions:

1. What causes the engine to develop progressively more power with increased rpm?

2. What causes the delivered power fall off when the rpm has been extended beyond the critical period in the rpm range?

In effect, increasing the rpm is much like extending the length of a lever: the further distant the end from the fulcrum, the greater is the lifting power. For example, a single cylinder two (stroke) cycle engine delivers one power impulse (stroke) per each revolution. If its stroke is 6 inches and the engine is operating at 1,000 rpm, the piston on its combined power strokes travels 500 feet per minute; when running at 2,000 rpm, the piston mathematically travels a distance of 1,000 feet to deliver power, thus increasing the leverage to achieve greater lifting ability. It is simply a matter of more power impulses per minute. Basically, the greater the engine speed, the greater is the leverage or power developed. Breathing and internal resistance, however, are also factors which affect engine performance.

Breathing, when associated with reciprocating internal combustion engines, describes the conduct of fuel vapour passing through the engine—from the beginning to the end of the cycle, or through induction (intake) compression, combustion (power), and exhaust. For example, volumetrically, at cranking speeds with the carburetor shutter fully open, a single cylinder engine of 19 cubic inch displacement should draw or "take in" 10 cubic inches of fuel vapour for compression and combustion on each downward stroke of the piston. But, as the engine starts and begins to run under its own power, fuel vapour inertia and friction must be overcome as the rpm increases. The normal tendency of matter is to remain motionless until energy is applied to move it, or to continue in motion unless energy is applied to stop it (inertia).

Friction exists between the incoming fuel vapour charge and the walls of the intake manifold, the cylinder, and (in the two cycle engine) the transfer channels. Both fuel vapour inertia and friction affect engine performance, since time and energy are required to overcome both. Time in this instance is controlled by the rate (rpm) at which the piston passes through the cylinder wall port area on its up and downward strokes to uncover (open) and cover (close) the transfer ports. It becomes obvious then that the time element available for charging of the crankcase and fuel vapour transfer to the cylinder and combustion chamber is proportionate to the rpm at which the engine is running—correspondingly less with increasing rpm. The exhaust port is similarly affected.

As long as the engine is able to "breathe" effectively, power increases with increasing rpm. Nevertheless a period is eventually reached when with further increasing rpm, time available for overcoming fuel vapour inertia and friction and for effectively charging the crankcase is not of sufficient duration to maintain rated horsepower. Consequently, as "breathing" becomes restricted, power begins to fall off. The faster the engine runs the less is the time available to complete the events of the cycle—intake, compression, combustion (power), and exhaust.

Though they are not ordinarily applied to outboards, some engines use manifold blowers or super chargers to

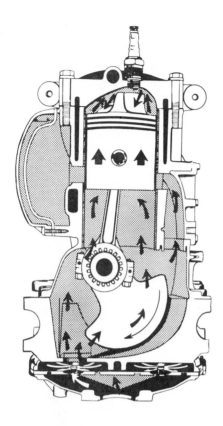

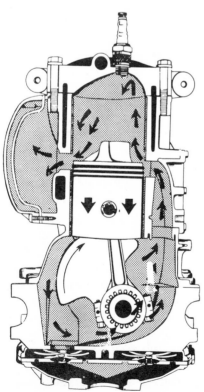

Outboard Marine Corporation of Canada Ltd.

Figure 19.24   Taking in Fuel

build up fuel vapour flow through the induction system in order to achieve improved breathing in the higher speed ranges for greater power output.

Internal counter-resistance also affects performance.

Power is required to start and stop (accelerate and decelerate) the piston-rod assembly at each end of the stroke (twice per revolution). Energy is used to shear the oil film (lubrication). Energy is required to overcome resistance presented by the bearings. Energy is similarly consumed to overcome other internal resistance such as inducing, compressing, and transferring the fuel vapour charge prior to ignition.

It takes power to operate the magneto and power merely to drive the gears in the gearcase, generator and alternator if installed. The faster the engine runs, the greater the internal counter forces become to have their combined effects on ultimate power available for driving the boat. It follows, then, that up to a certain critical point (rpm range for best performance), power developed as result of the rapidly expanding fuel vapour charges after compression and ignition is sufficient to overcome the effects of internal resistance with energy to spare for propulsion of the boat. But, in time and with a further increase of rpm and an eventual diminishing of the engine's breathing capacity, the ever-increasing effect of combined internal resistance acts to reduce power output further.

Beyond this critical point (rpm range for best performance), the force of counter-resistance increases to the extent that the engine now consumes considerably more energy to drive itself and less power is available for driving the boat. Theoretically, then, an engine running under "no load" conditions at full open throttle reaches its maximum rpm when internal counter-resistance and the force (energy) created by the running engine enter a state of equilibrium—that is, when the engine consumes all of the power it develops merely to drive itself.

The above illustration points out the effect of rpm on power output: power progressively increases with increasing rpm, then rapidly falls off with further increase. Clearly, an engine turning over at an excessively high rpm is not necessarily indicative of greater power output (rpm in excess of rpm range established for maximum effective performance and safe operation).

The correct propeller installation, then, is essential for the realization of best optimum performance. Many factors, however, enter into the correct selection of a propeller in this respect. What will do for one motor/boat combination may not do for another. The first details to be taken into consideration are the type of boat, shape of hull, weight of the boat and motor (without a load), load normally carried (some boaters run with heavier loads than others), distribution of load in the boat, angle of propeller drive, transom height of the boat as it affects depth at which the propeller operates below surface of the water, speeds expected. Total weight of the unit, incidentally, is not always the criterion of performance—of most significance is the design of the hull and how it rides the water. The lightest boat may not always be the fastest or the best performing.

Since propeller specifications (pitch and diameter) determine the rate of motor rpm, the importance of the correct propeller selection and installation cannot be overestimated. It critically affects the successful operation and performance of the unit. And the responsibility of correct propeller selection for best performance and owner satisfaction at this stage falls upon the installer (dealer).

Propeller specifications are given as (1) diameter—the diameter of a circle described by the tips of the turning propeller blades; and (2) pitch—the "twist" or angle given the propeller blade in relation to the direction of boat travel. Given in inches, it simply means that figuratively, a propeller of 6 inch pitch will advance 6 inches in one full turn—much like turning a nut down on the threaded end of a bolt. The propeller in reality, however, does not quite act in this manner, principally because water is liquid and not a motionless solid. Consequently, in its effort to advance, the revolving propeller draws in or pulls water from the front and discharges it to the rear to create what is known as the slip stream. During the process, some water slips or glides off the rapidly turning blades to have its effect, but for practical purposes, propulsion (of the boat) may be described as the effect of thrust developed by the effort of the propeller to advance and the resultant fast-moving slip stream acting against the surrounding body of water.

Light and lightly loaded planing boats present relatively little resistance to forward motion; consequently they are naturally faster with a given motor and propeller installation than the heavy and heavier loaded displacement boats, which offer proportionately greater resistance.

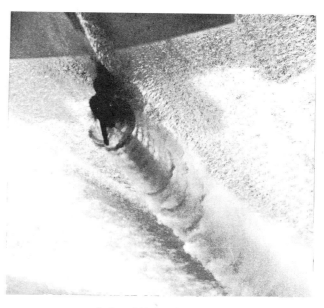

Figure 19.26   Propeller Slippage

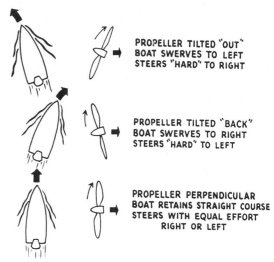

PROPELLER TILTED "OUT"
BOAT SWERVES TO LEFT
STEERS "HARD" TO RIGHT

PROPELLER TILTED "BACK"
BOAT SWERVES TO RIGHT
STEERS "HARD" TO LEFT

PROPELLER PERPENDICULAR
BOAT RETAINS STRAIGHT COURSE
STEERS WITH EQUAL EFFORT
RIGHT OR LEFT

Figure 19.27   Effect of Thrust Adjustment

Propeller slippage and slip stream loss (depending upon the type of propeller and its performance characteristics) may often run as low as 10 per cent for the light, lightly loaded planing hull, possibly 15 per cent to 20 per cent for the average planing runabout, and as much as 40 per cent for the heavier, heavily loaded, non-planing displacement boat (large runabout and heavy cruisers(with perhaps up to 50 per cent for barges. From this, it can be seen that pitch and propeller blade area are the factors involved when seeking a selection for best results. Pitch is given first consideration in preference to blade area when planning for the light planing installation, while blade area (with less pitch) enters more prominently into propeller choice for the heavier, planing and displacement type of hulls (runabouts, cruisers), since the force of driv-

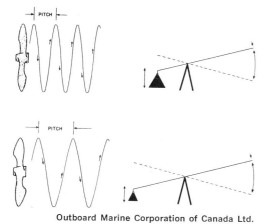

PITCH

PITCH

Figure 19.25   Propeller Pitch—Leverage

ing effort must be applied against a greater area of water for maximum effect. Pitch and blade area are not to be considered independently of each other entirely, however. Pitch in either event is adjusted or selected to permit the motor to turn within its desired rpm range when full capacity is attained. Hence, greater pitch and correspondingly less blade area (two blade propellers) is appropriate for the lighter boat, but greater blade area (three blade) and proportionately less pitch is desirable for the progressively heavier installation to realize full power capacity.

Beyond certain basic mathematical calculations, the process of propeller manufacture and selection for light or heavy duty outboard performance is largely a matter of "cut and try" in view of the many variables involved: variations in hull design and construction; variations in hull characteristics and load carrying characteristics; the nature of service and performance expected. Boats of the same general overall design manufactured by different builders often reveal different performance characteristics as a result of varying water absorption (wood) or of the condition of the individual hull bottom exposed to water, barnacles and/or moss. The practical, ideal situation is a propeller installation of such proportions (diameter, pitch, and blade area) as to permit the motor operating within its desirable rpm range to achieve the benefits of maximum motor capacity and of sufficient blade area, in relation to characteristics of the individual hull and nature of service for maximum average top speed performance.

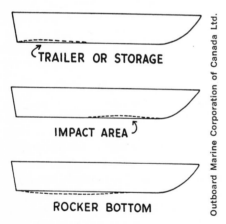

Figure 19.28 Hull Conditions Affecting Performance

Conditions for best performance eventually should permit the planing type of boat to ride fairly "flat" on the water with possibly the rear (stern) 30 per cent to 40 per cent, of the linear length of the boat) actually in contact with the water. At water level there should be a slight tilt (up) at the bow—a slender and gradually tapering light streak between the keel and water line which diminishines at a point of about 30 per cent to 40 per cent of the overall length of the boat from the stern, depending upon inherent characteristics of the particular boat, load carried, and distribution of the load.

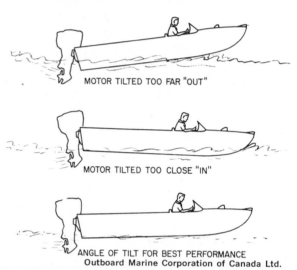

Figure 19.29 The Effect of Motor Tilt Angle on Performance

Ordinarily, the less of the hull area which is in physical contact with the surface water, the greater is the speed of the boat—other things being equal.

The average displacement, non-planing boat should ride on a fairly level keel with a very slight tilt (up) at the bow.

The following problem indicates what might be expected (mathematically) of a propeller of given pitch and turning at a known rpm. If the actual speed of the motor (by tachometer count) and pitch of a given propeller are known, it is not too difficult to determine possible mathematical boat speed by this simple equation.

$$\frac{(\text{Motor RPM's} \times \text{Gear Ratio} \times \text{Propeller Pitch in inches}) \times 60}{5{,}280 \text{ (Ft. per mile)}} = s$$

Mathematical or pitch miles per hr.

Example—Motor RPM's —4500
Gear Ratio — .572
Propeller —12½"

$$\frac{(4{,}500 \times .572 \times 12.5") \times 60}{5{,}280 \text{ (ft. per mile)}} = 30.5 \text{ pitch miles per hour}$$

This problem naturally does not take into consideration the effects of slippage and slip stream, always present but in various degrees depending upon the nature of propeller and hull design, normal boat weight plus boat load, and so on. But if the average boat speed is known (clocked on an accurately measured straight line course), it is relatively easy to approximate loss to slippage and slip stream.

Ideally, say the unit clocked 28 mph (a good planing boat with a fair load); the difference between 28 miles accurately "clocked" and 30.5 pitch miles per hour is 2.5 miles of "slippage" per hour or $\frac{2.5}{30.5}$—an 8 per cent loss to slippage; at 26 mph $\frac{4.5}{30.5}$, a factor of 14.7 per cent is lost to slippage and slip stream.

The same details may be worked out with any combination of motor rpm, gear ratio, and propeller pitch, but bear in mind that the result will be mathematical not actual. Slippage and slip stream always enter into the system of final results—there is less slippage for the light, lightly loaded "planing" boat and progressively more for the heavier heavily loaded planing boat (runabouts) and the heavier non-planing or displacement hulls.

Propellers for water-skiing present a somewhat different situation. Usually the fairly light or medium type of runabouts are employed, depending upon the size of the motor weight and number of skiers, and number of passengers in the runabout (regulations require at least two). In many instances where the skiing load is not particularly heavy, the propeller ordinarily provided or suggested for best optimum use is satisfactory.

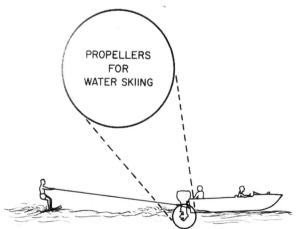

Figure 19.30 Propellers for Water Skiing

Propeller thrust requirements for water-skiing are normally greater than necessarily demanded for average runabout use, since the skier or skiers must be brought up to skiing position as quickly as possible and maintained at

that position. Experience will reveal the best suited propeller specifications for individual conditions.

The operator of a water-skiing unit provided with a lower pitched propeller than required for ordinary runabout use should refrain from running at full open throttle when running "light" (no skiers) to guard against excessively high motor rpm.

Some operators riding alone or with only one passenger may prefer top speed performance at the expense of quick get-away and ability to include additional passengers. In this event they will want a higher pitched propeller. Others with an identical unit may prefer quicker get-away and the ability to include several extra passengers at the expense of higher top speed. A propeller of lower pitch (best suited for average performance) would be suggested here.

The unit with the normally lower pitched propeller installation naturally will arrive at planing position in a shorter run and in less time than the unit with the higher pitched installation.

After both have reached the planing position, however, the lighter loaded unit with the higher pitched installation will out-run the former with the lower pitched propeller installation. On the other hand, the unit with the higher pitched propeller may fail entirely to attain planing position with the addition of two or more riders, while a like number of passengers could be carried in the boat with the lower pitched propeller with no appreciable decline in overall performance.

In either of the above situations, both propellers should be tailored to their respective units and conditions of operation so as to permit the motors in each event to operate as nearly as possible within the rpm range established for best peak performance. Obviously, they will not turn at identical rpm but will vary perhaps as much as 100 to 150 rpm.

For the heavy and heavier loaded runabouts, cruisers, and displacement type of boats, propellers of lower pitch than that suggested for lighter service are demanded. Correspondingly increasing resistance (water) to forward movement of the boat demands the greater "leverage" gained by the lower pitched installation to permit the motor to turn within the rpm range recommended for best performance. In summary, clearly the most important objective is to maintain the recommended rpm under any and all conditions of operation for best performance.

FUEL CHARGING, POWER TRANSFER, AND EXHAUST

The automatic reed valve (intake to crankcase) is, as its name implies, automatic in its performance as it is activated by existing conditions of crankcase pressure. The piston on its upward stroke creates a negative pressure or suction in the crankcase and in the process, the reed plate is caused to lift from its seat in an effort to equalize atmospheric and crankcase pressures. During the process, fuel vapour is drawn in from the carburetor to charge the crankcase.

Being automatic in its action and because of the variables involved, it is difficult to determine precisely when the reed actually starts to open and when it closes. But it is reasonable to assume that opening commences approximately when the piston reaches bottom centre position, beginning its upward stroke, and closing occurs perhaps near the end of the stroke. The reed valve closing might possibly occur somewhat later or after top centre position of the piston, however, as a result of inertia of the incoming fuel vapour charge. Pre-determined tension in manufacture of the reed may affect its action.

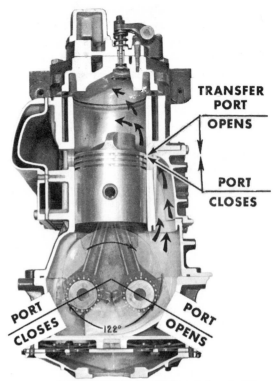

Outboard Marine Corporation of Canada Ltd.
Figure 19.32   Intake Combustion Chamber

at 4,500 rpm. At 5,100 rpm it reduces to 1/250 second, 13.3 per cent less time.

Exhaust port opening is ordinarily confined to 146 degrees of crankshaft rotation; consequently, the time permitted for exhaust escape is limited to 1/185 second at

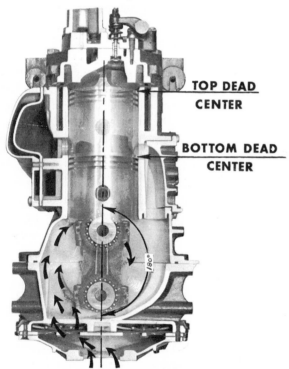

Outboard Marine Corporation of Canada Ltd.
Figure 19.31   Intake-crankcase

Charging of the crankcase (induction) must occur sometime during the upward stroke of the piston, within the limits of the time required for the crankshaft to rotate 180 degrees (half a revolution). Thus, only 1/150 second is consumed to traverse this distance at 4,500 engine rpm. At 5,100 rpm, time consumed to cover the same distance is restricted to 1/170 second, approximately 13.3 per cent less time at the higher rpm range.

Since transfer port opening extends over 122 degrees of crankshaft rotation, actual time permitted fuel vapour transfer from the crankcase to the cylinder is 1/220 second

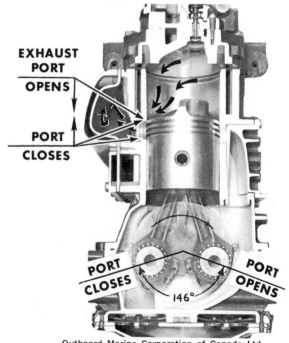

Outboard Marine Corporation of Canada Ltd.
Figure 19.33   Exhaust

4,500 rpm and to 1/210 second at 5,100 rpm—again, 13.3 per cent less time.

Thus, the time element allotted (1) to charge the crankcase, (2) to transfer the charge to the cylinder, and (3) to exhaust the spent fuel gases diminishes with increasing rpm affect overall performance.

For best performance and efficiency of operation, the compressed fuel vapour charge must be ignited and fully developed for combustion by the time the piston has reached its top centre position. This process, too, involves an element of time. Obviously, then, ignition must be introduced at a precise time or position of piston travel on its upward compression stroke.

The desirable degree of ignition (spark) advance prior to top dead centre position, as predetermined by engine design and performance characteristics, is relative to rpm. Fundamentally, the higher rpm demands a greater degree of spark (ignition) advance while at lower rpm, a lesser degree is needed to achieve fully developed combustion. Spark advance in outboards is manually controlled by the operator; there is partial advance at part throttle, and full advance at full throttle.

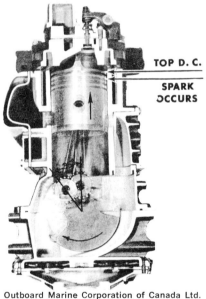

TOP D. C.

SPARK OCCURS

Outboard Marine Corporation of Canada Ltd.
Figure 19.34   Ignition or Spark

At recommended operating rpm range, the predetermined spark advance for best performance may be 35 degrees at full open throttle—35 degrees of piston travel upward to fully develop fuel vapour combustion. Spark advance in excess of this causes combustion to be developed too early—prior to top dead centre while the piston is still on its upward stroke.

The resulting counter-action causes engine knocking and a falling off of power. Spark or ignition advance of lesser degree at recommended rpm results in delayed development of combustion, and again power fall off; combustion is not fully developed until the piston has passed its top centre position and commenced its progress downward on the subsequent power stroke.

Depending upon performance characteristics of a given engine, combustion should be fully developed at or near piston top dead centre position for maximum power and efficient operation at 35 degrees of spark advance. Time allowable to develop combustion is limited to 1/771 second when operating at 4,500 rpm. At 5,100 rpm the time element is calculated at 1/874 second (less by 13.3 per cent, and this normally would require a slightly greater degree of spark advance.

FINAL TESTING AND TUNING

The function of final testing and tuning of any outboard motor is best performed under actual conditions—on a boat in open water where all conditions of normal operation may be observed. But, it is not always possible or convenient to do so; thus, the propeller test wheel has been developed for tank use.

The use of test wheels need not necessarily be confined to the shop test tank. Under certain conditions it becomes advantageous to run a check of motor performance at dockside without removing the motor from the boat. In this case the boat is anchored firmly to the dock, where there is ample water around and below the gearcase for test wheel running. The propeller is removed for installation of the test wheel. The tachometer leads are attached in the usual manner, then the motor is started and its performance observed. The desired operating range (rpm) for the specific model must be taken into account.

Dockside test running provides an excellent opportunity to make final adjustments and complete tuning, and to check remote control adjustments, overall rigging, and the electric harness/junction box installation.

Propeller thrust, the force required to drive the boat, is greatest at full throttle between the time the boat starts to move and the instant at which it breaks over to assume planing position—the point of greatest thrust. After reaching the planing position, propeller thrust for a moment falls off abruptly, but it commences to gradually build up again as boat speed increases and engine rpm approaches the range established for best performance—normal operation for the particular unit.

The propeller test wheels have been designed, constructed, and calibrated for each specific model horsepower range to simulate in the test tank, as nearly as possible, thrust and load conditions approximating those encountered during normal performance of the motor. At this time all final adjustments and tuning should be completed for maximum results.

It is a waste of time to attempt to check out or tune a

ILLUSTRATION 1

Outboard Marine Corporation of Canada Ltd.

ILLUSTRATION 2

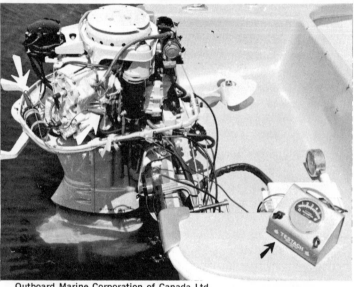

Outboard Marine Corporation of Canada Ltd.

Figure 19.35   Testing with Test Propeller

motor labouring at low rpm in the shop test tank or at dockside. Rpm must be "up" for the required adjustments to be made, particularly for the slow and high speed carburetor needle settings.

Because the high speed needles have been removed from some carburetors and replaced with fixed jets, test tank running within the desired rpm range becomes very important since the jets are calibrated for best performance.

Several variables other than mechanical fitness enter the picture to affect testing performance:

1. The type and size of test tank and resultant turbulence created by the rapidly turning test wheel.
2. Dissipation or dispersion of exhaust gases from the tank.

3. Area elevation above sea level.
4. Atmospheric conditions (principally barometric) at time of testing.

Using the chart as a guide, average tank performance (rpm) should not be too difficult to determine. The performance of several motors of each model should be recorded over time to establish an average of all tests on each model.

Any internal combustion engine fundamentally develops its maximum horsepower at sea level, where the air taken in with fuel vapour for combustion is denser than at elevations above sea level. Developed horsepower tapers progressively off at a rate of approximately 3 per cent per 1,000 feet of elevation up to about 8,000 feet.

Constantly changing atmospheric conditions (baro-

ENGINE TROUBLE CHART

A	B	C	D	E	F	G	H	POSSIBLE CAUSE
X		X						Fuel tank empty
X	X	X				X		Fuel filter in need of cleaning
	X		X					Carburetor low speed mixture valve out of adjustment
	X				X	X	X	Carburetor high speed out of adjustment
					X	X	X	Wrong oil in fuel mixture
	X				X	X	X	Wrong gasoline in fuel mixture
					X	X	X	Not enough oil in fuel mixture
	X		X		X	X	X	Too much oil in fuel mixture
X								Motor flooded
X	X				X	X		Spark plugs fouled or defective
	X		X		X	X	X	Wrong type spark plugs
X								No spark
	X	X	X		X			Weak or intermittent spark

A	B	C	D	E	F	G	H	POSSIBLE CAUSE
	X	X	X		X	X	X	Magneto contact points in need of attention
X								Spark plug leads interchanged
							X	Water pump failure
					X	X	X	Cooling system in need of cleaning
			X		X			Cavitation
					X	X		Propeller damaged
							X	Tilt angle not correctly adjusted
			X		X			Transom too high
					X			Transom too low
	X	X						Air vent hole in fuel cap clogged

A—Does Not Start

B—Runs Irregularly or Misses

C—Starts Momentarily and Cuts Out

D—Does Not Idle Properly

E—Motor Speed Faster Than Normal

F—Motor Speed Slower Than Normal

G—Does Not Develop Normal Boat Speed

H—Motor Overheats

---

metric and humidity) similarly affect engine performance; rpm increases to a minor degree on a high barometer, declines on a low barometer. Variations of 100 to 150 rpm may be noted when testing, or during normal operation of the motor, as a result of changing atmospheric conditions.

The test wheel chart should be used as a guide when testing or tuning in the test tank or at dockside, and the above mentioned variables taken into account.

REPAIR PROCEDURES
When the Motor Will Not Start

If a motor refuses to start despite persuasive efforts, it should be put through a simple trouble-shooting procedure. This usually will locate the cause of the trouble. (Refer to manual sections for specific remedy or repair.)

Suggestions

In conjunction with the following suggestions, refer to appropriate sections for further details.

1. Make sure there is gasoline in the tank. This seems almost too obvious to mention, but sometimes the fuel supply burns up faster than the operator realizes. Many an outboarder, confident he has plenty of gas, has spent half an hour hunting for trouble elsewhere before finally checking the tank and finding it empty.

2. Make sure that the air vent in the fuel tank filler cap is open, as well as the gasoline shut-off valve leading from tank to carburetor (the latter on integral tank engines).

3. Go through the procedure for starting a flooded motor: completely close the needle valve (or valves, if there are two) and spin the flywheel several times. This will clean out excess fuel from cylinders. Then reopen needle valves to correct starting position.

4. Check the carburetor. To see if water has got into the fuel, spill a little of the gasoline in the palm of your hand. Gasoline and water will not mix but will remain in separate beads or bubbles. If you blow on the mixture, the gasoline will evaporate rapidly leaving the water on your hand.

If the float bowl is dry, look for some obstruction between the fuel tank and the carburetor. (Usually, you will find that the fuel strainer has been stopped up by dirt or moisture in the fuel mixture.) The only way of checking is to loosen the screw on the bottom of carburetor to see whether gas is entering the carburetor.

Before you disconnect the gas line at the carburetor, open the shut-off valve and make sure that the gas flows through the line freely. If it does not, the line is stopped up. Disconnect the other end from the fuel tank and blow out the line. Also clean out connections at the tank and carburetor.

Fuel lines are disconnected by unscrewing the nuts. Always use wrenches on these nuts, never pliers. Pliers will round off the edges so badly that the nuts will have to be replaced. When replacing the gas line, do not tighten the nuts too severely, especially at the carburetor. Most of the castings on the outboard are aluminum, and threads can be stripped rather easily if a little care is not exercised.

5. If carburetor seems all right, or if it is difficult to get to the carburetor, remove a spark plug and look at it. A dry plug means that fuel is not getting into the cylinder, and it indicates that the trouble is in the carburetor or fuel line.

If the carburetor float bowl is full, there must be some obstruction between the float bowl and the cylinder—probably in the jets.

Remedying any of these problems by complete disassembly of the carburetor on a rough sea would be difficult with almost any carburetor. The only suggestion or recommendation that can be made, as stated previously, is to be sure that any obstruction in the passages of the fuel line to the carburetor, and from the carburetor, does not restrict the flow of fuel.

6. If a spark plug is cracked or damaged, replace it. (It is always a good idea to carry an extra plug in tool kit or tackle box.) If the plug is very oily, and there is no replacement, soak it in gasoline and burn off the oil.

7. Check the leads to the spark plugs. Disconnect the lead from the plug, hold end of the lead about 3/16 of an inch from the outside of crankcase and spin the flywheel. There should be a bluish spark. If not, there is something wrong with the magneto. Since magneto repairs necessitate the removal of the flywheel, this procedure is not recommended while out on the water. Only in an extreme emergency is it wise for an inexperienced individual to at-

tempt repair of the magneto, and only if proper tools are available.

If the engine has two or four cylinders, check the ignition leads to the other plugs. If one lead fails to spark when the others do, look for a bad connection or a short in that lead.

8. Check the plugs individually. Connect the lead to the plug, lay the plug on the cylinder block to ground it, and spin the flywheel. If there is no spark across the points, the plug is defective and must be replaced. Even if there is a spark, the spark gap should be checked before the plug is replaced. The gap should be set at .025″ in all cases, as recommended in the manual. In an emergency, if a gauge is not handy, use two thicknesses of an ordinary postcard or business card.

If it is necessary to change the size of the gap, move the outer electrode. Trying to bend the centre electrode may crack porcelain part of plug.

If the Motor Stops Running

If motor has been running and stops unexpectedly, the trouble-shooting procedure is the same as that previously given, with the omission of the flooded motor procedure, as that obviously cannot be the trouble.

The manner in which the motor stops abruptly tends to apply more to the electrical system. If it slows down gradually, sputters and coughs, and then stops, the difficulty usually will be found in the fuel system. It may be out of gasoline, there may be stoppage in the fuel line or carburetor, or the air vent screw on the fuel tank cap may be closed. Sometimes, when the tank is partly full, the motor may be tilted so much that gasoline is unable to flow to the carburetor, or the gasoline is tipped away from the tank outlet.

MOTOR TROUBLES CAUSE AND EFFECT

If after checking out a motor for erratic or faulty operation according to the simple trouble-shooting procedure and engine trouble chart, the cause cannot be determined, a major reconditioning of the motor is needed. On disassembly of the motor, inspect each part carefully. (Refer to specific sections in this book for repair.)

Other causes of erratic or complete breakdown of motor, as a result of faulty or careless operation, follow.

Trouble Chart
Starting Trouble
Engine will not start but spark is OK:
    A.   If there is no fuel at carburetor, check for
          Empty gas tank
          Clogged fuel filter
          Restricted vent in gas tank

Defective fuel pump
Air leak in line from tank
Closed main adjusting screw
Clogged carburetor screen
Clogged or broken fuel line

B. If there is fuel at carburetor, check for
Flooding at carburetor
Choke not operating
Water in gasoline
Restricted carburetor jets

C. If there is flooding at carburetor, check for
Choke out of adjustment
High float level
Excessive fuel pump pressure
Float saturated beyond buoyancy
High speed adjustment needle not seated
properly

D. If the fuel and spark are not OK, check for
Defective spark plugs
Spark plug gap set too wide
Improper spark timing
Water in cylinders
Poor fuel

ROUGH OPERATION

1. Engine misfires at idle:
    A. Trouble may be in ignition; check for
    Incorrect spark plug gap
    Defective or loose spark plugs
    Spark plugs of incorrect heat range
    Sticking breaker arm
    Incorrect breaker point gap
    Breaker points not synchronized
    Loose wire in primary circuit
    Defective distributor rotor
    Corroded or pitted breaker points
    Cracked distributor cap
    Leaking or broken high tension wires
    Weak armature magnets
    Worn cam lobes on distributor or magneto shaft
    Worn distributor or magneto shaft bushings
    Defective coil or condenser
    Defective ignition switch
    Spark timing out of adjustment

    B. Trouble may be in carburetion; check for
    Dirt or water in fuel
    Reed valve open or broken
    Incorrect fuel level
    Carburetor loose at flange
    Throttle shutter not closing completely
    Throttle shutter valve turned to one side or
    wrongly placed

C. Crankcase
Magneto adaptor flange worn out-of-round

2. Engine misfires at high speeds
    A. Check for conditions under No. 1
    Float loose or spinning on stem

    B. Check spark for
    Weak breaker arm spring
    Coil breaks down
    Coil shorts through insulation
    Breaker points improperly adjusted
    Poor breaker point contact
    Spark plug gap set too wide
    Too much spark advance
    Wrong type of spark plugs
    Excessive carbon in cylinders
    Poor compression
    Dirty carburetor
    Lean carburetor adjustment
    Crankcase magneto adaptor flange worn out-of-
    round

3. Engine backfires:
    A. Through exhaust; check for
    Cracked spark plug porcelain
    Carbon path in distributor cap
    Crossed spark plug wires
    Air leak at intake deflector
    Improper timing

    B. Through carburetor; check for
    Poor quality fuel
    Air-fuel mixture too lean
    Excessively lean or too rich mixture
    Improper ignition timing
    Engine pre-ignition
    Improperly seated or broken reed valves
    Improperly adjusted carburetor

4. Engine Pre-Ignition:
    A. Ignition causes; check for
    Spark advanced too far
    Incorrect type spark plugs
    Burned spark plug electrodes
    Incorrect breaker setting

    B. Fuel causes; check for
    Excessive oil in fuel
    Poor grade of fuel
    Lean carburetor mixture

    C. Other causes; check for
    Excessive engine temperature
    Carbon deposits in combustion chamber

ENGINE NOISES

1. Knocking in powerhead:
   - Loose flywheel
   - Excessive bearing clearance
   - Spark advanced too far—pre-ignition
   - Out-of-round bearing journals
   - Bent or twisted crankshaft
   - Crankshaft broken

2. Knocking at the connecting rods; check for
   - Excessive bearing clearance
   - Worn connecting rod
   - Misaligned connecting rods and cap
   - Bent or twisted connecting rod
   - Worn crankshaft journals

3. Piston noises; check for
   - Excessive piston-to-cylinder bore clearance (worn)
   - Out-of-round cylinder
   - Loose piston pin
   - Carbon in top of cylinder
   - Piston pin bent
   - Excessive clearance at ring groove
   - Broken piston ring

4. Centre main bearing; check for
   - Improper installation (too high or too low)
   - Crankshaft striking reed stops

5. Gear housing noisy; check for
   - Propeller shaft worn or sprung
   - Bearing worn
   - Broken gears
   - Propeller hub rubbing gearcase cover

6. Gears; check for
   - Improperly fitted (too tight or loose)
   - Worn
   - Wrong conical angle
   - Incorrect back lash
   - Oil seal leakage (water in gear housing or no grease in gear housing)

COMPRESSION LOSSES

1. Check for compression failures:
   A. Engine performance shows up in
      - Loss of power
      - Poor acceleration
      - Poor idle or no idle

   B. Engine sounds indicate
      - Clicking—broken piston ring or crankshaft strikes reed stops
      - Knocking—piston slap, broken piston, or bad bearing
      - Backfiring through carburetor—reed valve
      - Engine miss at all speeds
      - Engine drops on one or more cylinders

   C. A compression gauge shows
      - Low compression reading, all cylinders
      - Low reading, one cylinder

2. Check piston ring condition:
   A. If rings are broken, check for
      - Top ring striking ridge in cylinder
      - Worn ring grooves
      - Rings sticking in ring groove (gum-carbon-varnish)
      - Insufficient ring tension
      - Insufficient gap clearance
      - Excessive slide clearance in ring groove
      - Undersized pistons
      - Scored, wavy cylinder walls
      - Overheating

   B. If there is ring sticking, check for
      - Compression blow-by
      - Incomplete combustion
      - Engine detonation
      - Improper engine cooling
      - Insufficient ring land side clearance
      - Poor grade of oil or fuel
      - Carbon-gum-varnish

3. Piston Failures:
   A. If there are piston noises, check for
      - Carbon accumulations in head
      - Broken piston, skirt or ring land
      - Insufficient clearance at top of ring land
      - Out-of-round, tapered or worn cylinders
      - Excessive piston-to-bore clearance (worn)

   B. If there is piston breakage, check for
      - Inadequate lubrication
      - Overspeeding—wrong propeller, excessive rpm
      - Water taken in through carburetor or submerged
      - Pre-ignition
      - Engine overheating
      - Worn pistons
      - Eccentric or tapered cylinders
      - Warped cylinder sleeves

4. Cylinder Failures:
   A. If there is excessive wear (scoring), check for
      - Inadequate lubrication
      - Contaminated or poor oil
      - Exhaust ports clogged with carbon (no power)
      - Incomplete combustion

Incorrect type rings
Improper cylinder finish
Hole in cylinder
Insufficient ring gap clearance
Distorted block and crankshaft

5. Valve Seating:
    Check for
    Incorrect reed valve seating
    Broken or weak reed valve

ELECTRICAL FAILURES

1. Battery:
   A. If frequent charge is necessary, check for
       Corroded battery terminals
       Alternator grounded or shorted
       Worn out, inefficient battery
       Rectifier defective
       Short circuit in charging circuit
       Excessive use of electrical units
       Short circuit in ignition switch

   B. If there is high battery water loss, check for
       Too high charging rate
       Old, inefficient battery
       Leaking battery cell
       Worn out battery
       Cracked case
       Defective current regulation

   C. If battery will not take full charge, check for
       Low water level
       Worn-out battery
       Cracked case
       Spilled electrolyte
       Internal short circuit
       Impure electrolyte

2. Starter Motor:
   A. If there is excessive current draw, check for
       Broken, jammed starter drive
       Dirty, gummed armature
       Shorted armature
       Shorted field or brushes

   B. If there is excessive noise at starter, check for
       Defective starter drive
       Chipped or broken flywheel teeth
       Insufficient lubrication
       Worn armature shaft bearings
       Misaligned starting motor
       Loose starter mounting
       Sprung armature shaft

   C. If there are burned commutator bars, check for
       Excessive arcing at brushes

Excessive battery voltage
Improperly seated brushes
Open circuited armature coils
Open field circuit

3. Excessive Voltage Drop:
    With lights as a guide, check for
    Corroded, rusty grounds
    Loose or corroded connections
    Cracked, leaking wire insulation
    Frayed, broken cable strands

4. Generator Fails to Charge:
    With generator as a guide, check for
    Open circuit
    Grounded wire in charging circuit
    Grounded field coil
    Short circuit in field

5. Rectifier Fails to Put Out:
    With rectifier as a guide, check for
    Defective rectifier
    Broken wire
    Generator—no output (see above)
    Burned, crossed battery leads

DISTRIBUTOR SYSTEM
With Ignition System as Guide:
   A. If there is breaker point oxidation, check for
       High battery voltage
       Resister of incorrect capacity
       High resistance in condenser circuit
       Incorrect type ignition coil

   B. If there is ignition coil failures, check for
       Extremely high voltage
       Moisture formation
       Excessive heat from engine

   C. If spark plugs burn and foul, check for
       Incorrect type of plug
       Too rich fuel mixture
       Engine pumping oil
       Inferior grade of gasoline
       Overheated engine
       Too much carbon in combustion chamber

HIGH GAS CONSUMPTION
1. When trouble is in carburetor:
   A. Flooding or leaking; check for
       Cracked carburetor casting
       Leaking line connections
       Defective carburetor bowl gasket
       High float level
       Plugged vent hole in cover

Loose float needle seat
Defective needle valve seat gasket
Worn needle valve and seat
Foreign matter clogging needle valve
Ridge worn in lip of float
Worn float pin or bracket
Float binding in bowl
High fuel pump pressure

    B.   An over-rich mixture; check for
        Choke level stuck
        High float level
        Warped or bent bowl cover
        High fuel pump pressure

2. Trouble is in fuel pump:
    Check for
    Leaking around diaphragm cover
    Leaking fuel pump diaphragm
    Warped check valves
    Dirt, sediment in valves
    Corroded valve seats
    High fuel pump pressure

3. Fuel loss:
    Check for
    Leakage at lines and connections
    Leaking gas tank
    Leakage at filler cap

4. Trouble is caused by ignition conditions:
    Check for
    Incorrect spark timing
    Leaking high tension wires
    Incorrect spark plug gap
    Fouled spark plugs
    Worn breaker points
    Faulty spark advance
    Defective condenser
    Weak ignition coil
    Pre-ignition

5. Trouble is caused by poor compression:
    Check for
    Worn or broken piston rings
    Worn pistons or cylinders
    Sticking reed valves
    Poorly seated reed valves

6. Other Factors:
    Check for
    Loose carburetor flange
    Improperly adjusted or worn throttle linkage
    Restricted exhaust system
    Carbon in manifold

Overheating engine
Use of poor grade of gasoline

VALVE FAILURES
When reed valve breaks, check for:
    Improper valve opening
    Corrosion of reed valve
    Poor valve seat

BEARING FAILURES
Check for premature wear:
    A.   Caused by dirt from
        Careless service methods
        Contaminated oil

    B.   Caused by improper fitting because of
        Distorted connecting rods
        Mixed connecting rod caps
        Dirt between bearing and connecting rod bore
        Out-of-round, tapered, or worn journals
        Warped crankshaft or block
        Excessive crankshaft end play
        Scored bearing surface
        Improper clearance
        Use of wrong service tools

    C.   Caused by corrosion from
        Overheating
        Storage in damp place
        Water entering powerhead

    D.   Caused by improper operation, such as
        Overspeeding
        Spark detonation
        Improper engine break-in

    E.   Caused by lubrication failures resulting from
        Excessive engine temperature
        Insufficient engine warm up
        Insufficient quantity of oil

COOLING SYSTEM TROUBLES
1. There is internal leakage:
    Check for
    Loose cylinder cover bolts
    Damaged cylinder cover gasket
    Warped cylinder cover or block
    Cracked cylinder wall
    Porosity of cylinder head

2. There is restricted overheating and circulation:
    Check for
    Pump impeller loose on shaft
    Water inlet pipe rubber ring not in place
    Pump blades broken or worn
    Waterpump cartridge worn

Clogged water jacket passages
Water tube mislocated
Water tube cracked or corroded
Cover not securely tightened

3. Spark conditions:
   Check for
   Incorrect ignition timing
   Improper fuel mixture
   Lower oil level
   Defective spark advance linkage
   Pre-ignition

ABNORMAL SPEEDS
1. Motor speed faster than normal:
   Check for
   Cavitation

Transom too high
Propeller clutch slipping

2. Motor speed slower than normal:
   Check for
   Carburetor out-of-adjustment
   Too much oil in fuel mixture
   Wrong oil in fuel
   Wrong type of gasoline
   Spark plugs fouled
   Wrong spark plugs
   Propeller damaged
   Tilt angle not correctly adjusted
   Transom too high
   Transom too low
   Cavitation
   Weeds tangled on gear housing

MERCELECTRIC TESTING AND TROUBLE CHART

TROUBLE	CAUSE	REMEDY
Starter does not start	Run down battery	(1) Check battery with hydrometer. If reading is below 1.150, recharge or replace battery. Use battery charger.
	Poor contact at terminals	(2) Remove terminals, scrape clean, and tighten bolts securely. Coat with sealer to protect against further corrosion.
	Wiring or key switch	Check for resistance between: a) positive (+) terminal of battery and large input terminal of starter solenoid; b) large wire at top of starter motor and negative (−) terminal of battery; and c) small terminal of starter solenoid and positive battery terminal (key switch must be in "Start" position). Repair all defective parts.
	Starter solenoid	Disconnect wire from starter solenoid to starter motor. With key switch in "Start" position, check resistance between two large terminals of starter solenoid. Replace defective solenoid.
	Starter motor	(3) With a fully charged battery, connect a negative (−) jumper wire to upper terminal on side of starter motor and a positive jumper to large lower terminal of starter motor. If motor still does not operate, dismount for overhaul or replacement.
Starter turns over too slowly	Low battery	Complete (1) preceding.
	Poor contact at battery terminal	Complete (2) preceding.
	Poor contact at starter solenoid or starter motor	(4) Check all terminals for looseness and tighten all nuts securely.

TROUBLE	CAUSE	REMEDY
	Starter mechanism	Disconnect positive (+) battery terminal. Rotate pinion gear in disengage position. Pinion gear and motor should run freely by hand. If motor does not turn over easily, clean starter and replace all defective parts.
	Starter motor	Complete (3) preceding.
Starter spins freely but does not engage engine	Low battery	Complete (1) preceding.
	Poor contact at battery terminals	Complete (2) preceding.
	Poor contact at starter solenoid or starter motor	Complete (4) preceding.
	Dirty or corroded drive pinion	Clean thoroughly and grease the spline underneath pinion with multi-purpose lubricant.
Starter does not engage properly	Pinion or flywheel gear	Inspect mating gears for excessive wear.
	Small anti-drift spring	If drive pinion interferes with flywheel gear after engine has started, inspect small anti-drift spring located under pinion gear. Replace all defective parts. (NOTE: If drive pinion tends to stay engaged in flywheel gear when starter motor is in idle position, start motor at $\frac{1}{4}$ throttle to allow starter pinion gear to release flywheel ring gear instantly.)
	Starter arm sticks against overload spring	Grease overload spring at point where starter arm contacts overload spring.
Starter keeps spinning after key is turned to "On" position	Key not fully returned	Check that key has returned to normal "On" position from "Start" position. Replace switch if key constantly stays in "Start" position.
	Starter solenoid	Inspect starter solenoid to see if contacts have become stuck in closed position. If starter does not stop running with small yellow lead disconnected from starter solenoid, starter solenoid should be replaced.
	Wiring or key switch	Inspect all wires for defects. Open remote control box and inspect wiring at switches. Repair or replace all defective parts.
Choke does not open or close sufficiently	Choke linkage	Check for interference between moving parts of choke linkage. Adjust any pins or clips which may interfere. Replace all defective parts.
	Choke solenoid improperly located	Loosen base bolts on choke solenoid and readjust for improved action.
	Wiring between rectifier and battery or key switch	With key in "On" position, check for resistance between: a) positive (+) terminal of battery and the spade terminal located at the "red" terminal of the rectifier; and b) negative (−) terminal of battery and mounting bolt at rear of rectifier. Inspect all soldered joints. Repair or replace all defective parts.

TROUBLE	CAUSE	REMEDY
	Wiring between rectifier and alternator	Rectifier: With an ohmmeter, measure the DC resistance between: a) red wire on rectifier and mounting (ground) bolt (reverse the two leads from ohmmeter and measure resistance again; ratio of two readings should be 10 to 1 or greater); and b) two yellow leads on rectifier (reverse the two leads from ohmmeter and measure resistance again; ratio of two readings should be no more than 2 to 1). Replace a defective unit.
		Alternator: With the two spade terminals open, check for continuity between two yellow leads from alternator.
		Also, check that there is no continuity between alternator wire and ground (base of stator or engine block). Repair or replace all defective parts.
Rectifier is over-heating	Battery terminals improperly connected	Check that negative marking on harness matches that of battery. If battery is connected improperly, severe burning of rectifier will occur.
	Rectifier is damaged	Inspect rectifier for damaged protective coating of plates. Replace a defective unit.
Wires are over-heating	Battery terminals improperly connected	Check that negative marking harness matches that of battery. If battery is connected improperly, red wire to rectifier will overheat.
	Short circuit in wiring system	Inspect all connections and wires for looseness or defects. Open remote control box and inspect wiring at switches. Repair or replace all defective parts. Check for high resistance.
	Short circuit in choke solenoid	If blue choke wire heats rapidly when using choke, choke solenoid may have internal short. Replace if defective.
	Short circuit in starter solenoid	If yellow starter solenoid lead overheats, there may be internal short (resistance) in starter solenoid. Replace a defective solenoid.
Circuit tester	Circuits on MercElectric models	To check performance of various components of MercElectric system use Magneto Analyzer.
Battery voltage	Battery voltage	Battery voltage is checked with ampere-volt tester only when battery is under starting load. Battery must be recharged if it registers under 9½ volts. If battery is below specified hydrometer readings (1.150), it will not turn engine fast enough to start.

CHRYSLER OUTBOARD TROUBLE CHECK LIST

Probable Cause	*Problem*
Remote control does not function correctly	1. Check the remote control adjustments and installation. 2. Check the gear shift rod adjustment. 3. Check synchronization of controls. 4. Adjust throttle stop.
Engine does not shift properly	1. Check the gear shift rod adjustment. 2. Check the remote control adjustments and installation.
Engine does not idle properly	1. Adjust the carburetor idle adjustment needles. 2. Adjust throttle stop. 3. Check synchronization of controls.
Engine does not obtain full throttle	1. Check remote control adjustment and installation. 2. Check synchronization of controls.
Electric starter inoperative	1. Perform starter circuit check. 2. Check neutral interlock switch. 3. Check remote electric cable installation.
Electric choke inoperative	1. Perform choke circuit check. 2. Check remote electric cable installation.
Engine does not start	1. Check the starting instructions as covered in the owner's guide. 2. Check remote electric cable installation. 3. Check complete engine wiring.
Engine misses on one or more cylinders	1. Remove and inspect spark plugs. 2. Check the breaker point adjustment. 3. Check the ignition coils and condensers. 4. Adjust carburetor idle adjustment needles.
Generator inoperative	1. Check rectifier. 2. Check field exciter brush assembly. 3. Check generator circuit. 4. Check and adjust the voltage regulator if necessary.
Generator charges but does not produce full output	1. Check field exciter brush assembly. 2. Check and adjust voltage regulator if necessary.
Generator over-charges	1. Check and adjust voltage regulator.
Battery discharges when engine is not running	1. Check and replace voltage regulator if necessary. 2. Check the complete engine wiring and the field exciter brush assembly.
Engine not receiving sufficient fuel supply	1. Check all fuel lines, fuel tank, and prime bulb assembly. Also check fuel line couplers and bushing for air leaks. 2. Check fuel pump.
Fuel tank gauge inoperative	1. Check fuel tank gauge float assembly.

TROUBLE CHECK LIST

A	B	C	D	E	
X	X				Remote fuel tank not connected
X	X				Battery cables not connected
X					Battery discharged
X					Remote electric cable not connected
X			X	X	Remote controls in need of adjustment
X	X				Fuel tank empty
X	X				Fuel shut-off valve closed
	X		X		Puddle drain system dirty or clogged
X	X		X	X	Fuel line kinked or pinched
	X		X	X	Fuel filters dirty or clogged
X	X		X	X	Vent screw gasket obstructing air flow
X	X		X	X	Vent screw on fuel tank filler cap closed
	X	X	X	X	Air leak in engine
	X		X	X	Air leak in fuel system
X	X		X	X	Carburetor passages clogged or dirty
X	X	X	X	X	Incorrect fuel-oil mixture
X	X	X	X	X	Carburetor out of adjustment
X					Engine flooded
X	X	X	X	X	Wrong type spark plugs
X	X	X	X	X	Defective or fouled spark plugs
X	X	X	X	X	Breaker contact points out of adjustment
X	X	X	X	X	Breaker contact points burned or pitted
X	X	X	X	X	Weak ignition coils
X	X	X	X	X	Weak or defective condenser
X					Spark plug lead wires interchanged
X		X			Frayed or cracked lead wire insulation
X		X			Disconnected, grounded or loose wiring in electrical system

A—Engine does not start   B—Starts but does not run
C—Engine misses   D—Does not idle   E—Does not develop full power

PART 3
SNOWMOBILES

CHAPTER 20
SAFETY
IN SNOWMOBILING

Snowmobiling can be a lot of fun for everyone, parents and children alike, if proper precautions are taken. Failure to follow these precautions may cause injury and in many cases, even death.

It may seem ridiculous to the average person that injuries and death can occur in such a fun-making machine, but the hospitals and cemeteries are full of these misadventures; newspaper stories are plentiful.

"Mr. Smith broke his leg on his ski-mobile . . ."

"Mr. Jones and his two children were killed yesterday while ski-mobiling . . ."

These articles could not have been written if simple but necessary precautions were taken or observed.

This chapter will endeavour to list a few important safety rules and some advice that will insure a safe and happy sport. It would be wise if the following items were practiced and memorized because, as it has been said many times, *"The life you save may be your own!"*

SAFETY PREPARATIONS
Dress

Particular care must be taken in the way a snowmobiler dresses. Being comfortable and warm keeps the sport fun; being cold or uncomfortable causes not only discomfort but spoils the fun of other people as well. The proper clothing is sold by many sports and department stores.

Long thermal underwear is a must; it must keep in body heat and yet let the skin breath. Heavy woolen socks should be worn over regular socks. An extra pair should be taken just in case.

All clothing should be light. A long sleeved sweater and warm slacks under the suit is sufficient, but these should be loose enough to provide movement.

The snow outfit should be warm but very light. A heavy suit will cause fatigue, make muscles sore, and will cer-

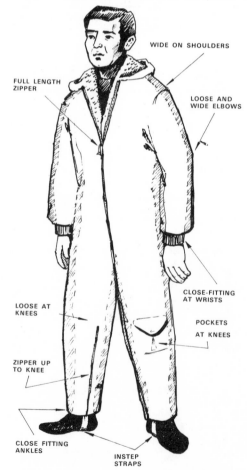

FULL LENGTH ZIPPER

WIDE ON SHOULDERS

LOOSE AND WIDE ELBOWS

CLOSE-FITTING AT WRISTS

POCKETS AT KNEES

LOOSE AT KNEES

ZIPPER UP TO KNEE

CLOSE FITTING ANKLES

INSTEP STRAPS

Figure 20.1 Fitting of Suit

tainly slow reflexes and body movements. Heavy suits *do not* always provide protection from cold weather.

The suit should be made from a nylon material to give it flexibility. Nylon does not get hard in the cold and provides complete freedom of movement. Nylon is water-proofed and resists snagging. The suit should be in one piece to stop the possible chance of catching branches, wind, snow or water. The suit should have zippered pockets with an outer, domed flap to protect the contents of the pockets. The pocket should be placed low on the leg to prevent its contents from pressing into the body when sitting. The pocket should be large and roomy.

It must be realized that control of the turns on the snowmobile is managed with the body, and that the driver may be sitting, standing or kneeling, depending on the land in which he is operating the machine. The suit, therefore, should be large, wide and not tight. Such a suit might seem embarrassing and out-of-style at first, but after a few hours outside, its advantages will be obvious.

The suit should be light cloured; if it is not, strips of light coloured material should be fastened in conspicuous places, so that in shadow or at night, they can be seen by those following.

The footwear is another important item of the outdoor sportsman. Very little movement is required of the feet; therefore, particular care should be taken to keep them warm and dry.

The boot is usually manufactured in two separate parts. The inner boot part is a thick, roomy warm felt with a

zipper front for easy removal. The outer boot is rubber; it has a drawstring top to keep the snow out and a zipper front with a water-proof web behind.

The boot is large to allow for heavy socks and for movement of the toes. The size of the boot also provides an area of warm air around the foot itself. This acts as insulation.

The mitten must be larger than the hand to allow the warm air around the hand to act as an insulator. The mitt is long and extends up the sleeve. It is secured to the wrist and arm with an elastic to keep snow and cold air out.

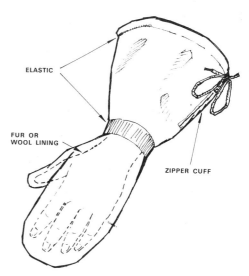

Figure 20.3   Snow Mitt

A pair of light gloves should be carried as well in case repairs to the machine are necessary.

The head should be protected at all times both from

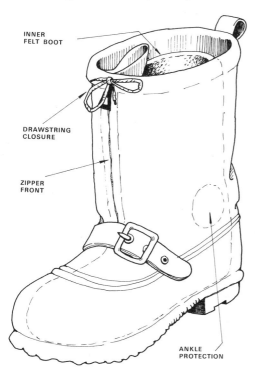

Figure 20.2   Snow Boot

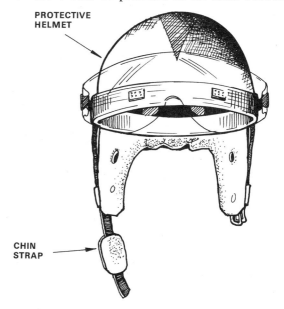

Figure 20.4   Hard Helmet

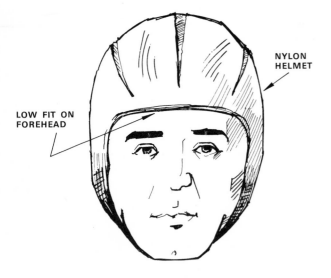

Figure 20.5 Nylon Helmet

NYLON HELMET

LOW FIT ON FOREHEAD

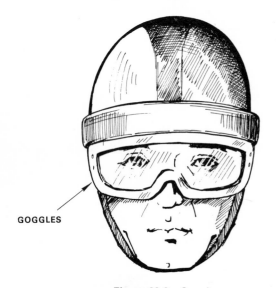

Figure 20.6 Goggles

GOGGLES

the cold and from severe injury from low limbs or falls. A close fitting nylon helment should be worn in near-zero weather to protect the head from the cold. A protective, hard helmet should be worn at all times to ward off serious injuries from falls or accidents.

Goggles should be worn to save the eyes from the cold

and from hidden branches. Lenses should be changed according to the light. Clear lenses should be worn at night. On dull or misty days, yellow lenses are necessary. On bright sunny days, lenses should vary in colour from grey to green. Any other colour will distort vision.

In temperatures of 0°F and below, a face mask should be worn, but not a Balaclava because it might move and its small eyelets block the vision. A leather face mask is available in most sporting goods stores. It must be remembered that a machine travelling at 40 mph at zero degrees F. has a chill factor of approximately 50° below zero.

Safety Belts

It is wise to wear a wide safety belt around the waist. The passenger belt has two loops for a passenger to hold on to, allowing him to follow the driver's leaning movements without danger of falling. The wide belt also helps to support the back and kidneys in case of a fall.

RACING   PASSENGER

Figure 20.8 Safety Belts

Spare Equipment

It is important that this safety precaution should be followed, as it could be the difference between life or death. (This statement may sound ridiculous but many people have perished because of this neglect.)

Spare spark plugs are a must; because of the oil content in the gasoline, the spark plugs have a tendency to foul in cold weather. Another item of equal importance is the spark plug wrench to remove and to replace the plugs when required.

A spare drive belt is essential for the machine as well as a brake cable, throttle cable, starter cord, bolts and screws, and, last but not least, spare bulbs for the lights.

A well-chosen tool kit should be carried at all times. (Gloves could be kept in the tool kit.)

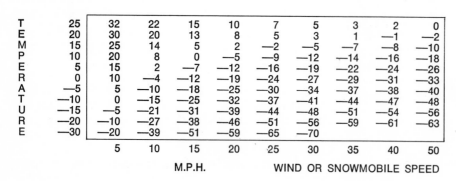

TEMPERATURE	5	10	15	20	25	30	35	40	50
25	32	22	15	10	7	5	3	2	0
20	30	20	13	8	5	3	1	—1	—2
15	25	14	5	2	—2	—5	—7	—8	—10
10	20	8	0	—5	—9	—12	—14	—16	—18
5	15	2	—7	—12	—16	—19	—22	—24	—26
0	10	—4	—12	—19	—24	—27	—29	—31	—33
—5	5	—10	—18	—25	—30	—34	—37	—38	—40
—10	0	—15	—25	—32	—37	—41	—44	—47	—48
—15	—5	—21	—31	—39	—44	—48	—51	—54	—56
—20	—10	—27	—38	—46	—51	—56	—59	—61	—63
—30	—20	—39	—51	—59	—65	—70			

M.P.H.   WIND OR SNOWMOBILE SPEED   **Figure 20.7 Chill Factor Chart**

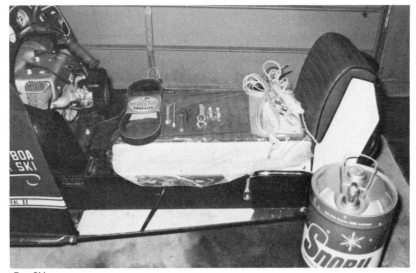

Figure 20.9a   Accessories

Boa-Ski

Figure 20.9b   Licence, Driver's Manual, etc.

Boa-Ski

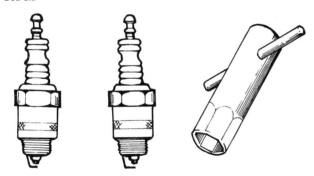

Figure 20.9c   Spare Spark Plug and Socket

The need for these items can easily be realized on reflection. If the machine fails in the woods, it may leave the driver and passenger stranded. It has been travelling at thirty miles per hour and the trip back for repairs would be exhausting on foot. (In some cases, the trip in heavy snow could produce complete exhaustion and perhaps death.)

What about the light bulbs? It was noted that a father and his two children were killed when a car struck their unlighted snowmobile while travelling on a sideroad. An-

other snowmobile could easily overrun an unlit machine in the dark and cause the same problem.

Other items of safety are as follows:

(1.) nylon rope and pulleys for pulling the machine out of ditches or holes (a block and tackle);

(2.) gasoline antifreeze;

(3.) a small, unbreakable flashlight

PREPARATION OF THE SNOWMOBILE

The manufacturer's specifications for the gasoline and oil mixture should be followed. The tank must be full before starting out. The machine should be rocked back and forth to ensure that the fuel is well mixed since fuel has a tendency to separate after sitting. A proper ratio is 20:1; 25:1 and some manufacturer's rate their mixtures at 50:1.

Starting the Engine

The throttle cable and linkage must be free and operating properly. (Some machines have been known to stick at high speed and to speed off, doing considerable damage.)

Electric Starter

Some machines are equipped with an electric starting

mechanism operated like an automobile. Key positions are usually OFF-ON-START. On some, the light switch is also included.

The starting procedure is as follows:
(1.) the choke is pulled;
(2.) the key is turned to START;
(3.) the throttle is slightly squeezed;
(4.) as soon as the engine has started, the key is released to the ON position;
(5.) the choke is returned to the original position when the engine is running smoothly.

The starter must not be engaged longer than thirty seconds as it could burn out.

Every machine is equipped with a manual starter to start the engine in case the electric starter fails to operate. The same procedure for starting is used, except that the key is turned to ON and the cord is pulled quickly and returned slowly to the original position. A decompressor lever is used to release compression. This lever should be returned to the closed position as soon as the engine starts.

Check List After Starting Engine

(1.) Turn the steering handles back and forth to be sure of full turns.
(2.) Try the lights to see if they are operating.
(3.) Tip the machine on its side and slowly accelerate the engine to see if the belts hold well in operating condition and are free of ice or snow. (Rotation of the tracks also frees the material which may be hard from the cold; the gradual movement will free the belt.)
(4.) If the machine is new, follow the manufacturer's rules closely until the machine is *"broken in"*. Failure to follow the manufacturer's instructions will cause expensive repairs that will not be covered by warranty.

Driving the Snowmobile

Driving the snowmobiles may be performed in one of three positions, depending on the condition of the area.

The feet should be kept on the running board when driving or turning. Failure to observe this rule could cause a broken leg.

When travelling on level or flat fields, speeds up to almost full power may be used. The machine should never be run at full power except in an emergency.

On level or flat ground, the driver may sit or kneel, with one foot on the running board. If operating at a low speed, it is more enjoyable to sit while driving. When at high speed, it is better to kneel or stand.

On bumpy trails, a kneeling position is more comfortable as the continuous bouncing movement is absorbed by the arms and shoulders. Kneeling in this type of ground adds extra control of the machine.

Turning a snowmobile is accomplished in much the same fashion as turning a motorcycle—by leaning to the inside of the turn. The added weight to that side of the machine helps the track grip the snow more firmly. By leaning ahead at the same time the inside ski takes a firmer grip from the weight, increasing the sharpness of the turn.

The heavier a machine, the farther the driver must lean forward for the inside ski to grip. The greater the speed, the wider the turn will be.

If there is a passenger on the snowmobile, it is wise to take a few practice turns, thereby allowing the passenger to familiarize himself with leaning for turns. As mentioned previously, a wide belt with handles for the passenger will help him to follow the drivers motions.

Powder or Wet Snow

Turning a machine on this snow condition requires common sense.

First, slow speeds are essential since there may be ice, soft ground, or even sand under the snow. The machine should be kept in a slow, controlled turn to avoid spinning out or even a sudden stop.

Ice

It is impossible to make a sharp turn on ice. Slow speeds and heavy leaning to the inside of the turn are needed. The machine is then braked and accelerated again.

If a trail has become icy from rain, the driver should head to the base of the banked edge of the trail opposite to the turn. The tilt or lean of the machine will help to control the turn.

In turns down on an ice slope, the speed must be reduced, and the handle bar turned without any leaning in the direction of the turn. The driver remains seated. If the operator leans in the direction of the turn, the machine could turn over.

Turns up on an icy slope are accomplished in much the same way as any icy turn, except the driver remains seated. The turn is accomplished by turning the handle bars very heavily in the direction of the turn; the machine is accelerated and braked; this process is repeated several times until the turn is accomplished. No attempt is made to turn all at once.

It may be important to reverse the direction of the machine in a confined area on ice. This can be accomplished in several ways.
(1.) *The first and simplest method.* The driver gets off and lifts the rear of the machine around to the reverse direction.
(2.) *The second method* of reversing direction is simple

but requires a very strong person to control the operation. The driver gets off the machine, grasps the handlebar, accelerates slightly, and pushes the rear of the machine with his left hand. He must be careful in this operation, as the machine could snap away from him suddenly.

(3.) *In the third method* of reversing the direction on ice, the driver kneels on the seat and with his right foot on the ground, pushes with his left foot which should be placed against the back of the seat. He accelerates slightly at the same time. This type of turn requires a lot of space.

The first reversal turn described is the safest and most practical method of turning a machine.

When operating a machine up a hill, it is important to let the motor run at a slower speed to provide reserve power. A standing position, leaning forward, is the proper method.

If the hill is icy, any machine ahead must reach the top first. (He may slide backward and have to jump off.) If the hill is known and there are no obstacles on the other side, the operator could take a longer run at the hill to maintain speed. It is wise to stand with feet placed behind the foot guard and both hands on the handlebars. The operator should release the throttle if the slope is very steep and let the compression of the engine slow the machine, using the hand brake very gently from time to time. A sudden jamming of the brake could cause the machine to tip over.

When travelling on side slopes, the driver should kneel with the other foot on the high side. While breaking a new trail on a side slope, a gentle slope should be chosen. If the slope is steep it is wise to stand and lean as far up-hill as possible. The driver must watch out for snow slides.

Sometimes it is impossible to avoid a jump. The machine must not turn. The throttle is released and the driver stands up with knees slightly bent to take the impact. When the machine touches ground it is accelerated and the driver gradually straightens his elbows and legs.

CHILDREN AND SNOWMOBILES

The family snowmobile is supposed to be fun for everyone. Children will always ask, "Can I drive, Daddy?" The answer should be a firm "No", but if the parent agrees then proper precautions should be considered.

An adult's mind is quicker to respond than a child's. What to do in case the throttle sticks when heading for a tree or a hole in the ice? An adult will change direction and turn off the key, but a little person could panic and an accident result.

Young children do not have the sense of responsibility that an adult is supposed to have. They could cause pro-

perty damage without realizing it. The child under fifteen should not be allowed to operate a machine on his own. He should be thoroughly familiarized with the machine before he operates it. All the questions that he asks should be answered. When teaching the younger ones about operating the machines, the teacher must *practice what he preaches*. Children are the greatest imitators; the careful and calm actions of the adult are almost completely accepted by the younger children.

When a boy or girl is old enough to solo, the speed of the machine can be cut in half by changing the position of the throttle cable on the carburetor. The screw is loosened and the cable allowed to move until the throttle can be squeezed halfway before the machine starts to move. The cable screw is then tightened and the machine will operate at a very reduced speed.

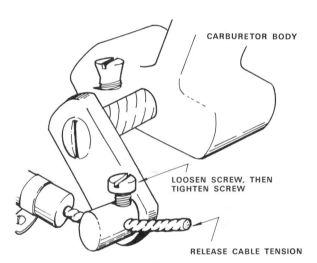

Figure 20.10 Adjust Throttle for Half Power

A flat field, away from buildings or trees, should be used. The route taken should not cross a road or rail crossing. Then the boy or girl may solo under a watchful eye. Any mistakes which can be corrected immediately are carefully noted. A correct and careful driver is a safe driver, not only to himself but others.

Safety Habits

This part of the chapter will try to familiarize the operator with good safety habits. It is wise to evaluate oneself and others continually on these habits to avoid a serious problem that could arise. Some people have said that such problems could not happen to them, but they never really know. It is better to be safe than *sorry* or *dead*.

A safety checklist is provided below:

(1.) Always tell somebody the approximate area of travel and the time of return. Someone will then locate you in an emergency at home or if the machine breaks down. Remember—exhaustion will come quickly if you try to walk any distance in deep snow.

(2.) Never snowmobile alone. It is wise to be with one more machine or a group. If one machine breaks down, the other can either tow it or go for help.

(3.) Never depend on someone else for emergency supplies. Always keep a package of matches in a water proof container of sealed wax paper.

(4.) An extra container of gasoline is a must if a long outing is planned.

(5.) The operator is required to carry his licence and insurance in some areas. It is wise to contact the local police for special rules and regulations.

(6.) Keep a spare key in a safe place in case you lose the ignition key. Always take the key out of the ignition when leaving the machine.

(7.) When making a new trail, drive very slow and carefully. Notice sudden dips and obstacles. If you travel in a strange area, try to carry snowshoes to walk ahead, searching for hidden rocks or bumps.

(8.) Always ask permission of the owner when crossing private property and keep to the trail he gives you.

Figure 20.11 Trailing Signals

(9.) Do not swerve from side to side on the trail as this will spoil the trail and create a "washboard" effect on it. This bumpy effect on the trail tires other people and shakes their machines, sometimes causing breakdowns. When crossing a trail, always yield the right of way to those on the trail.

(10.) When trailing with a group, always watch for hand signals and leave at least thirty feet between machines for braking room.

(11.) Groups of trail riding machines should have one or two machines free of passengers in case of breakdowns. The spare seats can be used for bringing the extra people home.

(12.) When approaching a snowbank, stop and climb to the top to see what lies on the other side. Many a driver has hurtled over a bank to find a secondary road or a hole on the other side.

(13.) Crossing a road is easily accomplished if you follow the safe routine:

(a) do not jump the machine over the road bank;

(b) stand up and climb the bank; then let the machine come down slowly to prevent any damage to the machine; the skis could be bent or broken in jumping;

(c) cars have the right of way over snowmobiles on the road; a collision between a machine and automobiles leaves the snowmobile operator little chance for survival;

(d) if you must travel on the road for some reason before crossing it, keep to the far right on the shoulder and drive slowly; it is against the law for even a licenced snowmobile to travel on the paved surface of a road.

(14.) When operating on a lake or river the following safety precautions should be observed fully.

(a) In an unfamiliar area, follow a guide who knows the lake currents and outlets. These currents or outlets generally cause thin ice. Always consider temperature; this affects ice by causing crevices that open or close.

(b) If a group of machines is travelling across ice, leave extra room between the machines to stop if the machine ahead breaks through the ice. This will help in rescue.

(c) Always cross the ice in single file, as cracks will zigzag.

(d) When crossing ice at night, speed must be greatly reduced because your field of vision in the headlight beam is small. (Do not operate your machine at high speed anywhere at night; shadows hide dangerous obstacles.)

(15.) Never operate a snowmobile on railroad right-of-ways. Besides the danger of an accident, it is illegal to walk or to drive on railway property. When the machine is operating, it is impossible to hear an approaching train. If you must cross a railroad be sure to use a crossing. Stop. Turn off the engine and listen. Then restart the engine and proceed. This is the only way to be sure that a train is not approaching the crossing.

(16.) After an hour's travel take a few minutes to rest and to let your body relax. This will relieve the fatigue that eventually leads to exhaustion.

(17.) When the trip is over and the machine is loaded on the trailer, be sure that the machine is securely tied down and the trailer lights are operating.

(18.) Never start a return trip home when you are tired. The heat of the car and any tobacco smoke will definitely make you drowsy. If time permits, stay overnight and return on the next morning when you are refreshed. (This is a must if you are a long distance from home.)

(19.) Always fill your machine's fuel tank at the end of the day. The fuel tank, when partially full, will condensate and the water droplets will freeze in the fuel lines.

(20.) When going in for meals, take off your suit and boots or you will feel the cold when you return to the outdoors.

(21.) Do not drink alcoholic beverages when operating your machine. It dulls your sense of judgment. If you are drinking outside and then return to the heat of a chalet or a restaurant, the alcohol will act like an unpredictable bomb.

(22.) Be sure that you have insurance on your snowmobile. You are responsible for damage to private property and injury to others. Remember: Your insurance becomes null and void if you speed, test, or race your machine. Contact your insurance agent for a complete explanation of insurance coverage in your area.

The next portion of this chapter will explain what to do if special difficulties arise in snowmobiling. The following information should be studied closely; it could save your life or that of others. Some of this section can be used in the newest of all sports.

CARAVAN CAMPING

The snowmobile has brought two new ways of life to us. It first brought a winter sport for the family that could not ski. It took the family out into the fresh air to see the country in its winter beauty. The fresh air relaxes the tensions of city life and exercises the body.

The newest winter sport developed through the snow-

Figure 20.12   Tent Trailers and Caravan Camping

mobile is Caravan Camping. Many trailer companies have built small camper trailers on skis that can be towed by snowmobiles. This, in turn, has lead to travelling greater distance with these machines, for longer periods of time and usually into strange and unknown areas. Observing the following material can turn this sport into enjoyment, but failure to use these ideas could cause panic or a terrifying experience.

Caravan Camping

The first item on the agenda for caravan camping is choosing a leader. He should be well-acquainted with the area to be travelled and trained in first aid. He could be a resident of the area.

The group should have one or more persons qualified to repair their machines in case of breakdown.

It would be wise to have someone who is familiar with winter camping or camping outdoors. This person will have a wealth of ideas to make the camping enjoyable.

The caravan should not operate after dark since it is hazardous even without the trailers. It is foolish to operate the machines after dark away from campsite; the driver could become lost.

The leader's signals and directions should be followed without question.

The caravan should have extra fuel, drive belts, tools and ample food for the trip. It is a must that the direction and destination of the trip be given to someone at the start so that if trouble occurs, they can find the caravan.

When a machine gets stuck in loose snow, the driver should stand with his feet toward the rear of the machine and rock the machine gently to pack the snow. With a firm grip on the handlebars, he then accelerates. In most cases, the machine will pull itself out. This operation is handy on a slope or in a ditch.

It is advisable to carry a rope and pulley, especially in

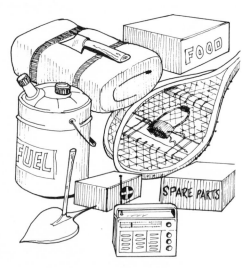

Figure 20.13 Caravan Supplies

a caravan. The rope can be fastened to the front of a machine. With the opposite end of the block and tackle, a machine can be pulled out with ease.

If a disabled machine must be towed, the drive belt is removed and the machine can be towed easily. Care has to be taken when braking as the machine behind could collide with the rear of the front machine. Towing a machine with a disabled or jammed track can be accomplished by loosening the spring ski bolts and turning the skis around to face the track. The back of the disabled machine is lifted and fastened to the bumper of the towing machine. This machine can now be towed with little effort.

If a member of the party becomes injured in a fall, he must not be moved unless in danger. Then the move should be taken with caution as there could be internal injuries. If the injured party must be moved, he should be pulled lengthwise, after a trailer cover is placed under him. (Send a member of the party who is familiar with the area for help.) The victim should be covered to avoid shock. (This is why it is important to have one or more of the caravan trained in first aid.)

Travel supplies should include a complete map of the course and the destination. No one should travel blind in an unknown area.

The caravan should make camp with a few hours of daylight to spare.

The Trailer and Tents

The trailer should be strong and low. Hitches should be sturdy and reinforced to prevent breakage. The camper trailer will come fully equipped, but it is wise to check the hitch on both trailer and snowmobile to ensure adequate reinforcement.

If a tent is used, it must be small and low. A high tent catches too much wind and is hard to heat. The tent should have a canvas floor, but an oil cloth or ground sheet would help to keep the dampness down.

Equipment

Special equipment is a must for full enjoyment of the outing. The necessary equipment is listed below:
—a camp stove;
—a tent heater;
—a lantern;
—a can opener;
—a sleeping bag for each member;
—fresh underwear (when the tent is warm, underwear should be changed to prevent sweat and dampness);
—a transistor radio to provide weather forecasts;
—a saw;
—an axe;
—a light rope;
—a small mallet, and
—a shovel.

Food

The amount of food taken on the trip will depend on the length of time for the journey, but allowance should be made for emergencies.

Special attention should be given to types of food and the way it is packaged. A list of possible provision is given below:
—sliced meat, individually wrapped (large frozen chunks are hard to cook);
—no liquids (they freeze and are wasted);
—sliced bread;
—bacon or sausage;
—no fruit as they freeze;
—no eggs (breakable and easily frozen);
—no greens as they will freeze and spoil;
Do not place any food near the fuel containers as the food will take on a fuel taste.

These are just a few items that should be observed for provisioning a caravan. One good set of provisions is frozen T.V. dinners; while they may be expensive to purchase, they cause no trouble and take less space to carry.

Preparation For Camp

The first item for camp is setting and warming the tent.

The size of the floor area is traced in the snow and the snow removed to a depth of one foot inside the rectangle.

Fir or spruce boughs are placed six inches in depth where the tent floor will be and the tent erected. It helps if a row of cedar or fir boughs are placed around the outside of the tent to insulate the floor of the tent.

No one should smoke in the tent as it makes the air stale and is a dangerous fire hazard.

Something should always be worn on the head during sleep; a touque or ski cap is sufficient.

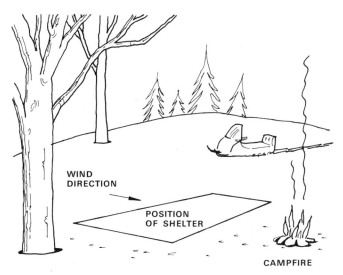

Figure 20.14 Camp Layout

The tent should not be covered with any type of material to keep out the cold. This prevents the air in the tent from circulating and the occupants could asphyxiate in their sleep.

Important

All fires must be away from the tents because of the cedar or fir boughs around the floors.

When the camp is broken, all campfires must be spread and extinguished. Hot ashes may be buried in the snow.

All garbage should be taken away and the area kept clean.

What to Do When Lost

Many people that have snowmobiles have never been in the area before.

People do not realize the distance that can be covered in an hour, and in an unfamiliar area, they get lost very easily, especially after dusk. (Darkness comes very quickly in wooded areas.)

If in doubt about the direction to travel, the driver must not panic or try to search for a trail. Trying to find a trail could place him farther away and the machine could run out of fuel. He should stay where he is!

The first problem is to prepare a shelter for the night and to build a fire for warmth.

Not everyone has been a scout or camper; therefore, it is important to follow details in the checklist below.

   (1.) Check for wind direction.

   (2.) Build the campfire 2 feet away from shelter for safety. (Always carry matches in waterproof wrapping.)

   (3.) Scoop out the snow approximately 8 inches to 10 inches deep and fill with pine, cedar, or fir boughs to keep dampness to a minimum.

Figure 20.15 Types of Campfires

   (4.) Place two limbs 6 feet long, with a "Y" in them, into the snow, approximately six feet apart.

   (5.) Place another pole across as a ridge pole. Then lean the poles against the ridge poles 4 to 6 inches apart. (These act as rafters.)

   (6.) Lay cedar, fir, or other green boughs across the rafters as thickly as possible to form the roof. The shelter is complete.

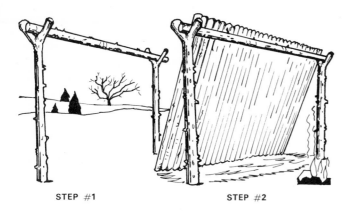

STEP #1   STEP #2

Figure 20.16   Building Shelter in the Forest

(7.) The fire should be banked with six inches of snow to keep the embers from blowing. (The fire will gradually sink in the snow.)

(8.) A supply of dry wood should be gathered to keep the fire going. Dead trees will supply all that is needed. By shaving the dead limbs with a knife good tinder for starting a fire will be provided. If a dead birch is nearby, the bark will make an excellent fire starter.

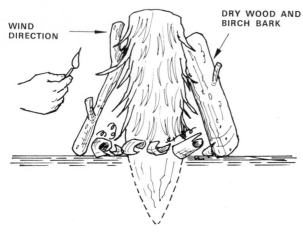

WIND DIRECTION

DRY WOOD AND BIRCH BARK

Figure 20.17   Starting a Fire

(9.) If your emergency kit has a chocolate bar or two, a nibble at the chocolate will ease your hunger.

(10.) The next morning, the surrounding area may look more familiar and perhaps a direction from other trails may help you find a way out. Remember, moss is always on the north side of trees. If you are still in doubt, stay still so that a search party can find you.

(11.) Keep your mind and body occupied by planning survival tracks, and place a snare in a well-travelled path.

(a) Tie a loop in a boot lace with a sliding knot; when a rabbit is running, his head will enter the loop and tighten it.

(b) Support the loop from a branch 6 to 8 inches above the track.

(12.) If you have an axe, do not use it in freezing weather until the axe head has been warmed. Frozen steel has been known to shatter like glass in below-freezing temperatures.

STANDARD TRAIL SIGNS

Snowmobiles are blazing trails into areas that have never been travelled by man. These trails are becoming highways for the sportsman and his family on sunny weekends.

Many snowmobile owners have formed clubs and are trying to reduce the number of serious accidents. The clubs have been formed to provide safety, not only for their own members, but for distant neighbours that will travel in their area.

Clubs throughout North America have standardized trail symbols that are understood by people throughout the continent. The snowmobile manufacturers have cooperated with the clubs and will provide the signs at cost.

Rail or Road Crossing

A serious problem has arisen over trails approaching and crossing roads or railroads.

The sign should symbolize a road or railroad along with a stop sign. The crossing symbol should be a hundred feet from the actual crossing. The stop sign, white letters on a red background, should be at least fifteen feet from the crossing.

Fences

Some clubs have arranged with farmers to allow trails through their property. Since the snow often covers trails where the fence openings are, two red circles are placed on a post at least 8 feet high, to show the actual opening. If the signs are not erected, it would be very easy for a machine to cross at the wrong place and result in a severe injury to the operator.

Danger Beside Trail

A few snowmobile adventurers often leave a trail only to fall prey to an unseen obstacle or trap. These traps include a hidden cliff, a ditch, an unfrozen watercourse, holes or even thin ice. A sign should be placed at the side of the trail to indicate the danger of leaving the trail.

Steep Slopes

Drivers should be warned in advance about steep slopes

ahead. This warning lets the driver prepare himself or others for a possibly dangerous situation.

Trail Forks and Crossings

All trails do not lead to the same place; therefore, a sign should show the place and distance. If the other trail is a lesser trail, the proper trail should be shown.

Distance

The distance between two points shoud be shown at least every two or three miles.

Lakes

Lake names should be marked clearly wherever the trail leaves the lake. If the trail is used at night, a yellow light (lantern) should be left to indicate where the trail leaves the lake.

SNOWMOBILE CENTRES

The snowmobile has brought a new concept in entertainment, the Snowmobile Centre.

The *centre* may be a short distance from the city or many miles in the country. The centre provides a base of operation. Some places have storage areas for machines for the year round, and mechanics to service and to repair machines.

The centre may be a club, a chalet or even a farm, with trails running from it like the spokes of a wheel. Clubs often provide barn dances and outdoor barbecues for entertainment. They are a completely new concept in outdoor living. Most snowmobile magazines have information about these centres; they often help the owner to avoid taking a machine and trailer back and forth to the city.

WARRANTY - MERCURY SNOW VEHICLE

1. *We warrant each new Kiekhaefer Mercury Snow Vehicle and accessories thereto (hereinafter referred to as "Product") manufactured by us and still owned by the original retail purchaser, to be free from defects in material and workmanship.*

2. *This warranty shall become effective only upon our receipt of a completed Warranty Registration Card, which shall identify the Product so registered by serial number. The Warranty shall remain in effect for a period of one (1) year from date of purchase by the original non-commercial purchaser. In case of commercial use, said Warranty shall be for a period of three (3) months from date of first use but in no event for a longer period than one (1) year from date of the purchase by the commercial user.*

3. *This warranty shall not apply to any Product which has been damaged due to: (1) neglect, accident, abnormal operation or by repairs or alterations performed elsewhere than at one of our authorized repair facilities; or (2) operation with accessories or parts which have not been recommended by Kiekhaefer Mercury for use on the Product and certified in writing by its Engineering Department as having design characteristics suitable for use with or on the Product; (3) operation with a lubricant of a type or grade which has not been recommended by Kiekhaefer Mercury in the Mercury Snow Vehicle Owners Operation and Maintenance Manual for use with the Product; or (4) racing.*

4. *Claim shall be made under this Warranty by delivering the Product for inspection to an authorized Kiekhaefer Mercury Snow Vehicle dealer or by giving notice in writing to the area Kiekhaefer Mercury Snow Vehicle distributor, branch manager or to the Company. Any parts, sent to us for inspection or repair, must be shipped with transportation charges prepaid.*

5. *Our obligation under this Warranty shall be limited to replacing, free of charge, such part or parts found by us to be defective as shall be necessary to remedy any malfunction resulting from defects of material or workmanship as covered by this Warranty. Except as herein expressly provided, we make no warranty, express or implied with respect to any Products manufactured by us, and we reserve the right to change or improve the design of any Products without assuming any obligation to modify such Product which we have previously manufactured.*

6. *This warranty is in lieu of all other warranties expressed or implied and may not be modified or extended by anyone except pursuant to a written authorization signed by an officer of the Company. There are no warranties which extend beyond the description on the face hereof.*

KIEKHAEFER MERCURY
DIVISION OF BRUNSWICK CORPORATION
FOND DU LAC, WISCONSIN 54935

Kiekhaefer Mercury

YOUR MERCURY SNOW VEHICLE WARRANTY

Kiekhaefer Mercury wants you to know the terms of your warranty in event your Snow Vehicle requires warranty service.

Warranty replacement parts and labor are limited to the terms of the "Warranty Agreement" on the back cover of this manual. Labor payments are made according to the times shown in the dealer's "Labor Rate Manual". There are, however, certain types of service (parts and labor) which are required for general maintenance and, therefore, not covered by warranty. These include:

1. *Minor adjustments and tuneups, which involve checking, cleaning or replacing spark plugs, carburetor adjustments, checking lubrication, ski alignment, drive chain tension, track tension and track alignment.*

2. *Additional service work requested by you over-and-above that necessary to satisfy the warranty obligation.*

3. *Claims for replacing complete assemblies, unless the assembly cannot be placed in first class mechanical condition by the replacement of one or more parts.*

4. *Transportation charges and/or travel time to and from another servicing point. Delivery must be made to any franchised Mercury Snow Vehicle dealer for service.*

We cannot over-emphasize the importance of proper maintenance and care and proper operating habits. The little time, which they require, will assist you in keeping your over-all operating and maintenance costs at a minimum.

Kiekhaefer Mercury

Figure 21.1a (above) Typical Warranty

Figure 21.1b (left) Items Not Covered by Warranty

the engine; the model, type and serial number must be given when ordering parts for the engine.

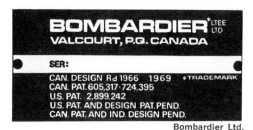

Bombardier Ltd.

Figure 21.2   Frame Number

Bombardier Ltd.

Figure 21.3   Engine Number

CHAPTER 21 SNOWMOBILE MAINTENANCE

The contents of this chapter will aid the student or owner in the care and maintenance of the snowmobile.

Chapter 20 explained safety and operation; this chapter is also important for the operator. A machine improperly maintained can be a dangerous hazard, not only to the operator but for others as well.

Although this chapter will cover maintenance procedures for snowmobiles, it is very important that the operator's manual be kept on hand, *at all times.* The manual has specific information for each model of snowmobile.

WARRANTY

It is important to know what is covered by the warranty of the manufacturer. This can be found by reading the warranty printed in the manual carefully.

Warranties differ from one manufacturer to another. Some models are warranted for 30 days and others for one year from the date of purchase. It is interesting to note that all machines used in racing or for abnormal use will not be warranted.

IDENTIFICATION

There are three ways of identifying snowmobiles: by the frame, by the engine and, sometimes, by the track. Each unit has its own serial number. These serial numbers are used in warranty claims, loss, theft or disputes over ownership.

Frame numbers are stamped in a prominent place, usually on the left or right rear section of the frame.

Engine numbers are stamped on the blower housing of

Bombardier Ltd.

Figure 21.4   Track Number

Some manufacturers have a serial number stamped in the rubber track for identification.

It is important, when contacting the dealer for parts and accessories, that the following information always be given:

(1.) the vehicle serial number;
(2.) the vehicle model;
(3.) the engine serial and model number;
(4.) the date purchased and the dealer;
(5.) the approximate number of hours used;
(6.) the details of the trouble experienced;
(7.) the date of any previous problems.

Warranty Service

The manufacturer's warranty appears in the service manual along with a list of items not covered by the warranty. Minor adjustments can be performed by the owner with the standard tools, but major repairs should not be attempted unless the special tools are available. Without the special tools, severe damage could be caused to the machine.

Repairs that require disassembly or replacement of internal parts should be done only by the service dealer. The dealer is trained and has the factory-designed tools and equipment to do the job properly and economically.

OPERATION AND CONTROLS

When the snowmobile is delivered, it is ready for normal service; but like all machines, it requires a little consideration during the first several tanks of fuel.

Most manufacturers recommend that their snowmobiles be operated at reduced speed and full throttle should not be attempted in the first 5 to 10 hours. If this advice is followed, it will give the engine and other components a chance to "break-in" and it will prevent the possibility of premature wear to the internal parts of the engine.

The operator should familiarize himself with the controls. The throttle is located on the right handle and the brake on the left; the throttle must be released when the brake is applied. This will aid the stopping capability and will prolong brake life.

The ignition switch is usually made in a three-position style. The manual models have *Off, Run* and *Run/Lights* positions.

The electric starters have *Off, Run* and *Start* positions.

The key can only be removed in the *off* position. The keys must not be left in the switch when the machine is alone.

The choke, light switch, and decompression levers are fully explained in the operators manual.

Fuel Mixture

A good grade of regular gasoline must always be used. It is a good practice to follow the manufacturer's advice on oil use and oil ratios.

Outboard oil must not be mixed with the gasoline. It will break down under the heat in an air-cooled engine. If possible, the gasoline and oil should be at room temperature when mixed.

Fuels must be mixed outside or in a well-ventilated room and no one should smoke in the fuel area.

Recommended oil-fuel ratios are as follows:

MAKE OF ENGINE	FUEL	OIL
JLO, Kohler, Arctic, Mercury	20	1
Hirth and Sachs	25	1
Fichtel-Sachs Rotary Combustion	40	1

A clean container, half-filled with gas, is used and then the full amount of oil is added. It is shaken vigorously, and the remaining gas filled and it is reshaken. The fuel should not be mixed in the machine's tank.

Excessive oil will cause carbon deposits on the pistons, spark plugs, parts and exhaust systems. Too little oil may cause piston seizure, overheating, rod and bearing failure.

Carburetor Adjustment

Carburetors are adjusted at the factory, but altitude and temperature differences may disturb these settings. The proper adjustments are usually made by the dealer prior to delivery.

There are many types and styles of carburetors used on snowmobiles; therefore, it is recommended that the settings of the manufacturer's manual be followed carefully.

WEEKLY MAINTENANCE: A CHECKLIST

(1.) Remove the front cowl and oil or lubricate the steering mechanism.

(2.) The chain case oil level must be checked; if the level is not at the level plug hole, it should be filled with the proper transmission grease.

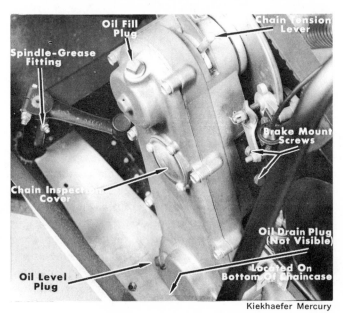

Figure 21.5 Drive Chain Lubrication

(3.) Remove the upper inspection port. The chain tension should not exceed $\frac{1}{4}$ inch free play. Check the manual for the proper tension and the adjustment.

(4.) The battery should be checked carefully. Fill the battery with distilled water to bring the electrolyte to the proper level (the ring at the bottom of the filler hole). Be sure that all connections are tight and corrosion free. Use a solution of baking soda and water to remove corrosion build-up. A stiff brush will help to remove stubborn corrosion.

Do not allow the solution to enter the battery as it will neutralize the electrolyte.

(5.) The track condition must be checked weekly, with the machine supported so that the track is clear. Rotate the track by hand, visually checking for bad cuts or missing inserts. (See the dealer for any missing inserts.)

2½ to 3″
FREE-PLAY

Bombardier Ltd.

Figure 21.6   Track Tension

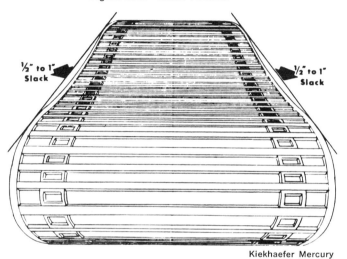

½″ to 1″
Slack

½″ to 1″
Slack

Kiekhaefer Mercury

Figure 21.7   Slack in Track

(6.) The track tension can be checked, while the machine is supported with your hand on the middle part of the track. The free play should be 2½ inches to 3 inches on most machines, but Keikhaefer Mercury specify ½ inch to 1 inch slack when the machine is sitting with the track supporting the weight. If the track is too tight, it will thump, and the tightness will cause differences in speed and wear. Check the manufacturer's manual for proper adjustment procedure.

(7.) The track alignment can be viewed during the proceeding inspections. Start the engine and accelerate gradually so that the track turns slowly. See that the track is centred and the sprockets turn evenly.

The distance between the edges of the track and the side plates should be the same on both sides, approximately ⅛ inch. Improper alignment will cause excessive wear on the tracks edges and the sprocket teeth. See the manufacturer's manual for the alignment adjustments.

(8.) The ski assembly should be checked for noticeable wear and for alignment. Apply grease to the spring slider cushions and lubricate all coupling bolts with oil.

(9.) The bogie wheels and suspension should be lubricated and checked for wear. (Replace weak or broken springs.)

(10.) The drive belt should be checked daily for wear and alignment. If the belt is under ⅞ inch (Skidoo) or 1⅛ inch (Mercury) outer surface measurement, it must be replaced. (Remember: it could be a long exhausting walk out of the bush.) Start the engine and gradually accelerate it. Watch for the belt alignment; if the belt twists,

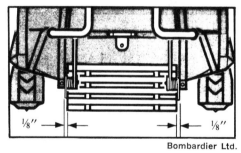

⅛″   ⅛″

Bombardier Ltd.

Figure 21.8a   Track Alignment

Figure 21.8b   Dual Track Alignment

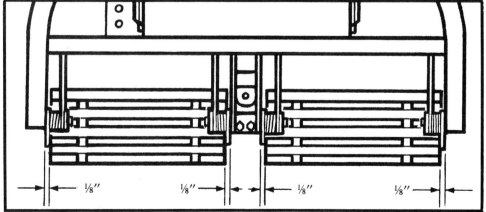

⅛″   ⅛″   ⅛″   ⅛″

Bombardier Ltd.

wobbles or vibrates, contact the dealer for the proper pulley adjustment.

When accelerating, the drive pulley should close, and the driven pulley should open.

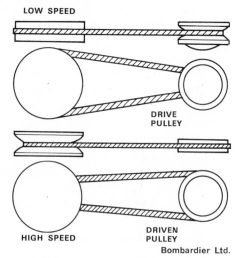

Figure 21.9   Drive Belt

(11.) Spark plugs should be checked weekly (every 10 hours). A normal spark plug is "brownish" in colour. If the spark plugs are black or light gray, the engine is not operating properly. This abnormal condition can be caused by an incorrect fuel mixture, incorrect adjustment or the wrong type of spark plug (heat range). Follow the manufacturer's instructions for gapping and cleaning. (Always keep a spare set of spark plugs with you.)

(12.) Lights, wiring, and fuses (if applicable) must be checked and replaced if necessary. Most manufacturers claim this to be a weekly check, but it

would be wise to take a few minutes and check them every day.

The figure below shows the weekly items that should be checked. Failure to do so could cause a loss of holiday trips and expensive repairs.

SUMMER STORAGE

The snowmobile will give its operator many years of enjoyment if he cares for it. A few minutes of precaution will save extensive repairs in the fall. The following steps for storage will increase the life of the machine.

(1.) All excess dirt and oil must be cleaned from machine and engine.

(2.) The hood and chassis should be cleaned and waxed; automotive cleaner wax will do.

(3.) The vinyl upholstery should be rubbed down with lemon oil.

(4.) The track and suspension should be hosed and allowed to dry thoroughly.

(5.) Rust or bare spots on the metal should be painted to retard rust.

(6.) Grease should be applied to all fittings and suspension arms.

(7.) The steering bushings and all spindle shafts should be oiled. A light coating of oil on the ski surfaces keeps rust a minimum.

(8.) Gas should be siphoned from the fuel tank and the engine run until it stops. The spark plugs should be removed and a small amount of oil applied into the spark plug holes. The engine should be turned over a few times to allow

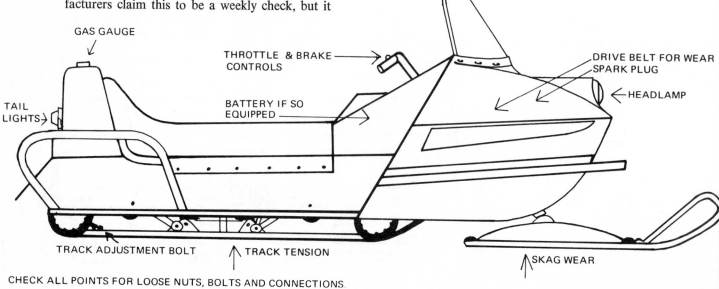

CHECK ALL POINTS FOR LOOSE NUTS, BOLTS AND CONNECTIONS.

Arctic Enterprises Inc.

Figure 21.10a   Weekly Check Items

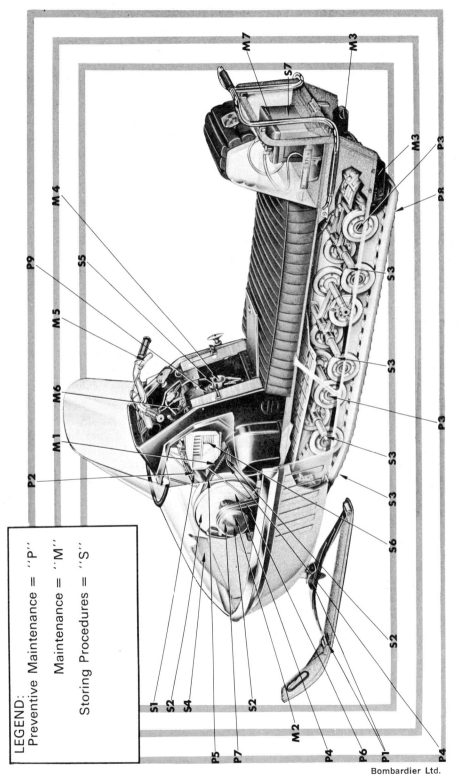

LEGEND:
Preventive Maintenance = "P"
Maintenance = "M"
Storing Procedures = "S"

Figure 21.10b Preventive Maintenance Chart

the oil to pass around the cylinder walls and rings. Some manufacturers will void the warranty if the tank is not drained for summer storage.

(9.) On machines equipped with electric starters, the battery should be removed, cleaned, charged and stored in a cool dry place, but not placed on a floor. It is a recommended procedure to trickle-charge the battery every 30 days.

(10.) The machine should be stored, in a shed, off the ground or cement, on wooden blocks or boards. If the machine is stored outside, it should be covered with a tarpaulin, and the windshield protected from the sunlight.

(11.) Ski-doo requests that on models equipped with built-in metal fuel tanks, the rubber filler necks be removed and spray protector be sprayed into the tanks for 5 seconds.

POOR PERFORMANCE

Even a well designed, properly maintained snowmobile may develop minor troubles caused by wear, damage, or faulty adjustments. The chart below will assist in determining the cause of low performance. The dealer should be informed of the details to assist him in repairing the vehicle. Repairs should not be undertaken unless a thorough knowledge of the machine is known and the proper tools available.

A	B	C	D	E	F	G	H	Possible Cause
●		●						Fuel Tank Empty or Shut-Off Valve Closed
●		●						Motor is Cold
●	●	●	●		●		●	Fuel Line Pinched or Kinked
	●		●	●	●			Fuel Filter Screens in Need of Cleaning
●	●	●	●	●	●		●	Air Leak in Vacuum Fuel System
●			●					Low Speed Mixture Screw Mal-Adjusted
	●	●		●	●		●	High Speed Mixture Screw Mal-Adjusted
			●	●	●			Carburetor Icing
			●		●		●	Wrong Oil in Fuel Mixture
	●		●	●	●		●	Wrong Gasoline in Fuel Mixture
			●	●	●		●	Not Enough Oil in Fuel Mixture
	●		●	●	●		●	Too Much Oil in Fuel Mixture
●								Motor Flooded
●	●		●	●	●		●	Spark Plug Defective
	●		●	●	●		●	Wrong Type Spark Plug
●								No Spark
			●	●	●	●		Track Binding and/or Freezedown
●	●	●	●	●	●		●	Weak Spark or Intermittent Spark
				●	●	●		Drive Chain Out-of-Adjustment or Broken
				●	●	●		Variable Speed Belt Worn or Broken
				●	●	●		Incorrect Track Tension and/or Alignment
●	●			●	●		●	Incorrect Spark Timing
●	●	●	●	●	●		●	Breaker Points Mal-Adjusted

A Does Not Start
B Runs Irregularly or Misses
C Starts Momentarily and Cuts Out
D Does Not Idle Properly
E Engine R.P.M. Slower Than Normal
F Vehicle Does Not Develop Normal Speed
G Vehicle Fails to Move When Throttle Is Depressed
H Engine Overheats

Figure 21.11 Trouble Chart

Kiekhaefer Mercury

INDEX